Social Dimensions of U.S. Trade Policies

Social Dimensions of U.S. Trade Policies

Alan V. Deardorff and Robert M. Stern, Editors

Ann Arbor

THE UNIVERSITY OF MICHIGAN PRESS

2003   2002   2001   2000   4   3   2   1

A CIP catalog record for this book is available from the British Library.

Library of Congress Cataloging-in-Publication Data

Social dimensions of U.S. trade policies / edited by Alan V. Deardorff,
   Robert M. Stern.
      p.   cm. — (Studies in international economics)
   "This volume contains the papers and comments that were commissioned
for a conference on the 'Social dimensions of U.S. trade policies,' which was
held at the U.S. Library of Congress in Washington, D.C. on April 16–17,
1998"—Introd.
   Includes bibliographical references and index.
   ISBN 0-472-11099-3 (cloth : alk. paper)
   1. United States—Commercial policy—Congresses.   2. Trade adjustment
assistance—United States—Congresses.   3. Foreign trade and employment—
United States—Congresses.   I. Deardorff, Alan V.   II. Stern, Robert
Mitchell, 1927–.   III. Studies in international economics (Ann Arbor, Mich.)

HF1455.S696   2000
382'.3'0973—dc21   99-059371

Contents

Preface

This book contains the papers and discussants' comments prepared for a conference on the "Social Dimensions of U.S. Trade Policies," which was held on April 16-17, 1998 at the U.S. Library of Congress in Washington, D.C. [Each of the papers was revised subsequent to the conference to take into account the comments of discussants, conference participants, external reviewers, and the editors.] The discussants' comments are based on the conference versions of the papers and thus have not been altered to reflect the changes that authors made in their papers.

The impetus for the conference was provided by a grant received from the Ford Foundation to study the role of interest groups in U.S. trade policies. We are grateful to the Foundation for its support and to Seamus O'Cleireacain and Bernard Wasow for their encouragement of our research and policy outreach program. The conference was co-sponsored by the Congressional Research Service (CRS) of the U.S. Library of Congress. Arlene Wilson of the CRS was instrumental in arranging this collaboration and for overseeing the organization and implementation of the conference.

We also wish to thank Judith Jackson for her superb assistance in helping to organize the conference and especially for editing and preparing the manuscript for publication.

Alan V. Deardorff
Robert M. Stern

CHAPTER 1

Introduction and Overview

Alan V. Deardorff and Robert M. Stern

I. Introduction

This volume contains the papers and comments that were commissioned for a conference on the "Social Dimensions of U.S. Trade Policies," which was held at the U.S. Library of Congress in Washington, D.C. on April 16–17, 1998. This conference was part of a program of policy outreach activities supported by a grant from the Ford Foundation to the University of Michigan School of Public Policy to study the role of interest groups in U.S. trade policies. Previous activities included a conference on "Constituent Interests in U.S. Trade Policies," held in Ann Arbor in November 1996. The proceedings of this November 1996 conference were published by the University of Michigan Press in 1998 (see Deardorff and Stern, 1998). We also had a one-day workshop on "U.S. Trade Policies and the Public Interest," in Ann Arbor in November 1997.

Our Washington conference provided an opportunity to address the salient issues of the social dimensions of U.S. trade policies in a setting on Capitol Hill where we were able to attract a number of Congressional staff as well as representatives from the broader trade policy community comprising staff from a number of Executive Branch agencies, international organizations, think tanks, public interest organizations, and universities. All of the papers were made available in advance to conference participants in hard copy and to a wider audience via the web site of our University of Michigan Research Seminar in International Economics. This helped considerably to focus the discussion and comments in each of the sessions.

The conference papers were revised following the conference to take into account the discussants' comments as well as points raised during the floor discussion. It was decided to include the discussants' comments as they were originally prepared based on the conference versions of the papers, in order to capture the concerns and criticisms raised in the conference sessions. The panelist remarks are also based on the conference versions. We trust that readers will find the comments and panelist remarks interesting and informative in their own right and useful supplements to the individual papers.

To assist the reader in determining which chapters may be of greatest interest, we provide brief summaries in Section II that follows. Then, in Section III, we reflect on what we have learned from the papers and commentaries about the social dimensions of U.S. trade policies and offer our suggestions on a number of issues that merit further exploration.

II. Overview

In **Chapter 2, Foreigners and Robots: Assistants of Some, Competitors of Others**, Edward E. Leamer notes that over the last three decades, unskilled workers in the United States and Europe have been experiencing stagnating or declining real wages and higher rates of unemployment. This has stimulated an intense academic debate in the United States that has focused on two potential drivers: skill-biased technological change associated with the computer revolution and the economic liberalizations in the third world that have greatly increased the effective global supply of unskilled workers with no commensurate increase in physical or human capital. His chapter reviews the theory and evidence, particularly regarding the role of trade.

It is apparent that there exist differences in wages at different points on the globe. Arbitrage might be expected to eliminate these differences, which suggests a fundamental question. If it is inward-looking isolationist government polices that have historically prevented arbitrage from eliminating geographic wage differences for equivalent workers, what will happen now that these barriers are being torn down? To answer this question we ought to use a clear conceptual framework. A one-cone fully diversified Heckscher-Ohlin (HO) model has been the implicit or explicit foundation for most of the data analysis regarding trade and wages. An HO diversified equilibrium has wages set completely by external competitiveness conditions, but the HO model also allows specialized equilibria in which the internal margin affects wage rates. Specialization is one way to limit international labor arbitrage and leave substantial wage differences among countries. Another isolating force is distance. Leamer discusses both distance effects and specialization effects.

Both the diversified and the specialized HO models suggest looking at relative prices to determine the impact of *globalization* on the world's labor market. The Stolper-Samuelson Theorem implied by the one-cone fully diversified HO model maps product prices into wage rates. This theorem has served as a theoretical foundation for several studies of the prices of tradables. At least one of these studies argues that there were significant price declines of labor-intensive tradables in the 1970s. But the relative price of labor-intensive tradables stabilized in the 1980s when most of the rise in U.S. inequality occurred. To argue that the 1980s rise in inequality is driven by trade forces us to look at mechanisms not captured by HO models. There are many other ways that trade could matter, the most promising of which may be threat effects or *contestabilty*.

Lawrence Mishel notes in his comment that Leamer's paper is a corrective to the writings and views of most trade economists and policy makers that globalization and its trade consequences have a minimal impact on wages and income distribution. But he takes issue with Leamer about how bad U.S. schools are and notes that there has been a deterioration of wages for high school graduates irrespective of the alleged decline in school quality. Mishel also questions the impact of changes in technology on wage inequality, citing evidence from the 1990s that is contrary to the experiences of the 1980s that Leamer considers. To help explain wage inequality, Mishel cites especially the erosion of the U.S. minimum wage and the erosion of union power as well as the redistribution of income from wages to capital as important factors. He suggests that Leamer's conception of the policy options available to deal with wage inequality needs to be broadened to make allowance for the variety of social safety net and wage-shaping policies that the U.S. and other governments pursue. Furthermore, he is critical of the claim that U.S. productivity levels exceed those in Europe, and he questions whether "more education" is a sufficient policy option in its own right. He takes issue, finally, with claims of high tech firms that there is a shortage of technology workers in the United States.

Also commenting on Leamer's paper, T. N. Srinivasan notes that it offers a varying set of conclusions derived from different highly stylized models. But it does not provide what Leamer once characterized as "good empirical estimates of the relative effects of technological change, globalization and education on the U.S. labor markets." Instead it offers a variety of conclusions based on a variety of models, with the connections between conclusions and models not always clearly identified. For example, some models suggest that a fall in the relative price of labor-intensive goods arising from increasing import competition from labor-abundant developing countries need not result in a fall in the relative wage of unskilled labor in skilled-labor abundant developed countries. Nor is it the case competition in world markets for, say, apparel by developed and developing countries necessarily implies that the wages of unskilled labor have to be the same in both. Attention is drawn to some recent theoretical and empirical works that arrive at conclusions different from Leamer's on the role of innovation and the use of computer-based technology in explaining trends in the relative wages of U.S. unskilled labor.

In Chapter 3, **Economic Research and the Debate Over Immigration Policy**, George J. Borjas notes that in the next few years, the debate over immigration policy will begin to stress the character and consequences of *legal* immigration. Although economic factors alone will not decide the outcome of this debate, economics has often set the questions that frame the immigration debate: Who benefits? Who loses?

The existing research establishes a number of stylized facts:

- The relative skills of successive immigrant waves declined over much of the postwar period. In 1970, for example, the latest immigrant arrivals had .4 fewer years of schooling and earned 17 percent less than natives. By 1990, the most recently arrived immigrants had 1.3 fewer years of schooling and earned 32 percent less than natives.

- Because the newest immigrant waves start out with such an economic disadvantage and because the rate of economic assimilation is not very rapid, the earnings of the newest arrivals will probably not reach parity with the earnings of natives.

- The large-scale immigration of less-skilled workers had an adverse impact on the economic opportunities of less-skilled natives. Immigration may account for almost one half of the recent decline in the relative wage of high school dropouts. The new immigrants have higher rates of welfare recipiency than earlier immigrants, as well as higher rates of recipiency than natives.

- The net gains from immigration are relatively small, on the order of .1 percent of GDP per year.

Borjas investigates the implications of these facts for immigration policy. He argues that every immigration policy must resolve two distinct issues: First, how many immigrants should the country admit? Second, which types of persons should be awarded the scarce entry visas? Before these issues can be solved, however, we have to ask ourselves: What does the United States want to accomplish with its immigration policy? In other words, what is the nation's objective function?

In the conclusion, Borjas stresses that if the social welfare function places a heavier emphasis on the well being of the U.S. native-born population, the "optimal" immigration policy would probably lead to a smaller immigrant flow, as well as a mix of immigrants more heavily weighted towards skilled workers.

In his comment, Jack Otero is in agreement with the main points made by Borjas, especially with regard to the importance of economic factors that condition the national debate on immigration. Otero notes that there is an apparent lull in this debate because of favorable economic conditions, but a variety of events could occur that might rekindle the debate. He calls attention to the special role that Hispanics play in the California economy especially and to their potential vulnerability as they are singled out in anti-immigrant political campaigns. He is also critical of the use of non-immigrant H-1 Bond D-1 visa programs designed to permit employers to bring in workers with specialized skills that may serve to undercut the employment and earnings of U.S. workers.

Jagdish Bhagwati, in his comment, disputes most of Borjas's claims on the effects of immigration and nearly all of his recommendations in regard to U.S. immigration policy. Bhagwati's differences arise on several issues: (1) Borjas's reliance on partial equilibrium rather than general equilibrium tools of analysis; (2) a range of theoretical and policy issues that have been considered by others in recent decades but are absent from Borjas's analysis; (3) Borjas's failure to consider ethical and sociological factors in his analysis; (4) Borjas's cautious and skeptical view of immigration; and (5) Borjas's view that U.S. policy should favor skilled over unskilled immigrants.

In **Chapter 4, U.S. Trade Adjustment Assistance Policies for Workers**, Gregory Schoepfle notes that since the early 1960s, the U.S. Department of Labor has maintained a variety of programs to assist displaced workers—those with some labor market attachment who lose their jobs and are unlikely to be recalled—in finding new employment. In the case of those adversely affected by expanded international trade, special trade adjustment assistance programs have been established to meet their needs. Qualified dislocated workers are provided job search assistance, job counseling, retraining, and other supportive services to assist them in finding suitable jobs. Recipients may also receive income support while in training. The intervention of government in the process of worker adjustments, both to international trade and to other changes in government policies, has been based on several underlying motivations. These have included equity notions of compensating those injured by governmental policies undertaken in the national interest, improved labor market efficiency, and political efficacy in the pursuit of further liberalizations of international trade and investment policies.

The Trade Adjustment Assistance (TAA) program for workers displaced by U.S. imports was first introduced as part of the Trade Expansion Act of 1962. However, the requirement to establish a direct link between specific trade liberalizations and a worker's dislocation resulted in few worker groups applying for assistance and even fewer being certified as eligible for benefits under the program. In 1974 legislation authorizing U.S. participation in the Tokyo Round of multilateral trade negotiations, TAA eligibility criteria and benefits were substantially streamlined and liberalized. Worker groups could now qualify for assistance if an increase in imports "contributed importantly" to their dislocation, i.e., increased imports—not necessarily linked to a specific trade liberalization—were an important cause but not necessarily more important than any other cause. With less stringent program requirements and procedures, TAA worker certifications began to increase rapidly. During the 1975–79 period, the permanently displaced were a fairly small portion of TAA recipients and the program provided mainly income support to workers on short-term layoff who eventually returned to work with their previous employer. As a result, few certified workers took advantage of the program's retraining opportunities. Major changes were introduced to the TAA program in 1981 and the number of TAA petitions submitted and approved declined when income support benefits were reduced to the level of weekly unemployment insurance payments and were only available after exhaustion of regular unemployment benefits, making TAA a program of extended unemployment insurance with training. As conditions changed in the 1980s and trade-induced layoffs became more long-term and permanent, the assistance that was provided shifted more to a mix of income support and the provision of training and other reemployment services. Since in many cases reemployment meant finding a job in another industry or profession, training was emphasized and eventually required in 1988 for certified workers to receive extended income support.

To address workers' concerns about further North American economic integration under the North American Free Trade Agreement (NAFTA), a special trade adjustment assistance program was introduced as part of the NAFTA implementing legislation in 1993. This NAFTA-Transitional Adjustment Assistance (NAFTA-TAA) program provides early and rapid response by state units as well as the opportunity to engage in long-term training while receiving income support. Assistance is available not only to those directly affected by import increases from Mexico or Canada, but also to those affected by a shift in production to Mexico or Canada. In addition, assistance is available for secondarily affected workers in plants that provide materials to or process further the products produced by a directly affected firm.

While the benefits available to certified workers under the TAA and NAFTA-TAA programs are similar, program certification criteria and procedures differ slightly. The Clinton Administration is considering measures to expedite the application and certification process and to improve the timing and delivery of assistance and services. Proposals have also been made to extend TAA eligibility to those affected by a shift in production to another country and to secondarily affected workers.

While trade-related worker dislocations may account for a small portion of all long-tenured dislocated workers in the U.S. economy, they may represent a significant portion in some manufacturing industries, and reemployment for some of these workers in the industry of their last employment may be more difficult than for other displaced workers seeking reemployment. For these workers, the income support payments and other adjustment assistance services (such as training, job search, and relocation allowances) may be vital in securing their reemployment.

Over the last quarter century, questions have been raised about the appropriateness, adequacy, and utilization of the TAA programs. Evaluations of the TAA program have provided mixed results on the usefulness of training, with some observing that provision of job search services may be more effective than training. Others have proposed additional modifications such as some form of wage insurance program to allay fears of displacement due to further globalization. What emerges from the popular debate and workers' concerns about globalization is a clear message to policymakers that they must take account of transitional adjustment costs and distributional issues (a more equitable distribution of the gains from trade and investment) in designing policies aimed at easing adjustments to changing economic circumstances brought on by globalization if they expect to garner popular support for further trade liberalization.

In his comment on Schoepfle's paper, Steve Beckman notes that UAW members have been important "consumers" of the Trade Adjustment Assistance program. That experience has led to the UAW suing the Labor Department numerous times over various aspects of the TAA process, including certification and regulatory interpretations. This indicates the contentiousness of the program, and its inadequacy in the eyes of those it is intended to benefit. Too few workers are certified for benefits due to the excessively narrow certification criteria. "Secondary workers," those making parts for products that are displaced by imports, remain outside coverage of the program despite the obvious connection between increased imports and their job losses. The reality of training opportunities often fails to live up to its promise. There are not enough effective training options available in the areas where workers have been laid off. The tight rules for the training requirement of the NAFTA-TAA program are a serious impediment to qualifying for benefits under that program.

While laudatory of Schoepfle's survey of the motives and programs for U.S. worker adjustment assistance and the special adjustment program under the NAFTA in his comment, J. David Richardson identifies a variety of recent studies that are especially deserving of attention and that are not covered by Schoepfle. These include analysis of job-mobility and earnings-insurance policies, studies of the effectiveness of different policies, equity issues, and how trade adjustment assistance programs actually impact workers. These new avenues of research, Richardson notes, suggest ways in which labor adjustment programs can be redesigned and improved in effectiveness.

In **Chapter 5**, John Kirton addresses the question, **Has Trade Strengthened or Weakened U.S. and Foreign Environmental Quality? The NAFTA Experience**. He notes that the experience of the United States under NAFTA shows that trade liberalization has a weak but positive effect on environmental quality, both in the United States and its partner countries of Mexico and Canada. An analysis of NAFTA trade liberalization that emphasizes the role of foreign direct investment, of the intervening processes of production, infrastructure, social organization and government policy in specific sectors, and of NAFTA's intergovernmental institutions demonstrates isolated instances of increased ecological pressure, but several channels and areas of environmental advance.

Consistent with recent findings about the environmental impact of trade liberalization in general, NAFTA-associated trade and foreign direct investment, through an intensification of comparative advantage and technology transfer, are fostering general region- and economy-wide positive environmental effects. Post-NAFTA trade is not concentrating in environmentally-intensive sectors, but in environmentally-friendly intermediate goods and service sectors, while NAFTA is not adding to the environmental burdens of the maquiladoras. NAFTA-induced FDI shows no migration to pollution havens or general tendency to concentrate in geographically stressed areas, but has encouraged environmentally-enhancing technology transfer, investment, subsidies and voluntary standardization among regionally integrated firms and industries.

Studies of how NAFTA-associated trade and investment flows interact with processes of production, management and technology, physical infrastructure, social organization and government policy in key sectors suggest generally favorable environmental impacts in the automotive and cattle-feedlotting industries, with outcomes in the electricity sector critically dependent upon national policy choices yet to be made.

Among the 50 trilateral intergovernmental institutions created or catalyzed by the core NAFTA (trade) agreement, those with the most direct environmental responsibility have had a mixed record in fostering a regular, balanced, trilateral communication, capacity building, high level regulatory convergence, and regional co-operation in multilateral forums and dispute management. The successful performance of bodies dealing with chemicals, in contrast to the poor performance of those in the automotive field and the mixed performance of those in agriculture, can be explained by the presence of visible ecological intervulnerability, a multilateral nest, government insulation from societal pressures, a functional need to harmonize in order to reap trade gains, low cost to powerful industries, MNC support, and the regional export interests of U.S. industry.

On balance, the record suggests that NAFTA's dedicated environmental organization, the Commission for Environmental Co-operation (CEC), has autonomously engendered balanced environmental co-operation and improvement amidst the trade liberalization brought by NAFTA. However, it has done little to foster trade-environment equality and integration, and it is currently in danger of being rendered less effective.

In his comment on Kirton's paper, David van Hoogstraten agrees with most of Kirton's conclusions, although it is still relatively early to draw conclusions concerning the effects of NAFTA. Also, he notes that more documentation is needed in a number of places in the paper, particularly on the key issue of enforcement of environmental regulations and the lack of adequate resources in Mexico to achieve effective enforcement. In general, van Hoostraten views the NAFTA as an environmentally activist document, which is an objective sought by the U.S. negotiators. While it may be said that the NAFTA has had a week positive impact on the environment, there is concern about population pressures on the Mexican side of the border and resulting stress on the delicate and diverse ecosystem. Finally, van Hoostraten approves of the role of the NAFTA Committee on Environmental Cooperation (CEC) in publicizing information on environmental issues, and he urges that more attention be paid to these issues in the broader hemispheric context.

Also commenting on Kirton's paper, Alan Deardorff notes the importance of Kirton's conclusion that the NAFTA has not brought any significant environmental degradation and that the institutions created by the NAFTA have on the whole worked well to date. Aside from some questions about Kirton's terminology and the interpretation of his sectoral analysis of trade, Deardorff notes that some ex post analysis would have been useful to learn the mechanisms by which the NAFTA has affected the environment. That is, did the cleaner industries in Mexico tend to expand? Can it be established that techniques of production used in Mexico have become more friendly to the environment? How important was the peso crisis and subsequent decline in Mexican income and employment for the environment? Has the NAFTA in fact fostered a "race to the top" as Kirton suggests, and if so how? Deardorff offers some suggestions to explain why a race to the top may be occurring, but concludes that more information is needed to establish the facts and interpretations.

In **Chapter 6, The Role of Labor Standards in U.S. Trade Policies,** Gary S. Fields makes the following principal points:

- Absent an agreement on international labor standards, a stalemate is quite possible. On the one hand, it might not be possible to push trade liberalization forward, as most in the trade community want. On the other hand, the current world trading environment will not be rolled back, as some in the labor movement want.

- The international labor community has now coalesced around a set of "core labor standards" that deal with freedom of association and the right to organize and bargain collectively, forced or compulsory labor, equal remuneration for men and women, and non-discrimination in employment, and child labor. Minimum wages, maximum hours of work, and fixing other conditions of employment are *not* being called for at the present time. It would be well for those in the trade community to know what is and is not on labor's agenda. If these core labor standards or ones like them were to be linked to international trade, opposition to trade agreements might be overcome, helping international trade.

- The alternative to "core labor standards" would be a set of "international labor rights," defined by the criterion that it would be better to have no production at all than to have production using such "illegitimate means." Although such discussions are not prominent in international debate at the present time, they deserve discussion in the future.

- Wages, employment conditions, and other social benefits have improved dramatically for workers living in countries that have achieved rapid export-led economic growth. Of course, problems remain, which is precisely why those who have an interest in workers overseas seek to harness the strengths of both trade and labor standards to improve conditions for these groups.

- Although freer trade might be good on the whole for the United States, it is not good for all workers in the United States. The small number of people who are hurt a lot by freer trade have every reason to be much more vociferous in expressing their opposition to freer trade than are the large numbers who benefit relatively a little. Policies can be enacted that will mollify the opposition, and they deserve serious consideration. Absent such measures, the agenda of the trade community is seriously jeopardized.

In his comment on Fields's paper, Pharis Harvey is critical of relying on market mechanisms alone to deal with poverty, child labor, and other problems of poor countries. He also notes that the emphasis on trade expansion via Fast Track in the United States needs to take labor's interests explicitly into account. Harvey maintains that there exists a much broader consensus on what constitutes core labor standards than Fields implies. He is critical of Fields's suggestion that certain labor rights be dropped from consideration on the grounds that the enforcement would be impractical. He suggests instead trying to determine whether enforcements and punishments can be devised that would help to improve compliance with labor rights. Finally, he is critical of Fields's reliance on economic growth as the primary vehicle for improving labor rights in the absence of explicit policies that are designed to improve labor rights. In this connection, Harvey's interpretation of the Korean growth experience is quite different from what Fields maintains has led to increased real wages and per capita incomes.

Dani Rodrik in his comment notes and provides empirical evidence suggesting that, while workers' earnings are determined by productivity, labor standards and civil liberties matter as well. He notes further the need to be clear whether the policy objective is to help workers abroad or instead to help domestic workers whose earnings might be impacted by low foreign labor standards. Under some conditions, he argues that gross violation of core worker rights abroad might be grounds for protecting the interests of domestic workers. Finally, he suggests that more attention be given to designing the best set of policy instruments for helping foreign or domestic workers.

In **Chapter 7, The Simple Economics of Labor Standards and the GATT**, Kyle Bagwell and Robert W. Staiger ask: how should the issue of domestic labor standards be handled in the GATT/WTO? This question is part of a broader debate over the appropriate scope of international economic institutions such as the GATT (and now its successor, the WTO). Member countries are considering proposals for a new round of negotiations that would move beyond GATT's existing focus on trade barriers and cover "domestic" issues such as labor and environmental standards and regulatory reform which have traditionally been treated with "benign neglect" within GATT. Such proposals encroach on traditional limits of national sovereignty, and they raise fundamental challenges to the existing structure of international economic relations among sovereign states.

Bagwell and Staiger consider in their chapter several approaches to the treatment of domestic labor standards within a trade agreement. They use simple economic arguments to show that, while the benign neglect of labor standards within a trade agreement will result in inefficient choices for both trade barriers and labor standards, direct negotiations over labor standards are *not* required to reach efficient outcomes. Specifically, they describe two tariff negotiating structures that deliver efficient outcomes while preserving varying degrees of national sovereignty over policy choices. A first approach combines tariff negotiations with subsequent *Kemp-Wan adjustments*, under which each government is free to alter unilaterally its policy mix so long as trade volumes are not affected. A second approach adds to the first approach GATT's rule of *reciprocity*, under which subsequent to tariff negotiations each government is free to alter its tariff unilaterally, but its trading partner is then free to recipro-cate with a tariff response that stabilizes export prices. They show that both approaches will deliver governments to the efficiency frontier, but that the second approach provides governments with greater sovereignty over their policy choices and bears a strong resemblance to the negotiating procedures spelled out in GATT.

In his comment on the Bagwell-Staiger paper, John H. Jackson expresses reservations concerning the conceptualization of economic efficiency as ap-plied to child labor in view of the considerable cultural differences that exist across countries. He also questions the feasibility of lump-sum payments as a practical matter and the problems involved in implementing reciprocity in the Bagwell-Staiger analysis. Jackson's view on labor standards is that they must become internalized within the GATT/WTO process. The question becomes one of how this can be most effectively accomplished. He discusses several possible approaches, but acknowledges in the final analysis just how difficult it will be to deal with issues of labor standards in the GATT/WTO. This is es-pecially true because of the fears of many developing countries that the United States and other major industrialized countries will use issues of labor stan-dards to respond to domestic protectionist pressures.

Also commenting on the Bagwell-Staiger paper, T. N. Srinivasan notes that they have applied the same methodology to analyzing labor standards as employed in a series of papers analyzing the roles of GATT's principle of non-discrimination, and the ill-defined notion of reciprocity in multilateral trade negotiations on tariff reductions in reaching an efficient (Pareto Optimal) and stable outcome. However, with two policy instruments (viz. tariffs and labor standards) at the disposal of the governments, if they are free to set one of them unilaterally in a non-cooperative fashion, it is intuitive that negotiations to set the other instrument will result in neither instrument being set at levels consistent with efficiency. The choice of the two instruments, one of which is a purely domestic policy instrument, has to be linked to get around this prob-lem. The authors propose three such linkages, two of which allow some free-dom for countries to choose labor standards unilaterally. However, the authors' modeling of labor standards does not take into account some essential features. An alternative model that incorporates these features is set out in an appendix. Srinivasan agrees with the authors that using trade sanctions to en-force labor standards is harmful and unnecessary. Doing so is to take the first step on a slippery slope of avoidable and welfare-worsening use of trade sanc-tions to enforce other purely domestic policies.

In **Chapter 8, A Transactions Cost Politics Analysis of International Child Labor Standards**, Drusilla K. Brown addresses some of the issues that pertain to the treatment of child labor in the international arena. A review of the standard prescriptions for reducing child labor provides little hope that the welfare of children can be improved in the absence of world-wide economic growth, development and increased adult wages.

Familiar prescriptions such as import tariffs levied against goods produced with child labor are likely to leave children with lower wages and/or in more damaging occupations. Similarly, product labeling, intended to identify goods produced without child labor, can have adverse consequences for working children. If the premium paid for labeled products is not sufficient to compensate firms for the cost of using adult labor only, then no firms will label. If the premium paid for labeled products is just barely sufficient to cover the cost of using adult labor only, then all of the label premium will be dissipated by the use of an inefficient technology. Some firms will use only adult labor and label their products to that effect, but the wages and employment of adult and child workers will be unaffected. If the labeling premium is more than enough to compensate firms to shift to adult labor-only production, then adult wages will rise and child wages will fall. Children will be made better off only if the increase in adult wages is sufficient to place family income above the threshold level where child labor begins to decline. As a consequence, if the labeling premium is effective in improving the welfare of children the reason is that the label premium raises family income, not because it provides a disincentive for firms to hire children.

The allocation of the task of monitoring child labor to the ILO rather than the WTO is also analyzed using the transactions cost politics approach. One interpretation of the separation of the dual tasks of monitoring trade and labor standards between the two agencies stems from the fact that fair trade standards can be established without regard to level of income of participating countries. This is not the case for many labor market outcomes which depend critically on the level of economic development. As a consequence, compliance with fair trade standards is more easily observable than compliance with labor standards. In an agency with the responsibility of monitoring both trade and labor standards, compliance with trade standards would receive closer scrutiny, while labor markets would be inadequately monitored. However, as a historical matter, the separation of monitoring tasks between the two agencies has been sought by those principals who want little or no monitoring of labor standards, not by those principals who seek greater monitoring of labor practices.

An alternative explanation is that the separation of monitoring tasks across agencies stems from the fact that international agencies are controlled by multiple principals. The United States has sought both to include labor standards in the WTO and to use a logical connection between labor market practices and WTO rules to enforce those standards. The U.S. position has been ardently and successfully opposed by developing countries who fear that the United States is motivated by an attempt to protect domestic labor from low-wage competition. The discrepancy between the abilities of the principals to agree on trade rules compared to labor standards argues in favor of high trade standards with strict punishments for violations and labor standards with weak punishments. However, the United States was unable to pre-commit successfully not to exploit the incompleteness of the WTO charter and apply strict punishments to labor standards violations.

Partitioning the labor and trade monitoring tasks between two agencies allows each standard and the associated punishment for deviations to be set at the highest level to which the principals are able to agree. The comparatively strict rules of the WTO reflect the high degree of consensus for an open trading regime. The consequent ease of monitoring improves compliance. By comparison, the low level of agreement on labor standards is reflected both in the weak language of the ILO and the absence of any meaningful enforcement mechanism.

The final issue discussed is that of agency shopping. The United States, having failed to achieve its objectives with regard to labor standards in the WTO, has most recently turned to the IMF as a vehicle.

In his comment, Mark Silbergeld expresses a number of points of agreement with Brown's paper, including the view that child labor is perhaps the most painful aspect of poverty, but that there are very difficult cultural aspects to consider in dealing with the problems of child labor and a danger of introducing measures that may turn out to worsen the situations of some child laborers. He also agrees that the WTO may not be an effective forum for addressing the issues. In addition, however, he expresses disagreement and notes some considerations that Brown omitted. These include the need to take a broader social view of the problems of child labor, the need to improve general working conditions for all workers in developing countries, the need to provide better information to workers on labor market conditions and to consumers about the use of child labor, and the political necessity of using trade actions to deal with abuses of child labor as a means of gaining public acceptance of trade agreements.

Also commenting on Brown's paper, Avinash Dixit establishes conditions under which industrial country protection may be counterproductive and aggravate problems of child labor in developing countries. He acknowledges Brown's use of transaction cost ideas and her argument that it would be preferable to use separate agencies (i.e., the ILO and WTO) to deal with labor standards and trade rather than assign both of these to a single agency such as the WTO. But he notes that Brown's analysis needs to be broadened especially to take into account what he calls the repeated game of common agency that will engender cooperation among the principles in providing credible penalties for countries that do not adhere to the disciplines involved. He argues finally that the best way to eliminate child labor is for the United States and other advanced countries to foster trade expansion and foreign direct investment so as to increase the demand for labor and raise adult incomes in the developing countries.

Chapter 9 contains remarks of a group of panelists providing their perspectives on **The Role of Interest Groups in the Design and Implementation of U.S. Trade Policies.**

Claude Barfield notes that U.S. trade policy provides a rich and fascinating chronicle of the intermix of policy objectives played out and reshaped by strategically placed political actors and interest groups. Compared to other countries, the U.S. system is more open and interest-group friendly, and the role of interest groups in the trade area has increased dramatically in scope and depth. Because the trade policy bureaucracy, centered especially in the Office of the U.S. Trade Representative (USTR), is relatively small, the U.S. government is dependent on interested parties for analysis and for support of actions to further trade liberalization or deal with infractions of trade rules by trading partners. It is also the case that ever closer relations between U.S. trade officials and the private sector have been mandated in the successive trade acts since the 1970s. There have been positive consequences of increased private sector involvement particularly in liberalizing trade and enhancing access to foreign markets. But there have been negative consequences as well. One example is the 1987 Semiconductor Agreement with Japan, when powerful companies promoted welfare-reducing trade interventions. Other examples include very strict insistence on reciprocity as in the WTO financial services and telecommunications agreements and the decision to pursue the Multilateral Agreement on Investment (MAI) in the OECD. But, granting various negative consequences, Barfield concludes that the present system of random intervention by interest groups is preferable to an expanded and more powerful government trade bureaucracy.

In her remarks, Phyllis Shearer Jones draws on her four years of experience with IBM as a program director for international trade and two and a half years as Assistant USTR for Intergovernmental Affairs and Public Liaison. She notes that the North American Free Trade Agreement (NAFTA) debate provided a wake-up call for the supporters of freer trade and discusses how IBM mobilized its employees and suppliers to back NAFTA and to counteract the activities of the anti-NAFTA interest groups. There is a need for continuous involvement of interest groups favoring freer trade to avoid starting from scratch every time a new liberalization effort is to be undertaken. Her experience with USTR leads her to ask what makes some interest groups more effective than others in achieving their trade policy objectives. In her judgment, interest groups are most effective when: their message has emotional and intellectual appeal; active support can be enlisted from members of Congress, the Executive Branch, and the media; a large and influential constituency can be mobilized to demonstrate their support; the message for or against a particular policy measure is short and succinct; and the groups are continuously actively seeking their objectives.

Robert Naiman addresses the question of the role of "public" interest groups in U.S. trade policy. He notes that organizations such as Public Citizen take every opportunity available to call attention to what he refers to as the

"...failed economic model, the failed trade model, the deformed model of democracy which is being pushed by the Clinton Administration, the multinational corporations, the leadership of both political parties, the professors of economics." For this purpose, he uses the example of how the negotiations for the Multilateral Agreement on Investment (MAI) were conducted in secret and how the exposure of the MAI to public scrutiny resulted in the disruption of the negotiations. He is critical of the role that the International Monetary Fund may now play in pursuing the MAI agenda under the guise of capital account liberalization. Citing the public opposition to President Clinton's request for fast-track negotiating authority in the fall of 1997, he chides the advocates of freer trade for their dogmatic insistence on the need for better and more effective public education and their arguments about the gains from trade and compensation of the losers from freer trade.

In his panel remarks, Mike Jendrzejczyk notes that human rights groups believe that U.S. trade policy is relevant to their objectives. These groups try to influence U.S. policy via publicity, providing documentation to policymakers (at USTR, on the Hill, and to other relevant agencies) and meeting with government officials. Minimally, the groups press for consistent, effective implementation of U.S. trade laws such as GSP, OPIC, and MFN that take into account human rights and/or worker rights. But in addition, the groups have tried, with mixed success, to influence multilateral trade organizations, for example, the Asia Pacific Economic Cooperation (APEC) forum, and the issue of China's entry into the World Trade Organization.

Nancy Dunne, in her panel remarks, writes from the perspective of a *Financial Times* journalist. She praises interest groups for making her job easier because they provide so much useful information via press conferences and press kits. She notes further that interest group coalitions are usually very effective in getting their case before the Congress and members of the Executive Branch and for their contacts with journalists. Of course, there are many different interest groups with different agendas, which makes it necessary for the journalist to try to balance conflicting views. Interest groups also tend to stick with issues for long periods of time and make efforts to communicate their views to the public and the press. Dunne concludes by noting that non-economic interest groups have become increasingly important and active on issues of trade policies. Thus, whereas trade policy was once a backroom issue inside the beltway, this is no longer the case. Trade issues have now gone to the court of public opinion.

III. What Have We Learned?

As we expected and hoped, the conference brought together people with a wide range of interests and opinions, and the discussion was lively and informative. There was a great deal to learn from the papers, the discussant comments, and the group discussion. The interested reader will therefore have to read the papers carefully to get maximum benefit from these exchanges of views. However, we will try to report here a few of the lessons that we think we learned ourselves from the experience. Others, no doubt, will have learned different things, and will disagree with some of what we say below.

Indeed, it is precisely that disagreement that may be the most important message that we got from this conference. Almost everyone agrees that social issues, including especially labor standards, are now permanently a part of any discussions of trade policy, whether they are pleased with that development or not. But they disagree strongly from that point on, regarding whether and how social issues should be linked with trade issues, and even regarding what society's objectives concerning many social issues should be.

As trade economists, we are accustomed to discussions in which the intellectual case is clear and both the objective and the means of achieving it are largely agreed upon. That is, national (consumer) welfare is the objective, and free trade is the means. For half a century, GATT negotiations worked to move the world in this direction, and the only dispute was how quickly one should move vis-a-vis one's trading partners. There were frictions, of course, and many pressures from within countries to slow down the process. But these were understood to be only that, not genuine competing national interests.

That was fine, apparently, as long as trade was a sideshow in the international economic panorama. But as trade barriers have come down, as developing countries have become a larger and more open presence in the global economy, and as technological innovations have linked national markets more closely than ever before, trade has moved to center stage. Trade now matters for many domestic issues, including this social dimension, and the domestic issues interact inextricably with trade. Trade policy can no longer be made in isolation, for its domestic and social implications are manifest. In the conference, we learned about many of these implications.

To grapple directly with these issues along with trade however, is far more difficult than are the problems of trade policy alone. We must worry not only about a broader range of problems and also policies. But also, the objectives in these social dimensions are often much less clear than we are used to for trade alone, because they require tradeoffs. We deplore children in developing countries having to work, for example, but we also are critical of depriving them of the income that may be keeping them alive. We all want a clean environment, but not perhaps at the cost of pushing the poorest of countries further into poverty. Human rights are sacrosanct, but so too is national sovereignty. Of course we want the poorest among us to have higher incomes, but should this be accomplished with higher wages, and at what cost in terms of economic efficiency and longer-run growth for all? In all these cases, we must perform a balancing act among competing objectives, and disagreements about the right balance are inevitable. Add to that our limited understanding of how various issues do in fact interact, and it is not surprising that the usual policy consensus among trade economists was noticeably absent at the conference.

In spite of ten years of research by trade and labor economists, for example, we still do not really know how globalization has affected wages. Nor, therefore, do we know what to do about it, if anything. The effects of immigration on wages are, it seems, even more controversial, involving as they do a more direct confrontation between groups of affected workers. Most do seem to agree that workers who are displaced by trade and related aspects of globalization should be helped in some way, but there is disagreement about the effectiveness and adequacy of our existing TAA regimes. It is difficult to infer from any of this what exactly should be done. But it does seem clear that future changes in trade policy will have to acknowledge and deal with their implications for wages, more than they have in the past.

Labor standards abroad seem to be here to stay as part of negotiations on trade, whether or not they become incorporated as a formal part of the WTO institutional mechanism. Several of the papers in the conference examined how the interaction between trade and labor standards could be structured, but again there was far from a consensus.

It seems unlikely, therefore, that academic discussion will ever achieve the same kind of agreement on the interaction between social issues and trade that it has had on trade alone. That being the case, policy decisions will be guided even less by economic science and even more by the interactions among the groups involved and between them and policy makers/negotiators. At the conference we got a glimpse of how this interaction works, primarily in the panel discussion at the end.

It is clear that the advocates for particular interests play an important role in Washington and presumably elsewhere as well. This has been true for trade policy for a long time, as we learned from Phyllis Shearer Jones. Until now, when trade could be considered on its own merits alone, the intellectual case for liberal trade also played an important role, much to the frustration, evidently, of Robert Naiman. But as social issues have come more into contact with trade, we may expect the views expressed by Naiman and others with a similar agenda to become increasingly influential. On the other hand, at present it appears that those advocating different social objectives also disagree on whether trade is an obstacle to, or a facilitator of, their objectives, as witness Mr. Jendrzejczyk versus Mr. Naiman. As long as that remains the case, the outcome of these policy debates will be far from clear.

One would like to think that academic-style researchers, such as ourselves, could be counted upon to remain objective, even when we cannot agree. Although it is not evident in the papers reproduced here, we can report from the conference discussion, however, that this is not always the case. Advocates for particular policy positions can and do get carried away and exaggerate their case, even when not driven to do so by narrow self interest. It was refreshing, therefore, to hear from Ms. Dunne about the journalist's effort to balance conflicting views. Perhaps it is to journalists we should be talking and expressing our opinions, if we can ever figure out what our opinions on these difficult issues are.

References

Deardorff, Alan V. and Robert M. Stern (eds.). 1998. *Constituent Interests and U.S. Trade Policies*. Ann Arbor: University of Michigan Press.

CHAPTER 2

Foreigners and Robots: Assistants of Some, Competitors of Others

Edward E. Leamer

I. Setting

Much of the economic energy of the globe after World War II concentrated on integrating the war-torn areas of Europe and Japan with the powerhouse economy of the United States. This was a happy time for all the participants. The three decades after WWII witnessed very high rates of GDP growth in Europe and Japan, excellent numbers for the United States, and even greater growth of global trade. The European countries and Japan had work forces with education levels comparable with the United States and the increased trade allowed substantial wage increases in Europe and Japan without much apparent downward pressure on wages in the United States. In other words, this economic integration caused convergence of living standards mostly "from below," raising living standards greatly in Europe and Japan without any apparent substantial downward pressure on wages in the United States. On the contrary, the emergence of export markets in Europe and to some extent Japan may well have contributed to the substantial wage increases that occurred in the United States.

This "comfortable" trade among the educated has been threatened by the economic liberalizations around the globe that are adding an enormous number of low-skilled workers to the global labor markets, with no commensurate increase in human or physical capital. With the rise of China as a great trading nation and Southeast Asia and Latin America and Eastern Europe, it seems certain that the global trading patterns of the 21st century will be very different from the patterns of 1980. The "comfortable" club of high-wage, highly-educated trading nations is having to make room for an enormous number of low-wage uneducated workers. Is convergence of living standards now working mostly "from above", dragging wages in the United States down toward the Chinese level? Or is the globe about to experience another burst of economic progress with benefits that are broadly distributed among all the participants?

The Europeans, and the Japanese have been competing with American workers since the 1960s. The Taiwanese and the Koreans joined the competition in the 1970s and the Mexicans and the Chinese entered in the 1980s. Waiting in the wings are the Indians and the Indonesians. That seems like pretty discouraging news for American workers since the Chinese and the Indians and the Indonesians are both extraordinarily numerous and extremely poorly paid. But things have gone from bad to worse. In the 1990s an entirely new kind of worker entered the global labor markets in huge numbers. These new entrants had very low wages in 1990, but year after year they are working harder and harder for less and less pay. Employers around the globe are exploiting these aliens by forcing them to work virtually around the clock in unsafe and unhealthy conditions that grossly violate U.S. health and safety laws. As extraordinary as it may seem, even the United States government has laws preventing unionization of these workers. And most of these alien workers are under the age of ten! You know of whom I speak—it's the Microprocessors.

Integration of all these low-wage workers into the global economy creates both opportunities and challenges for the high-wage workers of the world. Obviously things look pretty bleak for anyone who tries to compete with either the Chinese, the Indians or the Microprocessors. But workers who do not do the same tasks as these low-wage laborers, or even better, workers who use these low-wage workers as assistants, can expect to do quite well in the next Millennium. A critical public policy problem facing governments around the globe is therefore how to assure that workers benefit from the forces created by globalization and technological change. If governments and individuals do not respond effectively, and if these forces continue unabated, the consequent rise in income inequality in many communities will put terrific strain on economic and political systems. Looking backward, the rise in income inequality has already been historic and the strain on our social systems has been substantial. Looking forward, things are likely only to intensify. What now can communities and countries do to insulate their workers from ruinous competition with Microprocessors and Foreigners? How can we in the United States assure that these Microprocessors and Foreigners will be our assistants, not our competitors?

If there were no Microprocessors but only low-wage Foreigners, there are three pretty obvious "right" answers to this policy question: Education, Education and Education. The liberalizations that have swept the globe have created great new gains from trade to be had by skilled workers. But these same liberalizations have created hopelessly intense competition ahead for workers who have not much more to offer than raw labor power.

Education and training can raise wages of some Americans, but what about the less-than-average Joe and the less-than-average Sally, who have dropped out of high school or graduated with poor math and verbal skills? Do they have to compete with the Chinese and Indians? In this seamless global economy toward which we are heading, will geography no long matter? Will Joe and Sally in Los Angeles be paid the same as Chen in Shanghai? "Not necessarily," is the answer. Low-skilled workers can have decent wages if they reside in communities inhabited mostly by skilled workers. Using the schematic representation below, as a first approximation, it is useful to imagine three tiers of countries. The first tier is composed of skill- and capital- abundant communities that export chemicals, machinery, software and financial services to the emerging third world in exchange for apparel and textiles and toys and assembled electronics. Seattle is an example. The third tier consists of labor-abundant communities like Shanghai that compete in the crowded global marketplaces in apparel and textiles and toys. Communities with intermediate supplies of capital and skills form the middle, second tier. These second tier countries have competitors both above and below. They produce aircraft in competition with first-tier countries and apparel in competition with the third-tier. Think Los Angeles.

Whether low-wage, low-skilled foreigners are your assistants or your competitors depends both on your skills and also on the tier in which you happen to work. In first tier countries like Sweden and Switzerland both skilled and unskilled workers employ low wage third-tier workers as their assistants. These assistants do low-wage work making apparel and footwear. These assistants do not, of course, reside in Sweden and Switzerland, but they do not have to; they ship their labor services but not themselves in aircraft crates and ocean-going containers. These assistants free up first-tier workers to take high-wage jobs in aircraft and chemicals and financial services.

	Factor Supplies	**Product Mix**	**Example**
First Tier	Abundant Skills	Aircraft	Seattle
Second Tier	Moderate Skills	Aircraft and Apparel	Los Angeles
Third Tier	Scarce Skills	Apparel	Shanghai

In third-tier countries like China and Mexico, low-skilled workers have competitors, not assistants in other third-tier countries. (It is very bad news indeed for Mexican workers that the Chinese have entered the global product markets in such a big way.)

The second tier is different. In the second tier, foreign unskilled workers are the assistants of the skilled but the competitors of the unskilled. Here is why. Low-skilled workers who sew apparel in second tier countries have wages set to assure that the local apparel sector is competitive against third-tier locations of production. That means low wages. This competition with the third tier does not affect wages only in the apparel sector. Job mobility between apparel and aircraft and services in the second tier countries assures that all unskilled workers get paid the same low amount. Thus the third-tier unskilled workers are the direct or indirect competitors of all second-tier unskilled workers. The skilled workers in the second tier have an entirely different outcome; they are triply blessed. They have foreign low-paid assistants to make their apparel and footwear, and they have local low-wage, low-skilled assistants to help make the aircraft and the chemicals, and they have local low-wage, low-skilled assistants to tend the gardens, cut the hair and serve the meals in restaurants. Access to low-wage, low-skilled workers to help make the aircraft gives the skilled workers in the second tier a competitive advantage over first-tier skilled aircraft workers who have to pay high wages to their local assistants. When these skilled workers in the second tier take home their fat paychecks, they discover yet another blessing: haircuts and gardening and restaurant meals are a lot cheaper because the workers who provide these services have wages set indirectly in competition with the third tier. Consequently, it is in the second tier where skilled workers command the highest wages, both because they have high take-home pay and also because local services are cheap.

The right policy option for the first-tier countries is: Enjoy. Don't sit back and enjoy. Maintain your lead in education and infrastructure, and enjoy the great gains from trade. The third-tier countries, like the first-tier countries, should have no problem choosing trade policy. Although income inequality is most extreme in the third tier, the costs of closing down external trade are enormous and not really an option, as has been proven by many third-tier experiments over the last several decades.

The right policy option for the second-tier countries is not so clear. There are substantial gains from trade for these countries, which makes trade barriers seem undesirable. But free trade will also increase income inequality. Wages of low-skilled workers will be set low in competition with the third-tier. Wages of the highly skilled will be set high in competition with the first-tier. The quick fix for the income inequality in second-tier countries is trade barriers. This is almost surely trading modest short-term improvements in income equality for substantial long-term losses in living standards overall. A longer-run view would allow the rise in income inequality to create incentives for educational investments that would move this second-tier country into the first tier, or at a minimum keep it from falling into the third tier. In these countries it is probably best to think of income equality as something undesirable, namely poverty of opportunity.

The three tiers of countries are separated by education, market access (infrastructure) and history. The United States is blessed with a great history and excellent market access. History probably once mattered more than it does today. In the 1960s trade was said to be driven by a "technology gap" but that word pair is never mentioned today. Today, the playing field looks pretty level. That is not surprising. Multinational corporations have as their primary function the location of intangible knowledge assets where these assets have the highest rates of return. In addition, the global village that is today woven together tightly with trade and communication links does not long tolerate substantial gaps in access to knowledge. Still, anyone who looks at data carefully cannot help but be impressed by how slowly moving over time are the patterns of employment, production and trade. Thus although the first-mover advantages that the United States enjoys may not be as substantial as they once were, they remain an important consideration. Education is a different story. The United States once was the global leader in education, but the erosion of the U.S. educational system and the great human and physical capital investments being made in Europe and Asia threaten to turn the United States into a second-tier global competitor that produces some first-tier goods like aircraft and chemicals but also competes with the Chinese in the third-tier markets of apparel and textiles.

Immigration, by the way, is another concern. First-tier communities with restricted immigration suffer no arbitrage possibilities that link their low-skilled workers with low-skilled workers in the third tier. But free immigration from the third tier creates an arbitrage link that directly equates wages in the two tiers and that drags the first-tier community into the second tier. I like to contrast the city of Seattle, a first-tier community, with the city of Los Angeles (LA), a second-tier community. The tradables in Seattle are aircraft and software. The tradables in Los Angeles are aircraft, movies and apparel. It is the apparel sector that links LA unskilled workers with the Chinese. What supports the apparel sector in LA, and why is this one of the few tradables sectors that has experienced employment growth in the last decade? Migration of unskilled workers from Mexico and Central America is the answer. Thus free mobility of products is very different from free mobility of workers. Seattle can have high wages for unskilled workers with free trade in products, but if the enclave/social barriers that keep Latinos from migrating from Los Angeles to Seattle are eliminated, then Seattle also will be a second-tier community.

If it is not the third-tier, low-wage workers but the Microprocessors that drive the labor-market outcomes, then the right policy option may also be education. One difference between the Microprocessors and the third-tier workers is that there are no trade barriers that can keep goods made by Microprocessors out of our product markets and no immigration barriers that keep Microprocessors out of the U.S. labor markets. Microprocessors will therefore be paid the same everywhere in the globe, first-tier, second-tier and third-tier. Workers who offer to do the same tasks as the Microprocessors will receive the same low rate of pay, regardless of where they happen to be employed. Thus the need to upgrade our educational system is even more urgent if it is Microprocessors not Chinese who are driving the competition.

There is also a big difference between a container of Chinese apparel and a container of Microprocessors. It does not take a rocket scientist to unpackage the Chinese apparel and to put the products to use in American homes and businesses. But it does take the equivalent of a rocket scientist to unpackage a microprocessor, and put it to use. Innovations in microprocessing have greatly but temporarily increased the demand for skilled workers who can do the installations. I do not mean putting computer equipment on your desktop and plugging it in. I mean doing the computer programming that lets the machine speak with mere mortals. I mean Bill Gates. But this is a temporary phenomenon. It is highly unlikely that there will be another Bill Gates of desktop computing. Now that we have Microsoft Office installed on all our desktops, there is not much need for an entirely new installation.

Education may be a solution to the temporary and permanent income-inequality problems caused by the increased supply of Microprocessors. We just need to teach everyone how to write computer code. This might work, but it might not. I like to raise some doubts by posing the rhetorical question; "Is a computer more like a forklift or more like a microphone?" What I am getting at is that it does not matter much who drives the forklift, but it matters a lot who sings into the microphone. Think about the forklift first. You might be a lot stronger than I am, but with a little bit of training, most of us can operate a forklift with a reasonable degree of effectiveness, and all operators will receive about the same wage rate. Thus the forklift is a force for income equality, eliminating your strength advantage over me. That is decidedly not the case for a microphone. We cannot all operate a microphone with anywhere near the same level of proficiency. Indeed, I venture the guess that I would have to pay you to listen to me sing, not the other way round. And I seriously doubt that a lifetime of training would allow me to compete with Michael Jackson, or Pavarotti. The effect of the microphone and mass media has been to allow a single talented entertainer to service a huge customer base and accordingly to command enormous earnings. This creates an earnings distribution with a few extremely highly paid talented and trained individuals and with the vast group of slightly less talented working in LA restaurants, hoping someday to hit it big. Thus, opposite to the forklift, the microphone creates a powerful force for inequality.

A computer is both a forklift and a microphone. Clerks in McDonald's no longer have to be able to read or to compute—they only have to be trained to recognize the picture of a hamburger on the cash register. That is the forklift. It does not much matter who punches the buttons. But for many other operations it matters enormously who types on the computer. The vast majority of people are incapable of producing commercially viable computer code. That is the microphone. A talented architect with a computer assistant can serve a much enlarged customer base. A talented attorney, or a talented economist, or a talented radiologist, with computer assistants, can serve much enlarged customer bases. These talented individuals command high wages while the less talented struggle for customers.

In other words, the information revolution may be a powerful force for income inequality by raising the compensation for natural talents and also the interaction between talent and training. It is the interaction between talent and training that is particularly difficult to deal with. If talent and training had additive effects on earnings, then compensatory education for the disadvantaged could be a low-cost solution for income inequality problems. But if training is much more effective for the talented, the talented will naturally receive more of it, and the amount of compensatory training that is needed to equalize incomes may be enormous and a great social waste—think of me and Pavarotti again.

II. Theory and Evidence

The Rise in Inequality Begins in the Early 1970s

Throughout much of the twentieth century, the dream of improved economic well-being for all Americans was a reality The first seven decades of the twentieth century brought steady and substantial increases in real earnings in the United States in both manufacturing and agriculture. The 1960s was a particularly good decade with almost 5% per annum increases in agricultural earnings and almost 1.5% per annum in manufacturing earnings. Workers at every level of the skill distribution participated in these earnings increases. The American dream died early in the 1970s when overall wage growth terminated and the gap between the rich and the poor began a precipitous increase. The problem was not just with average wages; wage inequality has also increased. The Gini coefficient and the ratio of income at the 4th quintile to the 1st quintile which had generally been falling started a steady and substantial rise in 1970 (figure 2.1). Naturally, Americans have been sorely disappointed by the growing discrepancy between expectations and reality. They do not like seeing their earnings stagnate and even decline; they particularly do not like it when incomes of the very few continue to rise.

Is it International Trade that is Causing the Rise in Inequality?

Unlike the eyewitness accounts of the "damage" being done by a deteriorating educational system, by immigration and the information revolution, the evidence against international trade is mostly circumstantial and largely captured in figures 2.2 and 2.3. Figure 2.2 compares over the last several decades the levels of real wages in manufacturing(using both the CPI deflator and the PPI deflator) and displays on another scale the U.S. trade dependence ratio, the ratio of exports plus imports divided by GDP. Figure 2.3 illustrates the vast differences between wages earned by U.S. manufacturing workers and wages earned in much of the rest of the world.

Figure 2.2 reveals that the abrupt halt in the early 1970s to the previously very steady rise in real wages came suspiciously at a time when the United States was experiencing a rapid increase in trade dependence. The reason why increasing trade dependence might hold down U.S. wages is suggested by figure 2.3 in which each country is represented by a line segment with height equal to 1989 wages and width equal to population., and countries are sorted by wage levels. If this is the global labor pool, it is a very strange pool indeed, with the liquid piled high at one end and hardly present at the other. What could possibly be holding up the high end? Barriers is one answer. The arbitrage opportunities suggested by figure 2.3 have not genuinely been present

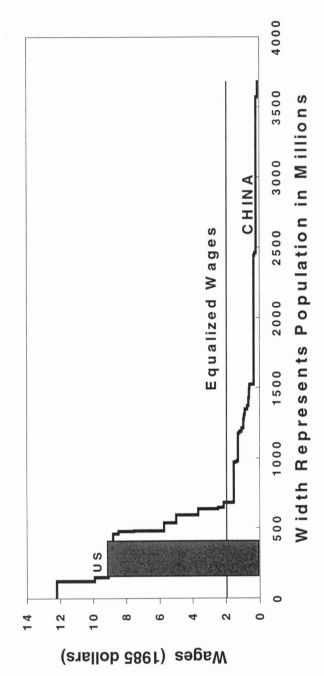

Figure 2.1. Measures of US Income Inequality
Source: US Census Bureau, Current Population Reports

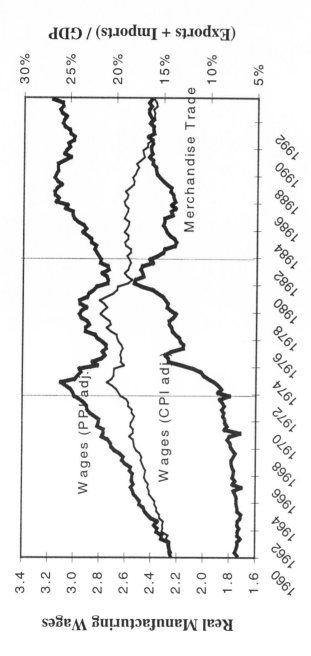

Figure 2.2. Wages and Trade Dependence.
Gross Hourly Earnings of Manufacturing Production and Non-supervisory Workers and Trade Dependence (1960 $)

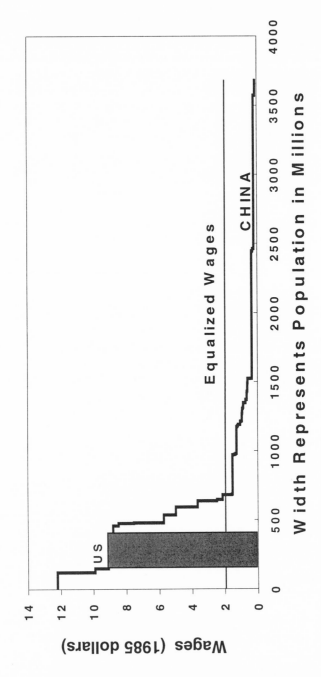

Figure 2.3. Industrial Wages and Population, 1989

because of the real and threatened interventions by governments which iso-lated workers in the high-wage countries from competition with workers in the low-wage third world. Now, according to this line of thinking, the liberaliza-tions that are sweeping the globe are bringing U.S. workers suddenly in direct competition with a huge army of workers who are receiving wages that are a tiny fraction of U.S. levels. If the workforces in China and India and Mexico and South America are integrated through the exchange of products with the U.S. workforce, how could the U.S. resist substantial downward movement of wages of unskilled workers?

Will U.S. Wages Fall to Chinese Levels?

The global labor pool illustrated in figure 2.3 is alarming since it suggests a potentially enormous fall in U.S. wages coming from the decline in barriers that have prevented workers at different points on the globe from competing against each other. If the global wage bill is kept constant and wages equally distributed, that is, if the liquid in the global labor pool is allowed to seek a common level, then U.S. wages would fall from $9 per hour to $2 (1985$). That would be a wrenching change indeed. But there are several reasons why U.S. wages need not be dragged down in competition with the Chinese and the Mexicans. After all, government barriers are not the only reason for differ-ences in wages across individuals or across countries, and economic liberal-ization does not mean that all workers on the globe will receive the same wage rate. Wage differences that come from productivity differences obviously will not be eliminated. Superior productivity of an individual can come from supe-rior effort, superior natural ability, superior education, superior tools and supe-rior teams. None of these sources of wage differences is necessarily eliminated by competition in the product markets, although technology and organizational forms can be hidden stowaways on the same ships and planes that carry prod-ucts internationally.

Clearly U.S. laborers who work harder, who are employed in superior or-ganizations, who have better natural ability, superior education and superior tools can expect to receive higher wages than Chinese workers not so well equipped. But what about the "average Joe" who is economically indistin-guishable from the "average Chen"? Doesn't economic liberalization mean the same wages for both? Maybe, and maybe not. A link between Chinese wages and U.S. wages is created when Chinese and U.S. workers produce the same products and sell in the same markets, for example, apparel. Then U.S. apparel wages have to be set to make the U.S. products competitive with the Chinese products in the global marketplace. Wages of unskilled workers in the U.S. apparel sector are of course linked to wages of unskilled workers in other sec-tors provided there is job mobility. Thus in communities that produce apparel in direct competition with Chinese apparel, every worker in the same re-gional/skill group is competing with the Chinese, even the restaurant workers and the gardeners. Chinese wages and U.S. wages can be unlinked, however, if

China and the United States have no common products. This can occur if the United States specializes in one set of products, aircraft for example, and the Chinese specialize in another set of products, say apparel. Then low-skilled U.S. workers could be employed at high wages either in the production of aircraft or they could provide local services like restaurant work and gardening. U.S. workers in neither aircraft nor gardening nor restaurants would feel their jobs threatened by an expansion of Chinese exports of apparel. On the contrary, they would welcome the lower prices of apparel that would come from the emergence of China. This rising tide of globalization would lift all boats.

This "world" model of global labor competition is translated into a diagram, figure 2.4, which illustrates a labor demand curve implied by a standard textbook model of international competition – the Heckscher-Ohlin (HO) model. This labor demand curve has two downward sloping segments in which increases in labor supply drive down wages and a horizontal segment in which the labor demand is infinitely elastic. In this horizontal segment, increases in labor supply do not affect wages. In this horizontal segment wages are set completely by external competitiveness conditions. How can this be? This horizontal segment of the labor demand curve comes from the assumptions that there are two factors of production (e.g., labor and capital) that can be freely divided between two tradables (e.g., apparel and aircraft). In each sector there is a zero-profit condition that equates the price of the good to the cost of production.[1] If product prices are set in the global product market, then these two zero-profit conditions can be inverted to solve for the prices of the two inputs. This mathematical manipulation does not depend at all on the supplies of labor and capital. It is enough to have the two zero-profit conditions. It is enough that both goods are produced. So what happens when labor supply increases? There is a shift of capital from aircraft to apparel, which raises the demand for labor just enough to keep wages at their initial level. This, by the way, is what trade economists call the Factor Price Equalization theorem, which would more accurately be called the Factor Price Insensitivity Theorem, meaning that wages do not depend on labor supply.

The economies that have labor supply relative to capital that place them in the two downward sloping segments of the labor demand curve in figure 2.4 produce only a single tradable. Then the one zero profit condition applicable to tradables is not enough to determine the two factor prices. For these economies, the demand for nontradables affects wages, and increases in labor supply drive down wages.

Figure 2.5 illustrates what happens to labor demand if the price of the labor-intensive tradable falls as a result, for example, of increased competition from China. The labor demand twists. Higher wages are awarded in communities that are richly endowed in capital. Lower wages are awarded in communities that are poorly endowed in capital. The former do not compete with the Chinese—they do not produce apparel. The latter do.

The Stolper-Samuelson Theorem describes the fall in real wages in those communities that are fully diversified before and after the fall in the apparel

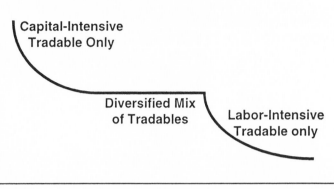

Real wages of workers in terms of the labor-intensive tradable

Capital-Intensive Tradable Only

Diversified Mix of Tradables

Labor-Intensive Tradable only

Labor / Capital Ratio

Diversified Economy

- Number of tradables = number of factors of production
- Wages set by external competitiveness conditions
  Input Costs = Product Prices
  $A w = p$
- Stolper-Samuelson Mapping
  $w = A^{-1} p$
- A trade deficit doesn't matter

Specialized Economy

- Number of tradables less than number of factors of production
- Wages depend on local demand for nontradables
- A trade deficit that finances local expenditures increases labor demand

---

Figure 2.4
Demand for Unskilled Workers: Wages are set on the margin
Heckscher-Ohlin General Equilibrium Model
Two inputs: Skilled and Unskilled Workers
Two Tradables and One Unskilled-Intensive Nontradable

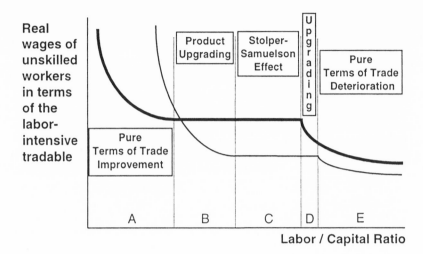

Figure 2.5
Effect of Decline in Relative Price of Labor-intensive Tradable
Heckscher-Ohlin General Equilibrium Model of Labor Demand

price. These communities have labor-to-capital ratios in the interval C in figure 2.5 that selects a horizontal labor demand both before and after the fall in the price of apparel. Communities with lower labor-to capital ratios in interval B experience product upgrading—they escape the Chinese competition by getting out of the apparel business altogether. Some communities in interval B have lower wages as a result of the fall in the apparel price, but others have higher wages. It depends on how much apparel was produced before the increased competition. If no apparel were produced, that is, if labor is very scarce relative to capital and the labor-to-capital ratio falls in interval A, then wages necessarily rise—there is a pure terms of trade effect.

As the price of apparel falls, the favorable product upgrading effect spreads even to communities that began with substantial apparel production. These communities will suffer wage declines initially as the price of apparel falls, but then the decline can reverse, and wages can rise back to, and even above, their initial levels. I suspect that this might have happened in the United States. Falling apparel prices in the 1970s were a force for lower U.S. wages, but by the 1980s the industry had product upgraded: t-shirts and jeans were no longer produced here. This product upgrading isolated the U.S. workers from Chinese competition, and the lower prices of t-shirts and jeans meant higher real wages for anyone who wore them.

This happy upgrading outcome is threatened by global capital mobility. If manufacturers of aircraft notice the low wages in China, they may be tempted to shift production from Seattle to Shanghai. In principle, a combination of trade and capital mobility is capable of eliminating all wage differences for equivalent workers in the United States, China and Mexico. But is this a likely outcome? What chance is there really that Boeing will move from Seattle to Shanghai? One important source of immobility is superior and cheaper human capital in Seattle. It is one thing to move the production facilities to China; it is quite another to move the designers, engineers, skilled craftsman, etc. Another reason to stay in Seattle is infrastructure. Thus although some forms of capital are or will become much more mobile, other forms are not and will not. Communities that make heavy investments in these immobile assets can attract the mobile assets and can end up with a product mix that economically isolates their unskilled workers from competition with the Chinese. Build it, and they will come—apologies to Kevin Costner.

Distance is an Important Isolating Force, Like 200% Tariffs

Even with complete capital mobility there is another powerful isolating force: distance. The distance effect on international commerce is described by the most successful empirical model in international trade—the gravity model. According to this empirical model, commerce between any two points on the globe is proportional to the product of the masses (GDPs) divided by the distance between them raised to approximately 0.6. The message of this gravity model is that the globe is not nearly as small as newspapers and business school curricula suggest. Merely eliminating government interference in international commerce is not enough to allow all the arbitrage opportunities that are suggested by the wage differences illustrated in figure 2.3 since many of the low-wage countries are very far from the high-wage marketplaces.

Neutral Transfer of Technology to the Third Tier is not a Big Problem

Both immobile assets and distance from Asia can protect American workers from the force of competition with the Chinese. There is another important reason why the global labor pool, figure 2.3, need not be too alarming. Wage equalization may work more from below than from above, mostly raising Chinese and Mexican wages, not much lowering of U.S. wages. This would occur if the wages in China and Mexico are low not because of abundance of unskilled workers but rather because these workers are equipped with technologically inferior tools and work in inferior organizations. Unlike physical capital, knowledge assets can be transferred to the developing countries without depleting their stocks in the United States. This transfer might, but need not, make U.S. workers worse off. According to the HO theory that is driving this discussion, the messenger that carries the news of third-world liberalization to first-world labor markets is relative prices—specifically a decline in prices of labor-intensive products. The transfer of technology and the improvements in organizations in the third world which raise productivity levels can, but need not, change relative product prices.[2] Indeed it seems probable that the high relative price of capital-intensive goods in the developing countries is partly a result of technological backwardness. Thus at least some product-price convergence can come from technological convergence without any international trade of products and without negative effects on U.S. wage levels.

Finally, do not forget the gains from specialization. The equalized wage line in figure 2.3 does not allow for any increase in global labor earnings. But the primary reason for international trade is to realize the gains from specialization, which gains will in principal be shared by all factors globally, increasing earnings in some countries by an amount that more than compensates for the loss in other countries.[3]

What Has Been Happening In the Apparel Sector?

Theoretically, we are now the proverbial "not-so-handy" economist: "On the one hand and on the other hand...." Some facts may help to sort out this bewildering set of possibilities. Apparel employment, producer prices and imports are illustrated in figure 2.6. From 1960 to 1972 import levels were low, prices were stable and employment rising. From 1972 to 1984 the import share of apparel production rose from under 5% to about 30%, prices relative to the overall PPI fell by over 30% and employment dropped from a peak of 1.4 mil-

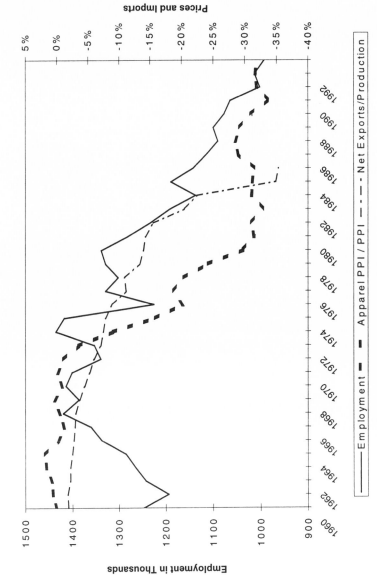

Figure 2.6. Apparel Employment, Prices, and Imports

lion down to 1.2 million. After 1984, apparel prices stabilized even as imports continued to increase and employment levels fall.

It seems pretty clear that rising import levels contributed to falling prices in apparel from 1972 to 1984. It seems surprising that after 1984 apparel producer prices stabilized even as imports continued to increase. Possibly, by the early 1980s most of the jobs in the "commodity" segment of the apparel industry were in Asia and what was left in the United States was mostly women's high fashion clothing in which there is a substantial advantage that comes from being near the market. In other words product upgrading and distance to Asia isolated the U.S. worker from low-wage global competition in the 1980s.

But Does the Tail Wag the Dog?

The apparel sector has only about 1 million workers out of workforce of 120 million. How could such a small sector matter so much? Does the tail wag the dog? Krugman (1995, p. 47), among others, does not think so: "Imports (other than oil) from low-wage countries—those where workers earn less than half the U.S. level—were a mere 2.8 percent of GDP." But one of the most important lessons of introductory economics is that *prices are set on the margin.* Remember the diamond and water paradox. Why is water so cheap and diamonds so expensive? Clearly the water is more valuable than diamonds. Yes, that is so, explains the instructor, but not at the margin. The first glass of water that you drink each day is worth an enormous amount, but the seventh is hardly worth anything. The beneficent feature of a market system is that you do not have to pay the full value; you pay the same price for every glass, the low marginal price. That is the source of consumer surplus. Fortunately there is enough water supply to drive down the marginal value to a very low level. Then the price of water is low, even though its value is high. Most economists think that the labor market if given enough time operates about the same as a product market and therefore wages of workers are also set on the margin. Imagine a labor demand curve like the one depicted in figure 2.4. The first workers are allocated to the highest value uses, but as more and more workers are added to the labor market, they must be assigned to tasks that are ever less valuable. A community with a very large number of unskilled workers may be forced to find jobs for some of these workers sewing garments. If these are the marginal workers, then all other workers in the same regional/skill group receive the same low wages. It does not matter if these workers are gardeners, waiters or janitors in aerospace firms. Their wages are all set in the garment district. Inframarginal workers may be highly productive, but it is the value of the product of the *marginal* worker that matters.

What job is the marginal worker performing? Quite possibly the marginal unskilled worker in your community is sewing apparel in competition with the Chinese. It then does not matter that trade in manufactures is a small proportion of GDP. It does not matter that employment in apparel is only one percent of the workforce. It does not matter whether your community is exporting apparel, or importing or has exactly balanced trade. What matters is whether or not the marginal unskilled worker is employed in the apparel sector, sewing the same garments as a Chinese worker whose wages are 1/20th of the U.S. level. If your community has so many unskilled workers compared with capital that it is forced to hang on to the apparel sector, (Segment C in figure 2.5), then the Chinese competition will drive down wages of the unskilled, not only in the apparel sector, but for all unskilled workers in the same regional labor pool as the directly affected garment worker.

There is, of course, a sense in which quantities matter. If your community has a very small initial share of apparel, it may respond to increased Chinese competition by product upgrading, as occurs in interval B in figure 2.5. The give-away signal that this did not occur is the retention of the apparel sector in response to the increased external competition. If the apparel sector is retained, any information about trade or production volumes is totally irrelevant—your community is certainly in the exposed region C in figure 2.5 in which Chinese competition has driven wages down.

Incidentally, your community may hang onto the apparel sector because an influx of unskilled immigrants raises the labor-to-capital ratio and pushes the community down the labor-demand curve. You may start in interval B in which there is a favorable product upgrading effect, but your workers may lose out because of the immigration. Incidentally, according to the demand curve in figure 2.5, immigration alone would not drive down wages. *The problem is neither trade nor immigration working alone. It is the two together that forces wages down.*

Do trade volumes matter?

Do you remember the case of Krugman Air, which uses a secret input—Mexican power—to fly its airplanes at low cost.? When Krugman Air started to compete in the U.S. market, it offered to fly U.S. routes at half the going price. The response of U.S. carriers was to match the price and find various ways to cut costs including lowering hourly wages by 30% and expanding hours per week by 10%. "Not us," explained the economists who worked for Krugman Air, "We couldn't have been responsible for all that reduction in wages. We are too small. We only have a 2.8% market share."

Will Rogers:

It's not what you know that will hurt you, it's what you know that ain't so.

III. Sectoral Price Changes

According to the HO model, the news of the liberalization of Asia is carried to U.S. labor markets by declines in prices of labor-intensive tradables such as apparel and toys. But Lawrence and Slaughter(1993) find little decline in the prices of labor-intensive tradables in the 1980s. This finding is echoed by Bhagwati(1994) and by Krugman and Lawrence (1993, 1994). Even Sachs and Shatz (1994) who are overall sympathetic to the idea that increased competition with low-wage developing countries is lowering wages of the unskilled nevertheless have a hard time finding supporting evidence in the price data. The findings of these authors seem based primarily on the subperiods over which they have measured relative prices. In fact, the two-digit relative price data in figure 2.7 evidence three distinct subperiods. Most of the relative price reductions of labor-intensive products occurred in the turbulent middle period stretching from 1972 to 1983. In the first period from 1960 to 1972 the price of the labor-intensive products (apparel and textiles) relative to the overall PPI fell modestly by about 4% and 8% respectively. In the second period from 1972 to 1983, prices of these labor-intensive products fell by another 30%. Then in the third period, there was little change in the relative price of apparel and textiles.[4]

What About Technology?

The increased competition with low-wage Asia has occurred at the same time as the "information revolution", and it is not at all clear which is the more important source of rising inequality. Whether you are studying trade or technology, it is a good idea to have your thinking organized by a clearly articulated model. Casual thinking by Luddites, journalists, and many economists makes them think that what matters is the factor bias of technological change. According to this way of thinking, unskilled workers are hurt by innovations that reduce the need for them in production. Even in a partial equilibrium framework, this is questionable. If the new equipment were robots that did the same work as the unskilled humans, but at lower pay, clearly there is something for the workers to worry about. But if the new robots are only assistants who help the unskilled carry out some of their functions more effectively, there is reason to suppose that the innovation could increase wages. In other words, one has to be careful in deciding just how a specific innovation shifts the derived demand for labor.

   More importantly, except in the very short run, workers are not tied to their initial industry, and wages are not determined in a single sector but rather in a general equilibrium. A general equilibrium model suggests a dramatically different conclusion: it does not matter that the technological change reduces the inputs of unskilled workers in every sector; what does matter is whether the technological improvement is concentrated in sectors that are intensive in unskilled workers, intensive in skilled workers or intensive in capital. *It is the sector bias not the factor bias of technological change that matters.*

   The surprising conclusion that the factor bias does not matter can be derived fairly straightforwardly from a definition of the growth in Total Factor

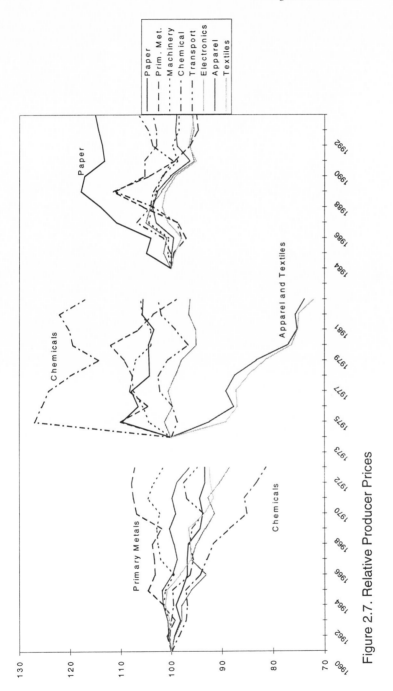

Figure 2.7. Relative Producer Prices

Productivity as the growth in compensation of the factors compared with the growth in the product price:

$$T\hat{F}P_i \equiv \theta_i' \hat{w}_i - \hat{p}_i \tag{1}$$

where the carats indicate percentage changes, the subscript i the sector, p the price level, θ the vector of factor shares, and w the vector of factor prices. This equation has to hold in order to maintain zero profits in sector i. For example, to maintain zero profits, an increase in TFP has to be accompanied by a rise in factor rewards.

To decide how compensation rates must respond if factors of production are mobile across sectors of the economy, simply drop the i subscript for wages in equation (1). Then if we are given TFP changes and product prices changes in all the sectors of the economy, we can solve for the factor price changes needed to keep zero profits. This calculation makes use of overall TFP changes, but it does not matter whether the overall change comes from labor-saving or capital-saving improvements. This is an implication of equation (1) because it depends only on the overall TFP growth in the sector. Thus, it is the sector bias that causes income inequality, not the factor bias.[5]

You are probably thinking that there must be something wrong with any model that does not allow labor-saving technological improvements to affect wages. Not to worry. There is a route by which factor bias can affect compensation levels even with equation (1) applicable. Labor-saving technological improvements can release workers who find jobs only if the labor-intensive sectors expand, which new output can be sold only at lower prices. In other words, *factor-biased* technological change can beget *sector-biased*, product-price changes which then requires changes in compensation rates to make Equation (1) hold. Thus the factor bias can matter. But be a little careful here. There is a critical intermediary in transmitting the news of factor-bias technological change to the labor markets—it is sector-biased product-price changes. This is exactly the same messenger that carries the news of the liberalization of China to the U.S. labor markets. The difficulties that many of us have had in finding sector-biased changes in product prices in the 1980s thus casts equivalent amounts of doubt on technological change as on globalization as explanations of increasing wage inequality.

This leads into a more general point. In order to determine the effect of technological change on wages, we need to be very clear about the effect that technological change has on product prices. For example, if TFP growth is exactly matched by price reductions, then equation (1) could be satisfied with no change in nominal factor earnings. The overall reduction in prices would then raise real compensation of all factors by the same percentage.

The problem of how properly to account for price changes induced by technological change is very great and entirely unresolved. The resolution requires a full general equilibrium system with a carefully specified demand side. Until this problem is resolved, we really will not have much idea of the impact of technological change on the labor market. Tentatively, from the results in Leamer (1997), I conclude that price declines of labor-intensive tradables have had a substantial effect on low-wage workers in the 1970s but this is offset in the 1980s. Technological change was a big driving force lowering wages of high-wage workers in the 1980s.

IV. What about the Increase in the Ratio of Skilled to Unskilled Workers? It's Outsourcing, not Technological Change.

Berman, Bound and Griliches (1992) decompose the changing "demand" for unskilled workers into a part that comes from the changing mix of industries (the between component) and a part that comes from changes in the "demand" for unskilled workers within industries (the within component). They base their analysis on an implicit assumption that events occurring *within* sectors must be due to technology and events *between* sectors must be due to trade. This is a commonly held opinion, for example, Krugman (1995, p.47): "The rise in demand for skilled workers was overwhelmingly caused by changes in demand within each industrial sector, not by a shift of the U.S. industrial mix in response to trade."

In a parallel argument, Lawrence and Slaughter (1993) attribute the rise in the ratio of nonproduction to production workers within most manufacturing sectors in the 1980s to technology, not trade. They point out that the trade model suggests that increased competition with foreign low-wage low-skilled workers drives down the wages of the unskilled, and if substitution is technologically feasible, businesses should use more of the unskilled, not less. Thus, they argue, the reverse movement in favor of nonproduction employment must be interpreted as evidence that it is technology, not trade that is driving wages.

I am unconvinced by either Berman, Bound, and Griliches or Lawrence and Slaughter. Let us take a look again at my favorite sector: apparel. The employment levels of production and nonproduction employment the apparel sector are displayed in figure 2.8. What you see is a rise in the ratio of nonproduction to production workers as Lawrence and Slaughter point out, and of course you are looking at something strictly *within* a sector, what Berman, Bound and Griliches would attribute to technology. But I look at this figure, and I do not see technology at work; I see trade. The increased foreign competition in apparel could not be met merely by lowering wages of production workers. Instead, the production jobs were moved offshore, even as the nonproduction jobs expanded at home, thus increasing the ratio of nonproduction to production jobs. Even if this reduction in production jobs is related to technological improvements, the fundamental driver may still be trade, which necessitated the installation of equipment to raise productivities.[6]

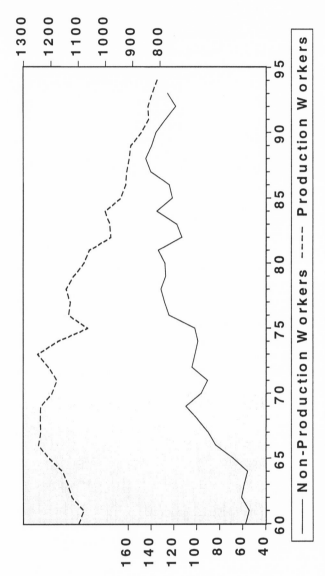

Figure 2.8. Outsourcing: Production and Non-production Workers in Apparel

V. Aren't There Other Forms of "Globalization"?

I think there is clear evidence that "globalization" drove down prices of labor-intensive tradables which produced "Stolper-Samuelson" forces that lowered the wages of unskilled U.S. workers in the decade of the 1970s. But the increase in earnings inequality continued in the 1980s even as relative producer prices stabilized. Thus if you are a trade-kook, you have a timing problem to deal with. It is possible that the relative product price changes in the 1970s take several decades to filter through the U.S. labor markets. Keep in mind that the Stolper-Samuelson theorem applies in a time frame that is long enough to allow complete detachment of workers and capital from their initial sectors. The persistence of country production patterns from decade to decade is very great, which makes one think that the Heckscher-Ohlin Stolper-Samuelson "period" is at least a decade and maybe several.

Thus if "globalization" is your favorite suspect, you can blame the damage in the 1980s on the price changes of the 1970s. But you are probably going to be more comfortable arguing that the Stolper-Samuelson relative price changes are not the only way that globalization affects U.S. labor markets.

To set the stage for a discussion of non-Heckscher-Ohlin models, take a look at figures 2.9 and 2.10. Figure 2.9 is a HO type of outcome. It shows employment levels in the labor-intensive sectors of apparel, footwear, leather and textiles. From 1970 to 1992 the United States lost about 800,000 jobs in these sectors. Germany, the United Kingdom, and Japan had almost the same experience. Where were these jobs going? Mostly to low-wage Asia. Korea gained about 400,000 jobs from 1970 to 1978, but experienced no growth thereafter, basically because its labor had priced itself out of this activity. This OECD data set does not include the other major apparel exporters, but you know the story. China, for example, expanded rapidly in the late 1980s. This movement of low-wage jobs to the third world is exactly what we want, isn't it? They can do the low-wage work and we will do the high-wage work. That is exactly the new international division of labor implied by the HO model. Unfortunately, it did not work out that way in the 1980s. Figure 2.10 shows the employment in machinery and equipment—the high paying jobs. The new international division of labor seemed very much in effect in the 1970s. The United States gained over 1 million jobs in these high-wage sectors. But these new jobs all disappeared in the 1980s. Where did they go? To Japan and Korea.

In order to understand the 1980s we need a model that allows for a new international division of labor, with jobs in labor-intensive sectors like apparel moving to the third world and with an expansion of jobs in the capital-intensive sectors to service the growing demand for capital-intensive goods in the expanding developing countries. But the model also needs to allow for special countries (Japan and Korea) in the high-wage regions to be the primary beneficiaries of this new international division of labor. The model needs to

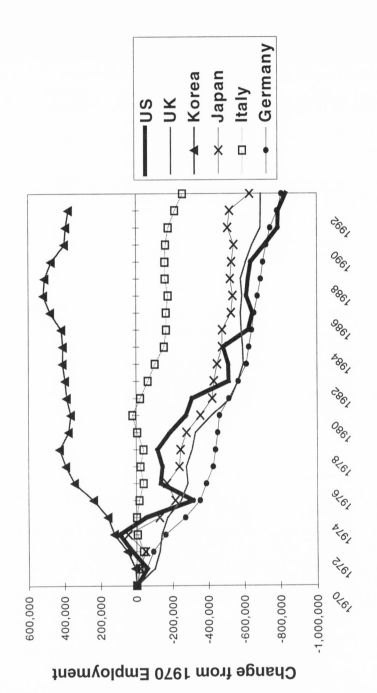

Figure 2.9. Employment in textiles, apparel, footwear, and leather, 1970–1993

Legend:
US
UK
Korea
Japan
Italy
Germany

Change from 1970 Employment

600,000
400,000
200,000
0
-200,000
-400,000
-600,000
-800,000
-1,000,000

1970 1972 1974 1976 1978 1980 1982 1984 1986 1988 1990 1992

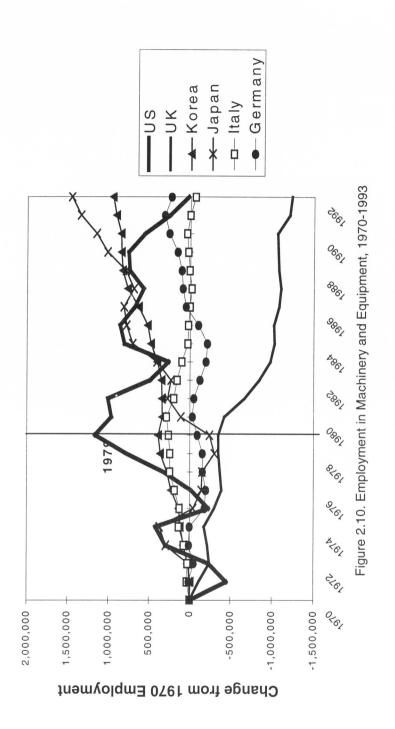

Figure 2.10. Employment in Machinery and Equipment, 1970-1993

deal with the huge U.S. trade deficit and the gyrations of the value of the dollar in the 1980s.

The model for the 1980s should probably allow foreign competition to *reduce market power* and put pressure on unions and other institutions that tend to cartelize an industry. I am inclined to think that the threat of competition, not from low-wage Asia, but from Japan and Korea was an important part of the story in the 1980s. Borjas and Ramey (1993) find that communities with manufacturing concentrated in the heavy, unionized sectors have tended to have worse wage outcomes than other communities. This supports the view that the threat of foreign competition is playing an important role in the job market. Incidentally, the foreign threat is very difficult to deal with empirically since it may not leave a behavioral trail. The threat alone may drive down wages; it need never materialize in actual imports.

If sector specific assets and diminished market power do not add up to a big globalization effect in the 1980s, do not worry, there are plenty of other ways that globalization can affect U.S. labor markets. *Increased international fluidity* of physical capital, human capital and knowledge capital allows mobile assets to escape overpriced complementary immobile inputs. Do you remember the "technology gap?" Once American workers had superior tools and were employed in superior organizations. The great increase in trade across the Atlantic and the Pacific oceans has been accompanied by a leveling of product, process and organizational technology. Indeed, the multinational corporation has as its primary reason for existence the transference of intangible knowledge assets from one country to another. This might or might not be contributing to the trends in wages. Models of multinationals, such as Markusen (1984), describe the impact on local labor markets of a flow of knowledge and other intangible assets to foreign locations.

Another globalization force is created by innovations in communication, transportation and organizational design that *turn nontradables into tradables*. One example is the delocalization of design, parts manufacture and assembly in manufacturing. Autos and engines and consumer electronics are now assembled by 600,000 Mexicans from parts designed and made in the United States and Japan. There are now over 600,000 Mexican workers in these operations. The growth in trade in services is another source of concern. HO models allow a country to select a high-wage equilibrium if its capital/labor ratio is great enough to allow concentration of tradable on the most capital-intensive products. Unskilled workers in these high-wage communities produce either capital-intensive tradables or nontradables. In neither case are these workers in competition with low-wage foreign workers. Innovations which allow trade in services threaten this equilibrium by reducing the number of jobs that are economically isolated from foreign competition. Trade in services will tend to increase income inequality if traded services use low-skilled workers. Casual observation suggests that most of the increased trade in services is at the high end of the skill distribution not the low end. Doctors and accountants and programmers are starting to compete globally. Gardeners, waiters, and taxi-drivers are not.

This is a very long and complicated list of globalization effects. We have some empirical evidence about many of these paths, but generally I think it is fair to say that we are pretty much in the dark regarding them.

VI. Don't Forget Immigration Which Interacts with Globalization

Immigration and trade can work together to cause increased wage inequality when neither working alone has any effect. This point is nicely captured in the two labor demand diagrams, figures 2.4 and 2.5. A favorable potential product upgrading effect may be eliminated by an increase in the ratio of unskilled workers to capital. In terms of figure 2.5, a community may start out in region B in which there is a product upgrading effect, but may slide down the labor demand curve to region C in which unskilled workers find themselves totally exposed to Chinese competition. The slide down the labor demand curve may be caused by a combination of immigration, increased native labor and slow capital accumulation. In other words, this crime of wage suppression might have been perpetrated by a conspiracy of four: globalization, immigration, increases in labor force participation and a low savings rate. Immigration or labor force participation might drop out of this conspiracy and the crime would still have occurred. But otherwise all the suspects would have to be working together to cause reductions in wages.

Figure 2.11 is my final piece of evidence. It depicts income inequality measures by state for 1969 and 1989. The coefficient of variation of incomes in 1989 was greatest in California, New Mexico, Texas, Arkansas and Florida. That has to be an immigration effect, doesn't it? [7]

VII. What is the Right Policy Response?

While public opinion holds educational deterioration, immigration, technological change and globalization all guilty of increasing wage inequality, the jury of academics seems to be rendering a very different verdict. Education, immigration and globalization have been found innocent and technological change guilty. Labor economists have not found evidence of much change in the relative supply of unskilled workers as a result of educational failures or immigration. They also do not find evidence of much change in the demand for labor coming from international trade. Like Sherlock Holmes who counsels, "Eliminate the impossible, and all that is left is the truth," once these economists found education, immigration and globalization innocent, they have chosen to convict technology, never mind that there is little organized evidence presented against this culprit.

My view is very different. First of all, I object, the evidence that has been presented in support of the innocence of globalization and immigration is "incompetent, irrelevant, and immaterial." Second, this is a crime that most likely

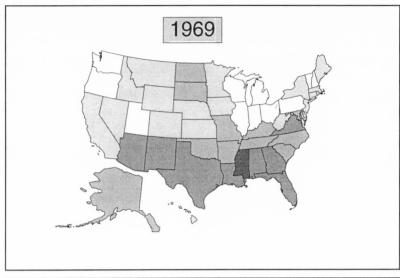

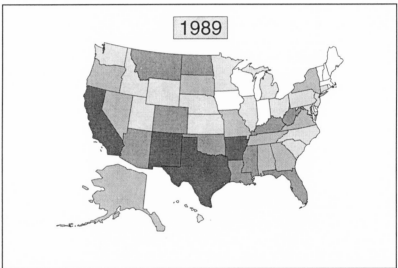

Figure 2.11. Coefficients of Variation of Income, Shaded by Quintiles

could not have been committed by any one of the culprits alone but requires all four to be working together. If, for example, the educational system had created a workforce in the United States that had very few unskilled workers, then economic integration of the goods markets with Mexico could benefit all U.S. workers, even the lowest skilled. Our fear of NAFTA speaks volumes regarding our lack of confidence in our educational system. Third, I would argue, the question is not: which is the guilty force? The real question is: what are we going to do about it? If we find education, immigration and globalization innocent, and technology guilty, we seem to me to be edging toward a very passive response: there is nothing that we can do to offset the march of technology through our culture. The continuing and persistent belief that immigration and globalization are guilty probably comes from the fact that these "problems" have an apparent remedy: economic isolation. A guilty verdict against education also points to a remedy, but educational investments have a very long gestation period, and we cannot expect to have much impact on the income inequality trends very quickly by pulling the education lever.

It is my view that education is the right solution. But education takes a long time to have much noticeable effect on the big trends in inequality. Unfortunately, the script for the next couple of decades for many Americans has already been written in our high schools and social systems that have put on the streets far too many illiterate and innumerate young men and women. I know of no evidence that would make us optimistic that remedial education for 20 year-olds could offset 12 years of substandard education. Thus we are stuck with a generation of workers poorly prepared to deal with the opportunities and challenges offered by globalization and the information revolution. But for heavens sake, let us recognize that this is a national emergency, every bit as important for our society as winning the Cold War. It's a paradox, isn't it, that no country struggled so hard to end the Cold War as it has, but no advanced nation seems so ill prepared for the economic consequences. So let's stop talking about education and start doing.

Even if today we did suddenly come to our collective senses and make a major push toward remedying our educational shortcomings, the inequality trends that we have experienced over the last several decades seem certain to continue. The very latest data do indicate some real wage increases, but I am inclined to think of this not as a trend but part of a cycle, associated with today's surprisingly low unemployment rates. If the inequality trends do continue, as I predict, you can be sure that we have not heard the last of David Duke, Pat Buchanan and Richard Gephart, all of whom have equally enlightened attitudes toward international trade. Can I hope that with both NAFTA and WTO now passed by Congress, the option of economic isolation is gone?

Our uncontrollable border with Mexico poses for us great problems with respect to immigration policy. I do not expect to see any increases in wages of the lowest skilled workers in Los Angeles as long as immigration from Mexico and from Central America continues so freely. But I cannot say that I find a Buchanan wall between Mexico and the United States a very attractive solution. Keep in mind that the biggest impact of these migrant workers in Los Angeles is in jobs requiring the very lowest levels of skills, and education of natives can greatly limit the number of natives who are adversely affected even by migration.

Education is thus the magic elixir, but it takes a long time for the cure to take hold. In the meantime, we have a patient that is in a lot of misery, crying out for trade barriers. A big problem is that Doctors Duke, Buchanan, and Gephart are all offering to sell the patient some trade barrier pills in exchange for votes. But a small dosage of trade barriers almost always gets the patient hooked and leads to demands for more and more. If we go down that road, and we give this patient all the pills of trade barriers she wants, she probably will stop taking the education tonic, since the immediate symptoms will have been alleviated, and since the education tonic does not taste very good, that's for sure. Much better for the long-run health of this patient to avoid those trade barriers. But we cannot just sit by and expect her to be able to resist the temptation without assistance. We have to offer something to ease the pain. Dare I say the word: progressive income taxation. I favor temporary progressive income taxation that partly offsets the rise in after-tax inequality, not so much that it eliminates altogether the rise in after-tax earnings inequality, but just enough to keep it within tolerable levels.

In conclusion I want only to say: There are two things I prefer not to talk about while I am in Washington in April 1998; one is them is the erection of trade barriers.

Notes

[1] I am assuming constant returns to scale, also, so that these zero-profit conditions do not depend on the scale of operations.

[2] For example, it is possible to imagine two isolated regions that have the same relative supplies of labor and capital and the same tastes but different pre-trade relative prices because of technological differences that vary by sector. Economic liberalization could mean a transfer of technology to the backward region, and an equalization of product prices without any trade at all and without repercussions for the advanced region.

[3] An autarchic labor demand curve awards low wages compared with an open-economy labor demand curve when labor is abundant (the abundant factor benefits from sales of its services to the global market) but also when labor is very scarce. The second, less well-understood, possibility arises because of the extreme specialization patterns that are available to open economies but not to closed ones. This is further discussed in Leamer(1996).

[4] The middle decade experienced a very large increase in the price of petroleum which, however, cannot account for the relative price decline of apparel and textiles since energy inputs are a small share of costs in manufacturing.

[5] In terms of an isoquant, this is saying that to a first order of approximation what matters is how much the isoquant is shifting in, not whether it is getting steeper or flatter.

[6] Thus, for example, as noted in an April 8, 1998 *Los Angeles Times* article by Marla Dickerson:

G.S. Dunbar is part of a modest but growing cadre of Southern California sewing contractors and apparel manufacturers using sophisticated technology to battle low-wage foreign competitors. In an industry that's synonymous with low-tech sweatshops, smart manufacturing is the future for domestic producers looking to scale the wage gap with superior quality and lightning-fast turnaround.

See also Feenstra and Hanson (1994) for a study arguing that outsourcing is extremely important.

[7] Borjas (1994) offers a good survey of the literature on immigration, but none of it effectively deals with the interaction of trade and immigration.

References

Baldwin, Robert E., and Glen G. Cain. 1997. "Shifts in the U.S. Relative Wages: the Role of Trade, Technology and Factor Endowments." NBER Working Paper No. 5934.

Berman, Eli, John Bound, and Zvi Griliches. 1992. "Changes in the Demand for Skilled Labor Within U.S. Manufacturing: Evidence from the Annual Survey of Manufactures." *Quarterly Journal of Economics* 107:35–78.

Bhagwati, Jagdish, and Marvin Kosters. 1994. *Trade and Wages*. Washington, D.C.: American Enterprise Institute.

Borjas, George J.; and Valerie A. Ramey. 1995 "Foreign Competition, Market Power, and Wage Inequality." *Quarterly Journal of Economics* 110:1075–1110.

Deardorff, Alan, and Dalia Hakura. 1994. "Trade and Wages: What are the Questions?." In *Trade and Wages*, Jadgish Bhagwati and Marvin Kosters (eds.), Washington, D.C.: American Enterprise Institute.

Dickerson, Marla. 1998. "Apparel Makers Respond to Need to Automate. *Los Angeles Times*, April 8.

Feenstra, Robert C., and Gordon Hanson. 1994. "Foreign Investment, Outsourcing and Relative Wages." Conference on "Political Economy of Trade Policy," Columbia University, November.

Katz, Lawrence F., and Kevin Murphy. 1992. "Changes in Relative Wages, 1963–1987: Supply and Demand Factors." *Quarterly Journal of Economics* 107:35–78.

Krugman, Paul. 1995. *Pop Internationalism*, Cambridge: The M.I.T. Press.

Krugman, Paul, and Robert Lawrence. 1993. "Trade, Jobs and Wages." NBER Working Paper No. 4478.

Krugman, Paul, and Robert Lawrence. 1994. "Trade, Jobs and Wages." *Scientific American* 270:44–49.

Lawrence, Robert, and Matthew Slaughter. 1993. "International Trade and American Wages." *Brookings Papers on Economic Activity* 161–226.

Leamer, Edward E. 1987. "Paths of Development in the Three-Factor N-Good General Equilibrium Model." *Journal of Political Economy* 95:961–999.

Leamer, Edward E. 1993. "Wage Effects of a U.S.-Mexican Free Trade Agreement." In Peter M. Garber (ed.), *The Mexico–U.S. Free Trade Agreement*. Cambridge: The M.I.T. Press.

Leamer, Edward E. 1994. "Trade, Wages and Revolving Door Ideas." NBER Working Paper No. 4716, April.

Leamer, Edward E. 1995a. "The Heckscher-Ohlin Model in Theory and Practice." *Princeton Studies in International Finance*, No. 77, International Finance Section, Princeton, New Jersey, February.

Leamer, Edward E. 1997. "In Search of Stolper-Samuelson Effects on U.S. Wages." In Susan Collins (ed.), *Imports, Exports and the American Worker*. Washington, D.C.: Brookings Institution.

Markusen, James R. 1984. "Multinationals, Multi-Plant Economies, and the Gains from Trade." *Journal of International Economics* 16:205–224.

Mishel, Lawrence, and Jared Bernstein. 1994. "Is the Technology Black Box Empty?: An Empirical Examination of the Impact of Technology on Wage Inequality and the Employment Structure." Economic Policy Institute, Washington, D.C.

Murphy, Kevin, and Finis Welch. 1991. "The Role of International Trade in Wage Differentials." In Marvin Kosters (ed.), *Workers and Their Wages*. Washington, D.C.: American Enterprise Institute.

Sachs, Jeffrey D., and Howard J. Shatz. 1994. "Trade and Jobs in U.S. Manufacturing." *Brookings Papers on Economic Activity*, 1–84.

Comment

Lawrence Mishel

The Leamer paper does not present any new evidence or analysis, at least to those of us who have absorbed Leamer's earlier work. The paper does, however, usefully present Leamer's perspective through a review of evidence and analysis.

I very much appreciate that Leamer is shouting, "Something is really happening here that we cannot ignore and we have really got to do something about it." Moreover, Leamer is speaking in a very conventional economics voice, with very conventional policy recommendations—progressive taxation along with education and training. As I will explain below, I think that that is a kind of very limited set of policy options. But, even on policy, one feels that Leamer is struggling to break out of the conventional policy box. And I think we ought to listen to Leamer when he says we really need to do something about this.

Leamer is a corrective for the mostly inexplicable hesitation of nearly all trade economists and policy makers to take seriously the economic costs and distributional consequences of expanding trade and globalization. This tendency, or if one is generous, this "oversight," has left trade policy weakened as public opinion and the losers from trade policy have gained enough political clout to challenge, or defeat, further moves towards liberalization, such as extending NAFTA, further "fast-track authority," MFN status for China, etc. The conventional view is that trade may have some costs or distributional consequences, but they are small (implicitly "inconsequential") relative to all other factors. Besides it being hard to understand why those who hold this view also believe that further trade liberalization will provide extensive *benefits* (with only trivial costs), the conventional view has no resonance with a public that correctly observes the costs of globalization in their communities, or who, at least, hear the unchallenged wisdom from leading employers (likely including their own) that globalization makes us need to tighten our belts (reduce employment) and lower our wage increases. The fear of openly discussing costs has thus isolated the internationalist position.

The only substantive problem I have with Leamer's paper is that it freelances quite a bit on education by talking about how bad the schools are and how much that is related to the wage problem. Once one moves out of simple theory and looks at education and labor market research, one would be hesitant to focus on school quality as the problem.

For instance, labor market economists, from right to left, have come to the conclusion that an erosion of school quality, assuming there has been one, has nothing to do with the growth of wage inequality. I can give you two reasons why. One is that when you analyze people with a high school degree, you find that wages have fallen for workers in their fifties, forties or twenties. Thus, whether you graduated with a high school degree in 1960 (when schools were "good") or in 1980 (a "bad" school year), high school wages have fallen, and by a lot. True, wages have declined more among the younger workers, but that does not necessarily mean that the schools are the problem. Two, if you look at direct evidence about schools you will not find a lot of deterioration in test scores or measures of school quality. And some studies, such as Murnane, Willett and Levy (1994) look at young workers with terminal high school degrees, and compare their wages from the mid-'70s to the mid-'80s, along with their test scores. They find that the students who graduated from high school in the mid-'80s with the *best* test scores earned less than people who graduated ten years earlier who had the worst test scores. So, what has happened is there has been a deterioration of wages for high school graduates, regardless of test scores (even if test scores do matter more).

Let me now turn to the continuing debate over the impact of technology on wage inequality. The Leamer paper, like most recent papers, mostly relates to 1980s data and to literature that analyzes the 1980s. I want to update this debate to the 1990s. My conclusion, so you do not have to hold your breath until the end, is that the 1990s data do not even provide prima facie evidence for a strong role of technological change in the growth of wage inequality. There is, I think, a legitimate debate about the 1980s, but I think there is really not much room for debate on this for the 1990s. Let me review some evidence. First, let us look at the non-production workers' share in total employment (in manufacturing). Think of this as the white-collar share of employment. One can look at both the "Annual Survey of Manufactures" and the Bureau of Labor Statistic's payroll employment data.

It has frequently been asserted that technology is the cause of wage inequality (or that skill-biased technical change exists) because the white-collar (non-production worker) share of employment has been going up. You should be interested to know, then, that for the last ten years this line has been totally stable, if not falling. Some, such as Berman, Bound and Machin (1998), actually argue that a rising non-production share is enough evidence to conclude that technology is the cause of wage inequality and trade is exonerated. If so, this logic suggests that the 1990s growth of wage inequality is all about trade. I do not believe that to be the case, but I just want to open up everyone's mind to the fact that over the last ten years the non-production worker's share has not grown.

You should also note that the estimated college/high school wage differential (excluding people with more than a college degree) has hardly grown at all, especially among men, in the 1990s (see Mishel et al., 1998). You should also note that there has been no acceleration of the supply of college graduates.

Thus, we have the price differential flat and the supply shifting at the same pace as in the '80s. This implies that there has been a *deceleration* of the growth of relative demand for education in the 1990s relative to the 1980s. So, the notion that we are going through a big technological wave in the 1990s leading to a growth of excess demand for education is contradicted by these basic data.

In discussions of wage inequality, there has been an understandable tendency to talk about the unskilled, a group that is never well delineated. Let us assume, however, that "unskilled" means the people who are way at the bottom, perhaps the bottom twenty percent. You might be interested to know that the only type of wage inequality we have seen over the last ten years is that between the top and everyone else, and there is really no differentiation between the middle and the bottom (in the latter years of the 1990s, the gap between the middle and the bottom actually narrowed). That is, you do not see the people at the bottom, who are the "least educated" and "unskilled" having their wages fall the most. So wage decline (at least through 1996) was happening to a wide group of people, not just a group that is unskilled.

So, I would say that if you update your analysis with 1990s data you would draw an even stronger view that technology is not the cause of wage inequality.

In policy terms, it may not matter what the cause is because the suggested solution is always more education. Let me try to broaden the discussion in two areas. Labor market economists talk about things other than trade and technology, such as labor market institutions—minimum wage and unions. There is a group of studies that shows that around one third of the growth of wage inequality is due to the erosion of the minimum wage and the weakening power of the unions. Deunionization was more important in terms of what happened among men, with the minimum wage being very important with what has happened among women. I do not think one needs to be for or against those types of institutions (witness those who blame trade but who are not protectionists) to acknowledge the role of weakened labor market institutions.

Another factor that is left out of the picture is the redistribution of income from wages to capital. Whenever this subject comes up, people start squirming as if it were impolite to discuss it. But this is a matter of facts and analyses that should be widely debated. Consider the trend in the return to capital in the corporate sector (all profits and interest relative to assets), the same measure used by Feldstein and Summers (1977) twenty years ago and used by Poterba (1997) more recently. The pretax return and the after-tax return of capital are very high relative to at least the last twenty years and, I think, high relative to history. Some analysts contend, "That's not the right thing—we should be looking at the share of income." Let me tell you, then, that the capital share of corporate sector income, which is where this is most relevant and best measured, has remarkably shot up. Is this trivial? No, you can actually calculate the counterfactual that would say that if there had not been this big surge in capital income relative to labor income, average wages could have been anywhere from three to six percent higher. That is an amount equivalent to almost any factor that anyone talks about in the wage inequality literature (see Mishel et al., 1998).

Let us just broaden the policy discussion a little bit. I do not know why, when we talk about trade, there are only two options: no trade or the status quo (or what anyone in any administration or congress wants to do for trade). This is implicitly how Leamer sets up the policy choices. But the debate in Washington is about "rights," intellectual property rights, the rights of capital and capital mobility around the world, and labor and environmental standards. There is very little discussion about stopping integration. There is a lot of discussion about how fast we want to globalize and on what terms. And I am not sure that anyone has shown that the next increment of globalization is just filled with benefits and that the particular paths for globalization being pursued, e.g., fast track legislation, maximizes net benefits. So, I think this conference should discuss how we globalize, not just whether we globalize (that is too easy).

There are other roles for government, besides progressive taxation and education, that are relevant. Issues such as national health insurance, what is going on with the pension system, and labor standards (like minimum wage institutions, unions, or other types of institutions) are also very important and play a significant role in shaping the wage and income distribution. These social safety net and wage-shaping policies create the entire context for trade policy discussions.

Having said that, people immediately pounce on Europe's economic problems. However, let me review some data with you (from the Conference Board [1997]). If you look at the productivity growth across advanced countries, you will note that OECD countries other than the United States have had productivity growth over the last 30 years that is twice as fast as ours. That is noncontroversial; it is usually explained, plausibly, by a technology convergence or leadership story, whereby it is harder for the leaders to move ahead and easier for the copycats, the imitators, to grow faster.

So, you would think that productivity growth rates would equalize when the two types of countries have similar levels of productivity. You might be surprised to learn that other countries have caught up or even exceeded U.S. productivity levels. I am not sure anyone should believe the exact numbers but I think the trend is probably unmistakably true. For instance, look at 1995, where France, West Germany, the Netherlands and Belgium have all basically caught up to the United States in productivity. These data reflect what other studies show, which is that the United States is a leader in some industries and other countries are the leaders in other industries. True, these are the countries that have high unemployment problems, but certainly these countries have not been doing everything wrong. Productivity growth and levels are measures of an important dimension of an economy. It is hard to understand how countries that are doing everything wrong have somehow managed to catch up to us and are now even pulling ahead in productivity.

Let me also introduce some skepticism that "more education" is a viable policy that is "sufficient." In Washington, more education means getting everyone to go to college. If you look at what has happened to the wages of young college (four-year) graduates, those with one to five years' experience, you will notice that young men graduating from college and working are earning somewhere between 8–10 percent less than those who graduated in the late 1980s. This is true for young women, too. Wages have risen a bit in 1997. I understand that these college graduates were earning wages higher than their cohort who did not go beyond just high school. Nevertheless, the question is how much can we push this "going to college" business?

My last topic is the issue of the technology worker shortage. Here, I have examined people with a four-year college degree and who have been out of school 1–10 years (to get a proper sample size). And this is in various occupations that we think are very high tech and are in great shortage right now. You will see that engineers—young, working engineers—are earning more than 10% less in 1997 than in 1990. These are people with a four-year college degree working in engineering. Those working in math and computer science occupations (the sample size is low so it is jumpy), show no instances where they are making more now in 1997 than in 1990. This is not very encouraging. We have a debate being led by high tech companies that says the following, which is very interesting for a debate on globalization: "We have a shortage of these workers. We cannot get them. Yet, we are the most competitive firms at the top of the world, right? Yet, we, the high tech firms, because of global competition, cannot raise our wages for these very highly-educated workers in order to attract more people into the occupation here in the United States. Higher wages would make us uncompetitive. Therefore, we have to go off-shore or bring in immigrants to do these jobs."

Now, I think that the high tech firms have some facts wrong. For this audience, I wonder why the trade economists of this country do not stand up and say, "High tech America, how can you be claiming to be the leaders of the world in your industry and yet you cannot raise wages because of globalization? You are giving globalization a bad rap." If you think it is important to fight against trade barriers, then you ought to speak truth-to-power when it comes to what firms are saying. You should not be surprised when the American public thinks that globalization depressed their wages, when they hear corporate titans in leading industries saying, "I cannot raise wages for my most skilled workers because of global competition."

References

Berman, Eli, John Bound and Machin. 1998. "Implications of Skill-Biased Technological Change: International Evidence." *Quarterly Journal of Economics* 113:1245–1279.

Conference Board. 1997. "Perspectives on a Global Economy, Understanding Differences in Economic Performance." Report Number 1187–97–RR. New York: Conference Board.

Feldstein, Martin S. and Lawrence Summers. 1977. "Is the Rate of Profit Falling?" *Brookings Papers on Economic Activity* 1:211–227.

Mishel, Lawrence, Jared Bernstein, and John Schmitt. 1998. *The State of Working America, 1998–1999.* An Economic Policy Institute Book. Ithaca, N.Y.: ILR Press, an imprint of Cornell University Press.

Murnane, Richard, John B. Willett, and Frank Levy. 1994. "The Growing Importance of Cognitive Skills in Wage Determination." Unpublished.

Poterba, James M. 1997. "The Rate of Return to Corporate Capital and Factor Shares: New Estimates Using Revised National Income Accounts and Capital Stock Data." Department of Economics, Massachusetts Institute of Technology, and the National Bureau of Economic Research, Cambridge, MA. Photocopy.

Comment

T. N. Srinivasan

When I was asked to be a discussant of Leamer's paper, I readily accepted it in the expectation that I would, as in the past, get to read and learn from a characteristically Leamer paper containing sound theory that is used in an integral way, rather than simply to motivate, or worse still added as decoration to, empirical analysis! But what I got instead, in time I might add, from the 'con' man from UCLA, is a paper from which he has taken out, if he had in fact put it in the first place, not only the 'con' but all of the econometrics! This is indeed a pity. Some years ago Leamer had said, rightly, that

> We are a long way from obtaining good empirical estimates of the relative effects of technological change, globalization and education on the U.S. labor markets, but we are most likely to make progress if the estimates are linked clearly with some understandable theory (Leamer 1994, p. 26).

and

> Recent discussions of the effects of globalization and technological change on U.S. wages have suffered from inappropriate or missing references to the basic international trade theorems: The Factor Price Equalization Theorem, the Stolper-Samuelson Theorem and the Samuelson Duality Theorem. Until the theory is better understood, and until the theory and the estimates are sensibly linked, the jury should remain out (ibid., abstract).

I thought he would provide in the paper for this conference "good empirical estimates" derived from a model "linked clearly with understandable theory." After all, for reaching meaningful and robust conclusions about the behavior of the structure of wages in the U.S. economy in the last few decades, we need to put together a coherent model in which all the important mechanisms that influence factor prices in general equilibrium are present. Also, the model should include the relevant stochastic disturbances, not simply as afterthoughts to a deterministic theory, but as elements integral to the theory itself. Such a model should be estimated using robust techniques. Only such an estimated model should be used to do *counterfactual* simulation exercises to generate effects of this or that policy, or the absence of this or that mechanism that influences factor prices.

I had indeed expected precisely such simulations. It is possible that he has already provided them in Leamer (1996), of which I should have, but did not, refresh my memory. Be that as it may, in the paper for this conference, Leamer offers a varying set of conclusions derived from different highly stylized models. The very good economist that he is, he skillfully uses conclusions from suitably chosen models to refute popular assertions about the observed behavior of factor prices from economists, politicians, and their think-tanks. This motley crowd includes labor economists who often analyze quintessentially general equilibrium effects with familiar partial equilibrium tools, protectionists and their agents in politics who see any and every twist in wage behavior as justifying the use of every imaginable tool of protection including labor standards, technology-phobes who see technological change as inexorably biased against the unskilled, and many others. When watching masters like Leamer or my good friend Jagdish Bhagwati use this almost rhetorical device to demolish the delusions of the demented, one can only applaud—but after the show is over, one is assailed with doubts: was one simply watching a gripping film, or are the masters on to something about the real world?

With these complaints and obiter dicta out of the way, let me turn to Leamer's paper. First of all, as I said, he works with many models, from the standard work horse, viz. the 2x2 Heckscher-Ohlin-Samuelson (HOS) model, to models in which there are two factors but more than two goods, to still others in which apparently there is product differentiation within an industry or sector, for example, when he talks about product upgrading. It is not always clear as to which model he is referring when he makes particular statements. On occasion he makes very loose statements—my favorite being—"A link between Chinese wages and U.S. wages is created when Chinese and U.S. workers produce the same products and sell in the same markets, for example, apparel." This might be read to mean that in such competition the U.S. wage for unskilled labor will sink to Chinese levels. But does it?

For example, consider Alan Deardorff's many commodity, two-factor model—to be specific, a three commodity (aircraft, apparel and food), two factor (skilled-unskilled labor) model. Let there be no factor intensity reversals, with aircraft ranked highest in skilled labor intensity, apparel coming next and food coming last. Suppose in equilibrium the United States produces aircraft and apparel while China produces apparel and food, with factor prices not being the same in the two countries. If we assume that the United States is abundant in skilled labor and China in unskilled labor, then the relative-wage of unskilled labor will be higher in the United States. This is depicted in figure 2.12 in which isoquants corresponding to one unit of value (at equilibrium international prices) of jet aircraft (JJ), apparel (AA) and food (FF) are shown. PQ represents the unit cost line of the United States and RS that of China, their slopes representing the relative wage of unskilled labor in United States and China, respectively. It is clear from the figure that compared to China the United States has a higher relative wage (w_{US}/w_s) as compared to (w_{US}^c/w_s^c)

for unskilled labor, and at common international prices, a higher absolute wage (w_{US} as compared to w_{US}^c) as well. Thus, in spite of United States and China producing and selling apparel at common world prices, wages for unskilled labor are higher in the United States.

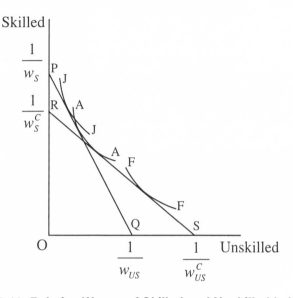

Figure 2.12. Relative Wages of Skilled and Unskilled Labor In a Three Commodity, Two-Factor Model

It can easily be shown that a fall in prices of labor-intensive commodities in the trade of a developed country such as the United States with poor countries need not necessarily result in a fall in the equilibrium relative wage of unskilled labor in the United States. For example, consider the case where the United States produces a nontraded service (haircuts, H in quantity) and a traded good (gadgets, G in quantity), using skilled and unskilled labor as inputs. The United States trades gadgets with poor countries for apparel at a price of λ gadgets per unit of apparel. Let the U.S. domestic transformation function be $G = F(H)$, $0 \le H \le \overline{H}$ where $F'(H) < 0$ and $F''(H) < 0$. Suppose the United States does not consume any gadgets but only apparel (quantity A) and haircuts. Let the U.S. social utility function be $U = \alpha \text{ Log } A + (1-\alpha) \text{ Log } H$ so that the elasticity of substitution between A and H in consumption is unity and the optimal shares of consumer expenditure on A and H respectively are α and $1-\alpha$. Clearly $\lambda A = G$ or $\lambda A = F(H)$. Substituting in U one gets, $U = -\alpha \text{ Log } \lambda + \alpha \text{ Log } F(H) + (1-\alpha) \text{ Log } H$. It is evident that the social utility maximizing value of H is independent of λ! Since the relative wage of unskilled labor depends only on the quantity produced of H, clearly it does not depend on λ. Thus, a fall in λ, while it increases U.S. social utility, does not affect the relative wage of unskilled labor. Of course, if the social utility function is of the constant elasticity of substitution form, depending on this elasticity, and whether gadgets are more or less intensive in skilled labor, a change in λ could raise or lower the equilibrium relative wage of U.S. unskilled labor. Thus, the fact that the price of imports from developing countries has fallen need not imply anything at all about the wages of unskilled labor.

Leamer is of course right in pointing to the unimportance of factor bias in technical change in different sectors in changing relative factor rewards. He is assuming that technical progress is exogenous. But one could instead assume that it is endogenous, more specifically it is influenced by considerations of profitability. In a recent paper, Acemoglu (1998) explains both the decline in the wage premium of U.S. college-educated workers in the 1970s as well as its large increase in the 1980s, using a model of induced innovation. In his model, a rise in the relative supply of college graduates reduces the premium in the short run. But it also induces skill-biased technical change to take advantage of the increased relative supply of skilled workers. Thus, in the longer run, the decline in the premium of the wage of college workers is reversed.

Finally, let me cite Autor et al. (1997) who use a simple supply-demand framework to analyze the changes in the relative quantities, wages and shares in the wage bill of college and non-college educated workers in each decade since 1940 and over the 1990–95 period. They find that

> The relative demand for more-skilled workers (college equivalents) grew more rapidly on average during the past twenty-five years (1970–95) than during the previous three decades (1940–70). In particular, the rate of growth of the relative demand for more-educated workers appears to have been more rapid in the 1970s and 1980s than in the 1960s. (p. 32)

Let me conclude by reiterating the need to build and estimate more complete econometric models of the interaction between changes in technology, increasing share of international trade in GDP, and changes in labor supplies. Partial analysis focusing on just one of the many mechanisms influencing relative factor rewards could be very misleading.

References

Acemoglu, Daron. 1998. "Why Do New Technologies Complement Skills? Directed Technical Change and Wage Inequality." *Quarterly Journal of Economics*, forthcoming.

Autor, David, Lawrence Katz and Alan Krueger. 1997. "Computing Inequality: Have Computers Changed the Labor Market?" National Bureau of Economic Research Working Paper 5956.

Leamer, Edward. 1994. "Trade, Wages and Revolving Door Ideas." National Bureau of Economic Research Working Paper No. 4716.

Leamer, Edward. 1996. "In Search of Stolper-Samuelson Effects on U.S. Wages." National Bureau of Economic Research Working Paper 5427.

CHAPTER 3

Economic Research and the Debate over Immigration Policy

George J. Borjas

I. Introduction

The United States is on the verge of yet another historic debate over immigration policy. Up to this point, the debate has focused primarily on illegal immigration or on welfare benefits received by immigrants, and these discussions have led Congress to increase penalties on illegal aliens and to severely tighten the eligibility restrictions for welfare use by non-citizens.

In the next few years, the debate will likely shift towards the larger and much more important issue of the character and consequences of *legal* immigration. Although economic factors alone will not decide the outcome of this debate, they will play an important role. Economics has often set the questions that frame the immigration debate: Who benefits? Who loses?

There have been two major shifts in immigration policy in this century. In 1924, the United States began to limit the number of immigrants admitted and established the "national-origins quota system," a visa-allocation scheme that awarded entry visas mainly on the basis of national origin and that favored Germany and the United Kingdom. This system was repealed in 1965, and family reunification became the central goal of immigration policy, with entry visas being awarded mainly to applicants who have relatives already residing in the United States.

The social, demographic, and economic changes initiated by the 1965 legislation have been truly historic.[1] The number of immigrants began to rise rapidly. As recently as the 1950s, only about 250 thousand immigrants entered the country annually; by the 1990s, the United States was admitting about 1 million legal immigrants annually, and an estimated 300 thousand aliens entered and stayed in the country illegally.

By several measures, immigration today is at or near record levels. Between 1901 and 1910, at the height of the Great Migration, 8.8 million legal immigrants entered the United States. If present trends continue, as many as 10 million legal immigrants and perhaps another 3 million illegal aliens will enter the country in the 1990s. The United States, therefore, will probably admit more immigrants in this decade than at any other time in the country's history.

Moreover, because of the decline in the number of children borne by American women, immigration now accounts for nearly 40 percent of the growth in population, as compared to about 50 percent at the beginning of the twentieth century. At least one of every three new workers who will enter the U.S. labor market during the 1990s will be an immigrant. By this yardstick, immigrants play a very crucial role in determining demographic and economic trends in the United States.

The 1965 legislation also led to a momentous shift in the ethnic composition of the population. Although persons of European origin dominated the immigrant flow since the country's founding until the 1950s, only about 10 percent of the persons admitted in the 1980s were of European origin. It is now estimated that non-Hispanic whites may form a minority of the population by the year 2050.

These economic and demographic changes have furnished the fuel that ignited the incipient debate over immigration policy. For the most part, the weapons of choice in this debate are statistics produced by economic research, with all sides marshaling facts and evidence that support particular policy goals. This paper addresses a question that seems quite simple, but is, in fact, very hard to answer: what does economic research imply about the type of immigration policy that the United States should pursue?

II. What Have We Learned?

The academic literature investigating the economic impact of immigration on the United States grew rapidly in the past decade.[2] This literature has provided important insights into such diverse issues as the process of assimilation, the impact of immigration on the labor market opportunities of native workers, and the fiscal impact of immigration.

Immigrant Performance in the Labor Market

Table 3.1 summarizes the key trends in immigrant skills over the 1970–90 period. The relative educational attainment of successive immigrant waves fell dramatically in recent decades. In 1970, the typical immigrant in the country had 10.7 years of schooling, as compared to 11.5 years for the typical native worker. By 1990, the typical immigrant had 11.6 years of schooling, as compared to 13.2 years for natives. The relative decline in the education of immigrants is partly responsible for a substantial increase in the wage gap between immigrants and natives. In 1970, the typical immigrant earned about 1 percent *more* than natives; by 1990, the typical immigrant earned 15.2 percent *less* than natives.

TABLE 3.1. Socioeconomic Characteristics of Immigrants and Natives in the United States, 1970–1990

Group/Variable	1970	1980	1990
Natives			
Mean educational attainment (in years)	11.5	12.7	
All immigrants			
Mean educational attainment (in years)	10.7	11.7	11.6
Percentage wage differential between immigrants and natives	+.9	-9.2	-15.2
Recent immigrants (less than 5 years in U.S.)			
Mean educational attainment (in years)	11.1	11.8	11.9
Percent wage differential between immigrants and natives	-16.6	-27.6	-31.7

Source: Borjas (1995a, Table 1). The statistics are calculated in the subsample of men aged 25–64 who work in the civilian sector, who are not self-employed, and who do not reside in group quarters.

The table also documents that part of the decline in the relative economic performance of immigrants can be explained by a sizable drop in the relative wage of successive immigrant cohorts. The latest immigrant wave enumerated in the 1970 Census (i.e., the 1965–69 arrivals) earned 16.6 percent less than natives in 1970. By 1980, the latest immigrant wave enumerated in the 1980 Census earned 27.6 percent less than natives; and by 1990, the wage disadvantage between the most recent immigrant wave and natives had grown to 31.7 percent. As long as we are willing to interpret relative wages as a measure of relative skills, the trend in the wage differential between recent immigrants and natives suggests that there was a rapid decline in the relative skills of immigrants during the 1970–90 period.[3]

The poor economic performance of immigrants at the time of entry would not be a cause for concern if their economic disadvantage diminished over time, as immigrants assimilated into the U.S. labor market. The available evidence, however, suggests that the economic gap between immigrants and natives does not narrow substantially during the immigrants' working lives.

Figure 3.1 illustrates the trend in the wage differential between a particular group of immigrants and similarly-aged natives, so that immigrants who arrived when they were between 25 and 34 years old in the late 1960s are compared to natives aged 25–34 in 1970, to natives 35–44 in 1980, and to natives aged 45–54 in 1990. Consider the group of immigrants who arrived between

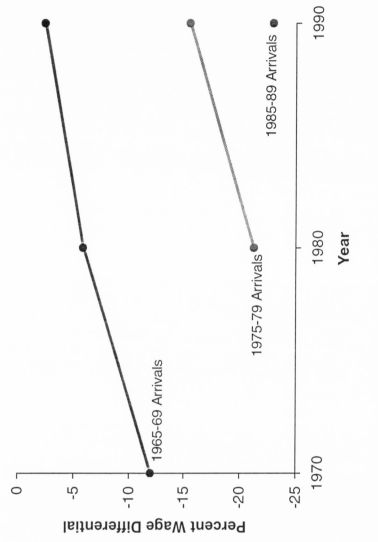

Figure 3.1. Wage Convergence Between Comparably-Aged Immigrants and Natives (Immigrants Aged 25-34 At Time of Entry)

1965 and 1969 and who were 25–34 years old in 1970. They earned 12.0 percent less than natives in 1970 and 2.5 percent less in 1990. Over a twenty–year period, therefore, the relative wage of this immigrant cohort increased by 10 percentage points.

It turns out that practically all immigrants, regardless of when they arrived in the country, experience the same sluggish relative wage growth. This result is significant because it suggests that more recent immigrant cohorts have not had faster wage growth despite their lower starting positions. Immigrants who arrived between 1975 and 1979 and were 25–34 years old at the time of arrival earned 21.3 percent less than natives in 1980 and 15.5 percent less than natives in 1990, an increase of only 5.8 percentage points. This wage growth is similar to that experienced by similarly aged immigrants who arrived between 1965 and 1969.

In short, the process of economic assimilation narrows the wage gap between immigrants and natives by only about 10 percentage points in the first two decades after arrival. If the recent waves experience the same extent of economic assimilation as earlier waves, the wage gap between recent immigrants and natives will remain at about 20 percentage points throughout much of the immigrants' working lives.

The Labor Market Impact of Immigration

Beginning in the early 1980s, a number of empirical studies began to estimate the impact of immigration on native earnings by comparing the earnings of natives who reside in immigrant cities (such as Los Angeles and San Diego) with the earnings of natives who reside in cities where few immigrants live (such as Atlanta and Pittsburgh).[4] These "spatial correlations" suggested that the average native wage is only slightly lower in labor markets where immigrants tend to cluster. If one city has 10 percent more immigrants than another, the native wage in the city with more immigrants is only about .2 percent lower.

This spatial correlation, however, does *not* necessarily indicate that immigrants have a numerically inconsequential impact on native workers. Suppose, for example, that immigration into California lowers the earnings of natives in California substantially. Native workers are not likely to stand idly by and watch their economic opportunities evaporate. Many will move out of California into other regions, and persons who were considering moving to California will now move somewhere else instead. As native workers respond to immigration by voting with their feet (and hence creating what has already been dubbed "the new white flight"), the adverse impact of immigration on California's labor market is transmitted to the entire economy. In the end, *all* native workers are worse off from immigration, not simply those residing in the areas where immigrants cluster.[5]

Recent work by Borjas, Freeman, and Katz (1997) provides what is perhaps the clearest evidence of a potential relation between immigration and native migration decisions in the United States.[6] Divide the country into three "regions": California, the other five states that receive large numbers of immigrants (New York, Texas, Florida, New Jersey, and Illinois), and the remainder of the country. Table 3.2 reports the proportion of the total population, of natives, and of immigrants living in these areas from 1950 to 1990. The resurgence of large-scale immigration into the United States began around 1970 and has continued since. It seems natural to contrast pre-1970 changes in the residential location of the native population with post-1970 changes to assess the effects of immigration on native location decisions.

The population counts reveal that the share of natives who lived in the major immigrant receiving state, California, was rising rapidly prior to 1970. Since 1970, however, the share of natives living in California has barely changed. However, California's share of the *total* population kept rising from 10.2 percent in 1970 to 12.4 percent in 1990. Put differently, an extrapolation of the demographic trends that existed before 1970—*before the immigrant supply shock*—would have predicted the state's 1990 share of the total population quite well. This result resembles Card's (1990, p. 255) conclusion about the long-run impact of the Mariel flow on Miami's population. Card estimates that Miami's population grew at an annual rate of 2.5 percent in the 1970s, as compared to a growth rate of 3.9 percent for the rest of Florida. After the Mariel flow, Miami's annual growth rate slowed to 1.4 percent, as compared to 3.4 percent in the rest of Florida. As a result, the actual population of Dade County in 1986 was roughly the same as the pre-Mariel projection made by the University of Florida.

Because labor (or capital) flows can diffuse the impact of immigration from the affected local labor markets to the national economy, Borjas, Freeman, and Katz (1992, 1997) proposed an alternative methodology to estimate the impact. The "factor proportions approach" compares a nation's actual supplies of workers in particular skill groups to those it would had had in the absence of immigration, and then uses outside information on how the wages of particular skill groups respond to increases in supply to compute the relative wage consequences of immigration. This approach predicts that about 44 percent of the 10.9 percentage point decline in the relative wage of high school dropouts observed between 1980 and 1995 can be attributed to immigration. This perspective thus implies that the adverse impact of immigration on the well-being of workers at the bottom end of the skill distribution has been substantial.

The Fiscal Impact of Immigration

Table 3.3 shows that immigrant use of welfare programs rose rapidly between 1970 and 1990. In 1970, immigrants were slightly less likely to receive cash benefits (such as AFDC and SSI) than natives. By 1990, the fraction of immigrant households receiving public assistance was 9.1 percent, or 1.7 percentage points higher than the fraction of native households. In fact, if one adds

TABLE 3.2. Regional Distribution of Adult-Age U.S. Population, 1950–90

| | Percentage of Total U.S. Population Living in | |
	California	Other Immigrant States
1950	7.2	26.9
1960	8.9	27.3
1970	10.2	27.1
1980	10.9	26.7
1990	12.4	27.0
	Percentage of Native U.S. Population Living in	
	California	Other Immigrant States
1950	6.9	25.4
1960	8.6	26.2
1970	9.6	26.2
1980	9.7	25.6
1990	10.0	25.5
	Percentage of Foreign-Born U.S. Population Living in	
	California	Other Immigrant States
1950	10.4	44.4
1960	14.6	44.9
1970	20.1	43.8
1980	27.2	41.9
1990	33.8	40.0

Source: Adapted from Borjas, Freeman, and Katz 1997, table 8. The calculations use the 1950-90 U.S. Censuses. The "other immigrant states" are New York, Texas, Florida, Illinois, and New Jersey. The adult-age population contains all persons aged 18–64 who are not living in group quarters.

TABLE 3.3. Welfare Use in the Immigrant Population, 1970–1990 (percentage of households receiving public assistance)

Group	1970	1980	1990
Native households	6.0	7.9	7.4
All immigrants	5.9	8.7	9.1
Recent immigrants (less than 5 years in U.S.)	5.5	8.3	8.3
Natives, aged 18–34 in 1970	5.1	6.4	5.6
Immigrants arrived in 1965–69, aged 18–34 in 1970	3.2	7.4	8.2
Immigrants arrived in 1975–79, aged 18–34 in 1980	—	5.8	7.8

Source: Author's tabulations from 1970, 1980, and 1990 public use samples of U.S. Census. The fraction of households receiving public assistance is calculated in the sample of households where the household head is at least 18 years old and does not reside in group quarters.

non-cash programs (such as Medicaid, Food Stamps, and housing assistance) to the definition of welfare, it turns out that 21 percent of immigrant households receive some type of aid, as compared to 14 percent of native households, and 10 percent of white non-Hispanic native households (Borjas and Hilton, 1996).

Two distinct factors account for the disproportionate increase in welfare use among immigrant households. Because more recent immigrant waves are less skilled than earlier waves, it is not surprising that more recent immigrant waves are also more likely to use welfare than earlier waves. In 1970, only 5.5 percent of the newly-arrived immigrant households received welfare, as compared to 6.0 percent for native households. By 1990, 8.3 percent of the newly-arrived immigrants received public assistance, as compared to 7.4 percent of native households.

In addition, the welfare participation rate of a specific immigrant wave *increases* over time. Consider, for example, the sample of immigrant households who arrived between 1965 and 1969 and who were 18–34 years old in 1970. This group of immigrant households had an initial welfare participation rate of 3.2 percent (much less than that of similarly aged natives). By 1990, the participation rate had risen to 8.2 percent (or about 2.6 percentage points above that of comparable natives). It seems, therefore, that the assimilation process involves not only learning about labor market opportunities, but also learning about the income opportunities provided by the welfare state.

The current debate over immigration policy seems to be dominated by the question of whether immigrants "pay their way" in the welfare state. The National Academy of Sciences recently conducted what is probably the most careful accounting of the fiscal impact of immigration for two states, California and New Jersey (Smith and Edmonston, 1997). The report concludes that immigration raises the annual taxes of the typical native household by about $1,200 in California and $200 in New Jersey.[7]

The Economic Gains from Immigration

Many observers claim that immigration is extremely beneficial for natives. It is typically argued that: immigrants spur economic growth; immigrant workers lower prices for American consumers; and immigrants increase the demand for goods and services produced by many native-owned firms. The available empirical evidence, however, indicates that these economic gains from immigration are quite small.

To see how natives gain from immigration, think first about how the United States gains from foreign trade. When we import toys made by cheap Chinese labor, workers in the American toy industry undoubtedly suffer wage cuts and perhaps even lose their jobs. These losses, however, are more than offset by the benefits accruing to consumers, who can now benefit from the lower prices induced by the additional competition.

Consider now the analogous argument for immigration. Immigrants increase the number of workers in the economy. Because of the additional competition in the labor market, the wage of native workers falls. *A* time, however, native-owned firms gain because they can now hire lower wages; and many native consumers gain because the lower lead to cheaper goods and services. As with foreign trade, the gai... ......g to the persons who use or consume immigrant services exceed the losses suffered by native workers, and hence society as a whole is better off. This does *not* mean that every person in the United States is better off. It simply means that the dollar value of the gains accruing to users of immigrant services exceeds the dollar value of the losses suffered by native workers.

Borjas (1995) and Johnson (1998) have shown that the net gains from immigration are on the order of .1 percent of GDP per year, or less than $10 billion. Put differently, immigration increases the per-capita income of native workers by less than $30 per year. At the same time, however, immigration induces a substantial redistribution of wealth. In particular, wealth is redistributed from native workers who compete with immigrant workers to the employers and users of immigrant services. Borjas (1995b), for example, estimates that native workers lose about 1.9 percent of GDP, or $152 billion in an $8 trillion economy. At the same time, employers and other users of immigrant services, such as owners of large agricultural enterprises, gain about 2.0 percent of GDP, or $160 billion in an $8 trillion economy. The net gain, therefore, is only about $8 billion annually.

III. The Parameters of an Immigration Policy

Every immigration policy must resolve two distinct issues: First, how many immigrants should the country admit? Second, which types of persons should be awarded the scarce entry visas?

It is useful to characterize immigration policy as a formula that gives "points" to visa applicants on the basis of various characteristics, and then sets a passing grade. The variables in the formula determine *which* types of persons will be let into the country, while the setting of the passing grade determines *how many* persons will be let into the country. For the most part, current U.S. policy uses a formula that has only one variable, indicating whether the visa applicant has a family member already residing in the United States. An applicant who has a relative in the country gets 100 points, passes the test, and is admitted. An applicant who does not gets zero points, fails the test, and cannot migrate legally. Moreover, current policy does not have strict restrictions on the number of immigrants—there are "pierceable caps" that essentially allow the number of certain types of visas (particularly those granted to close relatives of U.S. citizens) to expand with demand.

This description is, of course, a very simplistic summary of current policy. Current policy awards different numbers of points depending on whether the sponsor is a U.S. citizen or a permanent resident, and on whether the family connection is a close one (such as a parent, spouse, or child), or a more distant one (a sibling). These nuances in the policy help determine the speed with which the visa is granted, with closer family connections leading to speedier entry. In addition, a limited number of visas are distributed on the basis of skill characteristics, but these select workers make up only 7 percent of the immigrants.

Although the United States does not admit officially to using a "point system" in awarding entry visas, the immigration ministries of other countries maintain web sites that proudly advertise their formulas. The comparison of point systems across host countries reveals that the United States is unique in that its formula over-emphasizes family links between persons currently in the country and potential migrants. Canada, Australia, and New Zealand have more complex formulas, which include the applicant's educational background, occupation, English language proficiency, and age, as well as family connections. New Zealand's immigration policy, in fact, even creates financial incentives to speed along the process of assimilation by requiring certain immigrants to post a bond. Although the principal immigrant in the entering household must be proficient in the English language, accompanying family members need not pass the "English standard" at the time of entry. The family, however, must post a bond of NZ$20,000 (about $11,200) per family member who fails to meet the English standard. If the family member passes an English test within 3 months after arrival, the entire bond is refunded. If the family member fails this test but meets it within a year after arrival, only 80 percent of the bond is refunded. If the family member fails to meet the English standard within a year after arrival, the family forfeits the entire bond.

Sometimes a host country awards points to persons who are willing to pay the visa's stated price. Canada, for example, grants entry to those who are willing to invest at least $250,000 in a Canadian business. Although this "visas-for-sale" policy is a favorite proposal of economists, it does not seem to be taken very seriously in the political debate, perhaps because policy makers have a strong moral repugnance to what may be perceived as a market for human beings.

IV. What Should Be the Objective of Immigration Policy?

If economic research is to play a productive role in the immigration debate, the research findings should help us devise the formula that determines admission into the United States. We need to know the variables that are to be used to award points to the applicants, as well as the passing grade. Before we can resolve these issues, however, we have to address a very difficult question: What does the United States want to accomplish with its immigration policy? In other words, what is the nation's objective function?

The answer to this question is far from obvious, *even when posed from within a purely economic framework.* Suppose we divide the world into three distinct constituencies: persons born in the United States (the natives); the immigrants themselves; and those who remain in the source countries. To draw policy conclusions from economic research, we have to know whose

economic welfare the United States should try to improve when setting policy—that of natives, immigrants, the rest of the world, or some mix thereof.
The formula implied by economic research depends crucially on whose interests the United States cares most about.

Different political, economic, and moral arguments can be used to derive
objective functions that attach different weights to the three groups. Most participants in the policy debate probably attach the largest (and perhaps the only)
weight to the economic well-being of natives. This is not surprising. Natives
play the most important role in the U.S. political market, and most proposals
for immigration reform will unavoidably reflect the self-interest and concerns
of native voters.

Immigration, by definition, also improves the economic well-being of the
immigrants. If the immigrants are not better off after they enter the United
States, they are free to go back or try their luck elsewhere—and indeed many
do.

Finally, there is the vast population that remains in the source countries.
These people are affected by U.S. immigration policy in a number of ways.
Most directly, the policy choices made by the United States may drain the labor markets of many source countries from particular types of skills and abilities. A brain drain, for example, has a detrimental effect on economic growth
in the source countries, as the entrepreneurs and skilled workers who are likely
to be the engine of growth move to greener pastures. Similarly, the principles
of free trade suggest that world output would be largest if there were no national borders to interfere with the free movement of people. A policy that restricts workers from moving across countries unavoidably leads to a smaller
world economy, and will have a detrimental effect on many source countries.

Any serious discussion of immigration policy must begin with the specifi-
cation of an objective function detailing how the United States weighs the
costs and benefits accruing to each of these three groups. For the purposes of
the present discussion, I will simply assume that U.S. policy makers care only
about the economic well-being of the native population. One could argue that
the history of the United States—and its tolerance towards immigration—indicates that the objective function of the United States does not depend solely on
native economic well-being. Nevertheless, it is instructive to derive the "optimal" immigration policy implied by the assumption that the United States
cares only about native well-being.

Even after we settle the issue of how to weigh the interests of the three
groups, we still have to specify which dimension of native economic well-
being we care most about: the per-capita income of natives or the distribution
of income in the native population. As we have seen, immigration raises per-
capita income in the native population, but this does not mean that all natives
gain equally. We must, therefore, be able to judge an immigration policy in
terms of its impact on two different economic dimensions: the size of the economic pie and the splitting of the pie. In general, we can write the social welfare function as:

3.1 Social Welfare $= f$ (after-tax per-capita income of native population, distribution of income in native population).

When evaluating alternative social policies, economists are typically not concerned with their distributional impact. Policies are ranked solely in terms of their effect on per-capita incomes, with policies that lead to larger increases being considered better policies, regardless of their impact on the distribution of wealth. In other words, the typical policy discussion in economics simplifies equation (3.1) even further: social welfare depends only on per-capita income. In theory, one can justify this approach because it is possible to redistribute income from the winners to the losers so as to make every native in the United States better off. In fact, such redistribution seldom takes place; the winners remain winners, and the losers remain losers.

In my view, distributional issues are very important in the political arena, and they often drive the debate over many social policies. Throughout the discussion, therefore, I will emphasize how alternative immigration policies affect both efficiency and distribution in the U.S. economy.

V. Which Immigrants Should We Admit?

As we will see below, economic research does not tell us precisely what the "passing grade" should be in the admissions formula so that we have little idea of how many immigrants we should be admitting. Nevertheless, the research does suggest that the United States may be better off by shifting to a policy that favors skilled workers when awarding entry visas.

The case for skilled immigration contains two parts. Consider first how the *fiscal* impact of immigration affects the social welfare function in equation (3.1). Skilled immigrants require fewer social services, earn more, and pay higher taxes than less-skilled immigrants. From a fiscal perspective, therefore, skilled immigrants increase the after-tax per-capita income of the native population by more than less-skilled immigrants. Moreover, increasing the size of the skilled work force in a country with a progressive tax system implies that skilled workers will pay a larger share of total taxes, so that skilled immigration may also have a beneficial distributional impact.

Immigrants also affect the productivity of the native work force and of native-owned firms, and these productivity effects depend on how the skills of immigrants compare to the skills of natives. Skilled native workers, for example, have much to gain when less-skilled workers enter the United States. Skilled natives can specialize in their professions, while the immigrant work force complements the native work force by taking on a variety of service jobs. These gains, however, carry a cost. The jobs of less-skilled natives are now at risk, and these natives will suffer a reduction in their earnings. It does not seem far-fetched to assume that the American work force, particularly when compared to the work force of many source countries, is composed primarily of "skilled" workers. On aggregate, therefore, it would seem as if the typical American worker gains from *unskilled* immigration.

How does immigration affect the profits of firms? Firms that use less-skilled workers in the production line, such as sweatshops, gain from the immigration of the less-skilled. Less-skilled immigrants enter the country, reduce the earnings of less-skilled workers, increase the profits of the firms hiring these workers, and some of those excess profits are passed on to the consumers.

However, other firms might be better off with skilled immigrants. In fact, many studies suggest that there is, on average, more complementarity between skilled labor and capital than between unskilled labor and capital (Hamermesh, 1993, Ch. 3; and Goldin and Katz, 1996). Most firms, therefore, would gain more when the immigrant flow is composed of skilled workers.[8]

There exists a conflict between the type of immigrant that the "typical" native worker and the "typical" firm would like to see. The typical native worker would be better off with unskilled immigrants, while the typical firm would be better off with skilled immigrants. This conflict can be resolved only by measuring how much native workers gain from unskilled immigration and how much firms gain from skilled immigration, and by comparing the value of the two calculations (Borjas, 1995b). Although there is a lot of uncertainty in the literature, the productivity of capital is very responsive to the influx of skilled workers. The large increase in the profits of the typical firm, and the corresponding reduction in the costs of buying the goods produced by skilled workers, suggests that the United States might be better off with an immigration policy that favors skilled persons.

The gains from skilled immigration could be even larger if immigrants had "external effects" on the productivity of natives. One could argue, for example, that immigrants bring knowledge, skills, and abilities that native workers lack, and natives can somehow pick up this know-how by interacting with immigrants. It seems reasonable to suspect that the value of this external effect would be greater if natives were to interact with highly skilled immigrants.

The production complementarities between immigrants and natives, therefore, seem to increase the per-capita income of native workers most when the immigrant flow is composed of skilled workers. This type of immigrant flow also has the most benign distributional consequences: it narrows, rather than widens, the income gap between the skilled and the less skilled. Social welfare, therefore, is increased most when the immigrant flow is skilled.

VI. How Many Immigrants Should We Admit?

In theory, we should admit an immigrant whenever the immigrant makes a positive contribution to social welfare as defined in equation (3.1). The optimal number of immigrants could be calculated if we specify a particular functional form for the social welfare function. However, because different observers probably place different weights on the efficiency and distributional impacts of immigration policy, it is unlikely that reasonable participants in the immigration debate could ever agree on the magic number. In fact, no study has yet attempted to predict, purely on the basis of the empirical evidence, what the number of immigrants should be.

It is also worth noting that the U.S. demand for immigrants is not the only factor that determines how many immigrants enter the country. Suppose, for example, that the maximization of social welfare indicates that the United States should admit Q^* workers belonging to a particular skill group. It is far from clear that Q^* such workers would want to move to the United States. Many workers often find that income opportunities in the source countries (net of migration costs) are far better than those provided in the United States. By 1990, for example, 4.3 million Mexicans had chosen to migrate to the United States. But almost 85 million Mexicans had chosen *not to*. In the end, the size and skill composition of the immigrant flow are jointly determined by supply and demand.

The United States now admits slightly less than 1.0 million legal immigrants annually, and the Immigration and Naturalization Service (INS) estimates that the stock of illegal aliens permanently residing in the United States increases by about 300 thousand per year. It is worth thinking about whether 1.3 million immigrants annually are "too many" or "too few" relative to the optimal number.

It is tempting to interpret the heated debate over the social, political, and economic consequences of immigration as a sign that the United States is admitting too many immigrants. The symptoms include: the support of Proposition 187 by a vast majority of California voters, banning the provision of many types of public assistance and social benefits to illegal aliens; the enactment of the welfare reform legislation in 1996, with key provisions that restricted the eligibility of *legal* immigrants for many types of public assistance; and the recommendation by the presidential Commission of Immigration Reform to cut the size of the flow. However, one can also interpret these political events as responses to the perception that the United States is admitting the "wrong type" rather than the "wrong number" of immigrants.

An alternative way of posing the question is to imagine a counterfactual: what would be the nature of the immigration debate today if the immigrant flow had been composed exclusively of 1.3 million skilled workers? I think we would still be in the midst of a heated debate, but of a very different nature. After all, this type of immigration would also have substantial distributional consequences, reducing the wages of less-skilled workers. The political reactions of some professional groups—such as engineers or mathematicians—to increased immigration in these fields have been quite vocal, and have emphasized precisely the distributional impacts on the economic well-being of their professions.

Therefore, I interpret part of the political debate over immigration as a sign that the immigrant flow is too large, and is creating substantial economic, political, and social dislocations. The fiscal consequences of immigration on the receiving states are serious, and the labor market consequences of immigration on the affected workers are severe.[9]

VII. Immigration and Trade

In discussing the link between economic research on immigration and the setting of immigration policy, I have abstracted from the close link that exists between immigration and trade. Both trade and immigration have risen markedly in the past few decades. In 1970, the ratio of exports and imports to GDP stood at 8 percent; by 1996, this ratio had risen to about 19 percent. And much of this increase can be attributed to trade with less developed countries. By 1996, nearly 40 percent of all imports came from these countries.

Both trade and immigration increase the "effective" labor supply of particular groups of workers in the United States. As we have seen, immigration has substantially increased the labor supply of less-skilled workers. How has foreign trade changed labor supply? Not surprisingly, the United States exports different types of goods than it imports. And the workers employed in the importing industries tend to be disproportionately less educated, while the workers employed in the exporting industries are disproportionately well educated. Put simply, imports hurt the less-skilled while exports help the skilled.

The recognition that both trade and immigration change the nation's effective labor supply suggests that one could estimate the impact of trade on the income distribution by calculating the number of workers implicit in the observed trade flows. This calculation would construct, by skill group, the man-hour equivalent of each car that is imported and of each copy of computer software that is exported. One can then calculate the "factor content" of trade—the implicit number of workers in the traded flows—by adding up these man-hours over all imports and exports.

These calculations often reveal that the economic impacts of immigration and trade are quite different. In particular, immigration changes effective labor supply by a great deal more than trade (Borjas, Freeman, and Katz, 1997). The immigration that occurred between 1980 and 1995, for example, increased the number of high school dropouts in the United States by 21 percent, while trade increased the effective labor supply of these workers by only 4 percent. At the other end of the skill distribution, immigration increased the supply of workers with a high school diploma by only 4 percent, while trade increased it by less than 1 percent.

Because trade and immigration have such different effects on labor supply, it follows that they also have different effects on the income distribution. Between 1980 and 1995, the wage ratio between high school dropouts and high school graduates fell by 11 percentage points. The impact of immigration on the relative supply of high school dropouts can account for almost half of this decline in the relative wage. Trade, however, can only account for 10 percent of the decline.

Although this approach shows that immigration has a far larger impact than trade on the income distribution, one should be cautious about the interpretation. Both trade and immigration allow a country to employ resources that are scarce within its borders—and the same economic incentives that drive global trade flows motivate workers to move across international borders. If there were no foreign trade, for example, the United States would have greater incentives to allow the immigration of particular types of workers. Conversely, if there were no immigration, we would want to import the types of goods that are now produced by immigrants. As a result, the "small" effects of trade on wages might be larger if there were no immigration, and the effects of immigration would be larger if there were no trade.

Nevertheless, in the long run, immigration probably has a much larger impact than trade. If the United States stopped trading with its foreign partners, trade would no longer influence the effective labor supply of less-skilled workers. The goods that were imported in the past decade have long since been consumed, and trade leaves no "footprint." Immigration, however, is a permanent increase in the labor supply of the United States. Even if the United States were to stop admitting immigrants tomorrow, the impact of past immigration on labor supply would continue throughout the immigrant's working life—and beyond, as the children and grandchildren of immigrants entered the labor market. The debate over the consequences of globalization, therefore, should take into account the links between immigration and trade, and recognize that, in the end, immigration probably has a much bigger impact on the United States.

Notes

[1] Borjas (1990, chap. 2) provides a brief history of U.S. immigration policy.
[2] Recent surveys of the literature include Borjas (1994) and Friedberg and Hunt (1995).
[3] The income distribution also widened significantly during that period. Borjas (1994) shows that the deteriorating economic performance of immigrants cannot be explained by the changes in the wage structure.
[4] The first studies were by Grossman (1982) and Borjas (1983). More recent work using the spatial correlation approach includes Altonji and Card (1991) and Schoeni (1997). The literature estimates spatial correlations both in cross-section data, as well as in panel data (where changes in economic conditions in particular cities over some specific time period are correlated with variables that measure the change in the number of immigrants during the period). Both approaches tend to generate the same weak negative correlations.
[5] Note that capital flows across regions can also re-equilibrate the national labor markets after an immigrant supply shock.
[6] Filer (1992) and Frey (1995) provided the initial empirical evidence of this important demographic response to immigration.
[7] The National Academy report also estimated the long-run fiscal impact by "tracking" the fiscal consequences over a 300–year period after an immigrant is admitted into the United States (as the descendants of immigrants enter the labor market). This dynamic exercise revealed that admitting one immigrant today yields an $80,000 fiscal surplus at

the national level. The long-run net benefit from immigration, however, arises solely because the exercise assumes that the federal government will put its fiscal house in order in the year 2016, and pass a huge tax increase to ensure that the debt-GDP ratio remains constant after that point.

[8] The argument holds strictly when the capital stock in the United States is fixed. If the capital stock adjusts to the increase in labor supply induced by immigration, the gains to firms decline.

[9] It is worth noting that the optimal number of immigrants need not be an immutable constant, but might vary as the variables that determine social welfare in equation (3.1) vary. For instance, a good case can be made for linking immigration to the business cycle: admit more immigrants when the economy is strong and cut back on immigration when the economy is weak.

References

Altonji, Joseph G. and David Card. 1991. "The Effects of Immigration on the Labor Market Outcomes of Less-Skilled Natives." In John M. Abowd and Richard B. Freeman (eds.), *Immigration, Trade, and the Labor Market*. Chicago: University of Chicago Press.

Borjas, George J. 1983. "The Substitutability of Black, Hispanic, and White Labor." *Economic Inquiry* 21(1): 93–106.

Borjas, George J. 1990. *Friends or Strangers: The Impact of Immigrants on the U.S. Economy*. New York: Basic Books.

Borjas, George J. 1994. "The Economics of Immigration." *Journal of Economic Literature* 32(4): 1667–1717.

Borjas, George J. 1995a. "Assimilation and Changes in Cohort Quality Revisited: What Happened to Immigrant Earnings in the 1980s?" *Journal of Labor Economics* 13(2): 201–245.

Borjas, George J. 1995b. "The Economic Benefits from Immigration." *Journal of Economic Perspectives* 9(2): 3–22.

Borjas, George J., Richard B. Freeman, and Lawrence F. Katz. 1992. "On the Labor Market Impacts of Immigration and Trade." In George J. Borjas and Richard B. Freeman (eds.), *Immigration and the Work Force: Economic Consequences for the United States and Source Areas*. Chicago: University of Chicago Press.

Borjas, George J., Richard B. Freeman, and Lawrence F. Katz. 1997. "How Much Do Immigration and Trade Affect Labor Market Outcomes." *Brookings Papers on Economic Activity* 1: 1–67.

Borjas, George J. and Lynette Hilton. 1996. "Immigration and the Welfare State: Immigrant Participation in Means-Tested Entitlement Programs." *Quarterly Journal of Economics* 111(2): 575–604.

Card, David. 1990. "The Impact of the Mariel Boatlift on the Miami Labor Market." *Industrial and Labor Relations Review* 43(2): 245–257.

Filer, Randall K. 1992. "The Impact of Immigrant Arrivals on Migratory Patterns of Native Workers." In George J. Borjas and Richard B. Freeman (eds.), *Immigration and the Work Force: Economic Consequences for the United States and Source Areas*. Chicago: University of Chicago Press.

Frey, William. 1995. "Immigration and Internal Migration 'Flight' from U.S. Metropolitan Areas: Toward a New Demographic Balkanization." *Urban Studies* 32(4–5): 733–757.

Friedberg, Rachel and Jennifer Hunt. 1995. "The Impact of Immigration on Host Country Wages, Employment and Growth." *Journal of Economic Perspectives* 9(2): 23–44.

Goldin, Claudia and Lawrence F. Katz. 1996. "The Origins of Technology-Skill Complementarity." National Bureau of Economic Research Working Paper No. 5657.

Grossman, Jean Baldwin. 1982. "The Substitutability of Natives and Immigrants in Production." *Review of Economics and Statistics* 54(4): 596–603.

Hamermesh, Daniel S. 1993. *Labor Demand.* Princeton, N.J.: Princeton University Press.

Johnson, George. 1998. "Estimation of the Impact of Immigration on the Distribution of Income Among Minorities and Others." In Daniel S. Hamermesh and Frank Bean (eds.), *Help or Hindrance? The Economic Implications of Immigration for African-Americans.* New York: Russell Sage Press.

Schoeni, Robert F. 1997. "The Effect of Immigrants on the Employment and Wages of Native Workers: Evidence from the 1970s and 1980s." Unpublished paper, the RAND Corporation, March.

Smith, James P. and Barry Edmonston (eds.). 1997. *The New Americans: Economic, Demographic, and Fiscal Effects of Immigration.* Washington, D.C.: National Academy Press.

Comment

Joaquin F. Otero

I agree with the tone and direction of Borjas's paper, in particular that economic factors will influence and decide the outcome of the national debate, on both *legal* and *illegal* immigration.

I also agree that immigration policy in the U.S. will be dictated by the fortunes of the U.S. economy. At present there is an apparent lull in the national immigration debate, due to the enormous success of the Clinton economic policies and his incredible record of new job creation—15 million plus new jobs since 1993. The low key nature of the debate is also the result of the country's recent preoccupation with alleged sex improprieties in the White House, the threat of war related to the Iraqi weapons inspections and recent weather disasters attributed to the capricious "El Niño." However, we can expect a resumption of the debate at high decibel levels the moment that large American companies announce that they are moving their facilities to the "maquiladora" zones in Mexico, Panama, the Dominican Republic or to a "Tiger" nation in Asia. And if the Congress decides to revisit the President's request for "fast track" authority for more free trade in the hemisphere, the debate will really be heated. Because in the mind of most Americans, trade and immigration are issues they consider bad for U.S. jobs.

And, let us hope that there will be no more highly publicized immigration-related incidents, that is, police beatings of illegal aliens at the border. These are issues that, generally, trigger a warped combination of automatic public outrage and a bigoted knee jerk anti-immigrant response. From the analysis of these facts, I conclude that Borjas is right on target. So long as our economic ox is not gored, the response of Americans to immigration is not of the visceral kind.

Since Borjas focuses on California as an example of how the impact of immigration on that state's labor is transmitted to the entire U.S. economy, I find it compelling to say that, on the one hand, I agree with the empirical data available. On the other hand, it is also my view that the harsh reality of facts and figures is exacerbated by the demagoguery of politicians such as California Governor Pete Wilson, who has effectively played the race card to advance his own political designs.

In many parts of the country, but in California particularly, Hispanics have become the favorite punching bag of demagogues, racists, foreigners haters, and organized anti-immigration forces. The invaluable assistance that immigration labor lends to the huge California agribusiness is always played down or ignored. Without immigrant labor—most of it Hispanics—California and America in general would not be able to have fruits, vegetables, and other agricultural products at reasonable prices. And, indeed, well-to-do and middle income Americans would not have gardeners, maids, cooks, nannies, and other low-wage workers at their beck and call. Yet, that vital economic contribution of millions of legal immigrant workers is blurred by the argument that those immigrants abuse social services and public assistance programs. The problem is that we want to have our cake and eat it too. Because Hispanics are rapidly becoming the largest minority group in California and, indeed throughout America, they will suffer increased discrimination. And, adding to Borjas's arguments I contend that this discrimination will intensify as the United States increases trade with Mexico and Latin America.

It is predictable that the U.S. government will go to great lengths to dramatically increase free trade with Latin America in the next decade. The aggressive trade policies of the Asian countries and the European Union leave the United States no choice but also to aggressively seek other trading alliances in the hemisphere. If the United States blinks, it will pay dearly in economic losses for years to come. Yet, if the United States wins, there will be a loud hue and cry that trade is bad for American workers. Free trade would be more palatable to the average American if the government were to pursue expanded trade in tandem with social and economic policies that allow economic growth without major injury to the native force. And those policies should include a realistic and fair immigration component. That is a commitment that is crucially important for the growth of the U.S. economy, as well as for the preservation of the principle that America is and should continue to be a nation of immigrants.

Borjas is correct in that increased immigration has had an undeniable and substantial adverse impact on the well-being of American workers, especially on those at the lower levels of the education and economic ladder. It is my personal opinion that immigration policy in the United States is broken and needs urgent fixing. For example, our own failure to effectively curb illegal immigration is a fact that, unfortunately, enhances the dislike and distrust of low-skill immigrants. And when the U.S. government links poor immigration policy to insensitive trade policies, the negative impact on American workers is even more disastrous. For Americans of Hispanic descent, the effects are catastrophic in nature. Most Hispanic workers are usually at the bottom of the seniority rosters and, thus, since they were last hired, they are the first to be fired or laid-off.

In recent years, both the Congress and the Executive Branch have adopted policies that enable U.S. trade negotiators to offer non-immigrant visas in return for overseas business opportunities for U.S. companies. While it is fair that foreign business persons be allowed to enter the United States to oversee and manage their investments, the U.S. government needs to retain tight control over who is allowed to enter and remain in the country, including whether or not such a person has a right to enter the U.S. labor market. Trading immigration visas for business opportunities restricts the ability of the President and Congress to administer U.S. immigration law and protect the interests of U.S. workers, who have much to lose from U.S. government policies permitting government negotiators to use non-immigrant visas as a bargaining chip in trade and investment negotiations.

The Office of the U.S. Trade Representative negotiates trade and investment agreements that promote U.S. business interests abroad, including agreements that allow workers to cross national borders. Unfortunately, in the haste to open up previously closed foreign markets to U.S. businesses, U.S. trade negotiators often conclude agreements which bind U.S. immigration law. This practice limits the ability of policymakers to correct abuses or deficiencies in our immigration system. Under the current immigration system, an unscrupulous employer could be allowed to bring into the United States (under the H-1B program) 20 computer programmers from India at lower wages than their American counterparts and do so without any effort to promote the recruitment of U.S. workers. Many companies that engage in this practice hide behind a mountain of paperwork and a failed regulatory policy. It is a practice that is unfair to American workers and those businesses that follow the rules.

Because the United States has binding commitments on the movement of people under the World Trade Organization's General Agreement on Trade in Services (GATS), some of the measures used to correct these visa abuses could be considered inconsistent with our international obligations. The NAFTA treaty currently provides for the temporary entry and employment of business persons from Canada and Mexico. Canadian professionals are allowed to enter the United States without numerical limitations, labor market tests, or procedural requirements such as a visa or petition. NAFTA has unintentionally created a common labor market for professionals in North America that allows Canadian professionals to be in direct competition with U.S. professionals without any regard for labor market implications. Another example of bad public policy in this area is the NAFTA visas for Canadian nurses. Canadian nurses do not need visas to enter the United States, and there is no labor market test to determine entries and no numerical restriction on how many can be admitted. Presently, entries of Canadian nurses average 6,000 per year.

While many employers do not misuse the H-1B program, there are glaring abuses. During my tenure at the Department of Labor, I came across countless cases where abuses of non-immigrant visas resulted in massive layoffs of American workers. We found that computer companies, health care organizations, and universities routinely imported workers from Poland, Pakistan, India, Ireland, and other countries using H-1B visas, specifically to replace American workers in order to reduce costs of operation and maximize profits. The Department of Labor convinced the Administration to introduce legislation correcting these glaring abuses of the H-1B visa. But the Congress, under pressure from large corporations and other abusers of the H-1B visas, failed to enact the badly needed reforms. Another example of how non-immigrant visas are abused to the detriment of American workers can be found in the airline industry. U.S. commercial air carriers regularly use D-1 visas to hire foreign-national crews on international flights in positions traditionally held by U.S. based flight attendants. This practice displaces American workers. Some foreign airlines operating in the U.S. often use the D-1 visa, illegally employing foreign crews to work on U.S. domestic routes. Here again, we revert back to economic issues aggravated by bad public policy. U.S. and foreign employers, with the disguised blessings of the U.S. Congress and the Administration, routinely violate immigration policy as a tool to displace U.S. workers. These developments jeopardize the interest of the American worker and the nation at large, and further exacerbate the very difficult immigration problem besetting the United States.

I concur with Borjas's view that the economic impact on the U.S. labor supply, resulting from past uncontrolled immigration, will have long lasting effects even if the United States were to stop admitting immigrants tomorrow.

The United States needs an immigration policy that is fair, non-discriminatory and consistent with the national interest—not just the interest of those bent on profit at all costs. At the same time, legal immigration should be encouraged and regulated with wisdom and fairness. And illegal immigration must be controlled and stopped, or we will pay enormous social and economic consequences for years to come. And, as we move further into the globalization of trade and economic policy, we should recognize, as Borjas correctly argues, that the linkage between immigration and trade must be a priority item on the agenda of the national debate on immigration policy.

Comment

Jagdish Bhagwati

I should say at the outset that, much as I have found his empirical research on immigration into the United States to be a most useful and valuable addition to the many important contributions made over the years by U.S. immigration experts such as the late Julian Simon and the pioneering researcher, Barry Chiswick, I intend to express in a friendly and scholarly way my almost total disagreement with Borjas's analysis of the impact of immigration and, even more, with his views on immigration policy. I believe that my differences derive from several reasons, as follows:

(1) I started thinking and writing about immigration questions a quarter of a century ago and in the context of *general equilibrium* models that we trade theorists typically use[1] whereas Borjas got into the subject much later and from familiarity with the labor economist's typical use of *partial equilibrium* tools instead.

(2) The theorists and empiricists of immigration in the last quarter of a century considered a range of theoretical and policy issues (e.g., the conceptual question of how to define the social welfare function for a country in the presence of migration[2], the question of optimal income tax policy in the presence of international personal mobility[3], or the differentiated modeling of migration depending on the kinds of skills involved[4]) which are missing from, and hence handicap, Borjas's analysis[5];

(3) A sensible discussion of immigration policy requires in my view that the economic analysis both reflect, and be situated squarely within the context of, ethical and sociological analysis whereas Borjas typically ignores these aspects and hence is handicapped by his narrow focus.

(4) Like the late Julian Simon, I am strongly biased in favor of a relaxed view of immigration whereas Borjas inclines, I believe, towards a more cautious and skeptical, if not hostile, view of the matter.

(5) I find both morally unacceptable, and economically unconvincing, his view that we ought to favor skilled over unskilled immigrants.

Whose Welfare?

Let me begin with Borjas's definition of how we must evaluate the effects of migrants on U.S. welfare. Borjas, unlike in his earlier writings, now distinguishes clearly, as we learned to do in the 1960s[6], between the welfare of the "migrants" and that of those already here (whether native-born or naturalized or legal and illegal aliens), i.e., "us". That is all to the good.

But he is wrong to argue that we in the United States must be concerned only with the economic effect on us. This is sociologically and ethically an untenable viewpoint. As I have long argued, whether one treats migrants' welfare as part of "U.S. welfare" depends on the nature of the migration and also on the moral nature of our society. With permanent immigrants, it is likely that we will view their welfare as part of U.S. welfare: after all, the immigrants are joining our society. On the other hand, it is perfectly possible that, especially with the temporary and the "yo-yo" migrants who move back and forth, as with the guestworkers programs of Western Europe, some societies may not think so (though, even here, recall the solidarity expressed by some German labor unions with the guestworkers, the *gastarbeiters*, in their famous slogan: *ihr kampf ist unser kampf*)[7]. With illegal immigrants, the willingness to consider the welfare of immigrants as part of social welfare may be even more tenuous (though I plan to explore that too below). Equally, it is possible, in an analysis that embraces both the sending and the receiving countries, that the migrants' welfare will be considered part of neither country or as part of both countries' welfare.

Borjas therefore is wrong to think that the only plausible view to take is for our national economic welfare function to be defined purely on us and this, in turn, to be evaluated in terms of available goods and services as affected by the inflow of the immigrants. He considers that this is how Americans view immigration politically. I do not think so at all.

Thus, I believe that Americans, whose society has been uniquely formed by immigration, do have a morally-informed views on *both* which kinds of immigrants they would favor (thus implicitly indulging in interpersonal comparisons) *and* how immigrants must be treated, whether legal or illegal, once they are in their midst.[8] And, on both counts, *disregarding wholly the altogether separate question of how different immigrants will affect "our" economic welfare,* American are typically likely, even today, to show both decency and good moral sense.

Take the question of which kind of immigrants we would favor. Conduct a mental experiment. Assume that we have one immigrant visa to offer and there are two applicants: a skilled and well-heeled doctor and an unskilled and impoverished peasant. Banish all thoughts as to which of the two will add more to our economic welfare: it might help to think of either being settled sight unseen on a remote "paradise island" and being out of our lives before and after our choice. Whom would we then choose for the largesse? I have little doubt that most Americans would take in the peasant. *That* is what the Statue of Liberty is all about: taking in those whose needs are the greatest. In virtually ignoring this essence of American moral sensibility, Borjas unwittingly reduces the Statue of Liberty, with her outstretched hand holding the torch of liberty, to a monument instead to New York's subway rider with her raised hand holding on to the overhead strap as the train lurches along the labyrinthine tracks.

Nor does Borjas's focus on considering only *our* economic welfare come to grips with what I take to be the dominant American moral sense when he fails to consider also the immigrants' welfare once they are in our midst. In deciding how we should deter illegal immigration, for example, Borjas's focus would make us gladly put up with one or all of measures such as employer sanctions, the use of ID cards, deprivation of schooling for children[9] et al. which are likely, almost certain, to propel the illegals in our midst towards an underclass status without access to many of the economic and social "goods" enjoyed by the rest of us. In doing so, he and others so inclined discount the fact that, as I have argued recently in the *Boston Review:*[10]

> The explanation [of the American sense that we should "treat people who are here, whether native or naturalized or alien, with the basic decency that each of us owes to others"] lies in our history: the absence of an identity defined by shared memories that define "us" against "others", and a history of immigration that leads the culture to pride itself on ensuring chances for each and all. Our sensibility is offended at its core when we contemplate that any group, any individual, is denied fair access to the opportunities that our country offers. The notion that we can thus live alongside an underclass of humanity, denied access to social benefits and economic betterment simply because its members are illegal aliens, violates our fundamental sense of decency and morality.

I would even add that, in this regard, I have been struck particularly by a possible parallel between the way we wish to treat equally well all in our midst, and the absence in our culture of the Cinderella complex, the differentially advantaged treatment of one's natural over that of one's adopted or acquired children. I hazard the view, based on my casual observation of other cultures, that there is no particular opprobrium there in discriminating in favor of one's natural children, whereas in our culture, this is simply beyond the pale: all children, once in one's fold, are the same.

Economic Effects on Us

Having therefore rejected as indefensible for U.S. immigration policy analysis the exclusive Borjas concern with "our" economic welfare, let me now accept this focus and still disagree with his analysis and conclusions. There are three main issues I wish to comment on.

1. *Aggregate Income versus Income Distribution:* Borjas seems to accept that immigration will improve our welfare, in the aggregate.[11]

The problem is that, despite Borjas's conviction that unskilled immigration, which has to be largely illegal immigration (which is almost exclusively of the unskilled) but also includes some who come in on the refugee entries and others admitted under the familial programs, affects the real wages of our unskilled workers adversely, I would maintain that this case is hardly proven. The original Mariel boatlift study of David Card had first indicated that the effect of the influx of roughly 100,000 Cubans into Miami had left the average wages unchanged. What had happened then to "diminishing returns"? There were two answers to this puzzle once the partial-equilibrium habit of mind was abandoned. First, the normal influx of other migrants into Miami and the efflux of Miami residents elsewhere could have adjusted to the Cuban inflow and offset it. Second, the Cuban inflow may well have left Miami within the Chipman-McKenzie diversification cone, killing the diminishing returns as we well know from general-equilibrium analysis. By now, the labor economists are well aware of these possibilities. But their full import is not understood, in my view.

Thus, Borjas claims that the local effects in the states such as Florida, to which the unskilled and often illegal immigrants go, are masked by the net outflow of previous residents from these states, with the implication that the "problem" of adverse effect on wages is simply exported elsewhere, thus presumably is likely to surface there. But Rivera-Batiz (1998) has produced reliable refutation of Borjas's argument, which is based on shaky evidence from a sociological study. Breaking down the outflow by skills, it can be seen in Table 3.4 that the states receiving the unskilled immigrants have largely experienced outflows of skilled residents. In itself, therefore, the failure to show serious adverse impact in the states of immigration on wages from the unskilled immigration cannot be explained away in the fashion Borjas seems to favor.

But Rivera-Batiz's calculations suggest strongly that the diversification-cone argument may be the overriding reason why we have not observed the enduring and adverse impact anywhere on the wages of the unskilled here. It is obvious that the different labor markets around the country are connected, so that the diversification cone needs to be defined on more-than-local endowments. If it is defined over national endowments, and we reckon with the fact that capital accumulates at a rate more or less commensurate with the growth of the labor force (inclusive of all immigration) and of the unskilled labor force by itself as well, all at the national level, it becomes harder to expect that the immigration we have observed to date can be a source of any noticeable adverse effect on the wages of the unskilled. If so, the Borjas concerns about income distribution are simply exaggerated, at best, and ill-founded, at worst. In either case, we ought to dismiss them from the public discourse.

2. *Revenue Distribution*: The income distributional implications can arise also in a different sense which is fairly important, however. I believe that while there is some persisting disagreement whether immigration, on balance, leads to a drain on public revenues, the arguments going back well over a decade and raising a number of conceptual and measurement differences, there is general agreement that the Center tends to gain net revenues and the states of (immediate) immigration tend to lose them.

TABLE 3.4. Comparative Educational Distributions of Outmigrants and Mexican Immigrants, 1990 California, Texas, and New York (Persons 25 years of age or older)

	California	
Educational Distribution	Native outmigrants 1985–90	Mexican Immigrants 1980–90
Less than high school	14.6%	71.0%
High school diploma	26.7	12.5
Some college	34.9	11.7
College or more	23.8	4.8

	Texas	
Educational Distribution	Native outmigrants 1985–90	Mexican Immigrants 1980–90
Less than high school	16.0%	69.5%
High school diploma	27.8	12.8
Some college	30.6	12.1
College or more	25.6	5.6

	New York	
Educational Distribution	Native outmigrants 1985–90	Mexican Immigrants 1980–90
Less than high school	13.2%	46.2%
High school diploma	22.3	26.6
Some college	30.9	20.8
College or more	33.6	6.4

Source: Data from U.S. Department of Commerce, 1990 U.S. Census of Population and Housing. Francisco Rivera-Batiz, "Migration and the Labour Market: Sectoral and Regional Effects," paper presented at the OECD Seminar on Migration, Free Trade and Regional Integration in North America, Mexico City, January 15–16, 1998.

The problem then is that, even if the former gain dominates the latter loss, if nothing is done to compensate the losers, then the Governors of those states will have a huge political incentive to seek transfers by way of "compensation". Failing that, they will try to turn immigration, and the "drain on their exchequers" into a political issue. The competition for schools and health services will become an issue. In fact, I would venture to say that Texas earlier, and California Governor Pete Wilson later, may well have chosen to go after truly offensive proposals to deny schooling to children of illegal immigrants as a strategic political ploy to bring the entire issue to center stage, rather than because they genuinely believed that this ought to be our policy. What this points to, of course, is that the Federal responsibility for revenue transfers must match the federal immigration policy: the states should not be left in the lurch.

3. *Skilled versus Unskilled Immigration*: Let me conclude with the Borjas preference for skilled migration. I have already said why it offends our moral sense about what types of immigrants we ought to prefer. But I am presently addressing the separate issue: which type of immigrant is *better for us*.

Here, if we assume that migrants earn the value of their marginal product, there is little impact on the rest of us, one way or the other. So, the answer must be: we ought to be indifferent among different levels of skills, on economic grounds. But that is where you get into the question of (uncompensated) externalities. Are these externalities to us greater from the skilled? As skilled members of the elite, we are naturally disposed to vote for that proposition! But frankly, how do we know? I can readily imagine all sorts of externalities of importance from letting in a Haitian maid, or having her come in illegally, enabling women to go into the workforce in New York and yielding the social value of increased facilitation of female participation in the workforce. Again, unskilled immigrants who create economic opportunity for themselves in inner cities in all sorts of ways may well have a demonstration value for blacks who may otherwise take too seriously the notion, not entirely wrong of course, that the inner cities " lack economic opportunities." This demonstration value itself is an externality, lifting enlightened black leaders from defeatism into hope and action. One could go on.

In fact, the whole problem with externalities is that, as we have known from the industrial policy debates, they are the first refuge of the scoundrels. What I find ironic is that Borjas, who I suspect is suspicious of arguments based on externalities on industrial policy issues, is only too happy to assert them when it comes to favoring the skilled migrants! I believe therefore that the growing fetish for the skilled immigrants is just that, and we need to look at it straight in the face for the morally unacceptable, and economically unjustified, prescription for changing our immigration policy that it is.

Notes

[1] There were important contributions in this literature by Harry Johnson, Herbert Grubel, Tony Scott et al. For a synthesis and review of that literature, see Bhagwati and Rodriguez (1976).
[2] I take up this question immediately below.
[3] There is thus a huge literature in public finance on this question. See, for example, Bhagwati and Wilson (1989), Bhagwati (1991), Wilson (1982a;b), and Mirrlees (1982).
[4] Several theoretical models of professional migration and its consequences were developed by Koichi Hamada, myself and others in Bhagwati and Partington (1976), for instance.

[5] It is perhaps indicative that Borjas's references are almost entirely to himself (a failing that I share) and a narrow set of his associates, suggesting disregard of not merely the earlier literature by Johnson, Grubel-Scott, Berry, myself, Hamada, Mirrlees and many others, but also of recent literature by Barry Chiswick, Harriet Orcutt, Kar-yiu Wong and many others.

[6] Again, the first to draw this important distinction was Harry Johnson. It then became standard in the formal discussions of the so-called 'brain drain' that stimulated much of the theoretical and policy writings in the 1960s and 1970s.

[7] Translated, the slogan means: Their battle is our battle.

[8] Of course, Americans differ in what they think we owe to legal as distinct from illegal immigrants. Some, like me and Owen Fiss, the constitutional lawyer at Yale, would treat both alike, and pretty much the way we treat ourselves; but others would treat illegals less favorably. See the Symposium on "The Promise of Immigration" in the *Boston Review* 23(5), October/November 1998.

[9] Borjas himself does not approve of the deprivation of education for children. But he approves of nearly everything else, as far as one can tell from his public writings. E.g. see his *New York Times* op. ed. article, "Punish Employers, Not Children," July 11, 1996.

[10] The *Boston Review*, op. cit., page 21.

[11] I find it difficult to see, however, why he is unwilling to put a figure on this gain, considering he shows no shyness in turning out estimates that require even more heroic empirical assumptions. Such empirical estimates would help define the empirical trade-off between the income gain and the distributional problems that Borjas believes, but which I shall argue below to be implausible, to be the outcomes of current unskilled immigration, and hence also enable us to consider more meaningfully whether "compensation" to the damaged parties could be financed from the gains that the immigration brings.

References

Bhagwati, Jagdish. 1991. "International Migration and Income Taxation." In Douglas Irwin (ed.), J. Bhagwati, Political Economy and International Economics. Cambridge: MIT Press.

Bhagwati, Jagdish. 1998. "Getting Policy Wrong." *Boston Review* 23:21–22.

Bhagwati, Jagdish, and Martin Partington (eds.). 1976. *Taxing the Brain Drain: A Proposal.* Amsterdam: North-Holland Publishing Company.

Bhagwati, Jagdish, and Carlos Rodriguez. 1976. "Welfare-Theoretical Analyses of the Brain Drain." In J. Bhagwati (ed.), *The Brain Drain and Taxation: Theory and Empirical Analysis.* Amsterdam: North-Holland Publishing Company.

Bhagwati, Jagdish, and John Wilson (ed.). 1989. *Income Taxation and International Mobility.* Cambridge: MIT Press.

Borjas, George. 1996. "Punish Employers, not Children." *New York Times,* July 11.

Borjas, George. "Economic Research and the Debate over Immigration Policy." In this volume.

Grubel, Herbert, and Anthony Scott. 1966. "The International Flow of Human Capital." *American Economic Review* (May).

Hamada, Koichi, and Jagdish Bhagwati. 1976. "Domestic Distortions, Imperfect Information and the Brain Drain." In Bhagwati and Partington 1976.

Johnson, Harry. 1965. "The Economics of the 'Brain Drain': The Canadian Case." *Minerva*.

Johnson, Harry. 1967. "Some Economic Aspects of Brain Drain." *Pakistan Development Review* 3.

Mirrlees, James. 1982. "Migration and Optimal Taxes." *Journal of Public Economics* 18:319–42.

Wilson, John. 1982a. "Optimal Linear Income Taxation in the Presence of Emigration," *Journal of Public Economics* 18:363–80.

Wilson, John. 1982b. "Optimal Income Taxation and Migration: A World Welfare Point of View." *Journal of Public Economics* 18:381–98.

CHAPTER 4

U.S. Trade Adjustment Assistance Policies for Workers

Gregory K. Schoepfle

We should also offer help and hope to those Americans temporarily left behind by the global marketplace or by the
march of technology, which may have nothing to do with
trade. That's why we have more than doubled funding for
training dislocated workers since 1993—and if my new
budget is adopted, we will triple funding. That's why we
must do more, and more quickly, to help workers who lose
their jobs for whatever reason.

—President Clinton, State of the Union Address, January 27, 1998

I. Introduction

The effects of globalization and the rapid pace of economic change on U.S.
workers are hot topics of debate today in the press, on Capitol Hill, and among
the public at large. Since 1992, the Goldilocks U.S. economy (not too hot to
stir up inflationary pressures, not too cold to cause unemployment to rise)[1] has
been performing the best in a generation. But ironically, a large segment of the
workforce—described by former Secretary of Labor Reich as "the anxious
class"— is deeply concerned about job security and the implications of the ongoing economic change. The discussions leading up to and following the passage and implementation of the North American Free Trade Agreement
(NAFTA)—the most recent U.S. venture in the area of trade liberalization and
regional economic integration—and the recent discussions about extending the
President's authority to negotiate additional international trade agreements—
the so-call "fast track" debate—have rekindled angst among American
workers about threats to job and wage security brought on by a more open
U.S. economy linked more closely to other economies around the world.[2]

Although the benefits to the nation of international trade are widely accepted, the expansion of international trade has often been cited as the major culprit for the rising insecurity felt by many U.S. workers. However, many factors—in addition to international trade—have contributed to this concern: rapid development and diffusion of new technologies (especially in the areas of electronics, information, telecommunications, and transportation); declines in rates of unionization; changes in consumer tastes; and government policies of deregulation and reduced social spending.

The process of globalization and the introduction of new technologies in the workplace are occurring as the character and composition of the U.S. workforce are changing. Market forces indicate a need to develop a more skilled workforce, but a large number of U.S. workers are not prepared for the technical jobs that are becoming available. The skills divide raises questions of inclusion and exclusion and the potential to reap the benefits of economic growth in the new economy. The relationship between employer-employee is also changing as the rate of unionization continues to decline and employers use more part-time and contract workers—changes that may pose challenges to worker security and protections.

Economic restructuring and associated worker displacement are changing the industrial landscape. However, in a dynamic and growing economy like that of the United States, substantial job creation and substantial job destruction are to be expected.[3] The corporate downsizing in the 1980s affected white-collar workers as well as blue-collar workers. As layoffs become more permanent in nature (i.e., less cyclical and with fewer recalls), mismatches are created in terms of human capital (job skills) and industry/spatial location (where the jobs are). With both high-wage and low-skill jobs at risk in the new economy, workers will need to constantly upgrade their skills to keep (or get new) high-wage higher-skilled jobs. It is not just a question of change, but how to manage it.

When some workers, communities, industries, or firms might be adversely affected by the implementation of a new policy or legislative change, provisions are often made for the gradual implementation of the change and, in most cases, some form of adjustment assistance. For example, new international trade agreements usually include provisions to ease in changes so that adjustments can occur without severe disruptions; safeguard provisions are also included for disruptions that may occur after implementation of the agreement. Several recent trade agreements also have included provisions for an adjustment assistance program to help facilitate the reemployment of workers that might be adversely affected.

Since the 1960s, the U.S. government has attempted to ease structural economic adjustment through the implementation of a mix of active and passive labor market policies.[4] The trade adjustment assistance program for workers adversely affected by imports is an example of a targeted assistance program which offers a mix of active and passive labor market services. It is the subject of this paper. First, an overview is presented of general U.S. Department of Labor programs for dislocated workers—workers with labor force attachment (on the job for three years or more) who lose their jobs and are unlikely to be recalled—and the rationale for a separate program for workers dislocated as the result of changes in international trade. Next, two trade adjustment assistance programs specifically designed for workers affected by imports are discussed as well as plans to renew, expand, and consolidate them. The paper closes with some observations about these programs.

II. U.S. Department of Labor Assistance Programs for Workers Displaced by Trade

Overview of U.S. Department of Labor Programs for Dislocated Workers

The U.S. Department of Labor administers several programs to assist dislocated workers, their families, and their communities keep pace with changes in the new global economy. The federal-state unemployment insurance (UI) system, created by the Social Security Act of 1935, offers the first line of defense against the effects of unemployment. By providing compensation to laidoff workers (up to 26 weeks at an average gross wage replacement rate of 50%), UI helps ensure that basic necessities can be obtained during a short-term transition while searching for work.

For those displaced workers who face a more difficult or longer-term transition to reemployment, the federal government has specifically designed programs to assist these disadvantaged and dislocated workers. The first attempt to design an adult employment and training program dates back to the implementation of the Manpower Development and Training Act (MDTA) in 1962 when the unemployment rate was rising and concerns were growing about the adverse effects of automation on mid-career adult workers. As these concerns eased, interest shifted in 1972 to assisting the economically disadvantaged, and the MDTA was consolidated into a newly created Comprehensive Employment and Training Act (CETA) which offered disadvantaged workers a mix of classroom or on-the-job training and public service jobs. When CETA expired in 1982, it was replaced by the Job Training Partnership Act (JTPA) which sought to train and place workers in private sector jobs. The partnership aspect of JTPA involved a federal-state partnership to help expedite and customize the delivery of reemployment services in which state governors were given overall responsibility for administering their state's program and delegating to local business and labor representatives (private industry councils) the authority for design and administration of local programs, while the federal government monitored the performance of local program operators.

Title III of JTPA dealt specifically with adjustment programs for dislocated workers, providing for skills training, job placement services, relocation assistance, and support services such as child care and transportation while in training.[5] However, as a result of limited funding, few received assistance under these programs prior to 1987. Based on the results of a 1986 report by a

Secretary of Labor's task force,[6] which recommended development of a quick response to plant closings and mass layoffs and the delivery of services on site, the Economic Dislocation and Worker Adjustment Act (EDWAA) was passed in 1988; it amended the existing Title III of JTPA.

EDWAA (JTPA Title III, as amended) provides assistance to workers who have lost their jobs because of plant closings or individual or mass layoffs—regardless of the reason for job loss—and are unlikely to return to their previous occupations. The program is based upon a local delivery system that provides reemployment services, essential retraining services, and needs related payments. The program has expanded from assisting 290,000 individuals in 1993 to its current level of approximately 600,000. Of the 557,000 individuals receiving services during the program year 1995, 74 percent had a job three months after leaving the program in which they earned, on average, 96 percent of their pre-dislocation wage. In addition to providing services to individuals, states deploy rapid response teams to help communities handle mass layoffs. The Administration's budget for FY 1999 requests $1.45 billion to support an estimated 685,800 participants in the EDWAA program; this represents $100 million above the current level. Eighty percent of the EDWAA funds are allotted by formula to states which distribute at least 60 percent to substate areas for direct services to eligible individuals, and 20 percent of the funds are reserved for discretionary use by the Secretary of Labor (a national reserve) to provide services through direct grants in response to mass layoffs, plant closings, or military base closings.

The Department of Labor's other major programs for dislocated workers are special programs which target workers adversely affected by defense downsizing and international trade.[7] The Defense Conversion Adjustment (DCA) and the Defense Diversification Program (DDP) were added to Title III of JTPA in 1991.[8] The Department's program for workers dislocated by imports, however, has had a separate but parallel development to the general programs for dislocated workers, and it will be examined shortly.

Rationale for a Separate Program for Workers Dislocated by Imports

Historically, three broad and related reasons have been offered for the government to intervene in the process of worker adjustments to shifts in international trade or other shifts in government policies: equity, efficiency, and political efficacy. The goal is to provide compensation to the adversely affected, promote market adjustment, and facilitate expanded trade or acceptance of some other government policy change (Aho and Bayard, 1984).

Equity: The equity principle is based upon the notion of compensating those who are deserving and have been injured by government trade policy undertaken in the name of society's general welfare. While it is widely accepted that society as a whole benefits from a dynamic and open economy, economic change (due to trade liberalization, regulation or deregulation, changes in consumer tastes, technological innovations, etc.) rarely benefits all members of society. Typically, some individuals gain while others lose, both in the short and long run. Labor adjustment costs entail: temporary and permanent income losses, asset losses (savings, health benefits, pension, relocation), and the physical and psychological impact of job loss. It is also recognized that displaced workers usually bear the brunt of the inevitable adjustment costs. Income streams of dislocated workers are often linked to investment in less portable firm-specific human capital or accruing of economic rents due to factors such as unexplained inter-industry wage differentials, rate of unionization, or level of tariff protection. Workers with the longest tenure on the job from which they were displaced often suffer the greatest losses in subsequent wages and time employed. If adjustment costs due to trade-induced changes differ systematically from changes due to non-trade related changes, then there may be a need to develop a special program targeted at assisting groups of workers adversely affected by trade. On the other side of the equity issue (costs) is the fact that to the extent that a specialized assistance or compensation program for dislocated workers is successful, it may impose costs on new entrants to the labor market through longer job search or lower starting wages.

Economic efficiency: The argument here is that market imperfections or externalities may prevent or impede efficient adjustment and therefore government intervention in the adjustment process is warranted. It can be argued that labor market adjustment may be more difficult to achieve than industry adjustment since workers often are not able to adjust as quickly as firms (capital). Market adjustment problems include: imperfect information; uncertainty; incomplete factor mobility; wage-price rigidities; and insufficient access to the capital market to finance the human capital investments that are part of adjustment. Adjustment assistance programs also provide diagnostic signals for workers and firms to adjust without themselves distorting or weakening any of the natural market signals to adjust without significant change in product prices or foreign costs (Richardson, 1984).

Political efficacy: The argument here is that certain interest groups have sufficient political power to block or delay socially beneficial changes unless compensated or otherwise assisted. For example, it is generally accepted that the adjustment assistance provisions of both the 1962 and 1974 trade acts were important in obtaining legislative authority for and muting workers' opposition to the Kennedy and Tokyo Rounds of multilateral trade negotiations while offering something for business to support as a quid pro quo for escape clause and safeguard actions.

Targeted Programs for Trade Affected Workers

The Trade Adjustment Assistance (TAA) program for workers displaced by imports from any country was first introduced as part of the Trade Expansion Act of 1962 and was substantially modified in 1974, 1981, and 1988 (see table 4.1). A special program for workers displaced by imports from or production shifts to Canada or Mexico–called the North American Free Trade Agreement-

Table 4.1. History of the Trade Adjustment Assistance Program for Workers

Legislation/Date of Enactment	Major Features	Comments
Trade Expansion Act of 1962 (Public Law 87-794) 10/11/62	Created trade adjustment assistance program for workers directly affected by imports; to receive assistance, required that increases in imports due to trade liberalization be the main cause of the displacement. Workers qualifying could receive cash benefits (the lesser of 65% of their previous wage or 65% of the average weekly manufacturing wage) for 52 weeks.	Limited eligibility and usage of program; determinations that import liberalizations were the major cause of injury were made by the U.S. Tariff Commission (now known as the U.S. International Trade Commission), which made recommendations to the President for granting adjustment assistance.
Automotive Products Trade Act of 1965 (Public Law 89-283) 10/21/65	Created special authority during a transition period (01/21/66 to 06/30/68) for worker groups in a firm which produced automotive products and was directly affected by trade with Canada under this Act to apply to the President for adjustment assistance. Qualified workers were eligible for benefits like those under the Trade Expansion Act of 1962.	Substantially liberalized the procedures for granting workers adjustment assistance over those in the Trade Expansion Act of 1962 (criteria included a decline in domestic production and an increase in imports from or a decline in exports to Canada as the primary result of the agreement). After 06/30/68, worker groups could petition the Tariff Commission for assistance under the provisions in the Trade Expansion Act of 1962.
Trade Act of 1974 (Public Law 93-618) 01/03/75	Eligibility criteria eased ("imports contributed importantly") and benefits expanded. Workers qualifying could receive cash benefits (70% of their previous wage, but not in excess of the average weekly manufacturing wage) for 52 weeks. Job search assistance was added. The new worker adjustment program under this Act went into effect on	Resulted in a significant increase in the number of petitions received and approved; shifted authority for making determinations to the U.S. Labor Department.

Legislation	Provisions	Effect
	04/03/75, 90 days after the enactment of the Act, and was set to expire on 09/30/82.	
Omnibus Budget Reconciliation Act of 1981 (OBRA) (Public Law 97-35) 08/13/81	Reformed the program, particularly in terms of program eligibility and benefits, to reduce program costs and shift emphasis from income support for temporary layoffs to facilitating the reemployment of long-term unemployed through training and other adjustment measures. Reduced the level of cash benefits to that of unemployment insurance levels and stipulated that payment could only begin after unemployment benefits were exhausted. Extended program for one year, to terminate on 9/30/83.	Resulted in a decline in the number of petitions submitted and approved; made the program essentially one of extended unemployment benefits with training.
Amendments to the International Coffee Agreement Act of 1980 (Public Law 98-120) 10/12/83	Extended program for two years, until 9/30/85.	
Deficit Reduction Act of 1984 (Public Law 98-369) 07/18/84	Amended the program to increase the availability of training allowances and the level of job search and relocation benefits.	
Emergency Extension Act of 1985 (Public Law 99-107) 09/30/85	Extended program until 11/14/85.	
Public Debt Limit, Temporary Increase (Public Law 99-155) 11/14/85	Extended program until 12/19/85.	

Legislation/Date of Enactment	Major Features	Comments
Consolidated Omnibus Budget Reconciliation Act of 1985 (COBRA) (Public Law 99-272) 04/07/86	Reauthorized the program for six years, retroactively from 12/19/85 until 9/30/91. Required workers certified to participate in a job search program to receive benefits.	
Omnibus Trade and Competitiveness Act of 1988 (OTCA) (Public Law 100-418) 08/23/88	Made significant amendments in the program concerning eligibility criteria for cash benefits, funding, and administration; introduced a training requirement as a condition for receiving income support (effective 11/21/88) which replaced the job-search requirement introduced in 1986; and expanded coverage to include workers and firms in oil and gas exploration industries. Extended the program for two more years until 9/30/93.	Expanded the program to include supplier firms of directly affected firms, contingent upon the imposition of an import fee to fund program costs, but the fee was never imposed. Made appropriate training an entitlement.
Customs and Trade Act of 1990 (Public Law 101-382) 08/20/90	Extended the completion and reporting period for the supplemental wage allowance demonstration projects for workers required by the 1988 amendments.	
Unemployment Compensation Amendments Act of 1992 (Public Law 102-318) 07/03/92	Provided for weeks of active military duty in a reserve status (including service during Operation Desert Storm) to qualify toward the minimum number of weeks of prior employment required for TAA eligibility.	
Omnibus Budget and Reconciliation Act of 1993 (OBRA 1993) (Public Law 103-66)	Reduced the level of the cap on worker training entitlement funding from $80 million to $70 million for fiscal year 1997 only.	

08/10/93

Reauthorized the program for an additional five years, or until 9/30/98.

North American Free Trade Agreement (NAFTA) Implementation Act (Public Law 103-182) 12/08/93

Established the NAFTA transitional adjustment assistance (NAFTA-TAA) program for workers displaced by increased imports from, or domestic production shifts to, Mexico or Canada. Cash benefits and services available to certified workers are similar to those under TAA. Program is to terminate on 9/30/98.

Provided for certification based on a shift of production to Mexico or Canada. Established provisions for secondarily affected workers (upstream suppliers or downsteam processors of directly affected firms) to receive benefits under EDWAA (JTPA Title III). Introduced a timely enrollment in training requirement for receiving cash benefits, with no waivers of this requirement.

Transitional Adjustment Assistance (NAFTA-TAA) program—was authorized in 1993 in the NAFTA implementation legislation. Both programs provide dislocated workers with job search assistance, job counseling, retraining, and other supportive services to assist them in finding suitable jobs. Recipients under these programs receive income support while in training. Both programs were extended through June 1999. Legislation is pending regarding their further extension and consolidation.

Trade Adjustment Assistance (TAA)

The notion of special government programs to assist workers, firms, and communities adversely affected by trade dates back nearly 45 years to the work of the Randall Commission, established during the Eisenhower administration to advise the President and the Congress on future trade policy. In 1953, David McDonald, then president of the United Steelworkers and a Commission member, proposed the idea of a trade adjustment assistance program (a program of direct federal aid to firms, communities, and workers injured by imports). While the Commission members rejected the proposed idea (by a vote of 16 to 1), they did give mention of it in their report. The idea, however, caught the eye of some Democratic senators, in particular, the junior senator from Massachusetts who soon would become President of the United States.[9]

Trade adjustment assistance for industries, firms, and workers first became a component of U.S. trade policy when it was incorporated into the Trade Expansion Act of 1962 which authorized U.S. participation in the Kennedy Round of multilateral trade negotiations under the GATT. The purpose was to offer a constructive alternative to trade protection, by aiding industry and worker efforts to cope with import competition through retraining, reequipping, and restructuring.

At the time, Republicans in the Congress opposed the creation of a special adjustment assistance program:

> The lack of employment for a worker seeking a job, or the loss of a job in an industry in which a worker has spent the better part of his productive life, should be avoided, if at all possible. The cause of the worker's misfortune—whether foreign competition, increased automation, technological changes, or product obsolescence—is not a controlling factor. Every effort should be made—particularly at the State level—to assist the worker to recover from his misfortune. After careful consideration, upon the recommendation of the Committee on Labor and Public Welfare of the Senate and the Committee on Education and Labor of the House, Congress in this session enacted the Manpower Development and Training Act of 1962 to meet this need. . . . The problem of the worker displaced by foreign competition was thus

specifically considered in the enactment of the Manpower Development and Training Act. His needs were deemed to have been adequately provided for in that act. Without professing any extraordinary knowledge in this field, the Ways and Means Committee in reporting out the trade bill proposes a different and more liberal scale of unemployment compensation and training allowances, for a longer period of time, and irrespective of State unemployment compensation. Adjustment assistance provisions should be stricken from the bill. ...Adjustment assistance insures the U.S. negotiators will do a poor job of negotiating. Unemployment compensation and retraining, no matter how liberal, are a poor substitute for a job. The removal of the responsibility of U.S. negotiators in their trade negotiations to protect the job of the American worker represents a basic change of policy which we—and the American worker—should be unwilling to accept. ("Separate Views of the Republicans on H.R. 11970," Committee on Ways and Means, 1962: 93–95)

Provisions for workers to qualify for adjustment assistance under the Trade Expansion Act of 1962 were fairly stringent. Affected worker groups had to petition the U.S. Tariff Commission (now the U.S. International Trade Commission) for an eligibility determination that increased imports "as a result of in major part of concessions granted under trade agreements" (e.g., U.S. tariff cuts) have been "the major factor in causing, or threatening to cause," the group's unemployment or underemployment. After receiving a report from the Tariff Commission containing an affirmative finding, the President could provide that the affected worker group seek certification of eligibility from the Secretary of Labor to apply for adjustment assistance.[10]

In addition to being eligible for reemployment services and training, a certified worker was entitled to a trade readjustment allowance (TRA) which was available up to 52 weeks and set at a level of the lesser of 65% of their average weekly wage or 65% of the average weekly manufacturing wage. The weekly sum of remuneration for services performed, unemployment insurance, training allowances, and TRA allowances could not exceed 75% of the worker's average weekly wage.

As the result of the program's stringent rules and procedures—especially the need to establish a direct linkage between a worker dislocation and a specific trade liberalization—few worker groups applied for adjustment assistance, and even fewer were certified as eligible for benefits. No workers were certified as eligible to receive trade adjustment assistance benefits under the 1962 Act until 1969; between 1970 and 1974, about 47,000 workers received $69 million in benefits (Aho and Bayard, 1984).

The Automotive Products Trade Act of 1965 implemented the Agreement Concerning Automotive Products Between the Government of the United

States and the Government of Canada, signed January 16, 1965, (also known as the U.S.-Canadian Auto Pact) which provided for the mutual removal or reduction of duties on U.S.-Canadian trade of motor vehicles and original-equipment automotive parts. Provisions in the Act specified interim special procedures for adjustment assistance to U.S. firms and workers suffering dislocation resulting from the operation of the agreement. The Act provided that, during the period from January 21, 1966 to June 30, 1968, firms and workers applying for adjustment assistance as a result of the operations of the agreement would do so under special and more liberal procedures that differed materially from those previously established under the Trade Expansion Act of 1962. Under these special procedures, within 50 days after the receipt of a petition from a worker group for adjustment assistance, the U.S. Tariff Commission was to provide a factual report to the President on whether there were dislocations (or threat thereof), production of the U.S. automotive product concerned by the firm had decreased appreciably, and imports of like or directly competitive Canadian product had increased appreciably or exports to Canada by the firm (as well as U.S. exports to Canada) of the concerned product had decreased appreciably (and that decrease in exports was greater than the decrease, if any, of Canadian production of like product). Upon an affirmative finding by the Tariff Commission on these three points, the President was to certify the worker group as eligible to apply to the Department of Labor for adjustment assistance unless the President determined that the operation of the agreement was not the primary factor in causing (or threatening to cause) the dislocation. During this transition period, 21 worker groups petitioned for adjustment assistance, 14 worker groups covering 2,493 workers were certified; of these, 1,943 workers were found eligible for assistance payments. The total direct cost of the program (mostly in benefits payments to workers) was $4.1 million (USITC, 1976).

The Trade Act of 1974, which granted negotiating authority for the Tokyo Round of multilateral trade negotiations, liberalized the trade adjustment assistance eligibility criteria and expanded the benefits.[11] It also streamlined the process for worker groups to petition for trade adjustment assistance. A worker group, or its authorized representative (e.g., a trade union), could now submit a petition for assistance directly to the U.S. Department of Labor (i.e., the Secretary of Labor). The Department then had 60 days to make a determination whether the petitioning group met the following criteria specified in Section 222 of the Act:

> (1) that a significant number or proportion of the workers in such workers' firm or an appropriate subdivision of the firm have become totally or partially separated, or are threatened to become totally or partially separated,

> (2) that sales or production, or both, of such firm or subdivision have decreased absolutely, and

(3) that increases of imports of articles like or directly competitive with articles produced[12] by such workers' firm or appropriate subdivision thereof contributed importantly to such total or partial separation, or threat thereof, and to such decline in sales or production. For the purposes of paragraph (3), the term "contributed importantly" means a cause which is important but not necessarily more important than any other cause.

Thus, the Trade Act of 1974 severed the direct linkage between a worker dislocation and an increase in imports due to a specific trade liberalization as a basis for certifying a group of dislocated workers for TAA, replacing it with the less stringent requirement that an increase in imports "contributed importantly" to the workers' dislocation.

Certified workers were eligible for reemployment services, training, and job search and relocation allowances. In addition, they were entitled to a trade readjustment allowance (TRA) available up to 52 weeks,[13] set at a level of 70% of their average weekly wage (but not in excess of the average weekly manufacturing wage). The weekly sum of remuneration for services performed, unemployment insurance, training allowances, and TRA allowances could not exceed the lesser of 80% of the worker's average weekly wage or 130% of the average weekly manufacturing wage.

The initial emphasis of the new TAA program under the 1974 legislation was on expanded compensation, and relatively few participants received training or other adjustment services. The early period of the program (1975–81) was also the one of greatest program growth, with an average 168,000 individuals receiving cash benefits annually.

Evaluations of the early period of the program indicated that TAA recipients were, in many cases, not very different from other displaced workers although they were somewhat older, were somewhat less educated and less skilled, had longer tenure with firm, and were more likely to be a union member. In some instances, their earnings losses were somewhat higher than average and the desire for a higher replacement wage may have led to longer duration of unemployment. One of the more important characteristics of the early period of the program was that only a small fraction of TAA recipients actually changed jobs. As a result, very few TAA recipients utilized the adjustment provisions of the program. Most TAA recipients expected their layoff to be temporary, which may account for the relatively small fraction of recipients who received training. A substantial number of TAA recipients during this period included autoworkers and steelworkers who could draw on their union's supplemental unemployment benefits (subs) as well as drawing on their TRA payments. Prior to 1979, the permanently displaced tended to be a fairly small subset of TAA recipients. The TAA program primarily provided income support to workers who were, in fact, not permanently separated from their employers—over 70% ended their unemployment spells by returning to work with their previous employers (Corson and Nicholson, 1981; U.S. GAO, 1980).

Major changes to the TAA program were introduced again in 1981 when the benefits were restricted. TRA payments were reduced to the level of weekly unemployment insurance payments and were only available after the recipient had exhausted their unemployment benefits. Thus, the TAA program became essentially one of extended UI with training. With this change, assistance was targeted to the long-term unemployed, reflecting a shift in emphasis from providing compensation toward providing adjustment services, in particular, training. The shift became even stronger when in 1988 training was made an entitlement for eligible participants and enrollment in an approved training course was made a requirement for receiving weekly TRA allowances. However, waivers from this training requirement were given in certain circumstances.

During the 1980s, most TRA recipients received other reemployment services from the Employment Service at a rate higher than other UI exhaustees. TRA recipients also tended to remain jobless for a longer period of time on average than did other UI exhaustees. TRA recipients were more likely to experience extreme wage losses (20% of TRA recipients received less than half their previous wage, compared to 12–13% of other UI exhaustees). On average, reemployed TRA recipients were unable to achieve their previous wage level, even three years after their initial unemployment claim (Decker and Corson, 1995).

Prior to the 1988 amendments, 37% participated in TAA training; this ratio rose significantly to 47% after the 1988 amendments. The training requirement reduced weeks of TRA receipt among the average recipient, though the duration of training increased. The training requirement led to a decline in the duration of the initial jobless spell and to an increase in earnings due to more rapid reemployment. Training for displaced workers did not appear to have a substantial positive effect on the earnings of TAA trainees—compared to TRA recipients who did not participate in TAA training—at least in the first three years after the initial UI claim (Decker and Corson, 1995). Findings by Decker and Corson (1995) and Leigh (1990; 1995) have suggested that job search assistance might be more cost effective than a training program.

As a result of program modifications introduced in the 1980s, qualified TAA applicants now may receive up to 104 weeks of job training and up to 52 weeks of income support during training after exhausting their UI payments. During this retraining period, job search allowances are available and relocation allowances will pay for moving expenses beyond the normal commuting area. Since the tightening of the eligibility requirements, the TAA program has served about 33,000 workers annually (about 30% of those certified for benefits actually take-up or take advantage of the benefits available).

Workers from a wide variety of industries have been certified under the TAA program. Since 1975, the seven industries with the highest concentration of certified workers have been automotive equipment, wearing apparel, primary metals, leather products, electrical and electronic equipment, oil and gas production and services, and fabricated metal products.

The Trade Act of 1974 established an Adjustment Assistance Trust Fund in the U.S. Treasury Department (to be funded from customs duty revenues not otherwise appropriated) for the purposes of carrying out the provisions related to the TAA program for workers, including training. However, the Trust Fund was never implemented by Treasury, and, as a result, funding of the TAA program has depended upon appropriations from the Congress. TRA is an entitlement, while training and other reemployment services are capped-entitlements, i.e., ceilings are set on their funding.

The U.S. Department of Labor allocates funds to the states to provide TAA benefits (i.e., training, job search, and relocation costs) to workers certified under the program. During the early years of rapid growth of the program, administrative costs and benefits payments rose from $9.3 million and $150.3 million, respectively, serving 46,824 beneficiaries in fiscal year 1976 to $29.0 million and $1,630.0 million, respectively, serving 368,265 beneficiaries in fiscal year 1980.

More recently, the funds for TAA benefits (primarily training) allocated to the states by the Department amounted to $80.0 million in fiscal year 1993, $98.9 million in fiscal year 1994, $97.8 million in fiscal year 1995, $96.6 million in fiscal year 1996, and $85.1 million in fiscal year 1997 (when TAA training funds experienced a one-time reduction of $10 million). The Department's TAA funds for training allocations to the states are capped each fiscal year by law at $80 million. Prior to fiscal year 1993, all activities conducted were funded under that cap. In fiscal year 1994, the program experienced an increase in funding requests from the states for training activities and the Department requested and was granted funds for job search, relocation, and administrative funds over the $80 million cap, thus explaining the $18.9 million jump in funds available in fiscal year 1994 compared to fiscal year 1993. Since fiscal year 1994, the amount appropriated for job search and relocation has been reduced slightly each fiscal year.

In addition to funding the TAA benefits, the Department makes federal budget obligations for direct Trade Readjustment Allowances (TRAs) to TAA certified workers (i.e., extended unemployment insurance payments); the Department's budget obligations for TRA payments amounted to $64.0 million in fiscal year 1993, $127.8 million in fiscal year 1994, $170.2 million in fiscal year 1995, $191.0 million in fiscal year 1996, and $186.4 million as of the end of July fiscal year 1997. In fiscal year 1996, state agencies paid $163.3 million in TRA benefits to 30,673 certified workers, while in fiscal year 1995, $143.2 million was paid to 24,148 certified workers.

NAFTA Transitional Adjustment Assistance (NAFTA-TAA)

Throughout the debate leading up to NAFTA, concerns were expressed by some that U.S. workers might be displaced as the result of NAFTA, especially less-skilled and low-wage workers in the manufacturing sector. In May 1991, the Bush Administration indicated that it was firmly committed to an adequately funded worker adjustment program that ensured that workers displaced by NAFTA would receive prompt, comprehensive, and effective services—either through the expansion or improvement of an existing program or through the creation of a new program. Criticism and concerns about shortcomings of existing worker adjustment assistance programs had also been raised during the NAFTA discussions and several members of Congress felt that there was a need for a new program that would address the specific needs of workers who might be displaced as the result of NAFTA.[14] The expectations were that when the NAFTA implementing legislation came to the Congress for consideration, it would be accompanied by a more comprehensive worker adjustment program. By this time the in-coming Clinton Administration was already working on revamping existing worker assistance and adjustment programs in an effort to consolidate, simplify, and expedite the delivery of such services. Thus, the design of a new NAFTA-specific program was not considered initially. But as it became clear that the program redesign efforts would not be completed before NAFTA would come to a vote, the Administration decided to put forward a NAFTA-specific program—the NAFTA Transitional Adjustment Assistance (NAFTA-TAA) program—that was included in the NAFTA implementing legislation which was signed into law by the President on December 8, 1993 and entered into force on January 1, 1994.

The NAFTA-TAA program combines aspects of EDWAA (JTPA Title III) and TAA and provides rapid and early response by state units to the threat of unemployment as well as the opportunity to engage in long-term training while receiving income support. NAFTA-TAA not only provides assistance to workers who lose their jobs as a direct result of increased imports from Mexico or Canada, but also to workers who lose their jobs as a result of shifts of U.S. production to those countries. The Secretary of Labor has also extended assistance to workers in companies *secondarily* affected (i.e., upstream processors of articles produced by a directly affected firm or suppliers to a directly affected firm) by U.S. imports from Mexico or Canada, through administrative actions and authority under EDWAA. Responsibility for administering the NAFTA-TAA program is shared by the governor of the state where the firm is located and the U.S. Department of Labor, with rapid response being provided by the state and a full investigation of eligibility being conducted by the federal government.

A petition for assistance under the NAFTA-TAA program may be filed by a group of 3 or more workers (including farm workers), a union (or other duly authorized representative, including community-based organizations), or a company official. The workers on whose behalf a petition is filed must be (or have been) employed regularly at the firm identified in the petition and their employment must be (or have been) directly related to the production of an article (i.e., similar to TAA, the provision of a non-tangible service is not covered). NAFTA-TAA petitions must be filed within one year of the impact date of a layoff. When the program was initiated, the earliest reach back date for a NAFTA-TAA petition was December 8, 1993.

When the governor of a state receives a petition for assistance, the state is required to make a preliminary finding within 10 days as to whether the petition meets the eligibility criteria. Within 30 days of the receipt of the preliminary finding from a state, the Secretary of Labor is required to make a final determination. If a petition does not meet the eligibility requirements under the program, the petition is reviewed to see whether it may qualify for coverage under the regular TAA program.

In determining whether a significant number or proportion workers in a firm or subdivision of the firm covered by a NAFTA-TAA petition have become totally or partially separated, or are threatened to be totally or partially separated, the following criteria are applied:

> (1) the sales or production, or both, of the firm or subdivision have decreased absolutely; imports from Mexico or Canada of articles like or directly competitive with articles produced by the firm or subdivision have increased; and the increase in such imports contributed importantly—that is, be a cause that is important but not necessarily more important than any other cause—to the workers' separation or threat of separation and to the decline in sales or production of the firm or subdivision; or

> (2) there has been a shift in production by the workers' firm or subdivision to Mexico or Canada of articles like or directly competitive with articles which are produced by the firm or subdivision.

The NAFTA-TAA program is very similar to the existing TAA program. The type and extent of the assistance (training, job search, relocation, and TRA income support) offered is essentially the same under either program,[15] but the petition process, criteria for certification, and requirements for receiving TRA payments differ somewhat. Under the TAA program, affected worker groups must petition directly to the Secretary of Labor who must make a determination within 60 days; under the NAFTA-TAA program, the worker group must file first with the governor of the state who must make an initial eligibility determination within 10 days, and if affirmative, forward the petition to the Secretary of Labor for a final determination within 30 days. The TAA program offers assistance to displaced workers whose employment loss is the direct result of increased imports from any source, while the NAFTA-TAA program is restricted to imports from Mexico or Canada. The NAFTA-TAA program's coverage of workers displaced as the result of a shift in production to either Canada or Mexico is new; a shift in production to another country is not a criterion for certification of workers under the TAA program.

In order to receive TRA payments under either TAA or NAFTA-TAA, certified workers must be enrolled in an approved training program. However, the NAFTA-TAA program requires that a claimant must be enrolled in a timely manner (by the latter of the 16th week of the claimant's initial[16] unemployment compensation period or the 6th week of the certification of the claimant's worker group) in an approved training program in order to qualify for extended income support; waivers from this requirement are not permitted. Under the TAA program, waivers of the training requirement may be given. Finally, the NAFTA-TAA program's coverage under EDWAA (Title III of JTPA) of secondarily affected workers as well as family farms and farm workers who do not meet the group eligibility requirements (i.e., workers not eligible for UI) is new;[17] these groups are not covered under the TAA program.

Like TAA, the NAFTA-TAA program provides a comprehensive array of retraining and reemployment services tailored to meet a dislocated worker's individual needs. These include: (1) rapid response and basic readjustment services (e.g., information on available assistance programs, assessment of an individual's skills and abilities, and financial and personal counseling to help prepare for job transition); (2) employment services (e.g., career counseling and job placement services); (3) up to 104 weeks of training (e.g., in entrepreneurial and other occupational skills or for employment in another job or career); (4) up to 52 weeks of income support after the exhaustion of unemployment insurance compensation when enrolled in training (i.e., extended income support for those enrolled in training through the continuation of unemployment insurance benefits beyond the normal 26–week period for those payments); (5) job search allowances (e.g., to pay for expenses while searching for work beyond the normal commuting area); and (6) relocation allowances (e.g., to pay for moving expenses to an another area where reemployment is more likely).

Since the inception of the NAFTA-TAA program in January 1994, about 1,500 worker groups—covering approximately 183,000 workers—have been certified (through May 1998) as eligible to apply for benefits.

The U.S. Department of Labor allocates funds to the states to provide NAFTA-TAA benefits (i.e., training, job search, and relocation costs) to workers certified under the program. The funds for NAFTA-TAA benefits allocated to the states by the Department amounted to $8.5 million in fiscal year 1994, $21.4 million in fiscal year 1995, and $19.0 million in fiscal year 1996. The Department's NAFTA-TAA benefits allocations to the states are capped each fiscal year by law at $30 million; for the first (partial) fiscal year of the program, the cap was set at $8.5 million. In addition to funding the NAFTA-TAA benefits, the Department makes federal budget obligations for direct Trade Readjustment Allowances (TRAs) to NAFTA-TAA certified workers (i.e., extended unemployment insurance payments); the Department's budget obligations for TRA payments amounted to $2.0 million in fiscal year 1994, $8.1 million in fiscal year 1995, and $14.1 million in fiscal year 1996. For fiscal year 1996, the average weekly NAFTA-TAA trade readjustment allowance was $198.71 and the average number of weeks paid was 21, with 4,344 workers filing for TRA payments and 1,779 workers receiving their first TRA payment.

Experiences from the First Four Years of NAFTA-TAA

Since the NAFTA-TAA program is relatively new and less well studied (especially compared to its parent, TAA), it may be informative to examine some of the information available about the program's operation in the first four years of its operation. From January 1, 1994 through December 31, 1997, the U.S. Department of Labor made decisions on about 2,100 NAFTA-TAA petitions from 48 states covering approximately 267,000 workers. The Department certified 1,250 (60 percent) petitions covering approximately 156,000 (58 percent) workers who may apply for benefits under the program.

While the benefits under the NAFTA-TAA and the regular TAA program are virtually the same, some workers may only apply for benefits under the regular TAA program since there are less stringent timeframes required for a worker to enter training in order to receive income support benefits. However, compared to the requirements for certification under the regular TAA program, the requirements for certification under the NAFTA-TAA program are more liberal. For example, a shift in production would not qualify a petitioner for TAA benefits, so that workers certified for NAFTA-TAA benefits for this reason (slightly over half of all of the workers certified) might not have qualified for benefits under the regular TAA program. Also, some NAFTA-TAA petitions may have been certified that otherwise would not have been certified under the regular TAA program due to trade diversion resulting from the implementation of NAFTA—that is, an increase in U.S. imports from Mexico and Canada at the expense of other supplying countries. In this case, it would be possible for the overall level of imports of an item to remain unchanged with those from Mexico or Canada increasing due to reductions in U.S. barriers to those products under NAFTA and those from other country suppliers still facing those barriers decreasing due to the diversion (to Mexico or Canada) of their exports to the United States.

Not all worker dislocations are covered by the NAFTA-TAA program. Most displaced workers in the service-producing sector are not covered under either TAA or NAFTA-TAA unless they produce an article of commerce. Workers in firms that supply materials and inputs to or process articles from a firm directly affected by imports are not covered by either TAA or NAFTA-TAA, but secondarily affected workers processing articles from or supplying materials to a directly affected NAFTA-TAA firm may be eligible for assistance under the EDWAA program; however, only about 40 worker groups have been certified to receive such assistance.

In terms of workers certified under the NAFTA-TAA program, about 50 percent were certified due to a shift in production to either Mexico or Canada and about 50 percent were certified due to increased imports from those countries during the first four years of the program. Mexico was identified as the location of production shift or the source of imports for about 70 percent of the workers certified, Canada was identified as the location or source for about 23 percent of the workers certified, and the source was not separately identified for about 7 percent of the certified workers.

Nearly all (90 percent) of the workers certified for NAFTA-TAA benefits came from the manufacturing sector. Within the manufacturing sector, workers certified for NAFTA-TAA benefits were concentrated in a few industries: nearly half (49 percent) were in the apparel, electronic and other electrical equipment, and transportation equipment industries.

The source-country of industrial impact, based on NAFTA-TAA certifications, is not surprising, given Mexico's and Canada's relative resource- and comparative-advantages in certain areas of production. Production shifts to or imports from Canada were important in the certification of workers in mining, construction, lumber products, petroleum and coal products, and electric power industries. Production shifts to or imports from Mexico were important in the certification of workers in apparel; rubber and miscellaneous plastics products; stone, clay, and glass products; industrial machinery; electronic and other electric equipment; transportation equipment; and miscellaneous manufacturing industries (e.g., jewelry, sporting goods, toys, musical instruments, pens and pencils, brooms and brushes, etc.). These results tend to conform to the ongoing North American integration of production that was taking place long before NAFTA was implemented.

Some information is available on the utilization of adjustment services and the benefits actually received by those who were certified for NAFTA-TAA benefits, based on data for the first four years of the program. Surprisingly, a rather small percentage of workers certified for NAFTA-TAA benefits actually took advantage of them (the take-up rate). For example, of the approximately 156,000 workers certified under the NAFTA-TAA program, only about 9,900 workers (6 percent) actually received training or income benefits under that program. However, the apparent low take-up rate for NAFTA-TAA benefits is due to the fact that about three-fourths of all workers covered by NAFTA-TAA petitions are also covered by petitions submitted for consideration under the regular TAA program, and that about two-thirds of those workers certified as eligible to apply for benefits under NAFTA-TAA are also certified as eligible to apply for benefits under TAA. Workers may be certified under both programs, resulting in dual eligibility, but certified workers must make a decision to take-up benefits under one program or the other. Since certified workers can only draw benefits from one program, some NAFTA-TAA certified workers have chosen to draw their benefits under the TAA program, resulting in a lower take-up rate of benefits under the NAFTA-TAA program. In fact, about 21,200 dual certified workers took up their benefits under the TAA program during the first four years of the NAFTA-TAA program. When dual certification under NAFTA-TAA and TAA is taken into account, the actual benefit take-up rate for NAFTA-TAA certified workers is about 20%; this figure is slightly lower than the take-up rate of workers certified only under TAA which was about 35% for the same period.

Based on data from the BLS displaced worker survey, the number of workers certified under the NAFTA-TAA program during the first three years of the program represented about 2.4 percent of all long-tenure U.S. workers on permanent layoff. For some industrial sectors (such as textiles, apparel, electronics, lumber, and paper), the share of NAFTA-TAA dislocated workers relative to all long-tenure dislocated workers in the industrial sector was much higher than for other industrial sectors.

Because certified NAFTA-TAA job losers (as well as certified TAA job losers) must exhaust unemployment insurance benefits—which typically can be received for 26 weeks—before they can draw trade readjustment allocations (i.e., extended income support), the number of long-term unemployed job losers offers an alternative (upper bound) measure of program need. Based on labor force statistics from the Current Population Survey administered by BLS, workers with an unemployment duration of 27 weeks or more accounted for 17.4 percent of all unemployed workers in 1996 (20.3 percent in 1994 and 17.3 percent in 1995), historically, a fairly high proportion for this stage of economic recovery. Workers certified for NAFTA-TAA benefits in 1996 accounted for 3.6 percent of all U.S. workers with an unemployment duration of 27 weeks or more (1.3 percent in 1994 and 2.6 percent in 1995). By comparison, workers certified for regular TAA benefits in 1996 accounted for 7.9 percent of all U.S. workers with an unemployment duration of 27 weeks or more (5.0 percent in 1994 and 7.0 percent in 1995).

While reemployment data on the NAFTA-TAA certified workers are not available, a comparison with long-tenured dislocated workers in the U.S. economy suggests that while NAFTA-TAA related dislocations may be a small portion of overall dislocations, they may represent a significant portion in some manufacturing industries and that reemployment for some workers in the industry of their last employment may be more difficult than for other displaced workers seeking reemployment. For these workers, the trade readjustment benefits (i.e., extended unemployment insurance benefits) and the provision of additional adjustment assistance services (such as training, employment services, and job search and relocation allowances) may be vital in securing reemployment.

Future Directions

Both the TAA and the NAFTA-TAA programs were extended through June 1999, and legislation is pending for their further extension and consolidation. Proposals are being developed to modify both programs so that differences between them are reduced and the delivery of assistance and services is made in a more timely manner. The modifications under consideration include: reducing the time of the certification process for TAA to 40 days, the same as for NAFTA-TAA; extending coverage under TAA to workers affected by a shift in production to another country, similar to the current provisions under NAFTA-TAA for shifts of U.S. production to Mexico or Canada; making the rules under TAA and NAFTA-TAA for enrolling in training more similar (e.g., tightening the rules on granting waivers from the training requirement for receiving TRA payments under TAA or modifying the current requirements for NAFTA-TAA); expanding the training funds cap for TAA from $80 to $120 million; expanding coverage of secondarily affected workers under JTPA Title III; improving outreach efforts (videos and homepage web site[18]); and developing new tracking and program reporting procedures.

Program revisions are also being considered by the Administration to provide more effective rapid response services to workers who lose their jobs due to mass layoffs or plant closures. The proposed increase of $100 million for fiscal year 1999 for EDWAA (JTPA Title III) will not only expand available services to dislocated workers but permit the Department of Labor to earmark $50 million annually out of the Secretary's national reserve funds to assist secondarily affected workers, i.e., workers adversely affected by trade who are not directly certifiable under either the TAA or NAFTA-TAA programs. In addition, drawing upon its past experiences with the Department of Defense in helping communities and workers adjust to defense downsizing and military base closings, the Department of Labor plans to work with other executive agencies to help communities with economic development initiatives and other measures to help bring jobs to areas where significant dislocations have occurred due to trade or other reasons.

III. Conclusions

While U.S. trade adjustment assistance programs have often been maligned by some over the years as insufficient, inadequate, and underutilized, most accept that the economic benefits (welfare gains) accruing to the country as the result of a more open trading system outweigh the costs of worker displacement and adjustment. However, the adverse effects of imports are often more visible and concentrated—with mass layoffs, plant closures, or plants moving to another country—while the positive effects of trade are in many cases more diffuse and less visible, raising questions about the equity, efficiency, and political efficacy of a more open international trading system.

Since 1962, the United States has had a program to assist workers dislocated by imports. In its early years—especially after program revisions in 1974—assistance provided to those dislocated by imports was mostly in the form of income maintenance, since their layoffs were more short-term in nature with many being recalled back to their old jobs. However, as conditions changed and layoffs became more long-term and permanent, the assistance provided shifted more to a mix of income support and the provision of training and other reemployment services. Since in many cases reemployment meant finding a job in another industry or profession, training was emphasized and eventually required for workers to receive extended income support.

But evidence on the impact of training and employment programs in the United States on durations of unemployment of unemployed workers and on their post-unemployment earnings is mixed. Moreover, costs must be taken into account as well as benefits. Recent evidence for the United States suggests that the effects of placement services, counseling, and other types of job search assistance are often as effective as, or more effective than, training, and are considerably cheaper (Leigh, 1990; 1995; Ehrenberg, 1994). Since the type and nature of training varies widely as does the appropriateness of training for an individual, some have suggested more flexibility in requiring training for income support, while others have called for offering vouchers for training services that the individual can use at accredited training facilities (Samuel et. al., 1998; Carnevale and Jacobson, 1997). What seems clear is the need for lifetime learning to maintain one's employability, flexibility, and adaptability to the increased competition and the new technologies being introduced in the workplace.

Some have argued that while government intervention through adjustment assistance programs may help to reduce the costs of adjustment, this type of intervention alone may not be adequate to allay the fears of workers about the security of their jobs in the face of globalization. According to this view, some form of a wage or job insurance system is needed (Burtless, Lawrence, Litan, and Shapiro, 1998; Jacobson, 1996; 1998). Such a job insurance system would likely be very expensive and need to be carefully targeted. But the viability of such a system in a period of federal budget belt-tightening is questionable, especially since additional federal budget expenditures need to be offset by reductions elsewhere in the budget.

Others have suggested a need for a social vision for international economic integration as a way of allaying the fears of structural change induced by further globalization. In this case, the new politics of trade agreements are not so much the loss of jobs but more about aspects beyond the freer flow of goods, services, and investment—namely, the terms of engagement. From this perspective, the question is whether we can have further economic and financial integration without some degree of social integration or at least some attention being given to distributional issues and the social dimension.

What emerges from the popular debate and concerns about globalization is a clear message to policymakers that they must take account of transitional adjustment costs and distributional issues (a more equitable distribution of the gains from trade and investment) in designing policies aimed at easing adjustments to changing economic circumstances brought on by globalization if they expect to garner popular support for further trade liberalization. Since the joblessness faced by many dislocated workers is now less cyclical, more aggressive and active labor market policies may be required to assist the displaced in making the transition to new jobs in growing industries. Leigh (1995) has suggested a useful framework to think about these types of programs:

1. Program services should facilitate the transition of displaced workers to jobs in expanding industries and growing sectors within existing industries by responding to market signals.

2. Program activities must meet the needs of displaced workers. Displaced workers are interested in jobs, not training. On-the-job training may be preferred to classroom training for providing needed job skills, and there may be a need for stimuli for firm-based training. Usually, income maintenance is needed while enrolled in training.

3. Programs should serve the entire spectrum of displaced workers, not just those easiest to place.

4. Training programs must supply marketable skills to program graduates. Firm-based training is more likely to enhance labor market opportunities than classroom training since it is demand-related. Employer involvement usually is necessary.

5. Programs should effectively utilize existing educational and training institutions or performance-based contractors or community colleges—many of which provide non-degree courses for adults and create customized curricula to meet the needs of regional employers.

6. A broadening of job skills should be encouraged. The breath of skills required is increasing.

In comparison to other industrialized nations, the United States devotes a small fraction of its national resources to labor market programs.[19] Many of the available active labor market programs are fragmented, overlapping, and subject to wide fluctuations in funds and focus. In addition, funding for government-sponsored programs is less stable, often fluctuates dramatically, and the professional quality of program managers is uneven. But the Administration appears committed to streamlining and improving access, raising the quality and timely delivery, and consolidating and simplifying procedures of existing adjustment assistance programs. Building upon the federal-state delivery system should help facilitate these goals.

Notes

The views expressed in this chapter are those of the author and do not reflect the views or opinions of the U.S. Department of Labor or the U.S. Government. The author is solely responsible for any errors or omissions.

[1] A characterization of the U.S. economy given by then Secretary of Labor Robert Reich in comments on the release of employment figures in December 1996.

[2] For a discussion of perceived increasing job insecurity in OECD countries, see OECD (1997: Chapter 5).

[3] Davis, et al. (1996) find that in an average year, between 12–19% of workers change jobs or employment status; during the recessions of the mid-70s and early 80s, the rate rose to 16–24%. They conclude that high job destruction rates are pervasive. Because almost all industries and sectors exhibit high rates of job destruction, most workers face

some risk of job loss. However, they find no systematic relationship between the magnitude of gross jobs flows and exposure to international trade (job creation 9%, job destruction 10%); the only indication of a relationship (reduced job security) is the large rate of gross job destruction (12%) in industries facing very high levels of import penetration.

[4] Active labor market policies focus on trying to shorten the duration of post-displacement unemployment spells and restore long-run earnings potential (e.g., job search assistance and retraining), while passive labor market measures provide income support (a cushion or social safety net, such as unemployment compensation, pensions, early retirement benefits, continuation of health insurance, and welfare benefits).

[5] Other titles of JTPA relate to programs for economically disadvantaged adults and youth (Title II); programs for Indians and native Americans, programs for migrant and seasonal farm workers, and the Job Corps (Title IV); programs for Aid to Families with Dependent Children (AFDC) and supplemental security income (SSI) recipients (Title V); and the federal-state employment service program (Title VI).

[6] See Secretary of Labor's Task Force on Economic Adjustment and Worker Dislocation, 1986.

[7] In addition to targeted adjustment programs for trade and defense conversion, other targeted dislocated worker programs have included programs for those displaced by the Clean Air Act and federal legislation related to cutting of redwoods and other federally protected timber.

[8] DCA provides retraining and readjustment assistance to workers dislocated by defense cutbacks. Services include retraining services (educational and occupational), readjustment services, and needs related payments. The Department has funded over 125 projects to provide targeted reemployment assistance to Department of Defense employees at 48 installations affected by decisions of the Base Realignment and Closure Commission since 1988. A total of more than $295 million has been awarded to state and local areas and defense contractors to provide transition services to about 94,000 individuals as the result of defense downsizing. DDP specifically targets members of the armed services and full-time National Guard that were laid off during fiscal years 1990–94, and Defense Department and contractor employees who were laid off as a result of reductions in defense spending during fiscal years 1992–96. In addition to the standard services available through Title III programs, DDP offers skills upgrading for non-managerial employees and promotes the development of high performance workplace systems.

[9] See Hufbauer and Rosen (1986, ch. 3) and Destler (1998) for a discussion of the early political history of TAA.

[10] The 1962 Act also included provisions for trade adjustment assistance from the Department of Commerce for industries and firms adversely affected by imports. If the Tariff Commission determined that increased imports due to trade liberalization were a major cause of injury to an industry or firm (same test as for workers), the Commission's recommendations to the President could include recommendations for adjustment assistance for workers in the injured industry or firm as well as assistance to the industry or firm itself.

[11] The 1974 legislation also expanded coverage to communities adversely affected by trade. The industry/firm and community adjustment assistance programs are administered by Commerce Department, and they will not be discussed further. The trade adjustment assistance program for communities was discontinued in 1981.

[12] Since both the 1962 and 1974 TAA legislation required that a trade-affected worker produce an article directly affected by imports of a similar article, TAA, by its very design, was targeted toward and primarily served dislocated workers in the manufacturing or other segments of the goods-producing sector. Most workers in the last survey of the general population of dislocated workers were not previously employed in manufacturing. Based on the last BLS displaced worker survey covering the period 1993–95, the service-producing sector accounted for 53% of the dislocated workers in the United States, manufacturing for 29%, construction and government for 7%, mining for 2%, and agriculture, forestry, and fisheries for 1%. In contrast, most workers in the first survey covering the period 1979–84 were from manufacturing (49%), followed by service-producing (33%), construction and government (13%), and agriculture, forestry, and fisheries (2%).

[13] An additional 26 weeks was available to adversely affected workers to complete approved training or to adversely affected workers who had reached their sixtieth birthday on or before the date of total or partial separation.

[14] For example, given Mexico's proximity to the United States and the already strong U.S. investment in the Mexican maquiladora (assembly) sector, there was concern that not only would U.S. workers be affected by increased imports from Mexico, but also by U.S. firms shifting operations to lower-wage production facilities in Mexico.

[15] Funding for training is capped at $80 million per year under TAA, while the cap on training funds under NAFTA-TAA is set at $30 million per year.

[16] This was subsequently modified to "last" as a result of a court ruling.

[17] Technically, this was provided for in a Statement of Administrative Action (SAA) issued by the Secretary of Labor and further described in Training and Employment Guidance Letters sent to the states.

[18] The link to the web site address is: http://www.wdsc.org/layoff/index.htm.

[19] For comparative data on expenditures on active and passive labor market measures as a percent of GDP in various OECD countries, see OECD (1994, p. 101).

References

Addison, John T., Douglas A. Fox, and Christopher J. Ruhm. 1995. "Trade and Displacement in Manufacturing." *Monthly Labor Review* 118:58–67.

Aho, C. Michael and Thomas O. Bayard. 1984. "Costs and Benefits of Trade Adjustment Assistance." In Robert E. Baldwin and Anne O. Krueger (eds.), *The Structure and Evolution of Recent U.S. Trade Policy.* Chicago, IL: University of Chicago Press.

Aho, C. Michael and Thomas O. Bayard. 1980. "American Trade Adjustment Assistance after Five Years." *The World Economy* 3(3):359–376.

Aaronson, Daniel and Daniel G. Sullivan. 1998. "The Decline of Job Security in the 1990s: Displacement, Anxiety, and Their Effect on Wage Growth." *Economic Perspectives* (Federal Reserve Bank of Chicago), First Quarter 1998, 22(1):17–43.

Bednarzik, Robert W. 1993. "Analysis of U.S. Industries Sensitive to International Trade." *Monthly Labor Review* 116(2):15–31.

Burtless, Gary, Robert Z. Lawrence, Robert E. Litan, and Robert J. Shapiro. 1998. *Globaphobia: Confronting Fears About Open Trade.* Washington, D.C.: Brookings Institution, Progressive Policy Institute, and Twentieth Century Fund.

Carnevale, Anthony P., and Louis S. Jacobson. 1997. "The Voucher That Works: The Role of Pell Grants in the Welfare, Employment Policy, and Training System." Paper presented at The 25th Annual Pell Grant Conference. Washington, D.C.: The College Board, November 13–14.

Cline, William R. 1997. *Trade and Income Distribution*. Washington, D.C.: Institute for International Economics.

Committee on Ways and Means, U.S. House of Representatives. 1962. *Trade Expansion Act of 1962*, Report to Accompany H.R. 11970, House Report No. 1818, 87th Congress, 2nd Session. Washington, D.C.: U.S. Government Printing Office, June 12.

Committee on Ways and Means, U.S. House of Representatives. 1997. *Overview and Compilation of U.S. Trade Statutes, 1997 Edition*. Washington, D.C.: U.S. Government Printing Office, June 25.

Corson, Walter, and Walter Nicholson. 1981 "Trade Adjustment Assistance for Workers: Results of a Survey of Recipients Under the Trade Act of 1974." *Research in Labor Economics* 4:417–469.

Davis, Steven J., John C. Haltiwanger, and Scott Schuh. 1996. *Job Creation and Destruction*. Cambridge, MA: MIT Press.

Decker, Paul T., and Walter Corson. 1995. "International Trade and Worker Displacement: Evaluation of the Trade Adjustment Assistance Program." *Industrial and Labor Relations Review* 48(4):758–774.

Destler, I. M. 1998. "Trade Policies and Labor Issues: 1953–95." In Susan M. Collins (ed.), *Imports, Exports, and the American Worker*. Washington, D.C.: Brookings Institution.

Ehrenberg, Ronald G. 1994. *Labor Markets and Integrating National Economies*. Washington, D.C.: Brookings Institution.

Flaim, Paul O., and Ellen Sehgal. 1985. *Displaced Workers, 1979–83*. Bulletin 2240 [reprints article initially published in the *Monthly Labor Review*, June 1985, along with additional tabular material and an explanatory note]. Washington, D.C.: U.S. Department of Labor, Bureau of Labor Statistics, July.

Gardner, Jennifer M. 1995. "Worker Displacement: A Decade of Change." *Monthly Labor Review* 118: 45–57.

Hufbauer, Gary Clyde, and Howard F. Rosen. 1986. *Trade Policy for Troubled Industries*. Policy Analyses in International Economics *15*. Washington, D.C.: Institute for International Economics.

Jacobson, Louis. 1996. "An Assessment of Policy Responses Aimed at Reducing the Costs to Workers of Structural Change due to International Competition and Other Factors." Draft, September 26.

Jacobson, Louis. 1998. "Compensation Programs." In Susan M. Collins (ed.), *Imports, Exports, and the American Worker*. Washington, D.C.: Brookings Institution.

Jacobson, Louis S., Robert J. LaLonde, and Daniel G. Sullivan. 1993. "Earnings Losses of Displaced Workers." *American Economic Review* 83(4):685–709.

Jacobson, Louis S., Robert J. LaLonde, and Daniel G. Sullivan. 1997."The Return from Community College Schooling for Displaced Workers." Working Papers Series, Macroeconomic Issues, Research Department, WP-97–16. Chicago, IL: Federal Reserve Bank of Chicago.

Kletzer, Lori G. 1998a. "International Trade and Job Displacement in U.S. Manufacturing: 1979–91." In Susan M. Collins (ed.), *Imports, Exports, and the American Worker*. Washington, D.C.: Brookings Institution.

Kletzer, Lori G. 1998b. "Job Displacement," *The Journal of Economic Perspectives* 12(1):115–136.

Kodrzycki, Yolanda. 1997. "Training Programs for Displaced Workers: What Do They Accomplish?" *New England Economic Review* (Federal Reserve Bank of Boston), May/June, pp. 39–59.

Kruse, Douglas L. 1988. "International Trade and Labor Market Experience of Displaced Workers," *Industrial and Labor Relations Review* 38:402–416.

Leigh, Duane E. 1990. *Does Training Work for Displaced Workers? A Survey of Existing Evidence*. Kalamazoo, MI: W.E. Upjohn Institute for Employment Research.

Leigh, Duane E. 1995. *Assisting Workers Displaced by Structural Change: An International Perspective*. Kalamazoo, MI: W.E. Upjohn Institute for Employment Research.

Organization for Economic Cooperation and Development (OECD). 1994. The OECD Jobs Study: Evidence and Explanations; Part II The Adjustment Potential of the Labor Market. Paris: OECD.

Organization for Economic Cooperation and Development (OECD). 1997. *Employment Outlook*. Paris: OECD.

Richardson, J. David. 1983. "Worker Adjustment to US International Trade: Programs and Prospects." In William R. Klein (ed.), *Trade Policy in the 1980s*. Washington, D.C.: Institute for International Economics.

Rodik, Dani. 1997. *Has Globalization Gone Too Far?* Washington, D.C.: Institute for International Economics.

Ruhm, Christopher. 1991. "Are Workers Permanently Scarred by Job Displacements?" *American Economic Review* 81(1):319–323.

Samuel, Howard D., Lawrence Chimerine, Marvin Fooks, and Andrew Harig. 1998. "Strengthening Trade Adjustment Assistance." Washington, D.C.: Economic Strategy Institute, March.

Secretary of Labor's Task Force on Economic Adjustment and Worker Dislocation. 1986. *Economic Adjustment and Worker Dislocation in a Competitive Society*. Washington, D.C., December.

Shelburne, Robert C. and Robert W. Bednarzik. 1993. "Geographic Concentration of Trade-Sensitive Employment." *Monthly Labor Review* 116:3–13.

United States Department of Labor. 1994. *Reemployment Services: A Review of Their Effectiveness*. Washington, D.C., April.

United States Department of Labor. 1995. What's Working (and what's not): A Summary of Research on the Economic Impacts of Employment and Training Programs. Washington, D.C.: Office of the Chief Economist, January.

United States Department of Labor. 1997. *Career Success: Case Studies in Job Transitions*. Washington, D.C.: Employment and Training Administration, September.

United States General Accounting Office (U.S. GAO). 1980. "Restricting Trade Act Benefits to Import-Affected Workers Who Cannot Find a Job Can Save Millions." Report No. HRD-80–11, January 15.

United States International Trade Commission (USITC). 1976. "The United States-Canadian Automotive Agreement: Its History, Terms, and Impact." Report to the Committee on Finance of the United States Senate on investigation No. 332–76 Under Section 332 of the Tariff Act of 1930, Two Volumes, January.

Comment

Steven M. Beckman

From the vantage point of my association with the United Auto Workers (UAW), UAW members have been important "consumers" of the Trade Adjustment Assistance program. We have a great deal of experience and familiarity with this program. As a union economist covering trade issues for 20 years, working on heavily trade-impacted industries, my observations are based on considerable experience.

Schoepfle's paper provides a very good history of the TAA program. I would like to focus on some of the deficiencies that workers have experienced, and continue to experience, in the structure and operation of the program. In describing the experience of UAW members with the TAA program, it is relevant that the UAW has sued the Labor Department numerous times over various aspects of the TAA process—certification, regulatory interpretations, and other issues. This indicates the contentiousness of the system, and its inadequacy in the eyes of those it is intended to benefit.

The program's problems are of long standing and they are widely recognized. Then-Senator and candidate for Vice President Al Gore, in October 1992, responding to the denial of TAA benefits to some Tennessee workers and the release of a GAO study he requested to examine the denial, stated in a press release, "The Labor Department blames a 60–day deadline for most of the errors but the GAO report makes clear the Department has decided to meet that deadline at any cost without regard for the welfare of the workers. . . For too long, obvious deficiencies in the Labor Department's program have been ignored, and workers have paid dearly for it."

Recognizing the skepticism that greeted the adoption of this program, Schoepfle included in his paper an excerpt from the Separate Republican Views on the original 1962 TAA proposal that sums up the view of many workers toward the TAA program:

> "Unemployment compensation and retraining, no matter how liberal, are a poor substitute for a job. The removal of the responsibility of U.S. negotiators in their trade negotiations to protect the job of the American worker represents a basic change of policy which we—and the American worker—should be unwilling to accept."

When President Clinton tells American workers that "change is good", and that free trade agreements improve living standards, the sentiment above is what many workers are thinking in response. Losing the source of your liveli-hood, without any prospect of being able to replace it, is not considered desir-able by most workers. Still, the American labor movement endorsed the Ken-nedy Round of trade negotiations in 1962 and believed that the TAA program would provide relief from the relatively small anticipated displacement from trade expected at that time. In spite of the changes made in the program since 1962, noted in Schoepfle's paper, it remains a disappointment for American workers.

Looking over workers' experience with the TAA program, one of the amazing realities is how *few* workers have been certified. The explosion of the U.S. trade deficit and the value of imports since the late 1970s would lead to the expectation that utilization of the program would grow as well. However, except for limited time periods, that has not been the case. Some hint at an ex-planation is provided by looking at the period when utilization was very high, in the late 1970s and early 1980s when significant import displacement of auto and steel workers occurred. Because so many of these workers were union-ized, they were informed of the availability of TAA benefits and could get as-sistance from their union in petitioning for benefits and, if necessary, appeal-ing determinations.

An important part of the explanation for the underutilization of the TAA program is the excessively narrow certification criteria. To qualify for benefits, employment must decline within specific time periods, workers must have been employed for a minimum duration within that period and imports of the specific product made must increase. Regarding just the last of these criteria, the UAW has focused much attention on expanding TAA eligibility to "secon-dary workers." Thousands of workers have been denied TAA benefits because they make parts, components and materials for finished products that are dis-placed by imports. These workers are as certainly displaced by the imports as the workers making the finished goods. They are eligible for TAA benefits, though, only if they work for the same firm that makes the final product. De-spite years of effort to fix this problem (including a funding mechanism for secondary worker coverage included in the 1988 Omnibus Trade and Com-petitiveness Act which was rejected by the Bush Administration), the program continues to exclude secondary workers.

While strongly supporting the inclusion of payments for worker retraining in addition to income support payments, the UAW and the labor movement as a whole have also raised concerns about the requirement that training be un-dertaken by workers in order to receive TAA benefits. While training waiver provisions exist, all too often, the reality of training opportunities fails to live up to its promise. There are just not enough effective training options available in the areas where workers have been laid off. As Schoepfle's paper points out, quoting in its conclusions from a paper by Duane Leigh, "Displaced workers are interested in jobs, not training." Seldom is there a demonstrated demand for the skills obtained in the training programs that trade-displaced workers can find. And, without the prospect of a job utilizing the newly acquired skill, worker interest in training is greatly diminished. Under these circumstances, the training requirement does not serve to improve the employment prospects of workers; it only delays the time when the job loss will result in unemployment and/or declining income and living standards for a substantial share of the trade-displaced workers.

The often-raised question, why have a separate program for workers displaced by trade instead of putting all displaced workers into a common program, is addressed in the paper, but I want to emphasize the reason the UAW supports this status. The TAA program, and the income support benefits that extend beyond regular unemployment insurance benefits, are a legal entitlement. Other programs for displaced workers are not entitlements and are, therefore, subject to severe underfunding and other federal budget process uncertainties. If and when there is a proposal to merge all the worker adjustment programs that establishes the comprehensive program as an entitlement for dislocated workers, the UAW and the labor movement will give it very serious consideration. Until then, such proposals are viewed as a way to weaken the protections currently available to trade-displaced workers without any assurance that they, or other workers displaced by other causes, will be served as well as under current programs.

Finally, I would like to make a brief comment comparing the NAFTA-TAA program and the general TAA program in terms of their value to workers. At this point, each program has its own pluses and minuses. The NAFTA-TAA program covers a broader range of trade-displacing events: increased imports, investment in production in Canada or Mexico, production shifts to those countries. Only the first of these is covered in the general TAA program. Secondary workers can also be certified for benefits under the NAFTA-TAA program (though few have received benefits), which is an improvement over the general program. However, the tight rules for the training requirement of the NAFTA-TAA program are a serious impediment to qualifying for benefits under that program.

Without getting into all the differences between the general TAA program and the NAFTA-TAA program, the inflexibility of the NAFTA program's training requirement is one explanation for the low utilization of that program. The UAW advises our members eligible for both programs to use the benefits of the general TAA program because of this difference.

Comment

J. David Richardson

Schoepfle's paper is full of interesting and provocative detail. It is, for example, the best recent survey I know of the multiple motives and programs for U.S. worker adjustment assistance. It is also the best brief summary I know of the special adjustment program under the North American Free Trade Agreement.

So I am hesitant to complain that there was an *additional* paper to write with even more interesting and more provocative detail. But there was, and I will.

It seems to me that Schoepfle could have added more fruitful attention to a lot of recent research. The research involves both theory and practice and both efficiency and equity considerations.

For example, there has been important theoretical work on adjustment-assistance policies. A four-paper symposium edited by Robert C. Feenstra in the May 1994 *Journal of International Economics* found both job-mobility and earnings-insurance policies to have favorable effects relative to other forms of assistance. Job-mobility policies are found to be practically effective in Meyer's (1995) survey of authoritative controlled experiments on recipients of U.S. unemployment insurance (UI). Practical options for earnings-insurance policies are also proposed in Lawrence and Litan (1986) and in Burtless et al. (1998).

For example, there is an increasingly clear consensus on policy effectiveness—measured by cost-benefit tests. Job-search assistance looks effective; school-based retraining, advance notification, and cash bonuses for early withdrawal from UI programs look minimally effective at best (Kletzer (1998a), Meyer (1995), Ruhm (1992,1994)). But on-the-job training looks more effective than school-based training (Jacobson et al. (1993), Kodrzycki (1997)), and technically-oriented vocational courses and basic math and science help earnings recovery after layoff whereas generic courses do not (Jacobson et al. (1997)). *Any* training for younger workers has lower opportunity costs (of foregone work) than for older workers, and comprehensive training for entire communities of low-income workers seems to have some intriguing synergies (Bloom (1996), Bloom et al. (1997)).

For example, there is also a growing consensus on equity questions. Compensation policies are increasingly accepted as part of a society's commitment to "conservative social welfare" (Brander and Spencer (1994)); individual workers deserve policy help with transition and with job-market information;

but wage premiums and other "rents," including job-specific skills, are not so deserving of compensation, if at all. Up to half of a typical worker's $80,000 lifetime earnings loss from involuntary displacement is estimated to be rents, but workers who must switch industries to become re-employed have 1½ to 2 times larger losses (with a smaller share representing rents) (Jacobson et al. (1993), Jacobson (1998)). Kletzer (1998b) shows how hard it is, using the same Displaced Worker Surveys as these other researchers, to disentangle the distinctive effects of "trade displacement" from the way workers with high search costs and low search skills are over-represented in import-sensitive industries (see also Kletzer (1998a)).

Moreover, the paper does not mention relevant research that is specifically targeted to U.S. trade adjustment assistance (TAA) programs. For example, Polivka (1991) finds that when TAA increases wage replacement ratios, it also increases the duration of a displaced worker's job search without improving the quality of the eventual job match (contradicting the speculation by Richardson (1982) that increased duration "paid off" in more effective search). Or, for example, Magee (n.d.) discovers that TAA programs benefit workers more in high-unemployment industries than in others, ceteris paribus, but not in high-unemployment regions relative to others, a presumably desirable bias if such workers have higher search costs and lower earnings recovery.

My brief summary of this unrepresented research is that TAA's viability is today questionable, as is the usefulness of the chaotic assortment of historical U.S. labor adjustment programs alluded to in Schoepfle's paper. But *some* sort of re-distributive companion to global integration policy is needful. And some existing sub-programs are more useful than others. And creative new programs *do* show promise. So maybe it is time to bury some bodies and birth others?

References

Brander, James A., and Barbara J. Spencer. 1994. "Trade Adjustment Assistance: Welfare and Incentive Effects of Payments to Displaced Workers." *Journal of International Economics*, 36:239–61.

Bloom, Howard S. 1996. "Building a Convincing Test of a Public Housing Employment Program Using Non-Experimental Methods: Planning for the Jobs-Plus demonstration," manuscript, October.

Bloom, Howard S., Barbara Fink, Susanna Lui-Gurr, Wendy Bancroft, and Doug Tattrie. 1997. *Implementing The Earnings Supplement Project: A Test of a Reemployment Incentive*. Ottawa: Social Research and Demonstration Corporation, October.

Burtless, Gary, Robert Z. Lawrence, Robert E. Litan, and Robert J. Shapiro. 1998. *Globalphobia: Confronting Fears About Open Trade*. Washington, D.C.: Brookings Institution.

Collins, Susan M. (ed.). 1998. *Imports, Exports, and the American Worker*. Washington, D.C.: Brookings Institution.

Jacobson, Louis S. 1998. "Adjustment." In Collins (1998).

Jacobson, Louis S., Robert J. LaLonde, and Daniel G. Sullivan. 1993. *The Costs of Worker Dislocation*. Kalamazoo: W.E. Upjohn Institute for Employment Research.

Jacobson, Louis S., Robert J. LaLonde, and Daniel G. Sullivan. 1997. "The Returns from Community College Schooling for Displaced Workers," manuscript, December.

Kletzer, Lori G. 1998a. "Job Displacement." *Journal of Economic Perspectives* 12:115–36.

Kletzer, Lori G. 1998b. "International Trade and Job Displacement in U.S. Manufacturing, 1979–91." In Collins (1998).

Kodrzycki, Yolanda K. 1997. "Training Programs for Displaced Workers: What Do They Accomplish?" *New England Economic Review* May/June, pp. 39–57.

Lawrence, Robert Z., and Robert E. Litan. 1986. *Saving Free Trade: A Pragmatic Approach*. Washington, D.C.: Brookings Institution.

Magee, Chris. n.d. "Administered Protection for Workers: An Empirical Analysis of Trade Adjustment Assistance Certifications," manuscript.

Meyer, Bruce D. 1995. "Lessons from the U.S. Unemployment Insurance Experiments." *Journal of Economic Literature* 33:91–131.

Polivka, Anne. 1991. *Trade Adjustment Assistance and Workers' Employment Histories*, unpublished doctoral dissertation, University of Wisconsin, Madison.

Richardson, J. David. 1982. "Trade Adjustment Assistance Under the U.S. Trade Act of 1974: An Analytical Examination and Worker Survey." In Jagdish N. Bhagwati (ed.), *Import Competition and Response*. Chicago: University of Chicago Press.

Ruhm, Christopher J. 1992. "Advance Notice and Post-Displacement Joblessness." *Journal of Labor Economics* 10:1–32.

Ruhm, Christopher J. 1994. "Advance Notice, Job Search, and Post-Displacement Earnings." *Journal of Labor Economics* 12:1–28.

CHAPTER 5

Trade and Environmental Quality

John J. Kirton

I. Introduction

The debate over how international trade has affected environmental quality in the United States and in the foreign countries most closely tied to it dates back to the Stockholm era of the early 1970s and has now flourished in its intense form for well over a decade (Rugman and Kirton, 1998; Bhagwati and Hudec, 1996; Jaffe, Peterson, Portney and Stavins, 1995). Yet it reached a new level of analytic intensity, mass public awareness, and salience for U.S. foreign and domestic policy with the controversy over, and conclusion of, the North American Free Trade Agreement (NAFTA) taking force on January 1, 1994.

Such controversy was hardly surprising. NAFTA, representing a confirmation and geographic and functional extension of the Canada-U.S. Free Trade Agreement of 1988, marked an historic change in U.S. trade policy, from multilateralism to bilateralism and regionalism, from progressive liberalization to full free trade with the substantial economies (Canada and Mexico) that now constitute its two largest trading partners, and from historical sectoral liberalizations (such as the Maquiladora program, Defense Production Sharing Agreements, and Automotive Pact), to a comprehensive regime governing not only trade in goods, but also trade in services, foreign direct investment, and several once domestic areas. Moreover, NAFTA brought with it, uniquely for the United States in its relations with its North American neighbors, a dense array of trilateral intergovernmental institutions and regional organizations. It further came, uniquely for international free trade agreements, with a parallel agreement and institution for environmental co-operation, the North American Agreement on Environmental Co-operation (NAAEC), and the Commission for Environmental Co-operation (CEC) respectively. With international trade projected to account for a full third of U.S. GNP in five years (USTR 1997), with the NAFTA regime serving as a referent for U.S. regional free trade initiatives in the Asia-Pacific and Americas, and with a slow-moving process of WTO-based multilateral trade liberalization offering little additional impact on the U.S. economy, it is through an examination of NAFTA's effects that the environmental impact of trade on the United States and its major partners can best be assessed.

To identify such effects, analysts have offered a variety of analytical and methodological approaches. The United States and its two NAFTA partners have participated in the development, notably at the OECD and WTO, of frameworks for examining the environmental effects of trade and trade liberalization in general (OECD, 1994, 1997a,b). During the NAFTA debate and subsequently, several studies have employed partial and general equilibrium models to estimate NAFTA's impact on several welfare dimensions (Robinson et al. 1993; for a review see Esty 1996). Moreover, the years following NAFTA, and particularly the three-year Congressionally-mandated review of NAFTA in July 1997 have witnessed a host of studies (USTR, 1997; Weintraub, 1997; Lustig, 1997; Economic Policy Institute, 1997).

Notwithstanding their value, such studies often fail to capture some of the critical, environmentally-consequential characteristics of NAFTA—a full free trade agreement, including rules for investment and other areas, governing a region in which trade is closely tied to foreign direct investment (FDI) in a dense system of integrated production, and regulated by far-reaching regional rules and institutions to ensure ecological quality (Ramirez, 1996a; Stanford 1992). Moreover, many of the policy commentaries, focused on the public promises of U.S. politicians seeking support for NAFTA, rather than the autonomous operation of NAFTA-related trade as a cause of environmental change, fail to fully account for the array of macroeconomic and microeconomic forces simultaneously at work. In addition they often omit the complex linkages through which delayed, incremental and cumulative changes generate ecological pressures and supports that affect the ambient environment.

To provide a more comprehensive assessment, this chapter pursues three approaches.[1] First, it considers the environmental effects of NAFTA-associated trade in conjunction with the impact of FDI, in recognition of the fact that two-thirds of intra-North American trade takes place on an intra-firm or associated firm basis, that the United States has an intense FDI relationship with both Canada and Mexico and that a few large multinational firms account for most of this regional trade and investment. Second, it considers how trade and investment liberalization is translated into environmental change through often autonomous, powerful and complex processes of production, physical infrastructure, social organization and government policy, especially in such key sectors as automotive products and services, beef, electricity, and maize. Finally, it explores the autonomous environmental impact of the trilateral institutions created or catalyzed by both the core NAFTA and its accompanying NAAEC, with the express purpose of enhancing the favorable ecological impact of NAFTA's trade liberalization regime. In all three areas it builds on the analytic framework developed through NAFTA's Commission for Environmental Co-operation, as part of its mandatory responsibility to assess on an ongoing basis NAFTA's environmental effects (CEC 1999).

With only five years since NAFTA took effect, it remains too soon to provide a conclusive, comprehensive, integrated judgement of NAFTA's overall impact. Yet when one considers the patterns in these years since NAFTA took formal effect, and adds those since 1990, when the arrival of NAFTA was widely anticipated and corresponding strategic adjustments by firms and governments were made, several preliminary, partial conclusions emerge. NAFTA is generating both positive and negative ecological impacts in different domains. NAFTA-associated trade and FDI, through an intensification of comparative advantage and technology transfer, are starting to foster general region- and economy-wide positive environmental effects. Yet as a detailed analysis of key sectors demonstrates, the environmental impacts of this trade and investment depend critically on the particular production systems, physical infrastructure and social organization employed, and above all on government policy choices, nationally and internationally, regarding the sector specifically and the environment in general. The most environmentally relevant intergovernmental institutions created by NAFTA have had a mixed record, with robust environmentally-enhancing performances in the fields of dangerous goods transportation and pesticides, and weak performances in regard to automotive emissions. Finally the CEC itself has had some autonomous, environmentally-enhancing impact through its initial co-operative, surveillance-enforcement and trade-environment integration activities, although its future effectiveness has become uncertain. Taken together, these results suggest that thus far NAFTA has had a weak but positive effect on North America's ecology, and that its future environmental impact depends critically on government policy choices and regional institutional performance in the years ahead.

II. The Environmental Impacts of NAFTA's Trade and Investment Liberalization

There are now a host of studies of the post-NAFTA period which demonstrate the existence of an independent NAFTA effect on trade at the general, economy-wide level and for specific sectors in the United States, Mexico and Canada (USTR, 1997; DFAIT, 1997; Weintraub, 1997). The majority of such studies suggest that the economic effects of NAFTA are broadly positive or neutral on such major economic dimensions as trade growth and gains in GDP, income and employment. However a few point to specific negative effects on selected indicators such as income equality and trade diversion.

It is difficult to estimate, in overall terms, how much and how NAFTA trade-induced growth, demand and consumption have increased environmental stress, and how much NAFTA induced specialization has reduced such stress. In part, this is because there are in the general literature few empirically-based studies identifying the complex linkages between trade liberalization and environmental impact. The conclusions of the studies that do exist revolve around the attention and relative weight they give to three forces. The first is the composition effect, which, following the Heckscher-Ohlin approach, suggests that free trade leads a country relatively replete with environmental resources to specialize in the production of environment-intensive goods. However trade-induced income growth may also dynamically shift preferences toward more environmentally friendly goods. The second is the technique effect, which, following the Stolper-Samuelson theorem, suggests the relative price of environmental inputs will increase, inducing industries across the entire economy to switch to more environmentally-friendly processes. Here rising incomes also dynamically lead to a demand for a cleaner environment (through taxes or regulations) and push all industries toward cleaner production processes. The third is the scale effect, as the expanded economic activity and incomes resulting from trade increase the demands for all inputs, and hence the pollution involved in their production.

Early studies, focusing on the composition effect through a Heckscher-Ohlin-Vanek model, found that environmental abundance (measured by environmental control costs) had no effect on trade flows (Tobey, 1990; Grossman and Krueger, 1993). Indeed, rapidly growing open, as opposed to closed, economies had a lesser increase in the toxic intensity of manufacturing output, suggesting trade openness changes the composition of output to cleaner sectors (Lucas, Wheeler, and Hettige, 1992; Lucas, 1994). Most recently, a study of both static composition and dynamic income effects in regard to China indicates that trade liberalization directly generates water pollution through its impact on the terms of trade but indirectly reduces pollution through income growth (Dean, 1998). There is also good evidence that the growth in income strongly increases the demand for and level of environmental regulation (Eliste and Fredriksson, 1998b; Copeland and Taylor, 1994, 1995). Only in such specific cases as small open economies with an open access resource does trade liberalization have major negative effects on renewable resource management and economic development (Brander and Taylor, 1997).

A distinct line of inquiry, incorporating intervening political processes, argues that trade liberalization, especially with jurisdictions with lower environmental standards or enforcement, will lead to a regulatory race to the bottom (through relaxed standards or enforcement) or a regulatory chill (by preventing the passage of new environmental regulations) (Esty, 1994; Dua and Esty, 1997; Esty and Geradin 1997). Others point to the strategic behavior of ecological dumping, as countries adopt environmental policies at levels lower than those appropriate for the marginal damage (Barrett, 1994; Kennedy, 1994; Rauscher 1994).

The slender existing evidence suggests such phenomena are unlikely. Environmental regulations have small or insignificant impacts on trade (Jaffe et al., 1995), except in isolated instances (Low and Yeats, 1992; Lucas et al., 1992). There is also evidence that an increase in environmental regulations generates greater exports and reduced imports (van Beers and van den Bergh, 1997). Moreover, countries with homogenous populations set environmental policies optimally, despite competition for investment between them (Oates and Schwab, 1988). Indeed, the most recent study, exploring the agricultural sector, has found that countries with open trade have more stringent regulations, especially if they trade with countries with stricter regulations than their own (Eliste and Fredriksson, 1998a). This is particularly the case where there is a conscious calculation of the means to increase export access, high per capita income, highly visible environmental pressure, and a large producer lobby among which the costs of higher regulation can be spread. In short, in the face of higher environmental regulation, firms can remain at home and successfully export, rather than move production abroad or petition their government to lower the environmental regulations at home.

Such conclusions are sustained by research focused on the NAFTA region and western hemisphere. An application of the OECD-grounded TEQUILA model suggests Mexico's trade liberalization will decrease pollution-intensive activity, with the expanded pollution produced by increased scale offset by appropriate environmental reforms (Beghin et al., 1997). A more recent analysis of the harmonization of standards in the Americas indicates that trade liberalization and environmental policy intervention improve environmental quality, although relative convergence rather than full harmonization to U.S. levels is desirable (Tsigus et al., 1999).

The existing evidence from the NAFTA region itself tends to confirm many of these propositions, and thus points to the generally beneficial ecological impact which NAFTA-induced trade has had. In the first instance, the sectoral composition of post-NAFTA trade, and the dynamic changes in the share of such trade among sectors, is not having a negative effect on environmental quality. A matching of sectors where post-NAFTA trade is the largest and most rapidly growing, with the propensity to pollute of various sectors (as measured by the World Bank's Industrial Pollution Projection System) provides a mixed picture (CEC 1996:103). Post-NAFTA trade volumes and increases are highest in the low-polluting motor vehicle, photographic and optical goods industries, but also in the medium-polluting machinery and equipment industries, and in the high-polluting pulp, paper and paperboard, plastic products, furniture and iron and steel industries. More specifically, the export items that increased in value above the overall average from 1993 to 1994 were, in absolute increases, vehicles, machinery and oil and gas, and in percentage increases iron and steel (for Canada to United States, Mexico to United States, but also United States to Mexico trade).

Moreover, there are additional early signs that post-NAFTA trade is evolving in environmentally beneficial ways (Weintraub and Galbraith, 1996). Trade is increasing in intermediate goods, which provides an incentive to incorporate the same, high standard, firm-wide technologies in the production of such goods as part of an integrated production and liability system. Trade is increasing in service sectors, which are in general less polluting than manufacturing and natural resources ones. Finally, the overall effect of NAFTA on the maquiladoras, whose 2,000 plants produce primarily low polluting automotive and electronic equipment parts, is to reduce their tariff advantages, and thus the incentive to geographic concentration (and with it the environmental stress and transborder impacts) brought by such concentration. The existing strong growth in maquiladora production, and the resulting stress on fixed physical resources in the absence of adequate environmental infrastructure, is being driven by non-NAFTA factors, notably Mexico's need to export following the 1994 peso devaluation, the locational requirements of just-in-time inventory, and the regulatory requirement to send hazardous waste materials used in Mexican production back to the United States for disposal.

Of similar importance to, and closely associated with trade are transborder flows of FDI. In many ways NAFTA was an investment agreement as much as a trade agreement, and many of its most innovative provisions came in the new protections and dispute settlement mechanism it provided for transborder investment. Moreover, North American trade is integrally tied to such investment. About 65% of Canada's, and 60% of Mexico's manufactured exports to the United States are intra-firm transactions (Zeile, 1997; *New York Times*, 1997). A full 63% of all U.S. exports globally are made by transnational corporations (TNCs), many of them very large firms and a full 50% of Canada's exports come from only 50 firms, many of them foreign-controlled (Zeile, 1997; *New York Times*, 1997; *Wall Street Journal*, 1993; *Financial Post*, 1996).

The environmental effects of NAFTA-associated FDI involve several issues. The first and most publicly prominent is the way "pollution haven" seeking investment migration creates incentives for "environmental sanctuary" jurisdictions to lower or not impose their standards (or enforcement) to retain such investment, with consequentially negative effects on the environment. A second is the role of environmentally-enhancing technology transfer and diffusion through multinational corporations (MNCs) (Eliste and Fredriksson, 1998a; Reinhard et al., 1997). A third is the geographic concentration of such investment in environmentally stressed locales, or in those with low absorptive capacity. A fourth is the role of direct subsidies to offset environmental costs in attracting investment. And a fifth is the role of MNCs, with their integrated production systems, in fostering high level, region-wide, de facto or negotiated standardization as part of their corporate strategies.

Several analyses of FDI under NAFTA are consistent with the majority conclusions of the existing general literature in providing no support for the pollution-haven-seeking hypothesis. Preliminary evidence from 1994 suggested the widely-anticipated, NAFTA-induced FDI trends were taking place, with the United States giving a rising share of its outward FDI to Mexico (and a diminishing share to Canada), and Canada sharply increasing its FDI stock in Mexico (while holding steady in the United States) (Kirton, 1998a). However Mexican FDI in the United States, as anticipated, was also soaring from 1993 to 1994 (while remaining negligible in Canada). Moreover, after this initial NAFTA concentration in Mexico (and the United States), the trend slackened, and investment in Canada (including that from Mexico) increased. There is thus no longer term trend for the location of FDI to diminish in the United States and Canada, where environmental regulations and compliance costs are judged to be higher, and concentrate disproportionately in Mexico, where environmental enforcement and thus compliance costs are thought to be lower. Moreover, with U.S. FDI flows to Mexico in 1996 representing only 0.2% of U.S. gross private domestic fixed investment that year, there has been no general migration of U.S. firms (USTR, 1997; USITC, 1997).

Such a conclusion is sustained by an analysis of the composition of FDI on a sectoral basis (USTR, 1997). From 1993 to 1996, U.S. FDI flows to Mexico were negative in the high polluting sectors of chemicals (where total U.S. investment declined 47% over the period) and printed products. They were modest in the low-polluting automotive sectors (with the Big Three investing US$3 billion), and steady in the low polluting sectors of computers, household appliances and textiles-apparel. In the low polluting sectors of processed food and beverages, where more than 25% of total U.S. FDI in Mexico is concentrated, U.S. FDI stock rose from US$2.3 billion in 1993 to US$2.8 billion in 1994 but declined to US$2.3 billion in 1995. The sectoral pattern of new U.S. FDI into Mexico in the post-NAFTA period appears to be avoiding or declining in those sectors with a large ecological footprint (basic metals, industrial chemicals, and non-metal products) and concentrating in those with a smaller ecological footprint (textiles, metal products, food products). This is consistent with the pattern of initial post-NAFTA investment in Mexico (Ramirez, 1996b).

These results are confirmed by other studies. The most well developed of several studies demonstrates a trend of U.S. FDI into Mexico in industries characterized as lower polluting (Cole and Ensign, 1997). A recent study of the Canadian automotive parts industry casts doubt on corporate calculations or motives for pollution-haven-seeking behavior, by indicating that environmental regulatory compliance was almost non-existent as a factor governing corporate strategy and production location (Eden et al., 1997).

Casting further doubt on the race-to-the bottom hypothesis is the fact that this increase in FDI in Mexico has been accompanied by a sharp rise in its overall level of environmental regulations and enforcement capacity and action (Kirton, 1998b). Since 1992 Mexico has enacted five major environmental statutes and promulgated 87 regulations, most of which have used the U.S. equivalents as a referent (Steinberg, 1997). In 1993 Mexico established regulations on water quality, including wastewater discharges from industrial facilities and eliminated high sulfur diesel fuel. In 1994 it added regulations for air quality, which included the six substances specified in the U.S. Clean Air Act but added carbon monoxide as well. In 1994 it also set regulations for fossil fuel quality (including SO_2, NO_x, lead, sulfur, benzine, olefin and ash). In 1996 it joined with the United States to designate the El Paso-Juarez Valley an International Air Quality Management Basin. As of 1997 it had not introduced regulations for maximum levels of soil pollutants, but informally followed international (largely European) standards covering organic compounds such as hydrocarbons and inorganic compounds such as mercury and lead.

The years since NAFTA took effect have also seen a sharp increase in Mexican environmental enforcement capacity and action, despite the severe constraints on government expenditure induced by the economic crisis of 1994–95 (USTR, 1997: 112, 125). Mexico has created an environmental crimes unit in its Attorney General's office, increased the number and quality of environmental inspectors, and from 1993 to 1996 quadrupled the number of inspections (to 13,000 per year) and temporary, partial or permanent closures (to 1,377 per year). From 1992 to 1996 it increased to 49% the probability of an annual inspection for a maquiladora, conducted 12,347 inspections and compliance verification visits in the border, fined 9,884 facilities and partially or completely closed 548 facilities. The result has been, from 1993 to 1996, a 43% increase in the number of maquiladoras in complete environmental compliance and a 72% reduction in serious environmental violations in the maquiladoras.

The evidence on technology transfer through FDI is very limited. There is some evidence that FDI is a major source of technology transfer and diffusion (Hirshhorn, 1997). However, there are no studies dealing with these processes in regard to NAFTA on environmental technologies or impacts specifically. The outflows of U.S. and Canadian FDI to Mexico, reinforced by Mexican FDI in the United States should improve environmental performance in the recipient countries, through capital modernization (especially in greenfield plants), general technology transfer among affiliates, specific investments in environmental equipment, infrastructure and management systems, and the diffusion of such technology and practices across the sector, especially as the surge of new investment took place in 1994 when environmental consciousness in North America was at its peak. At a general level, a September 1997 survey of 125 companies operating in Mexico found that 86% of U.S.-owned firms and 84.2% of Mexican-owned firms reported incorporating new technology in its production/service processes to confront the increased competition brought by NAFTA (ACCM, 1997).

There is as yet no general evidence of a strong geographic concentration of FDI or NAFTA-associated domestic investment in particular regions such as north-south transportation corridors, or environmentally-sensitive areas. In particular, NAFTA-associated FDI does not appear to be geographically concentrating in already stressed locales such as the maquiladora region in northern Mexico. However the increasing scale of locally-sourced raw materials, greater use of packaging and plastics, and intensification of transport in intra-corporate trade may increase environmental stress.

There is little known about the effect of subsidies offered to offset environmental compliance costs in attracting investment to particular jurisdictions. The general evidence from the agriculture sector suggests that an increase in environmental regulation does lead governments to subsidize their producers in ways that distort trade but offset any tendency to industrial migration (Eliste and Fredriksson, 1998b). Anecdotal evidence from the NAFTA region suggests such a subsidy was employed, with apparent success, in attracting a U.S.-owned beef packing plant to Alberta.

There is also no systematic evidence about how FDI and resulting intra-corporate trade has led to uniform, high-level, region-wide industry environmental practices and standards. NAFTA has encouraged co-ordinated production in the automotive, telecommunications equipment, computer, electronic products, and textiles-apparel sectors, thereby increasing the export of high-value U.S. components and services to firms in Mexico, and allowing Mexican firms to displace extra-NAFTA competitors (USTR, 1997:40). This increases the incentive of such firms to adopt the generally high levels of environmental regulations prevailing in the United States. Operating in the same direction are corporate considerations of legal liability and customer and public reputation, as managers calculate that they will be held accountable for the environmental practices, both product and process embedded, of their subsidiaries, affiliates and suppliers. At a general level, a September 1997 survey of 125 firms in Mexico found that NAFTA had led 53.3% to establish a relationship with companies in the United States or Canada since 1994. A full 77.8% of Mexican-owned firms and 67.4% of U.S.-owned firms reported that the entry of new foreign firms into Mexico had been a complement rather than hindrance to their own companies operations (ACCM, 1997a).

Such activity has been encouraged by the Mexican government which in 1992 started to promote voluntary compliance through a new environmental auditing program. In 1996, 274 operations joined the program. By April 1997, 617 facilities had completed environmental audits and over 400 had adopted compliance Action Plans generating over US$800 million in new environmental investments (Kirton, 1998b). After 1996, Mexico's tax code has permitted up to 100% deductibility in the first year for private firm capital investments to comply with environmental standards (Steinberg, 1997).

Some tentative indication of the direction and strength of these various environmental effects from NAFTA-associated FDI can be obtained from two exploratory interview programs conducted in late 1995. The first, with five Fortune 500 companies in the automotive parts and petrochemical industries, suggested that U.S. companies operating in Canada and Mexico, motivated by cost-saving considerations, tended to use corporate environmental standards rather than individual country standards, especially in new facilities (Weintraub and Galbraith, 1996). Such standards exceeded those set by Mexican environmental regulations. Capital and operating costs for environmental purposes represented only a very small portion of the corporate total. Indeed, corporations were frequently unaware of the costs of environmental regulations (which were not specifically identified in internal audit procedures). Those firms operating on the Texas-Mexico border were concerned about the lack of environmental infrastructure and freshwater, although these concerns were not a significant factor in current plans for expansion or new investment.

A similar exploratory study of six firms in Mexico (in the automotive, auto parts, food, steel piping, chemicals and steel rods sectors) suggests that the anticipation and advent of NAFTA did lead to improved environmental investments in foreign-owned and domestically-owned firms in Mexico (CEC, 1996; Ramirez, 1996b). Such improvements were limited, however, because the MNC firms in the study already operated at high global corporate standards. After NAFTA, the foreign-owned firms added an environmental manager and established an environmental committee, while Mexican owned companies reported paying more attention to the environment at the production department level. The MNCs often imported machinery and technology from countries with high environmental standards or their parent firms and had an incentive to implement the latest technological processes (including for pollution) to remain competitive in the global marketplace. Both foreign and domestic-owned companies dealt speedily with the minor inconsistencies uncovered by government inspections and incorporated pollution treatment into their plans for expansion, although Mexican owned firms reported an increase in pollution as a consequence of increased production.

Such findings are consistent with those of the 1995–96 interview program conducted by Kirton, and of a survey of 125 companies operating in Mexico, conducted by the American Chamber of Commerce in Mexico in the immediate post-NAFTA period. This survey found that firms' 1992 spending for pollution controls and environmental protection increased by 85% (Steinberg, 1997). A similar study of 227 firms conducted in the spring of 1997 found that 57.1% reported investing in new technology to improve their environmental practices since January 1994, with an average of US$4.18 million invested by each firm. U.S. suppliers provided between 60% and 70% of Mexican imports of environmental technology and products (ACCM 1997b)

III. The Environmental Impacts of the NAFTA Regime in Key Sectors

The environmental effects of NAFTA on the United States and its neighbors can be identified in greater detail by examining four major sectors which together are of central economic and environmental importance in all three countries of North America. These are the major manufacturing sector of automotive products and services, the agricultural sector of cattle feedlotting broadly defined, electricity generation and distribution, and maize production in Mexico. Together these sectoral studies indicate that the environmental effects of NAFTA and its associated trade and investment flows are neither automatic nor direct, but are heavily conditioned by and dependent on specific, sectorally and nationally distinctive configurations of production, management and technology, physical infrastructure, social organization and government policy. Thus far trends suggest environmentally favorable environmental impacts from NAFTA-associated processes in the automotive and cattle-feedlotting industries. Outcomes in the electricity sector are critically dependent upon policy choices to come, while those in the maize sector to date have been neutral, as producers shift to a variety of new strategies.

Automotive Products and Services

This is the leading sector in North American production, trade and FDI. In this sector, NAFTA has reinforced three major trends, all of which bring net environmental benefit (Kirton, 1998b). The first is an intensification of the move toward a full scale rationalization and integration of the industry on a regional rather than national basis, with a corresponding production incentive to have a uniform set of production practices and relevant environmental standards in all three countries and across all their subfederal jurisdictions. The second is a new wave of regulatory harmonization at a higher level of environmental standards, as NAFTA's consciousness-raising, and to a lesser degree its institutions and dispute settlement mechanisms have inhibited any regulatory "race to the bottom" and inspired a "push to the top", driven and guided largely by the anticipatory and voluntary efforts of industry and its stakeholders. The third is the rapid spread of this push toward high-level harmonization, from the assembly to the original equipment manufacturers (OEM) parts and then aftermarket sectors, and from manufacturing standards to operating standards (for fuel, inspection and maintenance, and pollution prevention).

Prior to NAFTA, the United States, Canada and Mexico had possessed a substantially integrated automotive industry (for assemblers and OEM parts producers) but, especially outside the U.S.-Canada relationship, a widely varying set of environmental regulations and enforcement patterns. The result was that U.S.-based and owned larger manufacturers generally applied higher U.S.-level standards in their operations in Canada and Mexico. However, production in Mexico by smaller firms for the domestic Mexican market, separate California standards in the U.S., and the spread of such subfederal distinctiveness across the United States and Canada created an inconvenient and potentially very costly differentiation that was threatening to expand. At the same time, the move to an integrated total-systems approach to environmental control in the automotive industry increased the pressure for uniform standards over a wider range of industries and jurisdictions.

The advent of NAFTA brought a move toward more stringent and expanded environmental regulation, enforcement and regulatory convergence. With NAFTA came the prospect of the full incorporation of Mexico into the largely integrated U.S.-Canada-production system, new rules with targets and timetables for improved environmental performance, new trilateral institutions for ongoing dialogue and expanding cooperation, and an enhanced consciousness of the need for improved environmental enhancement throughout the North American region. Together these factors have led, even in the long integrated U.S.-Canadian case, to explicit upward environmental harmonization on U.S. standards for emissions, and the use of U.S.-pioneered pollution prevention programs among the industry on a multistakeholder basis. The process has extended, with greater difficulty, into fuel use, the adoption of U.S.-like inspection and maintenance programs at the subfederal level and other operating standards.

There has also been a notable improvement in compliance with environmental regulations, despite the severe reductions in public sector resources for environmental protection, inspection and enforcement in all three NAFTA countries. In their first five years, NAFTA's economic and environmental dispute settlement mechanisms have received no automotive related cases (with the exception of the MMT dispute), suggesting that the NAFTA rules and the regime's deterrent effect are operating so as to encourage effective government enforcement and industry performance. The pre- and post-NAFTA political need to demonstrate NAFTA's environmental effectiveness to the U.S. public has led to an increase in inspection and enforcement action in Mexico, while the larger need to secure and maintain the open NAFTA market, and satisfy customers, insurers and financiers, has led the larger firms to readily comply, often on a voluntary and anticipatory basis.

NAFTA's automotive institutions have identified as potential agenda items a full array of issues relating to manufacturing emissions standards, fuel standards, operating standards and enforcement. However outside of the transportation of dangerous goods, in core areas such as automotive emissions standards, it is not these institutions but industry forums for international dialogue and pressure on national governments, together with strong public environmental consciousness, that are driving the process of higher level, region-wide convergence. There have thus been limited costs and substantial benefits to industry in the area of manufacturing standards, as industry has largely shaped the regulatory process and reaped the rewards of rapid and pioneering pollution prevention action. However, there remain major challenges to the industry in the related areas of fuel standards and operating standards where less industry consensus and more diverse stakeholders exist.

Cattle Feedlotting

A second sector, centered in the United States and Canada, is cattle feedlotting and its associated upstream industry of feedgrains and downstream industry of beef slaughtering, packaging, and processing (Runge 1999). NAFTA, while not a primary cause of environmental impacts, has had a clear, direct and substantial impact on U.S. trade and investment in the sector (USITC, 1997; de Janvry, 1996; Canadian Cattlemen's Association, 1997). NAFTA's primary effect has been to intensify the existing pattern, whereby the United States and Canada slaughter and export beef products to Mexico and Mexico sends limited quantities of feeder cattle to the United States. Only over the very long term and with state-of-the-art technology and full harmonization of U.S. and Mexican food safety and heath regulations, could U.S. and Canadian-located feedlots and beefpacking plants migrate to Mexico and serve as a platform for increased Mexican beef exports to the United States (Melton and Huffman, 1993). For the foreseeable future, with the industry concentrated in a few large firms with modern production methods and increasing FDI in Canada, and geographically concentrated in the United States at the heart of a well developed North American transportation system, conditions are favorable for production at world class managerial and technological standards, transportation of inputs and products with very low degrees of additional environmental stress, and a high degree of environmental regulation and enforcement, including the regulation of cattle feedlots as point sources of pollution (Stabler, 1997; Williams and Garcia-Vega, 1996). Impacts on air, water, land and biota from NAFTA-associated trade, investment and production are thus environmentally favorable at a region-wide level. Negative impacts, such as stress on inadequate road systems in Alberta or cattle pens at Laredo and El Paso, are of a partial and localized nature (USDA, 1996:41). The overall environmental benefits, however, could be enhanced through greater progress intergovernmentally and through the NAFTA institutions in resolving animal health and plant inspection issues (Canadian Cattlemen's Association, 1997; Kirton and Fernandez de Castro, 1997).

Electricity

The third sector of electricity is one where the effects of NAFTA are heavily interrelated with, and conditioned by, the essentially autonomous and current move to deregulation and an "open grid" in the United States and Canada (Moscarella et al., 1999; USAID, SRP, CFE, 1997; Palmer and Burtraw, 1996; Canada, 1995). Here the combination is catalyzing four major processes, whose relative strength and precise impacts remain to be seen. First, NAFTA's overall liberalization, combined with the open grid, has intensified competitive pressures and induced industry to lower their input costs for electricity, by relying more on the low cost power provided by the U.S.-located coal fired generation that, through U.S. regulatory grandfathering, can pollute at levels 4 to 100 times higher than their competitors (Cohen, 1997). Second, where such regulatory subsidies for old coal generation do not exist, where new subsidies to cover the stranded costs of "dirty" generation are not imposed, and where the transmission capacity exists, NAFTA-bred competition and the open grid accelerate capital turnover by replacing U.S. generating capacity (two-thirds of which is twenty years old), with new, more efficient, cleaner generation, such as combined cycle gas turbines. Third, NAFTA's reduction of Mexican tariffs on clean generation technology and low sulfur U.S. coal, and NAFTA's procurement provisions that enable CFE to consider and accept bids from electricity suppliers in the United States and Canada, combine with open grid and international transmission interties to accelerate fuel switching from the high-sulfur residual oil that now provides half of Mexico's electricity supply. Fourth, the NAFTA institutions could foster, (although the NAFTA rules could prevent) the emergence of region-wide, harmonized regulations for uniform charges on distribution and transmission services (to finance clean power), minimum content (or "portfolio") requirements for clean power from all generation owners, and mandatory minimum standards for equipment and building efficiency.

Maize

The fourth sector, of maize in Mexico, is one where the NAFTA-defined lowering of Mexico's import restrictions has led, as anticipated, to increased imports of U.S. corn, but not to a decrease in Mexican maize production (Nadal 1999). Environmental impacts will depend on the long-term dominance of one of three adjustment strategies currently being pursued by Mexican producers: expanded production by traditional methods; a move to high technology mechanization and irrigation; or conversion into horticultural or other production.

IV. The Environmental Performance of the NAFTA Institutions

The importance of government policy in determining how NAFTA-induced trade and investment affect the environment in these key sectors points to the powerful role that co-ordinated intergovernmental action, especially embedded in international institutions and formal organizations, can have in shaping ecological impacts. This is particularly the case in NAFTA, which, unlike its CUFTA predecessor, and APEC, FTAA or WTO contemporary, was launched with a thick array of intergovernmental institutions, some of which had an explicit and precise environmental mandate, or clear environmental relevance. A comparative study of the negotiation and implementation of trade-environment rules in the NAFTA, WTO and EU concludes that such environmentally-enhancing rules develop more quickly, thoroughly and stringently as rich, "green" countries use their market access power (through coercion and compensation) to secure their interests vis-a-vis a smaller, weaker set of developing countries, as integration deepens, and as deepening integration leads ENGO's in the rich green countries to demand such rules (Steinberg, 1997).

Although not equal to the European Union (EU), NAFTA, in its stated principles, norms, rules and institutionalized intergovernmental decisionmaking procedures represented, by global standards, an innovative and far reaching trade-environmental free trade regime, unprecedented in the equality and integration provided for trade and environmental values (Krasner, 1983). NAFTA's principles, norms and rules brought a major change in the prevailing trade-environment framework, by affirming the value of trade-environment equality and integration and by expanding the force of environmental protection, while maintaining trade openness at the regional level (Munton and Kirton, 1994; Housman, 1994; Rugman and Kirton, 1998; cf. Audley, 1997). However the NAFTA regime's decisionmaking procedures, as operationalized in the institutions that interpret, implement and extend the rules, have given less emphasis to the values of environmental equality and integration at the core of NAFTA's embedded normative structure. Even so, among the 50 trilateral intergovernmental institutions created or catalyzed by the core NAFTA (trade) agreement, the dozen bodies with direct environmental responsibility have in several cases had an impact. They have fostered a regular, balanced, trilateral communication, capacity building, high level regulatory convergence, and regional co-operation in multilateral forums that tempers the autonomous actions of U.S. and trade actors (including their ability to impose environmental regulations with protectionist impact) and moves toward the trade-environment equality and integration upon which the core principle of sustainable development depends.

Normatively, the core NAFTA trade text made major advances. In addition, it gave many of the specific trilateral institutions mandatory powers to interpret, implement and extend specific responsibilities for environmental action. In some instances, notably dangerous goods transportation and automotive emissions, it identified a precise timetable and target for action. It also offered permissive mandates for some of these institutions to act on specified environmental subjects should they so wish. More generally, the mandates of other bodies, such as agriculture, dealt with issues of such clear environmental relevance that they too, with the Agreement's preambular authority, could operate in environmentally enhancing ways, if they so desired.

An analysis of the performance of NAFTA's environmentally-relevant trade institutions over their first three years of operation reveals five major patterns (Kirton and Fernandez de Castro, 1997; Weintraub, 1997). Firstly, following a slow start, 1996 witnessed a sharp takeoff in the activities of these bodies. Secondly, there has been a notable institutional proliferation, as the 26 bodies created by NAFTA have now doubled in number and new trilateral bodies with an environmental relevance have emerged within and outside the NAFTA structure across many issue areas. Thirdly, there is more balanced and open trilateral co-operation, as Mexico has become a fuller partner in the problem-solving spirit that has (amidst the inevitable differences of interest and hard bargaining) long characterized the Canada-U.S. relationship. Fourthly, there has been a wide variation in performance, with some bodies, such as those for the Transportation of Dangerous Goods and for Pesticides, having rapidly generated a high-level convergence of standards through mutual adjustment, while others, notably the Automotive Standards Council and Subcommittee on Land Transportation, have been slow to act. Finally, at the ministerial and lower levels, NAFTA's trade institutions and the CEC have done little to interact to produce the integrated, balanced trade-environment regime identified in NAFTA's normative core.

More specifically, the environmental impact of NAFTA institutional activity can be assessed through five functions these institutions perform. The first is communication, where the NAFTA institutions are leading to an understanding of legitimate geographic and environmentally-based differences in standards (for example, Mexico testing for automotive emissions at higher altitudes than does the United States). The second is capacity-building, where these institutions are encouraging and assisting Mexico to introduce environmental regulations where none existed before. The third is regulatory convergence, where they are identifying areas where Mexico has different but higher as well as lower standards than the United States, and incorporating an array of such features from all three member countries into a common approach. The fourth is broader international cooperation aimed at developing common North American positions in broader international forums, both to shape the broader regime to meet specific North American interests or to ensure broad multilateral harmonization as a value in its own right. The fifth is dispute settlement (through Chapters 11, 19 and 20). Here NAFTA's mechanisms, despite the initial concerns of critics, have operated in ways that have constrained national environmental regulations with protectionist effect, without inhibiting the emergence of high-level regional standards (Orbuch and Singer, 1995; Rugman and Soloway, 1997; Soloway, 1997).

Of particular importance is the impact of the NAFTA institutions in fostering regulatory convergence, at higher levels of environmental protection, among the three member countries and, equally importantly, their many subfederal units. Because NAFTA's environmental regime emphasized the effective enforcement of national regulations, it has thus far delivered less international regulatory convergence, in the myriad forms this process assumes, than the EU, where international harmonization formed the focus of the regime (Esty and Geradin, 1997; Jaffe et al., 1995). Yet the NAFTA environmental regime and institutions have created a clear bias towards regional convergence. This is best conceived of as a dynamic process unfolding in discrete, if partially overlapping, stages: (1) communication among actors to lower transactions costs and thus enhance market access and environmental learning; (2) capacity building to develop modern regulatory systems in partner countries; and (3) convergence of regulations, through individual mutual adjustment or coordinated agreement, toward a common system and state.

The NAFTA regime in its initial years has, despite the three member countries' large disparity in overall capabilities and initial diversity in economic and regulatory development, produced considerable convergence in environmental regulations, at higher levels of environmental protection. Only in the case of pesticides have concerns arisen that the NAFTA process is causing the higher national standards to be lessened. Moreover, the breadth of subjects covered by the 50 NAFTA institutions and the activities with which they deal (many of which are in subfederal jurisdiction) suggest that they will have an ever stronger constraining effect in the future on state-level environmental regulatory protectionism, and produce greater region-wide, high level regulatory convergence.

This high level harmonization is not primarily a hegemonic regionalization of U.S. regulations and preferences, driven by the activities of U.S. environmental NGO's (cf. Steinberg, 1997). The emergent trilateralism often does converge on state-of-the-art U.S. environmental regulations. But this process is not primarily one of the United States using NAFTA to impose its standards on its partners, particularly in ways that disproportionately benefit U.S.-based firms or the preferences of U.S. ENGO's. Rather, much activity takes the form of a dialogue aimed at understanding better the very different regulations and regulatory-standards-setting, testing/assessment, and enforcement/compliance systems within each of the three countries. The NAFTA process at a minimum lowers transaction costs, notably the information and confidence barriers, that otherwise inhibit access to all three markets. At a maximum it engenders a convergent movement upward through mutual adjustment.

The factors propelling such a movement toward high level regulatory convergence can be identified by examining, across the six institutions where NAFTA's work on environmentally-related regulations is concentrated, the wide variation in the degree of convergence sought and secured, the level of environmental standards aimed at and achieved, and the trilateral rather than bilateral or unilateral character of the bargaining and outcome (Krugman, 1997). In two of the six cases—the Working Group on the Transportation of Dangerous Goods (LTSSV) and the Technical Working Group on Pesticides (TWGP), there has been rapid, strong, high and balanced convergence based on a broadly multilateral rather than a U.S. national standard. In sharp contrast, in two cases—the Working Group on Vehicle Standards (LTSS I) and the Automotive Standards Council (ASC)—much less convergence has occurred and U.S. and trade/industry preferences have largely prevailed. In two cases— the Committee on Sanitary and Phytosanitary Standards (CSPS), and the Committee on Agricultural Trade (CAT)—there is a mixed record.

This variation across the six cases reflects the impact of several factors. The first is the visible, concentrated and obvious transborder character of the environmental harm and resulting ecological vulnerability of the United States, a factor which causes extensive, balanced, high-level regulatory convergence. An accident involving the transportation of dangerous goods is likely to attract publicity and damage political and corporate reputations and resources, in contrast to less visible, long-term, diffusely impacting automotive emissions (Oye and Maxwell, 1995; Eliste and Fredriksson, 1998b). Moreover sprayed pesticides flowing by air or water from Mexico into the United States are more likely to galvanize political pressure and action from geographically concentrated constituencies than are the more subtle issues dealt with by the CSPS. The direct ecological vulnerability of the United States to threats emanating from partner jurisdictions, especially Mexico, creates an effective chemical intervulnerability and a powerful incentive for action (Doran, 1985). At work is a process of dynamic intervulnerability as NAFTA's trade provisions increase transportation and truck travel in particular through the United States and with it the threat of chemical spills from trucks (more than rail cars or sea tankers) on U.S. soil.

A second cause of high level regulatory convergence, and one which corresponds to the logic and preferences of multilateralists who point to the costs of regional trade liberalization agreements, is the presence of a nested regime in the broader international system that fosters a nonhegemonic framework for regional action (Aggarwal, 1981). Work on the transportation of dangerous goods, where harmonization has proceeded fastest and furthest, is explicitly grounded in, and guided by, the established regime of the broader United Nations Economic Commission for Europe. The successful case of pesticides has the similarly multilateral OECD as its nest. In contrast, only very recently has the relevant automotive body become an effective multilateral as distinct from regional European forum.

A third cause is the insulation of the NAFTA institutions from direct, undiluted corporate influence. LTSSV on dangerous goods transportation contains only national government officials and is housed in national bureaucracies with an established mission according primacy to public health and safety. The TWGP incorporates a broad array of stakeholders, including both industry and ENGOs. In contrast, the ASC relies on national industry advisory committees to serve as its working group.

A fourth, but less salient, factor is the functional need to harmonize standards to reap NAFTA's trade gains. Thus transportation operations have seen rapid action as trade requires road transportation which enhances the probability of chemical spills. In contrast, in automotive emissions, the trade barriers and incentives are less apparent.

A fifth factor is the cost to powerful industries of the high-level harmonized standards. In dangerous goods transportation, work has proceeded rapidly on creating a regional emergency response guide for small packages. But progress has been slow for large containers, halogenated organic chlorides (where the chemical producing industry is seeking to shift the cost to the railroads by requiring super-strong tanker cars), and hazardous waste shipment (where the Canadian government was seeking to protect the commercial prospects of an Alberta disposal plant). In contrast, in the case of pesticides, action is spurred by the prospect that a single standard and test covering the entire region would facilitate trade by lowering costs (in money and time) to government and industry as well as lead to improved environmental protection.

A sixth factor is the support of MNCs most likely to be able to afford and benefit from a single, ultimately global system, and their relative influence over dispersed transportation interests and subfederal governments with a poor record of harmonizing on their own. In the case of dangerous goods transportation, officials in large national governments and large MNCs have a joint interest in preventing provincialism, with the transaction costs its autonomous regulatory activity brings.

There are few signs that the environmental achievements of the NAFTA institutions have come at the expense of trade liberalization values, through the promotion of national or regional protectionism rather than a broad multilateral regime. The absence of regional convergence in the failed cases is, on the whole, not driven by U.S. dominated "baptist-bootlegger" or "green and greedy" coalitions of environmentalists and firms insisting on unilateral autonomy and thus national environmental regulatory protectionism (De Sombre, 1995; Vogel, 1995; Vogel and Rugman, 1997). Indeed, with the exception of pesticides, environmentalists are notable by their absence across the spectrum of NAFTA economic institutional activity.

Nor have there yet emerged regional coalitions seeking to use the NAFTA institutions to gain environmental rules for the North American region at the expense of outside firms seeking to export into, or operate in the region, or in support of North American firms wishing to develop the critical regional mass to penetrate markets outside. Their general absence is apparent in the early preferences of members of the North American Trilateral Standardization Forum, the private-sector driven trilateral body that liaises with the government-only Committee on Standards-Related Measures (CSRM) and meets with the CSRM immediately before CSRM meetings. The Forum's Mexican members, representing an economy with 85 percent of its trade concentrated on the U.S. market on average, have displayed an initial affinity for co-operating with Canada, and a distrust of solutions embracing the United States. Canadian members, from an economy where 38% of GDP comes from goods and services exports, where 81% of merchandise exports go to the United States and where Canadian factories produce more for the export than the domestic market, prefer for reasons of diversification and a multilateralist ideology, not U.S. based or negotiated regional standards but a single, ideally universal multilateral regime of "one standard, one test, one mark." The U.S. members, coming from a country that sends only one-third of its exports to Canada and Mexico, rationally prefer (as defensive positionalists) multilaterally-compatible regional standardization.

Despite these multilateralist orientations, however, there is evidence of the impact of predominant U.S. power and interest, exercised in a trade liberalizing direction, but on a regional scale. For the cases of successful regional harmonization through the NAFTA institutions (dangerous goods transportation, pesticides) coincides with industries (chemicals) where regionally competitive U.S. business interests seek to secure a regional export market where they have enjoyed exceptional success. Successful regulatory convergence arises where the NAFTA market has expanded most for the home-based exports of the U.S. industry most affected from 1990 to 1994. More specifically, such convergence comes most in sectors in which the relevant U.S. industry has an export surplus with (1) its NAFTA partners; (2) with both NAFTA partners (and hence an incentive to harmonize on a trilateral basis); (3) where those surpluses are increasing from 1990 to 1994 (as NAFTA takes hold in anticipation and action); and (4) where the regional surplus is a large portion of U.S. industry's global surplus (Rugman, Kirton, and Soloway 1999).

V. The Impact of the Commission for Environmental Co-operation

The second dimension of the NAFTA regimes' institutional commitment to environmental enhancement came in the CEC. Analyses of the CEC's potential and performance varies, with the initial array of contingent optimists (Johnson and Beaulieu, 1996; Abbott, 1995) being replaced by a debate between disappointed critics (Public Citizen, 1995; Mumme and Duncan, 1996; Mumme and Duncan, undated; Audley, 1997; Council on Hemispheric Affairs, 1997; Economic Policy Institute, 1997; Lustig, 1997) and hopeful incrementalists (Munton and Kirton, 1994; de Mestral, 1996; Kirton and Fernandez de Castro, 1997; USTR, 1997; Weintraub, 1997; Kirton, 1997a). On balance, the record suggests that the CEC has autonomously engendered balanced environmental cooperation and improvement amidst the trade liberalization brought by NAFTA, but has done little to foster trade-environment equality and integration, and is currently in danger of being rendered less effective.

The CEC was created with three broad mandates—for environmental cooperation, for trade-environment integration, and for environmental surveillance-enforcement. To fulfill this mandate, the CEC currently maintains programs in eight broad areas, through a threefold institutional structure: a ministerial-level Council as the governing body; a single Secretariat; and a multistakeholder Joint Public Advisory Committee (JPAC) to advise the Council on any matter within the scope of the Agreement.

Each element of this institutional triumvirate has potentially important powers. The Council, which is, at a minimum, an annual meeting of the cabinet-level or "equivalent representatives" of the three countries normally operates by consensus (and thus equips each of the three countries with a veto) but moves from pure national control to supranational constraint in several areas. The CEC's single Secretariat is mandated to provide technical, administrative and operational support to the Council and to committees and groups established by the Council, under the authority of a somewhat autonomous Executive Director. The 15 member "Joint Public Advisory Committee," conceived as a single trinational body rather than three national sections meeting together, seeks to ensure that citizens of the three countries contribute strongly to the efficient execution of the CEC work and mandate. The governments also created additional bodies, at the Assistant Secretary level and below, as provided for in the agreement.

The CEC's Council has been active in giving political level direction. It moved swiftly into operation, meeting more regularly than its trade ministerial counterpart, and with one exception, always at the full ministerial level. By the time of its third meeting, in mid-1996, the Council placed the task of forging an equal, integrated trade-environment linkage in the interests of sustainable development at the forefront of the CEC's priorities (CEC, 1996). It also moved on environmental enforcement, authorizing, over Mexico's private opposition, an Article 14–15 factual investigation of the actions of the Mexican authorities in constructing a pier and supporting port infrastructure in Cozumel, allegedly without adequate environmental assessment. At its October 1997 meeting, the Council decided to make the completed factual record public.

The Secretariat has been equally active, moving faster than the other NAFTA-related organizations to select its professional staff, and become operational. Yet despite its successes (detailed below), there remain severe constraints on the Secretariat's ability to assist in accomplishing the purposes of the Agreement. Its budget, initially established at only two-thirds the anticipated level, has become increasingly inadequate as new responsibilities have been added (U.S., 1994:25). It is formally assigned no policy advisory responsibilities. It was created with and continues to face an inherent tension between its cooperative mandate (substantially dependent on the goodwill of member governments) and its surveillance-enforcement functions (overseeing their activities). Moreover, it has suffered from the forced departure of senior personnel, as U.S.-initiated government action secured the removal of the Executive Director (a Mexican national) at the outset of 1998, following his removal of the American Director immediately before (and the removal of a previous American Director at the outset of the CEC's operation). Further eroding the Secretariat's autonomy has been a tendency for national governments to become much more frequently engaged, in much more detail, in the Secretariat's operation, in the intervals between the annual ministerial meetings of the Council.

Through the Secretariat, the CEC has effectively employed several instruments to advance successfully its cooperative functions. One is the scientific credibility it has commanded and the broader support base and issue-specific epistemic community it is fostering through the many expert groups, study teams and consultations it has sponsored during its first four years. A second is its contribution to, and association with concrete progress on environmental priorities of governments and publics. A third is its role in fostering regional action plans to reduce and perhaps eventually eliminate from North America harmful pesticides and chemicals, notably DDT, PCBs, chlordane, and, prospectively, human-caused releases of mercury (CEC, 1997d). A fourth is its development of a modern, common and harmonized statistical base for measuring the environmental performance of the three Parties.

The real if limited impact of the CEC is further evident in regard to its surveillance and enforcement functions. These are contained in its ability to cast a "roving spotlight" on environmental issues under Article 13, to respond to NGO complaints about government non-enforcement of environmental regulations under Article 14 and 15, and to use its Part 5 powers for governmentally-initiated allegations of persistent non-enforcement by other governments.

The three Secretariat-initiated Article 13 reports initiated thus far have been directed first against Mexico (whose environmental practices were exonerated), then against all three countries, and most recently the United States and Mexico. The Article 14–15 process, which allows any NGO, business or other "interested party" to complain that a member government is failing to enforce its environmental laws, is also becoming more widely used and more trilaterally balanced in its application. In its first four years, the Secretariat received eleven such submissions, of which three dealt with the United States, two with Mexico, and six with Canada. In its first year, both cases came from the United States, and were terminated by the Secretariat on the grounds that the CEC lacked the legal authority to proceed. Of the four cases filed in 1996, the Secretariat terminated the two dealing with Canada, converted the one dealing with the United States into an Article 13 inquiry, and proceeded with the Mexican Cozumel case. Of the five cases (four Canadian and one Mexican) submitted in the first half of 1997, the CEC is proceeding with one, dealing with hydroelectric dams in British Columbia. Canada thus seems likely to join Mexico as the subject of Article 14–15 scrutiny. While the United States appears to be the great beneficiary, having escaped CEC investigation thus far despite its active array of ENGO's, the Article 14–15 process remains critically dependent on the actual enforcement performance of governments within each country.

There has been no use of the government-initiated Part 5 mechanism, which allows for the imposition of trade sanctions (in the case of the United States and Mexico) to punish a member government for its persistent non-enforcement of its environmental laws. All three governments appear to have accepted an implicit mutual non-aggression pact, choosing not to launch enforcement investigations against one another for fear that their partners could retaliate by launching similarly embarrassing investigations against them.

Far more modest has been the progress the CEC has made in securing the trade-environment equality and integration affirmed in the NAFTA regime. The relationship between the CEC and NAFTA's economic institutions is just beginning to develop, with both bodies at the ministerial level recognizing the importance of their interconnected agendas, asking for a joint meeting, but proving unable thus far to mount such an event. At the official level, there has also been little early contact between the CEC and those involved in NAFTA's economic institutions, despite the CEC's early move to implement in an ambitious fashion all of its trade-related responsibilities. More recently, the trade-environment dialogue has been strengthened, as co-ordinative centers and consultative processes have developed within national capitals.   Yet Mexican caution continues to constrain the CEC's flagship trade-environment project—to develop a framework to monitor NAFTA's environmental effects (De-Palma, 1997; America's Trade, 1997).

Also limited has been the movement to broaden and deepen the CEC as the institutional core of the NAFTA trade-environment regime. Only three of the ten Canadian provinces have acceded to the NAAEC and thus become full participants in the CEC. More broadly, the CEC is not reported as being involved in any of the 103 linkages between Canadian provinces and U.S. states on environmental matters operating in 1995, nor in the 649 such linkages covering all issue areas in the same year (Munton and Kirton, 1996; Kirton and Munton, 1996). On both its trade-environment and more environmentally-specific subjects, much of the CEC's work has come to be conducted with a conscious focus on how it can influence broader international forums, either as a means of asserting distinctive North American regional interests within them, or leading to the construction of a more multilateral regime (CEC, 1997b). Yet with the exception of the 1996 Canada-Chilean Free Trade Agreement, the NAFTA-NAAEC architecture, with an enlarged CEC as the foundation, has yet to be accepted as an integral element of any extension of NAFTA into the broader hemisphere.

A final sign of the environmentally enhancing impact of NAFTA's trade-environment institutions in general, and the CEC in particular, arises from an examination of the processing and outcome of 84 cases of environmental regulatory protection involving at least two of the North American countries from 1980 to mid-1998 (Rugman, Kirton, and Soloway 1999). A sharp move towards more balanced outcomes, across the three countries and between the region's trade-environment interests, comes in cases dealt with in the post-NAFTA, rather than the pre-NAFTA years. A similar movement appears when cases are dealt with at least partially through, rather than outside, the NAFTA institutions. And full balance is achieved in those cases dealt with by the environmental institutions of the CEC's, rather than those of NAFTA's trade institutions.

VI. Conclusion

The experience of the United States under NAFTA thus shows that trade liberalization has a weak but positive effect on environmental quality, both in the United States and its partner countries of Mexico and Canada. In keeping with the most recent findings about the environmental impact of trade liberalization in general, NAFTA-associated trade is not concentrating in environmentally-intensive sectors, but in environmentally-friendly intermediate goods and service sectors, while NAFTA is not adding to the environmental burdens of the maquiladoras. NAFTA-induced FDI shows no migration to pollution havens or any general tendency to concentrate in geographically stressed areas, even as it has encouraged environmentally-enhancing technology transfer, investment, subsidies and voluntary standardization among regionally integrated firms and industries. Studies of how NAFTA-associated trade and investment flows interact with processes of production, management and technology, physical infrastructure, social organization and government policy in key sectors suggest generally environmentally favorable environmental impacts in the automotive and cattle-feedlotting industries, with outcomes in the electricity sector and Mexican maize sector contingent upon national policy and producer-level choices still to come.

NAFTA's institutions have further strengthened this trade regime's environmental performance. The trade institutions with the most direct environmental responsibility for chemicals, in contrast to those for automotive products and agriculture, have fostered a regular, balanced, trilateral communication, capacity building, high level regulatory convergence, and regional co-operation in multilateral forums and dispute management. Propelling their success is the presence of visible ecological intervulnerability, a multilateral nest, government insulation from societal pressures, a functional need to harmonize to reap trade gains, low cost to powerful industries, MNC support, and the regional export interests of U.S. industry. NAFTA's dedicated environmental organization, the CEC, has also autonomously engendered balanced environmental co-operation and improvement amidst the trade liberalization brought by NAFTA, even if it has done little to foster trade-environment equality and integration, and is currently in danger of being rendered less effective. Indeed, when often trade-inhibiting and conflict-creating cases of environmental regulatory protection among the NAFTA members are processed through the NAFTA institutions, and in particular through the CEC, its is clear that NAFTA has achieved its overriding purposes of promoting sustainable development, and the advances in both trade liberalization and environmental enhancement at its core.

Notes

I am grateful for the contribution of my colleagues in the project on "Trade, Environment and Competitiveness" located at the University of Toronto's Centre for International Studies and the project on "NAFTA Environmental Effects" conducted by the Commission for Environmental Co-operation pursuant to Article 10 (6) D of the North American Agreement on Environmental Co-operation. I gratefully acknowledge the financial support of the Social Science and Humanities Research Council of Canada. The judgments presented in this paper are those of the author alone.
152

[1] Unless otherwise indicated, the judgments made in this chapter are based substantially on the results of two semi-structured interview programs. The first, conducted during the fall of 1995 and the spring of 1996, included 58 interviews, evenly balanced among the three countries, with 27 from government, 17 from business, 11 from NGOs and 3 from the academic community. Business respondents came from major industry associations and the automotive, chemicals, telecommunications, financial services, and natural resource sectors. The second, conducted from the summer of 1996 through the spring of 1997, embraced 88 individuals directly involved in the work of the NAFTA institutions. Of the 37 government officials interviewed in the initial phase, from the Assistant Secretary level downward and covering the major sector departments dealing with transport, agriculture and industry as well as finance and trade, 16 were from Canada, 15 from the United States, and 6 from Mexico. A draft was reviewed and modified on the basis of comments from a group of 51 individuals from government, business, academics and NGOs in the three countries, with the business reviewers covering economy-wide associations and the automotive, chemicals, metals and environmental technology industries. Additional specialized interview programs with Mexican industry were conducted by Rogelio Ramirez de la O in 1996, with U.S. Fortune 500 companies with operations in the region by Sidney Weintraub and Jan Galbraith in 1996, with stakeholders in the U.S. and Canadian automotive industry by John Kirton and Julie Soloway in 1997, and with Mexican stakeholders involved in NAFTA dispute settlement actions by Julie Soloway in 1997.

References

Abbott, Frederick. 1995. *Law and Policy of Regional Integration*. Cambridge: Kluwer.
ACCM. 1997a. *Business Planning '98: Analysis of the Mexican Marketplace*. Mexico City: American Chamber of Commerce of Mexico.
ACCM. 1997b. *NAFTA's Success: A Three-Year View from Mexico*. Mexico City: American Chamber of Commerce of Mexico.

Aggarwal, Vinod. 1983. "The Unravelling of the Multi-Fibre Agreement, 1981: An Examination of International Regime Change." *International Organization* 37:617–45.

Americas Trade. 1997. "NAFTA Institutions Should Go Further on Green Issues, Report Says." *Americas Trade* 4, December 11:11–13.

Audley, John. 1997. *Green Politics and Global Trade*. Washington, D.C.: Georgetown University Press.

Barrett, S. 1994. "Strategic Environmental Policy and International Trade." *Journal of Public Economics* 54(3):325–38.

Beghin, John, S. Dessus, D. Roland-Holst and D. van der Mensbrugghe. 1997. "The Trade and Environment Nexus in Mexican Agriculture: A General Equilibrium Analysis." *Agricultural Economics* 17:115–31.

Bhagwati, Jagdish, and Robert Hudec (eds.). 1996. *Fair Trade and Harmonization: Prerequisites for Free Trade?* Cambridge: MIT Press.

Brander, James, and Scott Taylor. 1997. "International Trade and Open-Access Renewable Resources: The Small Open Economy Case." *Canadian Journal of Economics* 30:526–51.

Canada, Embassy of Canada. 1995. "The Future of the U.S. Electric Industry and its Impact on Canada, " Washington, D.C., June.

Canada. 1992. *North American Free Trade Agreement: Canadian Environmental Review*. Ottawa.

Canadian Cattlemen's Association. 1997. "Pre-hearing Brief of the Canadian Cattlemen's Association before the U.S. International Trade Commission." In *Cattle and Beef: Impact of the NAFTA and Uruguay Round Agreements on U.S. Trade*. Washington, D.C., Investigation No. 332–371, March 10.

CEC. 1996. *Building a Framework for Assessing NAFTA Environmental Effects*, Report of a Workshop held in La Jolla, California on April 29–30, *Environment and Trade Series 4*. Montreal: Commission for Environmental Co-operation.

CEC. 1997a. *Independent Review of the North American Agreement for Environmental Cooperation*. Montreal: Commission for Environmental Cooperation.

CEC. 1997b. *Annual Program and Budget 1997*. Montreal Commission for Environmental Co-operation.

CEC. 1997c. *Continental Pollutant Pathways*. Montreal: Commission for Environmental Co-operation.

CEC. 1997d. *Taking Stock: North American Pollutant Releases and Transfers*. Montreal: Commission for Environmental Co-operation.

CEC. 1999. Assessing Environmental Effects of the North American Free Trade Agreement (NAFTA): An Analytic Framework (Phase II) and Issue Studies. Montreal: Commission for Environmental Co-operation.

Cohen, A. 1997. *Unfinished Business: Cleaning Up the Nation's Power Plant Fleet*. Boston: Clean Air Task Force.

Cole, Elizabeth, and Prescott Ensign. 1997. "An Examination of United States Foreign Direct Investment into Mexico and its Relation to the North American Free Trade Agreement: Towards a Balanced Understanding of the Effects of Environmental Regulation and the Factor Endowments that Affect the Location Decision." Paper Presented at the Annual Meeting of the Academy of International Business, Monterrey, Mexico, October 8–12.

Copeland, B. R., and M. S. Taylor. 1994. "North-South Trade and the Environment." *Quarterly Journal of Economics* 109:755–87.

Copeland, B. S., and M. S. Taylor. 1995. "Trade and Transboundary Pollution." *American Economic Review* 85:716–37.

Council on Hemispheric Affairs. 1997. "NAFTA's Failure to Deliver." Washington, D.C., June 27–29.

Dean, Judith. 1998. "Testing the Impact of Trade Liberalization on the Environment: Theory and Evidence." Paper prepared for a conference on "Trade, Global Policy and the Environment." World Bank, Washington, D. C., April 21–22.

DePalma, Anthony. 1997. "NAFTA Environmental Lags May Delay Free Trade Expansion." *The New York Times*, May 21.

De Sombre, Elizabeth. 1995. "Baptists and Bootleggers for the Environment: The Origins of United States Unilateral Sanctions." *Journal of Environment and Development* 4:53–75.

de Janvry, A. 1996. "NAFTA and Agriculture: An Early Assessment." *U.C.-Berkeley Working Paper No. 807*, Department of Agricultural and Resource Economics, November.

De Mestral, Armand. 1996. "Dispute Avoidance: Weighing the Values of Trade and the Environment under the NAFTA and the NAAEC." *Environment and Trade Series 3*. Montreal: Commission for Environmental Co-operation.

DFAIT. 1997. *NAFTA: A Partnership at Work*. Department of Foreign Affairs and International Trade Canada, Ottawa, June.

Doran, Charles. 1985. *Forgotten Partnership: U.S.-Canada Relations Today*. Baltimore: The Johns Hopkins University Press.

Dua, A. and Daniel Esty. 1997. *Sustaining the Asia Pacific Miracle*. Washington, D.C.: Institute for International Economics.

Economic Policy Institute. 1997. "The Failed Experiment: NAFTA at Three Years." *The Economic Policy Institute*, Washington, D.C., June 26.

Eden, Lorraine, Kaye Husbands, and Maureen Appel Molot. 1997. "Shocks and Responses: Canadian Auto Parts Suppliers Adjust to Free Trade and Lean Production." Paper presented to the annual meeting of the Academy of International Business, Monterrey, Mexico, October 12.

Eliste, Paavo, and Per Fredriksson. 1998a. "Does Open Trade Result in a Race to the Bottom? Cross-Country Evidence." Paper prepared for a conference on "Trade, Global Policy and the Environment." World Bank, Washington, D.C., April 21–22.

Eliste, Paavo, and Per Fredriksson. 1998b. "The Political Economy of Environmental Regulations, Government Assistance, and Foreign Trade: Theory and Evidence." Paper prepared for a conference on "Trade, Global Policy and the Environment." World Bank, Washington, D.C., April 21–22.

Esty, Daniel, and Damien Geradin. 1997. "Market Access, Competitiveness, and Harmonization: Environmental Protection in Regional Trade Agreements." *The Harvard Environmental Law Review* 21(2):265–336.

Esty, Daniel. 1996. NAFTA Effects: A Survey of Recent Attempts to Model the Environmental Effects of Trade: An Overview and Selected Sources. Montreal: Commission for Environmental Co-operation. Environment and Trade Series 1.

Esty, Daniel. 1994. *Greening the GATT: Trade, Environment, and the Future*. Washington, D.C.: Institute for International Economics.

Festa, David and Stacey Davis 1997. "Moving on Mercury: First Steps for Electric Utilities." *The Electricity Journal*, August/September, 76–84.

Financial Post. 1993. January 13, pp. 1–2.

Fry, Earl. 1997. "NAFTA and the Expanding Role of Non-Central Governments in North America." Paper presented at the Joint Conference of the Asociacion Mexicana de Estudios Internacionales and the International Studies Association, Manzanillo, Mexico, December 11–13.

Grossman, G., and A. Krueger. 1993. "Environmental Impacts of NAFTA." In P. Garber (ed.), *The U.S.-Mexico Free Trade Agreement.* Cambridge: MIT Press.

Hirshhorn, Ronald. 1997. "Industry Canada's Foreign Investment Research: Messages and Policy Implications." *Discussion Paper Number 5*, October.

Housman, Robert. 1994. "The North American Free Trade Agreement's Lessons for Reconciling Trade and Environment." *Stanford Journal of International Law* 30:379–422.

Jaffe, Adam, Steven Peterson, Paul Portney, and Robert Stavins. 1995. "Environmental Regulation and the Competitiveness of U.S. Manufacturing: What Does the Evidence Tell Us?" *Journal of Economic Literature* 33:132–63.

Johnson, Pierre Marc, and Andre Beaulieu. 1996. *The Environment and NAFTA: Understanding and Implementing the New Continental Law.* Washington, D.C.: Island Press.

Kennedy, P. W. 1994. "Equilibrium Pollution Taxes in Open Economies with Imperfect Competition." *Journal of Environmental Economics and Management* 27:49–63.

Kirton, John. 1997a. "NAFTA's Commission for Environmental Co-operation and Canada-U.S. Environmental Relations." *American Review of Canadian Studies* 27:459–86.

Kirton, John. 1997b. "NAFTA's Trade and Environment Regime: Regional Performance, Hemispheric Potential." Paper presented at the Joint Conference of the Asociacion Mexicana de Estudios Internacionales and the International Studies Association, Manzanillo, Mexico, December 11–13.

Kirton, John. 1998a. "NAFTA, Foreign Direct Investment and Economic Integration: A Canadian Aproach." In *Organization for Economic Cooperation and Development,* ed., *Migration, Free Trade and Regional Integration in North America*, OECD Proceedings. Paris: OECD, 1998, pp. 181–194.

Kirton, John. 1998b. "The Impact of Environmental Regulation on the North American Automotive Industry in the NAFTA Era." In Sidney Weintraub and Christopher Sands (eds.), *The North American Auto Industry under NAFTA.* Washington, D.C.: CSIS Press.

Kirton, John, and Rafael Fernandez de Castro. 1997. "NAFTA's Institutions: The Environmental Potential and Performance of the NAFTA Free Trade Commission and Related Bodies." Montreal: Commission for Environmental Co-operation, Environment and Trade Series 5.

Kirton, John, and Don Munton. 1996. "Canada-U.S. State-Provincial Relations in the NAFTA Era: The Societal Dimension." Paper prepared for a conference of the Association on Canadian Studies in the United States, Toronto, November.

Krasner, Stephen (ed.). 1983. *International Regimes.* Ithaca: Cornell University Press.

Krugman, Paul. 1997. "What Should Trade Negotiators Negotiate About?" *Journal of Economic Literature* 35:113–20.

Levy, Santiago, and Sweder van Wijnbergen. 1995. "Transition Problems in Economic Reform: Agriculture in the North American Free Trade Agreement." *The American Economic Review* 85(4):738–54.

Low, Patrick, and Alexander Yeats. 1992. "Do 'Dirty' Industries Migrate?" in P. Low (ed.), *International Trade and the Environment*, World Bank Discussion Paper 159, Washington, D.C.

Lucas, R.E.B. 1994. "International Environmental Indicators: Trade, Income, and Endowments." *Boston University IED Discussion Paper Series No. 46.*

Lucas, R.E.B. et al. 1992. "Economic Development, Environmental Regulation and the International Migration of Toxic Industrial Pollution: 1960–88." In P. Low (ed.), *International Trade and the Environment*, World Bank Discussion paper No. 159.

Lustig, Nora. 1997. "Setting the Record Straight." *Policy Brief 20*, June, The Brookings Institution, Washington, D.C.

Melton, B., and W. Huffman. 1993. "Implications of the North American Free Trade Agreement for Long Term Adjustment in U.S.-Mexican Beef Production and Trade." *Working Paper 93–WP 118*, Iowa State University, Center for Agricultural and Rural Development, December.

Moscarella, John Paul et al. 1999. "Electricity in North America: Some Environmental Implications of the North American Free Trade Agreement." In CEC. Assessing Environmental Effects of the North American Free Trade Agreement (NAFTA): An Analytic Framework (Phase II) and Issue Studies. Montreal: Commission for Environmental Co-operation, pp. 259–384.

Mumme, Stephen, and Pamela Duncan. 1996. "The Commission on Environmental Co-operation and the U.S.-Mexico Border Environment." *Journal of Environment and Development* 5:197–215.

Mumme, Stephen, and Pamela Duncan. Undated. "The Commission on Environmental Cooperation and Environmental Management in the Americas." Unpublished paper, Department of Political Science, Colorado State University, Fort Collins.

Munton, Don, and John Kirton. 1994. "North American Environmental Co-operation: Bilateral, Trilateral, Multilateral." *North American Outlook* 4:59–86.

Munton, Don, and John Kirton. 1996. "Beyond and Beneath the Nation-State: Province-State Interactions and NAFTA." Paper Presented at the International Studies Association Annual Meeting, San Diego, California, April.

Nadal, Alejandro. 1999. "Maize in Mexico: Some Environmental Implications of the North American Free Trade Agreement." In CEC. 1999. Assessing Environmental Effects of the North American Free Trade Agreement (NAFTA): An Analytic Framework (Phase II) and Issue Studies. Montreal: Commission for Environmental Co-operation, pp. 65–182.

New York Times. 1997. October 31.

Oates, W. E., and R. M. Schwab. 1988. "Economic Competition Among Jurisdictions: Efficiency Enhancing or Distortion Inducing?" *Journal of Public Economics* 35:333–54.

OECD. 1994. *Methodologies for Environmental and Trade Reviews*. Paris: Organization for Economic Cooperation and Development.

OECD. 1997a. *Economic Globalisation and the Environment*. Paris: Organization for Economic Cooperation and Development.

OECD 1997b. "Towards a New Global Age: Challenges and Opportunities", Draft Analytical Report, May 28, Paris.

OECD. 1997c. *The OECD Report on Regulatory Reform, Volume 1: Sectoral Studies*. Paris: Organization for Economic Cooperation and Development.

Orbuch, Paul, and Thomas Singer. 1995. "International Trade, the Environment and the States: An Evolving State-Federal Relationship." *Journal of Environment and Development* 4:121–44.

Oye, Kenneth, and James Maxwell. 1994. "Self-interest and Environmental Management." *Journal of Theoretical Politics* 6(4).

Palmer, Karen, and Dallas Burtraw. 1996. "Electricity Restructuring and Regional Air Pollution, Resources for the Future." *Discussion Paper 96–17–REV2*, July.

Public Citizen. 1995. *NAFTA's Broken Promises*. Washington, D.C.: Public Citizen.

Ramirez de la O, Rogelio. 1996a. "Literature Review of Econometric Models Developed to Assess Environmental Effects of NAFTA." *NAFTA Effects Working Paper No. 4*, April. Montreal: Commission for Environmental Co-operation.

Ramirez de la O, Rogelio. 1996b. "North American Investment Under NAFTA." *NAFTA Effects Working Paper No. 3*, April. Montreal: Commission for Environmental Cooperation.

Rauscher, M. 1994. "On Ecological Dumping." *Oxford Economic Papers* 46 (5):822–40.

Reinhard, S., C. A. Knox Lovell, and G. Thijssen. 1997. "Econometric Estimation of Technical and Environmental Efficiency: An Application to Dutch Dairy Farms." Agricultural Economics Research Institute, The Hague.

Robinson, Sherman et al. 1993. "Agricultural Policies and Migration in a U.S.-Mexico Free Trade Area: A Computable General Equilibrium Analysis." *Journal of Policy Modeling* 15:5–6: 673–701.

Runge, Ford et al. 1997. *Environmentally Sustainable Trade Expansion in the Latin American Region: An Analysis and Empirical Assessment*. Washington, D.C.: World Resources Institute.

Runge, Ford. 1999. "Feedlot Production of Cattle in the United States and Canada." In CEC, *Assessing Environmental Effects of the North American Free Trade Agreement (NAFTA): An Analytic Framework (Phase II) and Issue Studies*. Montreal: Commission for Environmental Co-operation, pp. 183–258.

Rugman, Alan, and John Kirton, with Julie Soloway (eds.). 1998. *Trade and the Environment: Economic, Legal and Policy Perspectives*. Cheltenham, U.K.: Edward Elgar.

Rugman, Alan, John Kirton, and Julie Soloway. 1997a. "Canadian Corporate Strategy in a North American Region." *American Review of Canadian Studies* 27:199–219.

Rugman, Alan, John Kirton, and Julie Soloway. 1997b. "NAFTA, Environmental Regulations, and Canadian Competitiveness." *Journal of World Trade* 31:129–44.

Rugman, Alan, John Kirton and Julie Soloway. 1999. *Environmental Regulations and Corporate Strategy: A NAFTA Perspective*. Oxford: Oxford University Press.

Soloway, Julie. 1997. "Environmental Trade Barriers in NAFTA: The MMT Fuel Additives Controversy." Unpublished paper, Trade, Environment and Competitiveness Project, Centre for International Studies, University of Toronto.

Stabler, C. 1997. "The River of Trade: Through the Heartland of America." *Industry Week*, 20.

Stanford, James O. 1992. "CGE Models of North American Free Trade: A Critique of Methods and Assumptions." Testimony to the United States International Trade Commission Public Hearing on Economy-Wide Modeling of the Economic Implications of Free Trade, Investigation No. 332–317, April.

Steinberg, Richard. 1997. "Trade-Environment Negotiations in the EU, NAFTA and WTO: Regional Trajectories of Rule Development." *American Journal of International Law* 91:231–268.

Tobey, J. 1990. "The Effects of Domestic Environmental Policies on Patterns of World Trade: An Empirical Test." *Kyklos* 43:147–62.

Tsigus, M. D., D. Gray and B. Krissoff. 1999. "Harmonization of Environmental Standards in the Western Hemisphere." Economic Research Service. U.S. Department of Agriculture.

USAID, SRP, CFE. 1998. *Study on Legal and Regulatory Factors Affecting Cross-Border Trade in Electricity Between Mexico and the United States.* Washington, D.C.: USAID.

USDA–Economic Research Service. 1996. *NAFTA: Year two and beyond, A report of the NAFTA Economic Monitoring Task Force.* Washington, D.C.: GPO.

U.S. Federal Highway Administration. 1994. *Public Roads.* Washington, D.C.: GPO.

USITC. 1997. "Cattle and Beef: Impact of the NAFTA and Uruguay Round Agreements on U.S. Trade." *Investigation No. 332–371.* Washington, D.C.: GPO.

USTR. 1997. *Study on the Operation and Effects of the North American Free Trade Agreement.* Washington, D.C.: United States Trade Representative.

Van Beers, C., and J. van den Bergh. 1997. "An Empirical Multi-Country Analysis of the Impact of Environmental Policy on Foreign Trade Flows." *Kyklos* 50(1):29–46.

Vogel, David, and Alan Rugman. 1997. "Environmentally-related Trade Disputes Between the United States and Canada." *American Review of Canadian Studies* 27(2):271–292.

Vogel, David. 1995. *Trading Up: Consumer and Environmental Regulations in a Global Economy.* Cambridge: Harvard University Press.

Wall Street Journal. 1993. September 27, p. A5.

Weintraub, Sidney. 1997. *NAFTA at Three.* Washington, D.C.: Center for International and Strategic Studies.

Weintraub, Sidney, and Jan Galbraith. 1996. "NAFTA's Trade and Effects" in CEC, *Building a Framework for Assessing NAFTA Effects.* Montreal: Commission for Environmental Cooperation.

Williams, G.W., and J. Garcia-Vega. 1996. "Liberalized Trade and the Mexican Livestock, Meat and Feed Industries." Symposium on "NAFTA and Agriculture: Is the Experiment Working?" San Antonio, Texas, November 1–2.

Zeile, William. 1997. "U.S. Intrafirm Trade in Goods." *Survey of Current Business*, February, http://www.bea.doc.gov/bea/ai/o297iid/maintext.htm.

Comment

David van Hoogstraten

Let me begin by noting that I was assistant general counsel of EPA for International Activities at the time that the NAFTA was negotiated and worked extensively negotiating the SPS and TBT chapters. I also worked a bit on dispute resolution and the "Green" provisions for NAFTA,when the Clinton Administration was negotiating the environmental side agreement.

Kirton, in my judgment, has written an excellent paper. It reaches many conclusions that I understand to be the correct ones, to the extent that we can draw definitive conclusions at this point in time since it is still relatively early in the life of all of these NAFTA institutions. I think though that, in a few places in the paper, the documentation is thin, and I wonder where the information comes from. For example, I am skeptical certainly when I read that in Mexico there has been a notable improvement in compliance with environment regulations despite severe reductions in public-sector resources for environmental protection.

Overall, this paper illustrates very well and effectively why those like Kirton who are willing to do the work and delve into the complex functioning of the large number of NAFTA environmental institutions are truly able to call themselves "hopeful incrementalists." Kirton puts himself in that category and I would put myself in that category too.

Let me now make a few specific comments on the paper itself. The paper confirms many of the findings that the EPA and the U.S. Government reached in 1991 and 1992 when the Office of General Counsel went down to Mexico on at least two occasions and assessed Mexican environmental health and safety regulations, standards, and laws. We of course found some gaps. There were areas where standards had not yet been developed, for example. But for the most part what was on the books we concluded was broadly comparable to what existed in the United States. The greatest problem was enforcement. In particular, there was lack of adequate resources to enforce Mexican laws. This is what gave rise to support in the United States for the environmental side agreement and for its focus almost entirely on enforcement of existing environmental laws that were presumed to be comparable among the NAFTA countries. We found, as Kirton suggested, that U.S. multinationals and Mexican multinationals were often manufacturing to a single world standard that provided for a high level of environmental health and safety protection.

We now also see that the emerging NAFTA trilateralism often does converge on state-of-the-art U.S environmental regulations. Kirton does not mention in his paper that the United States performed two voluntary reviews of the likely environmental effects of NAFTA. The first review was prepared by the Bush Administration and released in February 1992. Although it was not a mandated NEPA review, it tried to predict what the environmental impacts of NAFTA would be as well as the mitigating factors involved. It culminated in a series of recommendations to the negotiators about what needed to be in the agreement, in particular in the SPS and TBT chapters, dispute resolution provisions, and the so-called "green" provisions, most of which found their way into the agreement in the end. So I do agree with Kirton that the NAFTA itself is very much an environmentally activist document that evolved in the course of the negotiating process.

I remember in the summer of 1992 that USTR Carla Hills was very concerned about something known in those days as the Dunkel text, which was an earlier draft of the Uruguay Round agreement that was being widely circulated. Her concern was about what she called the invidious comparison between the Dunkel text and the NAFTA text relating in particular to the environmental health and safety aspects of the SPS and TBT agreements. She sent the negotiators back to the Watergate to rework these agreements to make more explicit some of the environmental protections and safeguards which we ended up with in the NAFTA. A number of mainstream environmental membership organizations supported NAFTA. At the conclusion of the NAFTA negotiations, the Clinton Administration performed a second environmental review that played off the first review. It was sent to the Congress at the time the NAFTA was concluded. It sought to assess whether the predictions that had been made in 1991 and 1992 were still valid and what the overall effects of NAFTA on the U.S. environment would be.

I think generally you could say what was predicted was exactly what Kirton has said would be the case, namely that NAFTA would have a weak positive impact on the environment. Nonetheless, we remained very concerned about some particular aspects of how things may have evolved in the wake of NAFTA certainly along the border, where, in the past ten years, there has been a remarkable increase of population particularly on the Mexican side that continues to strain a very delicate and diverse ecosystem. This strain on the ecosystem has not abated, contrary to some of the earlier predictions. One possible explanation is that, under our hazardous-waste bilateral arrangement with Mexico, we continue to ship waste back to the United States. This is of course very advantageous for Mexico and arguably for the regional environment, and it may have encouraged companies either to locate or to remain in the Maquiladora region.

One very significant political fact that is not brought out very well in Kirton's paper was why there was suddenly all this interest in the United States in dealing with the environmental issues raised by NAFTA. He refers to Mexico in 1991 as an advanced OECD economy. I think though that this was not the way most Americans viewed Mexico. Mexico was not yet then a member of the OECD. It is of course today. The concern was that global environmental issues were being viewed primarily from a developed country perspective rather than from a developing country perspective. This has continued to be the Mexican view and is apparently reflected in the continuing inability to reach common positions on environmental issues at the World Trade Organization (WTO) in the Committee on Trade and Environment (CTE). Mexico remains more concerned about issues of market access than about truly taking into account the environmental impacts of trade.

Let me now turn to consider the main environmental institution created by the NAFTA, which is the Committee on Environmental Cooperation (CEC), a trilateral international institution based in Montreal, Canada – the Clinton portion of the environmental side agreement as Kirton calls it. I would suggest that the CEC Article 14–15 process is considerably more important perhaps than Kirton suggests. There are merely factual investigations at issue, and there is no provision for the CEC Secretariat to analyze those facts and to report on their meaning and significance. It is left for the media and other analysts to interpret the facts. Nonetheless, bringing environmental issues into the spotlight of public opinion is potentially of great importance, particularly in a country like Mexico where historically there has been no mechanism to bring this information into the light of day.

Kirton mentions the inability to bring NAFTA trade and environment ministers together. That is true, and it is interesting to note that, in the discussions about moving towards a Free Trade Area for the Americas (FTAA), the United States has been pushing very hard to have a trade and environment ministerial in the hemisphere involving the 34 countries of Central and South America prior to June 1999. Thus far, the United States has been singularly unsuccessful in getting these countries to agree to such a meeting. But the United States has not given up. It may be necessary to bring in fewer than 34 countries. These are difficult issues, yet we must talk about them. I hope very much that we will.

Comment

Alan V. Deardorff

This is an admirable paper. It provides a complete and lucid overview of what has happened to both the environment and to environmental institutions since the NAFTA was initiated in 1994. It covers, to the extent this can be known, not only what has happened, but also what the market participants think has happened. It is a very useful description.

As we all know, a very prominent issue in the debate over the NAFTA was the effect that it would have on the environment. As a result, even though the originally negotiated agreement included substantial environmental provisions and secured the support of a sizable fraction of environmental community, the Clinton administration found it necessary to negotiate the additional environmental side agreement that would set up special institutions for the protection of the environment. In spite of this, many environmentalists continued to oppose the NAFTA. They feared that these provisions were not strong enough to prevent severe degradation of the environment as trade and investment between the United States and Mexico would expand. Despite academic research that suggested that the environmental consequences of the NAFTA would not be either large or harmful—most notably Grossman and Krueger (1993)—opponents of the NAFTA were hardly reassured. Considering the extreme difficulty even for the best researchers of ascertaining with any confidence how an issue like this will pan out, honest observers on both sides of the issue must have felt genuine uncertainty as to whether they were right. In the end, we could not know for sure what the environmental consequences of the NAFTA would be until they had happened.

We are hardly at the end, of course, and it will still be many years before the complete answers can be known. But enough time has passed for it to be useful to take stock, and that is what Kirton does. The evidence, not surprisingly for such a hard and controversial issue, is mixed. But on the whole Kirton's account of events is positive. Evidence does not suggest that major damage has been done by the NAFTA. Furthermore, the institutions created by the NAFTA have for the most part worked rather well. This should be reassuring to all, regardless of their position on NAFTA before it was created.

I have several small concerns about the paper in its current (pre-conference) form, plus two somewhat larger issues that I would like to raise here in my comments. But none of these diminish the major contribution that I think the paper provides in telling us what has happened.

My small questions are mostly those of a trade economist unfamiliar with both the literature and the terminology of environmentalists. The paper includes a large number of often intriguing terms that I do not know the meaning or significance of, such as "baptist-bootlegger" and "green and greedy" coalitions. What is meant by "intervulnerability," and what is a "multilateral nest"? I can imagine what most of these may mean, but I am not at all sure that I am right. I would like to see them defined so that I too can use such colorful language.

Kirton also speaks of the objective of "trade-environment equality," a phrase in which I understand all the words, but for which I cannot construct a meaning. If there is a sense in which trade and the environment could be made equal, I do not know what it is, and I am not sure I would approve of it if I did. To me, neither trade nor environment are ends in themselves, but instead, policies regarding both are means to the end of improving the well-being of the population. If treating trade-environment equality as an end in itself merely means that we should not forget the importance of either one, then of course I agree.

A final small concern is that the paper looks at how trade has expanded by sector, and it asks whether expansion has been predominantly in sectors that do environmental damage, or in sectors that do not. Kirton finds a "mixed picture," but I wonder what he was hoping for. If a sector is environmentally unfriendly, then even if our sole goal were to help the environment, would we want to see more trade there or less? I do not know, and I think the answer would have to depend at least on the direction of that trade, together with the identity of the country in which the industry's production would do the least damage.

Can We Update Grossman-Krueger?

But this brings me to my first main point about the paper. It seems to me that we have, in Grossman and Krueger's (G-K) *ex ante* analysis of NAFTA and the environment, an ideal framework for examining the issue *ex post*. G-K identified several channels through which the NAFTA could potentially affect the environment for good or ill, then attempted to forecast how each of these channels would respond. With hindsight we have the benefit of seeing what actually happened in each of these channels, or at least we should have. Kirton's paper touches on some of these, but it does not give us much hard information to draw upon.

For example, G-K noted the important issue of whether Mexico had a comparative advantage in clean or in dirty industries. If the former, then the expansion of production in Mexico due to NAFTA could be expected to help the environment there, not hurt it (with the corresponding expansion of dirty industries in the U.S. presumably being more effectively controlled by regulation). G-K did their best to anticipate what these industries would be, drawing incidentally on our computable general equilibrium work on NAFTA at Michigan.[1]

But Kirton has the advantage of being able to see which industries did in fact expand and contract after 1994. What he reports is consistent with what G-K anticipated – it was the cleaner industries that have tended to expand in Mexico. But I would have preferred to see some data on this, since to me this issue is of central importance.

Similarly, another issue identified by G-K was the effect that NAFTA would have on the techniques used in production in existing industries. Here too, Kirton reports usefully that techniques of production have been improving in Mexico in terms of their environmental friendliness. He attributed this improvement largely to foreign direct investment (FDI). This too is good to know, but I would have preferred more data to document the change.

A final and widely quoted issue raised by G-K was the per capita income level of Mexico. They argued that pollution tends to increase with economic growth only up to a point, after which as countries become richer they tend to use part of their increased income to clean up the environment. G-K examined this relationship empirically and found the turning point to be at a per capita income of about $5000. Since that was close to the per capita income of Mexico, and since NAFTA was expected to promote economic growth, they concluded that on this account too it would be environmentally friendly.

Of course what happened in the event was not a surge of economic growth in Mexico, but rather a rather severe decline that most of us would attribute not to NAFTA but to the peso crisis. The possible importance of this for the environment is not mentioned in Kirton's paper.

How Do We Race to the Top?

Perhaps the most tantalizing point that Kirton makes, for me, is his remark that worries about a "race to the bottom" have been unfounded. On the contrary, he says, what seems to have happened has been a "race to the top." That is, somehow the increased trade and/or FDI that has been stimulated by the NAFTA has caused producers to scramble to outdo each other in converting to cleaner technologies. I find this fascinating, but I want to know more about it. How exactly has this race to the top come about? And what evidence do we really have that it has been happening. Again, I would like to see more data rather than just anecdotes, but in this case I am even more interested in learning something that anecdotes could easily tell us. *Why* have firms behaved in this way?

I have tried to imagine for myself what the story may be. One possibility is simply that more modern technologies just happen to be both cleaner and cheaper, so that as NAFTA competition has pushed firms to reduce costs, they have adopted technologies that were also cleaner. I am sure this is the case in some instances, but I would be very surprised if it were broadly true. I just cannot believe that we are that lucky.

Another possibility is that Mexican firms seek to compete with U.S. firms by imitation, and that since the U.S. firms are using cleaner technologies in order to satisfy U.S. regulations, the Mexican firms inadvertently adopt cleaner technologies themselves. I am not sure that I would call this a "race" to the top, since the runners are then seemingly unaware of their direction. But I also doubt that it happens this way at all. For it assumes that Mexican firms fail to realize that they can reduce the cost of operating even the new technology by running it dirty, which I would think they almost always could.

The final explanation that I can think of for a race to the top, I rather like. Suppose that Mexican firms have resisted environmental regulations up to now by claiming that it is either impossible or too costly to satisfy them. Now, with the FDI permitted by NAFTA, foreign firms come into Mexico and bring with them the cleaner technologies that they had previously adopted to satisfy U.S. regulations. True, they (the U.S. firms now) could produce even more cheaply in Mexico by disconnecting the scrubbers and other such features of their technologies that make them clean. But they could not credibly resist the Mexican regulations as the Mexican firms had done. And now the Mexican firms cannot do that either. Their own credibility is undermined by the example of the U.S. firms. Again I am not sure I would call this a "race" to the top, but the movement in that direction at least seems plausible.

None of these may be the correct story, of course. Perhaps it is really the NAFTA institutions that have been pushing firms to improve, rather than the competitive forces that the "race to the top" seems to suggest. But if it is really true that Mexican firms have spontaneously been cleaning up their acts since the NAFTA, that seems extremely important. We need to know the extent to which this has occurred, and we need to know why. Only then will we know what to expect also in the future, in this and in other contexts.

Note

[1] See Brown, Deardorff, and Stern (1992).

References

Brown, Drusilla K., Alan V. Deardorff, and Robert M. Stern. 1992. "A North American Free Trade Agreement: Analytical Issues and a Computational Assessment." *The World Economy* 15:11–29.
Grossman, Gene M. and Alan B. Krueger. 1993. "Environmental Impacts of a North American Free Trade Agreement." In Peter M. Garber (ed.), *The Mexico-U.S. Free Trade Agreement.* Cambridge: MIT Press.

CHAPTER 6

The Role of Labor Standards in U.S. Trade Policies

Gary S. Fields

I. Introduction

The issue of labor standards and international trade is of interest to three different parts of the United States government. The Department of Labor aims to "foster, promote, and develop the welfare of the wage earners of the United States, to improve their working conditions, and to advance their opportunities for profitable employment." The Office of the United States Trade Representative is responsible for "developing and coordinating U.S. international trade, commodity, and direct investment policy, and leading or directing negotiations with other countries on such matters." Finally, the Agency for International Development seeks to "help the poor toward a better life" in a variety of ways, among which are helping client countries increase employment and earnings and achieve a more equitable distribution of income.

There are good reasons to address labor standards now. One is moral. The world has not gone far enough to ensure basic human rights in the workplace. It is time to establish these rights for working people everywhere.

A second reason is practical. As became clear during the debates on Fast Track authority in the fall of 1997, the labor community and its allies now have enough political force to be able to make future trade agreements difficult if not impossible to negotiate in the absence of safeguards regarding labor standards. One hears demands for fair trade on many grounds: to prevent our own country from unwarranted competition from competitors, to protect ourselves against trade with others, to avert a lowering of our own labor standards because of a "race to the bottom," and to express our concerns for human beings abroad (Bhagwati, 1995; Leary, 1996). As the trade community seeks to advance its agenda, it would do well to be aware of the concerns of the labor community.

A third reason is analytical. The rich literature on labor standards (see Bhagwati, 1996 and Stern, 1997 for summaries) contains careful theoretical models of the effects of labor standards (Brown, Deardorff, and Stern, 1996;

Casella, 1996; Srinivasan, 1996), cogent arguments for reducing diversity in labor standards (Bhagwati, 1996 for instance, presents philosophical, economic, structural, and political arguments along these lines), as well as good reasons for *not* harmonizing standards (e.g., Bhagwati and Srinivasan, 1996, and Krugman, 1997, discuss the unilateral nature of gains from trade, differences among nations as to what constitutes a reasonable standard, the ability to gain from trade with a country that has different standards from one's own, and the advantages of trading with countries that differ from one's own in endowments or technology). Despite all that has been learned, there is more modeling work to be done.

One big problem in establishing a dialogue in this area stems from the term "labor standards" meaning different things to different people. Clearly, it includes provisions regarding slavery, indentured servitude, forced labor, child labor, and workplace health and safety. But does it also include wages, fringe benefits, work hours, and paid holidays? Not only does the ambiguity of the term impede communication, but perhaps more importantly, it impedes analysis, since an argument based on one conception of "labor standards" may mean something entirely different from another conception. For instance, Bhagwati (1993, 1996) has proposed that the United States pass laws requiring that in order for the goods produced in U.S. subsidiaries overseas to be allowed into the United States without tariffs or other restrictions, corporations would have to adhere to U.S. labor laws in their overseas plants. Bhagwati intended to include due recognition of unions and collective bargaining, adherence to health and safety laws, and absence of child labor but *not* U.S. minimum wages or mandated benefits, but this restriction was not evident. Different conceptions of "labor standards" and "labor rights" are treated below.

The current levels of wages and working conditions are widely perceived as unsatisfactory, and the question arises what to do about wages and other employment-related benefits. The vital role of economic growth is also discussed in what follows.

Finally, it would appear that some of the most serious objections to free or freer trade could be met by taking action to address the concerns of the labor community. Some of these possibilities are taken up at the close.

II. The Defeat of Fast Track: the Labor Standards Lobby as a Force to be Reckoned With

Beginning in 1974, Presidents of the United States had "Fast Track" authority in trade negotiations. This gave the executive branch the authority to negotiate trade agreements, which would then be taken before Congress for ratification under a special set of rules: absolutely no amendments; a maximum of twenty hours of floor debate in each chamber; an up or down vote; legislation to be written by the executive branch; the bypassing of regular congressional committee procedures, such as mark-ups; and a vote within sixty legislative days after the legislation is submitted to the Congress. Each time that Fast Track authority was scheduled to lapse, Congress voted to extend it yet again – that is, until November 1997.

At that time, President Clinton's request for extended Fast Track authority passed the Senate and came up for debate in the House. The House Republicans, led by Speaker Newt Gingrich and Ways and Means Committee Chairman Bill Archer, supported Fast Track. The bill they put forth would have granted the President Fast Track authority but precluded the Administration from negotiating workers rights and environmental conditions in the main body of any trade agreement that might be brought for approval to Congress.

Ironically, these omissions appear to have reinforced the opposition of the overwhelming majority of House Democrats, led by House Minority Leader Dick Gephardt and House Minority Whip David Bonior. When it became clear that the votes were not there to pass Fast Track, the President and the House Republican leadership withdrew the bill. This was, at the time, labeled as the most damaging defeat of the Clinton Presidency.

Opposition to Fast Track came from many quarters: liberal Democrats, organized labor, environmental groups, isolationists, Ralph Nader, Pat Buchanan, and Ross Perot, among others. One argument held that previous trade agreements negotiated under Fast Track had been harmful, a position illustrated by a flyer put out by the AFL-CIO (1997), which said:

> The 'fast track' brought us NAFTA–and look where that got us:
>
> America lost 420,000 jobs as corporations shifted production to Mexico and Canada.
>
> Employers are using the threat of plant closures to drive wages down. People who found new employment after their jobs moved to Mexico took an average pay cut of $4,400.
>
> Air and water pollution along the U.S.-Mexico border has become significantly worse.
>
> Increased agricultural imports and inadequate border inspections have led to an increase in unsafe food in American supermarkets and unsafe trucks on our nation's highways.

(*The New York Times* has called such arguments "Fast-Track Falsities," but that is another matter.)

Others argued that trade agreements need to assure human rights and also protect the environment. In the words of House Democratic leader Dick Gephardt (1997):

> We must use our trade leverage to promote human rights as part of trade deals we sign in the future–I've argued for this as part of any new free trade arrangements. . . . Almost every other country in the world now has virtually unfettered ac-

cess to our market. Our goal is a world of middle-class consumers eager to buy our products – not a world where low-
priced imports flood our market, depressing wages in industries and sectors that have to compete with those imports.
We can't compete against workers who have no rights to
demand a higher wage in return for their hard work and increased productivity. We can't compete with slave labor. . . .
Our goal must be to promote open societies in a freer world
of fairer trade.

As I see it, the Fast Track debate was not about the authority to negotiate
trade agreements at all. Actually, it was a debate over the role of the U.S. in
the global economy and the national response to it. Should the United States
seek to maintain a position of leadership in world affairs? Would expanded
trade and foreign investment do more harm than good for worker, environmental, and public health interests? What ground rules should be set so as to
assure a "fair" distribution of the benefits of trade? Should the United States
enter into new trade agreements without an adequate social contract in place?
How can the threat of international trade to job stability and wage levels be
overcome? Is the average American helped or hurt by the emerging global
economy? And even if the majority gain, what should be done about those
who lose?

Some of these questions are matters of perception. A September 1997 poll
by *Business Week* found that 56% of Americans believe that "expanded trade
leads to a decrease in the number of jobs." Charlene Barshefsky, the U.S.
Trade Representative, has put it graphically: "All the statistics in the world
about export-related jobs don't offset one picture of a closed factory whose
loss is blamed on foreign competition." Of course, perceptions *do* matter, and
people are angry and fearful. President Clinton's own pollster found that 51%
of Americans believe global economic integration "benefits multinational corporations at the expense of average working families."

Debates on these and other questions are far from over. President Clinton
has repeatedly renewed his request for Fast Track authority, but there is no
reason to think he will get it any time soon.

Unless and until Fast Track authority is reinstated, any new trade agreements will be subject to amendment by Congress. This will make it more difficult for United States trade negotiators to reach agreement with other countries
– any piece of any deal struck in multilateral negotiations overseas can be un-
done in Congress, where interest groups will be able to express the full force
of their concerns in all of the standard ways. This was, of course, exactly the
point of opposing Fast Track: to strengthen labor's "voice" in trade agreements.

Those who favor further expansion of international trade would do well to
pay attention to what the opponents of Fast Track are saying, if only because,
at least for now, they have the votes. Failure to heed the voices of opposition

will jeopardize any move toward freer trade and will create an opportunity for protectionists to undo some of the hard-earned gains in the area of trade liberalization. What has been called "free trade without rules" is in jeopardy. Which will win out: "free trade with rules" or protectionism? I think rules are worth a try.

III. What "Labor Standards" Are We Talking About Here?

The International Labour Organisation (ILO) is the world agency charged with the responsibility of seeking the promotion of social justice and internationally recognized human and labor rights. There are now 176 ILO "conventions" setting standards in a wide range of areas for the 174 member countries: respect of fundamental human rights; protection of wages; employment security; working conditions; labor market and social policies; and industrial relations. The ILO's Director-General has said:

> "One of our major responsibilities, therefore, is to ensure that, once adopted, standards are widely ratified by States which solemnly pledge to apply them. We would be falling far short of our claim to universality if we were to insist on the universality of standards as a matter of principle without taking the same trouble to make sure that they were universally implemented." (International Labour Office, 1994)

It is important to recognize that universality is a dream, not a reality. More will be said on this later.

At the other end of the spectrum is the position that nothing should be done that might jeopardize free trade, including attention to labor and environmental matters in trade negotiations. On this view, concerns about labor standards are best dealt with in other fora, not in the WTO or other trade organizations (Srinivasan, 1994 and 1998; Bhagwati, 1998).

Thus far, we have only considered the "more is better" and the "fewer is better" ends of the spectrum. But that is not where the debate is taking place; it is, rather, on intermediate ground.

The U.S. Department of Labor has repeatedly upheld the following list of international labor standards:

- Freedom of association
- The right to organize and bargain collectively
- Prohibition of forced or compulsory labor
- A minimum age for the employment of children
- Guarantee of acceptable working conditions (possibly including maximum hours of work per week, a weekly rest period, limits to work by young persons, a minimum wage, minimum workplace safety and health standards, and elimination of employment discrimination)

For a non-technical explanation of the DOL standards, see Lyle (1991), Brown, Deardorff, and Stern (1995) or U.S. Department of State (1997). These standards have been included in U.S. trade legislation for many years. For example, Section 502 (b) (8) of the 1984 Trade and Tariff Act authorizes the President to withhold recognition under GSP, the Generalized System of Preferences, to a country that "has not taken or is not taking steps to afford internationally recognized worker rights to workers in the country (including any designated zone in that country)." GSP recognition has been withdrawn from some countries, but never because of labor standards violations. The most that can be said is that some countries have reformed their labor practices under threat of losing their GSP preferences (Charnovitz, 1995; Leary, 1996).

Efforts toward establishing a new set of international labor standards are taking place elsewhere. In mid-1994, after a draft agreement concluding the Uruguay Round of the GATT (General Agreement on Tariffs and Trade) had been tabled and was in the process of being ratified by the 124 member nations, the United States and France sought at the last minute to have international labor standards added to the agreement. Other countries refused, noting that they had spent seven years discussing the agreement which led to the World Trade Organization (WTO), that they had negotiated a mutually acceptable alternative, and that therefore they had no interest in reopening talks. The WTO agreement was then ratified as proposed (using, I might add, Fast Track procedures in the United States). In addition, following a Ministerial directive and a mandate from the G-7 countries, the OECD Secretariat was empowered to undertake an analysis of "trade, employment, and internationally recognized labor standards, including basic concepts, empirical evidence in trade and investment patterns, and current mechanisms for promoting higher labor standards worldwide."

The OECD issued its report in May, 1996. It proposed the following set of "core labor standards" for WTO member countries:

- Freedom of association and collective bargaining, i.e., the right of workers to form organizations of their own choice and to negotiate freely their working conditions with their employers.
- Elimination of *exploitative* forms of child labor, such as bonded labor and forms of child labor that put the health and safety of children at serious risk. [Emphasis in the original]
- Prohibition of forced labor, in the form of slavery and compulsory labor.
- Non-discrimination in employment, i.e., the right to equal respect and treatment for all workers.

Other desirable labor standards may perhaps be added to the agenda at a later time.

A number of reasons have been given for why the International Labor Organization (ILO) should be the principal implementing body on labor standards: because ILO conventions are likely to be the basis for international agreement; because the ILO enjoys international legitimacy for its competence in labor issues; because more than 170 countries comprising 98% of the world's people are members; and because the ILO has had considerable success in achieving tripartite agreement on labor matters in many countries. At the same time, it is felt that the ILO can and should be reinvigorated so as to play a greater role in emerging international law (Charnovitz, 1995). Furthermore, the role of the ILO might be supplemented by voluntary agreements on codes of conduct with monitoring done by independent observers.

We are now at the point where the OECD and the ILO designate seven of the 176 ILO conventions as "core labor standards," for which immediate and universal ratification is sought. These include:

- Convention 87 concerning freedom of association and protection of the right to organize and Convention 98 concerning the application of the principles of the right to organize and bargain collectively.
- Conventions 29 and 105 concerning forced or compulsory labor.
- Convention 100 concerning equal remuneration for men and women workers for work of equal value and Convention 111 concerning discrimination in respect of employment and occupation.
- A child labor convention. (ILO Convention 138 is deemed unsatisfactory, because it concerns only a minimum age for admission to employment.)

It is important to note what is *not* included: minimum wages, benefits, and standards regarding hours and other working conditions. They are excluded because the poorer countries of the world cannot afford them – in part, because their labor productivity is so much lower than that of the United States (Golub, 1997). At the forefront of this reconsideration is the ILO itself, whose then-Secretary-General, Michel Hansenne, has said:

> It must be understood that the competition provided by low salaries in some countries is not the consequence of what is commonly called 'social dumping' but is, rather, one of the major symptoms of underdevelopment. Defending human rights cannot be allowed to generate a new form of protectionism. (Hansenne, 1994)

Then-U.S. Secretary of Labor Robert Reich, in a keynote address to a symposium on international labor standards and global economic integration, said:

> It is inappropriate to dictate uniform levels of working hours, minimum wages, benefits, or health and safety standards. The developing countries' insistence that they must grow richer in order to afford American or European labor standards–and that they must trade if they are to grow richer–is essentially correct. (Reich, 1994)

Along the same lines, the International Confederation of Trade Unions, the World Confederation of Labor, and the European Trade Unions Confederation stated that the labor standards to be included in a social clause should be limited to basic human rights labor standards (World Confederation of Labor, 1994). So notwithstanding U.S. law, guaranteeing "acceptable" wages and other working conditions is effectively off the agenda.

As I see it, the seven co-called "core labor standards" have serious problems. First, the core standards, though nice-sounding, simply are not followed. Freedom of association and the right to organize and bargain collectively are routinely violated in many countries. Children are employed around the world. Acceptable working conditions are not guaranteed. Equal remuneration and non-discrimination in employment hold nowhere.

Second, failure to adhere to ILO conventions carries no significant stigma. Cynics might say that it is precisely for that reason that agreement could be reached giving the ILO the responsibility of implementing international labor standards. Supporters of labor standards argue for giving ILO standards some teeth.

Third, even the seven core conventions have not received universal ratification. The number of ratifications ranges from 143 (out of a total of 174 member countries) in the case of the forced labor convention to just 51 acceptances of the convention on minimum age for work. Some individual countries have ratified remarkably few ILO conventions. One of the most extreme is the United States, which has ratified only eleven conventions, just one of which is a "core" labor standard.

Finally, there is the question about what other countries will accept. Opposition to international harmonization of labor standards is widespread. Prime Minister Mahathir of Malaysia, hardly a friend of the West, put it strongly (Mahathir, 1994):

> Western governments openly propose to eliminate the competitive edge of East Asia. The recent proposal for a worldwide minimum wage is a blatant example. Westerners know that this is the sole comparative advantage of the developing countries. All other comparative advantages (technology, capital, rich domestic markets, legal frameworks, management and marketing networks) are with the developed states. It is obvious that the professed concern about workers' welfare is motivated by selfish interest. Sanctimonious pronouncements on humanitarian, democratic and environmental issues are likely to be motivated by a similar selfish desire to put as many obstacles as possible in the way of anyone attempting to catch up and compete with the West.

Other voices of opposition from the developing world include the Rio Group of Latin American nations, the member states of the Association of Southeast Asian Nations (ASEAN), the Latin American ministers to the Summit of the

Americas, and the 113 members of the non-aligned movement, among others. In response, U.S. Trade Representative Charlene Barshefsky has stated, "It is not realistic to suggest that countries will rewrite their domestic labor and environmental laws for the privilege of buying more of our goods."

It is sometimes said that there exists a long-standing consensus on international labor standards, dating back to the Treaty of Versailles in 1919, and since reinforced in the 1944 ILO Declaration of Philadelphia, the 1948 Universal Declaration of Human Rights and, more recently, by the World Social Summit in Copenhagen in 1995 and by the declaration adopted at the Ministerial Conference of the World Trade Organization in Singapore in 1996 (United Nations, 1995; World Trade Organization, 1996; Lee, 1997). I find the idea of consensus quite illusory and would ask these questions. What have the nations of the world agreed to when they pledge to "adhere to internationally-recognized labor standards"? All 176 ILO conventions? The seven core labor standards? Guarantees of minimum wages and working conditions? Some basic rights in the workplace? What agreements have been ratified? What penalties stand to be imposed on violators? Is consensus a symbol or a fact? Unless and until such standards are clarified, we have no consensus whatsoever. Pledging to honor something that is unspecific and ill-defined is no pledge at all.

Let me now try to clarify which international labor standards appear at the present time.

IV. A Process-Based Approach to International Labor Rights

People around the world care about the processes by which goods and services are produced: among them, whether they entail slavery, indentured servitude, or other types of forced labor; whether children are employed as workers; whether job conditions are unhealthy or unsafe; whether the workers are free to join the unions of their choice and to bargain collectively with employers. I have made this point in the past (Fields, 1990, 1995), and others have too (e.g., Portes, 1994; Rodrik, 1996; Compa and Diamond, 1996; Maupain, 1996; Langille, 1998).

This leads me to think in terms of guaranteed *labor rights*, which I define as basic human rights in the workplace (Fields, 1990, 1995). The defining criterion for such rights is that they entail those workplace processes and conditions which are so fundamental that it would be better to have no production at all than to have production using such illegitimate means. I contrast these with *labor standards*, which I define as those workplace processes and conditions that we would aim towards and rather have than not have. The difference, then, is that while some would urge international labor standards to prevent countries from competing with one another on the basis of "illegitimate advantages" (e.g., Wilkinson, 1994; Collingsworth, Goold, and Harvey, 1994;

Sengenberger and Campbell, 1994), my concern is with the establishment of international labor rights aimed at eliminating "illegitimate processes."

If this process-based criterion for establishing international labor rights were to be adopted, it would imply that labor rights would be set so as to apply *universally* to all working people, in rich and poor countries alike. Labor rights would be *guaranteed* by appropriate international agreements. They would be treated as *inviolable rights* (rather than targets, aspirations, statements of principle, or "promotional standards"). By assuring those labor rights that are fundamental, those productive *processes* that are deemed deplorable would be effectively banned.

What are such specific labor rights? Here is a list that I devised a while ago (Fields, 1995):

- No person has the right to enslave another or to cause another to enter into indentured servitude, and every person has the right to freedom from such conditions.
- No person has the right to expose another to unsafe or unhealthy working conditions without the fullest possible information.
- Children have the right not to work long hours whenever their families' financial circumstances allow.
- Every person has the right to freedom of association in the workplace and the right to organize and bargain collectively with employers.

This list of rights can and should be refined. (See, for instance, the discussions by Leary, 1996 and Swinnerton, 1997.) What is essential, though, is that violation of international labor rights be subject to all of the formal and informal sanctions that the international community might impose on human rights violators in this or in any other area.

I realize that there is no chance of such a set of "labor rights" being adopted by the ILO in the current round of negotiations. Still, the time for a debate on such rights may come in the not-too-distant future.

V. What Should Be Done About Wages and Other Employment-Related Benefits?

Ironically, all of this discussion about labor standards and rights leaves out what, to most working people and labor advocates alike, is undoubtedly the most important labor standard of all: the amount people earn for the work they do. Take for example the well-publicized case of workers in Indonesia, where wages are so low that poverty is endemic (e.g., *New York Times*, 1996; Greider, 1997). It has been reported that the 25,000 workers manufacturing sneakers carrying the Nike, Reebok, L.A. Gear, and Adidas brands together earn less than what Michael Jordan receives to endorse Nikes (Harvey, cited in Greider).

On May 12, 1998, Nike announced that it will stop hiring children under the age of 16 and that it will apply U.S. health and safety standards in its overseas plants. Wages, however, will not be raised.

Despite the importance of wages and other non-wage aspects of pay (including employer-provided housing and meals, health care, pensions, paid days off, and so on), wages and other job-related benefits are only tangentially included in current discussions of international labor standards. Does this mean that nothing can be done?

Some would say that wages can and should be raised by strengthening unions. A former United States Secretary of Labor put it thus: "Labor standards, especially the right of workers to organize and bargain collectively, make it possible for third world incomes to be higher and more equitably distributed" (Marshall, 1988). But unions can also be disruptive, and countries with reputations for unstable industrial relations may fail to attract international investors and may even lose their own domestic companies.

Others would say that the essential responsibility for higher wages rests with the State, and that government should therefore legislate minimum wages, provide a wide range of social services, and protect the old, the young, the unemployed, the sick, and anybody else needing help while combating social exclusion wherever it arises. Such "rights" have been institutionalized in a variety of agreements including the Universal Declaration of Human Rights, the International Covenant on Civil and Political Rights, the International Covenant on Economic, Social and Cultural Rights, and the European Social Charter. The problem is that these programs have proven to be unsustainably costly throughout Europe, compelling a re-evaluation of what is to be done with the limited resources available. In the developing countries of the world, a social safety net of this type can only be dreamed of.

What has worked well to facilitate higher wages and improved working conditions is economic growth. Despite the theoretical possibility that growth may be immiserizing, in the great majority of cases, it has proved not to be (Bruno, Ravallion, and Squire, 1998; Fields, forthcoming). To the contrary, when growth has been rapid, in most instances, full employment has been approached and sometimes achieved, real labor earnings have increased, and poverty rates have plummeted (World Bank, 1995). Furthermore, economic growth has enabled countries to afford to expand existing social programs and to institute new ones (United Nations, 1996). For this reason, the world's development banks, most international organizations, and most national development agencies regularly tout economic growth. To the extent that these organizations differ from one another, it is over the issue of whether growth can be counted on to increase living standards automatically or whether actions must be undertaken to overcome what the United Nations Development Program (1996) calls "bad growth."

The positive effects of economic growth can be illustrated by looking at one of the world's great development successes, the Republic of Korea (i.e., South Korea). Until recent months, the Korean economy was growing in per capita terms at more than 7% per year. As a consequence, real per capita GDP grew from $1,528 in 1965 to $13,269 in 1995, both in 1995 PPP dollars.

In the early stages of Korean economic growth, labor market conditions improved via a reduction in unemployment with real wages holding essentially constant. Then, once the Lewis-Fei-Ranis turning point was reached and there was no more surplus labor to be tapped, real earnings rose rapidly among a fully-employed labor force. Labor earnings and per capita growth proceeded apace of one another thereafter.

These gains led to marked improvements in standards of living, leading Korea to a place at or near the top of middle-income countries in such dimensions as life expectancy, infant mortality, access to safe water, adult literacy, and school enrollment rates (United Nations, 1996). The growing richness of the Korean economy permitted the country to introduce new social programs while improving and expanding existing ones. Minimum wages were introduced, employment insurance systems instituted, and social protection systems created.

At the same time, not every aspect of Korea's social situation was rosy. Labor unions were suppressed openly in Korea until 1987; the labor movement has only recently won some but not all of the battles in the struggle for free collective bargaining and freedom of association at the enterprise and federation levels. Wages were repressed, because of worries that increases in wages would undercut comparative advantage and threaten economic growth. (In my view, these worries were misplaced, as indeed is borne out by the continuation of very rapid economic growth in Korea throughout the 1980s and most of the 1990s.) The gap in earnings and job opportunities between men and women remains large, with discrimination against women playing an important role (Bai and Cho, 1995).

Notwithstanding these problems, Korea succeeded in dramatically improving the material well-being of working people. Real wages (adjusted for inflation) grew in Korea at the same rate that per capita Gross National Product did.) This was achieved not by being forced under international pressure to adhere to externally-set labor standards and not by setting an ambitious domestic labor code with which companies had to comply. Nor were their successes brought about by cracking down on unions, placing limits on wages, or disempowering women in the labor market. The lives of working people in Korea were improved by economic growth, which tightened the labor market to the point where full employment was achieved and maintained and wages and working conditions were pulled up by the rapidly-growing demand for labor. Employers raised wages not because the government told them to, not because the unions told them to, but because the *market* told them to – those that wanted to retain existing workers or attract additional ones had to pay more to compete in the labor market, while those that did not lost the workers they had, often going out of business in the process – a process institutionalized in Korea's annual "spring offensive," in which wage rates are renegotiated throughout the economy.

Korea's labor market success story is one that has been duplicated in kind in the other rapidly-growing economies of East and Southeast Asia (Fields,

1995; World Bank, 1995; Ahuja et al., 1997). The achievement of full employment, rapidly-rising real wages, improvements in the types of jobs that people are in, falling rates of poverty – all of these have happened because of the success of the East Asian types of growth models. (Note the use of the plural, "models." East Asian countries did not all follow the same growth model. Nonetheless, the different models they followed all succeeded.) Countries in other parts of the world would do well to study the elements that have made for success in East Asia, along with the elements that have now surfaced and have made for problems.

Korea's success also led to a quest for recognition of the country's attainment of advanced country status. Korea zealously sought admission to the OECD, which was granted in 1996. And in doing so, the country had to adhere to the labor standards set by the OECD. As the head of the Korean Industrial Relations Reform Commission told me: "If that's what they say we have to do to be regarded as one of the world's leading countries, then we'll have to do it."

The East Asian experience suggests a course for other countries to follow to improve conditions for workers: grow, using labor intensively in the early stages, producing world-class products. This takes us back to trade policy. In order for overseas workers to benefit from export-led growth, their products must be able to be sold in richer countries than their own. Free trade permits this, which is why an open trading environment is so important to workers elsewhere.

Meanwhile, what about workers in the United States and other advanced countries? We turn now to that.

VI. Getting the Labor Community to Buy Into Freer Trade

In my view, two things need to happen if the labor community is going to get behind freer trade, or at least not oppose it as strenuously in the future as they have in the past. First, they must be convinced that freer trade is good for most of their country's people. And second, they must be convinced that those who are hurt will not be abandoned.

The Generalized Benefits of Trade

Starting with the evaluation issue, the trade community for the most part analyzes trade policy in terms of the economic well-being of a *country*. This simply does not resonate with ordinary people. (Non-trade economists are not ordinary people, but I have not found a great deal of resonance there either.) The fact that the *country* may be better off does not matter nearly as much as whether *people themselves* (or in the case of policy analysts and advocates, the people they care most about) are better off. If working people believe that freer trade jeopardizes their economic position, they will oppose it. And that is exactly where many Americans, perhaps the majority, are in their thinking right now: they believe that they will be worse off under freer trade than they are at present.

Some trade economists' next line of argument is the compensation principle, viz., the idea that the winners from free trade could, in principle, compensate the losers, and everyone would be better off. This too is unconvincing, for two reasons.

First, the compensation principle says that the winners *can* compensate the losers, not that the winners *will* compensate the losers. If I lose from a policy action, I am not likely to be happy. If I lose from a policy action, if I know that there are winners who together gained more than I lost, and if I know that the winners *will not* compensate me, I may be furious. For the compensation principle to have any bite, there must be compensation in fact, not compensation in principle. This is hardly a new point, but still it bears repeating.

The second objection to the compensation principle is a more technical one, and it arises even if compensation is paid. The point is made in the literature on psychology and economics that people do not treat consumption gains symmetrically with income losses. Under most conceptions, an individual whose consumption starts at c^0, rises to c^1, then reverts to c^0 would end up with the same utility level that s/he started with. But an apparent anomaly is that the initial gain in going from c^0 to c^1 is outweighed by the loss in falling from c^1 to c^0, leaving individuals in a *worse* position than they started in (Loewenstein and Prelec, 1992). I do not know how important this possibility may prove to be in practice, but I suspect that it may be quite consequential.

Helping the Losers

As a practical political matter, it appears that the more that social programs reduce the number of losers and the magnitude of their losses, the more willing the labor community will be to buy into freer trade. I briefly present three formulations, not because I fully endorse them but because I believe that they need to be heard.

1. The Council on Foreign Relations has just completed a study of the impact of international trade (Feketekuty and Stokes, 1998). They concluded that while trade enriches the nation, "the living standard of the most typical income earner in the very middle of the income distribution *may not* rise" and that "global integration *may not* benefit middle-class citizens as a group." The result, the study concluded, is that "further global integration, *by itself, may not* be democratically supported." [Emphasis added.] Complementary programs are needed.

2. The AFL-CIO (1997) opposes a variety of free trade initiatives including the expansion of NAFTA to a proposed Free Trade Area of the Americas and Fast Track. They believe that the proposed arrangements "lack the rules and standards we need to protect our jobs, our wages, our environment and our safety" and call for:

- Rethinking trade and investment rules.
- Protecting core labor rights and environmental standards by writing them into the body of any new trade agreement as well as into any Fast Track legislation.
- Putting substantial resources into worker training and adjustment assistance.

Such measures, they argue, "will send the clearest possible message, both to our own negotiators and to our trading partners, that we are ready and willing to chart a new path in the global economy and that no country should be able to gain a competitive advantage by sacrificing its environment and its work force." (Trumka, 1997).

3. Robert Kuttner (1997) calls for a "social market," the major components of which would be:

- Full employment
- Stronger unions
- Wage subsidy and social income
- Education and training
- Gain-sharing commitments
- Responsible corporations

In his view, "These measures, on balance, would not hamper the vaunted 'flexibility' of the idealized labor market; they would certainly limit business's ability to pursue a low road, but on balance the result would be a more adaptable and dynamic labor force."

These three formulations give a flavor of the concerns of the labor community. It is not that free trade is opposed unconditionally. Rather, it is opposed in the absence of measures aimed at protecting labor standards, especially for the economically vulnerable.

VII. An Outline of a Program

What might be done to strengthen labor standards in the U.S. and abroad? Although there is no *logical* reason to link labor standards (or environmental standards or other standards) to international trade, there certainly are *political* reasons for supporters of such standards to link them to whatever they can, be it trade agreements, replenishment of commitments to international agencies, or anything else (Freeman, 1994; Krueger, 1996).

Here, then, are some possible ways to strengthen international labor rights for the twenty-first century:

- There needs to be widespread agreement on international labor rights, defined as basic human rights in the workplace. Working people everywhere, regardless of where they live or the kind of work they do, require assurances of workplace rights and protections against the most egregious forms of abuse. Violation of these rights must be treated harshly, both in the court of international public opinion and through direct penalties.

- Agreements on international labor rights should not extend to wages, working conditions, and other job-related benefits. Although the importance of improvements in these areas is undeniable, it would be a mistake to try to set such standards through international channels. To avoid jeopardizing possible progress in other areas, consideration should be given to deleting the clause on a "guarantee of acceptable working conditions" from the list of "international labor standards" promulgated by the U.S. Department of Labor and incorporated into U.S. trade law.

- Adhering to international labor rights should be rewarded, even through trade measures. For instance, the European Commission has proposed that additional trade access be granted to countries which have been certified as respecting international standards on free association, child labor, slavery, bonded labor, and prison labor, thus demonstrating "the essential fairness of open trade principles" (Brittan, 1995).

- Economic growth has brought about improvement in the living conditions of workers in the great majority of cases. When living conditions have not improved, it is usually because economic growth has not taken place. Moreover, countries that have participated actively in the world economy have grown faster and progressed more rapidly than those that have not. More economic growth and increased trade are therefore desirable, not only for their own sake but for the contribution they can make to raising people's standards of living.

- Fulfillment of international labor rights is of concern to many consumers in the economically advanced countries. One way of enabling developed country consumers to exercise their preferences for goods made according to productive processes that they find acceptable is to establish product labeling (Freeman, 1994; The Economist, 1995; Rodrik, 1996). Assuming that it is possible to create certifying agencies in which developed-country consumers have confidence and to devise counterfeit-proof labels, consumers who wish to purchase goods that are certified to have been produced using processes judged to be acceptable would be free to do so by looking for labels such as "No Sweat," "Rugmark," or "Child Labor Free."

- Corporate codes of conduct may also be established, either legislatively or through voluntary agreement. Reference has already been made to Bhagwati's proposal to grant unrestricted importing of goods produced in U.S. subsidiaries overseas only when these companies have adhered to U.S. labor laws in their overseas plants. The OECD (1996) recognizes product labeling and demands for multinational enterprises to avoid dealings with exploitative producers as possible means of action. Aggarwal (1995) notes that corporate codes of conduct have been adopted by individual U.S.-based multinational enterprises including Levi Strauss, Liz Claiborne, Nike, Reebok, Sears, Timberland, and Walmart. The Clinton administration has proposed five "model business principles" for U.S. corporations doing business around the world; in April 1997, such a Workplace Code of Conduct was agreed to in the apparel industry. For details, see Greenfield (1997). Finally, Duke University has just announced a code to prevent apparel bearing the university's name from being made in sweatshops, a code likely to be adopted by 160 other American universities (Greenhouse, 1998).

- Part of the demand for international labor rights is coming from citizens of one country telling those in another what it is we want them to do. To translate our desires into effective demand, we may need to pay them to take actions consonant with our interests (Ehrenberg, 1994; Bhagwati, 1998; Srinivasan, 1998).
- From a political point of view, those who lose their jobs because of freer trade cannot simply be neglected. They require cash assistance (which may be paid in the form of extended unemployment insurance benefits or in the form of wage insurance), retraining allowances, job search and placement assistance, counseling, and relocation assistance – that is, an "active labor market policy" (Katz, 1994; Ehrenberg, 1994; World Bank, 1995; Burtless et al., 1998; Schoepfle, 1998). Benefits to American workers who have been displaced from companies that have shut down their plants and moved production to Mexico or Canada are provided under NAFTA-TAA. Between January 1994 and December 1996, the total number of U.S. workers who were certified as eligible for such benefits was 90,000. Of these, only 6,000 actually used the benefits (the rest having found employment). NAFTA supporters conclude that the job displacement effect of the agreement was negligible, while NAFTA critics say that such figures show the inadequacy of the current trade adjustment assistance program. The Clinton Administration has called for extending TAA benefits to *all* workers displaced from companies that have shifted production to another country (Economic Report of the President, 1998). Those who fall into poverty might also benefit from an expansion of the Earned Income Tax Credit.

VIII. Conclusions

The following are the principal points that have been reached in this paper:
- Absent an agreement on international labor standards, a stalemate is quite possible. On the one hand, it might not be possible to push trade liberalization forward, as most in the trade community want. On the

other hand, the current world trading environment will not be rolled back, as some in the labor movement want.

- The international labor community has now coalesced around a set of "core labor standards" that deal with freedom of association and the right to organize and bargain collectively, forced or compulsory labor, equal remuneration for men and women and non-discrimination in employment, and child labor. Minimum wages, maximum hours of work, and fixing other conditions of employment are *not* being called for at the present time. It would be well for those in the trade community to know what is and is not on labor's agenda. If these core labor standards or ones like them were to be linked to international trade, opposition to trade agreements might be overcome, enabling international trade to be helped.

- The alternative to "core labor standards" would be a set of "international labor rights," defined by the criterion that it would be better to have no production at all than to have production using such "illegitimate means." Although such discussions are not prominent in international debate at the present time, they deserve discussion in the future.

- Wages, employment conditions, and other social benefits have improved dramatically for workers living in countries that have achieved rapid export-led economic growth. Of course, problems remain, which is precisely why those who have an interest in workers overseas seek to harness the strengths of both trade and labor standards to improve conditions for these groups.

- Although freer trade might be good on the whole for the United States, it is not good for all workers in the United States. The small number of people who are hurt a lot by freer trade have every reason to be much more vociferous in expressing their opposition to freer trade than are the large numbers who benefit relatively a little. Policies can be enacted that will mollify the opposition, and they deserve serious consideration. Absent such measures, the agenda of the trade community is seriously jeopardized.

Note

This paper was written while I was a Visiting Scholar at the Russell Sage Foundation. The foundation's financial support is gratefully acknowledged. I appreciate helpful discussions with Jagdish Bhagwati, Alessandra Casella, Allen Hunter, Lawrence Katz, Robert Merton, Robert Stern, and T. N. Srinivasan and the insightful comments of the conference discussants, Dani Rodrik and Pharis Harvey.

References

AFL-CIO. 1997. "Why the Fast Track is the Wrong Track." http://www.aflcio.org/ stopfasttrack/getthe.htm.

Aggarwal, Mita. 1995. "International Trade, Labor Standards, and Labor Market Conditions: An Evaluation of the Linkages." United States International Trade Commission, Office of Economics Working Paper No. 95–06–C, June.

Ahuja, Vinod et al. 1997. *Everyone's Miracle?: Revisiting Poverty and Inequality in East Asia*. Washington, D.C.: World Bank.

Bhagwati, Jagdish. 1993. "American Rules, Mexican Jobs." *New York Times*, March 24.

Bhagwati, Jagdish. 1995. "Trade Liberalisation and 'Fair Trade' Demands: Addressing the Environmental and Labour Standards Issues." *The World Economy*.

Bhagwati, Jagdish. 1996. "The Demands to Reduce Domestic Diversity Among Trading Nations." In Jagdish Bhagwati and Robert Hudec (eds.), *Fair Trade and Harmonization: Prerequisites for Free Trade?*, Volume 1. Cambridge: MIT Press.

Bhagwati, Jagdish. 1998. "Trade Policy and Human Rights." In Jagdish Bhagwati and Matthias Hirsch (eds.), *The Uruguay Round and Beyond: Essays in Honor of Arthur Dunkel*. Ann Arbor: University of Michigan Press.

Bhagwati, Jagdish, and Robert Hudec (eds.). 1996. *Fair Trade and Harmonization: Prerequisites for Free Trade?* Cambridge: MIT Press.

Bhagwati, Jagdish, and T. N. Srinivasan. 1996. "Trade and the Environment: Does Environmental Diversity Detract from the Case for Free Trade?", in Jagdish Bhagwati and Robert Hudec (eds.), *Fair Trade and Harmonization: Prerequisites for Free Trade?*, Volume 1. Cambridge: MIT Press.

Brittan, Sir Leon. 1995. "How to Make Trade Liberalisation Popular." *The World Economy*.

Brown, Drusilla K., Alan V. Deardorff, and Robert M. Stern. 1996. "International Labor Standards and Trade: A Theoretical Analysis." In Jagdish Bhagwati and Robert Hudec (eds.), *Fair Trade and Harmonization: Prerequisites for Free Trade?*, Volume 1. Cambridge: MIT Press.

Bruno, Michael, Martin Ravallion, and Lyn Squire. 1998. "Equity and Growth in Developing Countries: Old and New Perspectives on the Policy Issues." In Vito Tanzi and Ke-Young Chu (eds.), *Income Distribution and High-Quality Growth*. Cambridge: MIT Press.

Burtless, Gary, Robert Z. Lawrence, Robert E. Litan, and Robert Shapiro. 1998. *Globaphobia*. Washington, D.C.: Brookings Institution.

Casella, Alessandra. 1996. "Free Trade and Evolving Standards." In Jagdish Bhagwati and Robert Hudec (eds.), *Fair Trade and Harmonization: Prerequisites for Free Trade?*. Volume 1. Cambridge: MIT Press.

Charnovitz, Steve. 1995. "Governing the Global Economy." *The Washington Quarterly*, Summer.

Collingsworth, Terry, J. William Goold, and Pharis J. Harvey. 1994. "Time for a New Global Deal." *Foreign Affairs*, January-February.

Compa, Lance A., and Stephen F. Diamond. 1996. *Human Rights, Labor Rights, and International Trade*. Philadelphia: University of Pennsylvania Press.

"Consciences and Consequences." *The Economist*, June 3, 1995, p. 13.

Council of Economic Advisers. 1998. *Economic Report of the President*. Washington, D.C.: U.S. Government Printing Office.

Ehrenberg, Ronald G. 1994. *Labor Markets and Integrating National Economies*. Washington, D.C.: Brookings Institution.

Feketekuty, Geza and Bruce Stokes. 1998. *Trade Strategies for a New Era*. New York: Council on Foreign Relations.

Fields, Gary S. 1990. "Labor Standards, Economic Development, and International Trade." In Stephen Herzenberg and Jorge Pérez-López (eds.), *Labor Standards and Development in the Global Economy*. Washington, D.C.: U.S. Department of Labor.

Fields, Gary S. 1995. *Trade and Labour Standards: A Review of the Issues*. Paris: OECD.

Fields, Gary S. *Distribution and Development: A New Look at the Developing World*, forthcoming.

Freeman, Richard. 1994. "A Hard-Headed Look at Labor Standards." In U.S. Department of Labor, *International Labor Standards and Global Economic Integration*. Washington, D.C.: Bureau of International Labor Affairs.

Gephardt, Richard A. 1997. "Fairer Trade, Freer People." Address to the Detroit Economic Club, May 27.

Golub, Stephen S. 1997. "Are International Labor Standards Needed to Prevent Social Dumping?" *Finance and Development*, December.

Greenfield, Victoria. 1997. "Promoting Worker Rights in Developing Countries: U.S. Policies and Their Rationale." Congressional Budget Office, April.

Greenhouse, Steven. 1998. "Duke to Adopt a Code to Prevent Apparel From Being Made in Sweatshops." *The New York Times*, Sunday, March 8, p. 16.

Greider, William. 1997. "Why the Global Economy Needs Worker Rights." *Working USA*, May/June.

Hansenne, Michel. 1994. "The New Paths Towards Social Justice." *World of Work*, No. 8.

International Labour Office. 1994. *Defending Values, Promoting Change*. Geneva: ILO.

Katz, Lawrence F. 1994. "Active Labor Market Policies to Expand Employment and Opportunity." In Federal Reserve Bank of Kansas City, *Reducing Unemployment: Current Issues and Policies Options*, August.

Krueger, Alan. 1996. "Observations on International Labor Standards and Trade." Paper presented at the Annual Bank Conference on Development Economics, April.

Krugman, Paul. 1997. "What Should Trade Negotiators Negotiate About?." *Journal of Economic Literature*, March.

Kuttner, Robert. 1997. "The Limits of Labor Markets." *Challenge*, May-June.

Langille, Brian A. 1998. "Eight Ways to Think About International Labour Standards." *Journal of World Trade*.

Leary, Virginia A. 1996. "Workers' Rights and International Trade: The Social Clause (GATT, ILO, NAFTA, U.S. Laws)." In Jagdish Bhagwati and Robert Hudec (eds.), *Fair Trade and Harmonization: Prerequisites for Free Trade?*, Volume 2. Cambridge: MIT Press.

Lee, Eddy. 1997. "Globalization and Labour Standards: A Review of Issues." *International Labour Review*, Summer.

Loewenstein, George, and Drazen Prelec. 1992. "Anomalies in Intertemporal Choice: Evidence and an Interpretation." In George Loewenstein and Jon Elster (eds.), *Choice Over Time*. New York: Russell Sage Foundation.

Lustig, Nora Claudia. 1997. "NAFTA: Setting the Record Straight." Brookings Policy Brief No. 20.

Lyle, Faye. 1991. "Worker Rights in U.S. Policy." *Foreign Labor Trends* 91–154. Washington, D.C.: U.S. Department of Labor, Bureau of International Labor Affairs.

Mahathir, Mohamad. 1994. "East Asia Will Find Its Own Roads to Democracy." *International Herald Tribune*, May 17, p. 6.

Marshall, F. Ray. 1988. "Linking Workers' Rights and Trade." Paper presented to the International Metalworkers Federal Central Committee Meeting, Madrid, June.

Maupain, Francis. 1996. "La Protection Internationale des Travailleurs et la Libéralisation du Commerce Mondial: Un Lien ou Un Frein?." *Revue Generale de Droit International Public*, Jan/Feb.

Organisation for Economic Co-operation and Development. 1996. *Trade, Employment and Labour Standards: A Study of Core Workers' Rights and International Trade*. Paris: OECD.

Portes, Alejandro. 1994. "By-Passing the Rules: The Dialectics of Labour Standards and Informalization in Less Developed Countries." In Werner Sengenberger and Duncan Campbell (eds.), *International Labor Standards and Economic Interdependence*. Geneva: International Institute for Labour Studies.

Reich, Robert. 1994. "Keynote Address." In U.S. Department of Labor, *International Labor Standards and Global Economic Integration*. Washington, D.C.: Bureau of International Labor Affairs.

Rodrik, Dani. 1996. "Labor Standards in International Trade: Do They Matter and What Do We Do About Them?" in Robert Lawrence et al., *Emerging Agenda for Global Trade: High Stakes for Developing Countries*. Washington, D.C.: Overseas Development Council, Policy Essay No. 20.

Schoepfle, Greg. 1998. "U.S. Trade Adjustment Assistance Policies." Chapter 4 above.

Sengenberger, Werner, and Duncan Campbell (eds.). *International Labour Standards and Economic Interdependence*. Geneva: International Institute for Labour Studies.

Srinivasan, T. N. 1994. "International Labor Standards Once Again." In U.S. Department of Labor, *International Labor Standards and Global Economic Integration*. Washington, D.C.: Bureau of International Labor Affairs.

Srinivasan, T. N. 1996. "International Trade and Labour Standards from an Economic Perspective." In P. van Dijck and G. Faber (eds.), *Challenges to the New World Trade Organization*. Amsterdam: Kluwer Law International.

Srinivasan, T. N. 1998. "Trade and Human Rights." In Alan Deardorff and Robert Stern (eds.), *Representation of Constituent Interests in the Design and Implementation of U.S. Trade Policies*. Ann Arbor: University of Michigan Press, forthcoming.

Stern, Robert M. 1997. "Issues of Trade and International Labor Standards in the WTO System." *Joint U.S.-Korea Academic Studies*, Volume 7.

Swinnerton, Kenneth A. 1997. "An Essay on Economic Efficiency and Core Labour Standards." *The World Economy*, January.

Trumka, Richard L. 1997. "Testimony of Richard L. Trumka, Secretary-Treasurer, AFL-CIO, Before the Senate Committee on Finance on Renewal of Fast

Track Trade Negotiation Authority." http://www.aflcio.org/stopfasttrack/ trumka.htm, June 3.

United Nations. 1995. *World Summit for Social Development: The Copenhagen Declaration and Programme of Action.* New York: United Nations.

United Nations. 1996. *Human Development Report.* New York: Oxford University Press.

U.S. Department of Labor. 1994. *International Labor Standards and Global Economic Integration.* Washington, D.C.: Bureau of International Labor Affairs.

U.S. Department of State. 1997. *Country Reports on Human Rights Practices for 1996.* January 30, Appendix B. Available at http://www.state.gov/www/issues/ human_rights/1996_hrp_report/appendb/html.

Wilkinson, Frank. 1994. "Equality, Efficiency, and Economic Progress: the Case for Universally Applied Equitable Standards for Wages and Conditions of Work." In Werner Sengenberger and Duncan Campbell (eds.), *Creating Economic Opportunities: the Role of Labour Standards and Labour Institutions in Industrial Restructuring.* Geneva: International Institute for Labour Studies.

World Bank. 1995. *World Development Report.*

World Confederation of Labor. 1994. *The Social Dimension of International Trade: Joint Statement by World and European Trade Unions Confederations.* ICFTU, WCLL and ETUC 43/94.

World Trade Organization. 1996. *Singapore Ministerial Declaration.* Geneva: WT/MIN, December.

Comment

Pharis Harvey

It is a pleasure to respond to Fields's thought-provoking paper on the role of labor standards in U.S. trade policy. While we have substantial differences as well as many points of agreement, his paper provides a good launching pad for a necessary debate, not just among academics and activists but among those responsible for U.S. economic policies, including trade.

To start, I agree with Fields on the moral, practical and analytical reasons for this debate. A world in which one billion people, nearly one third of the global workforce, are unemployed or severely underemployed cannot simply allow market mechanisms to determine who survives and thrives. Market mechanisms alone, with this level of surplus labor, would drive wages to starvation levels. A world in which 250 million children are deprived of childhood and education in order to enter the workforce prematurely is morally, as well as economically, unsustainable. If market forces are, as anecdotal evidence suggests, increasing the disparity between the haves and have-nots and pressuring more children into the labor market, then other forces–moral, political, administrative, legal– have to be put in place as counterweights.

Practically, trade expansion at the expense of domestic economic health is not politically feasible. The Fast Track debate made clear that a constellation of forces does not exist in the United States to push forward the agenda of international trading firms at the expense of local communities, environmental degradation or sizable job losses. I would express the conundrum differently however, not as Fields does in seeing the "trade community" needing to be aware of the concerns of the "labor community," but the trade community needing to recognize that labor must be a part of the trade community itself.

I would like to focus my comments on three aspects of his paper: the definition and scope of international labor standards to be considered within the world of trade; the nature and scope of trade measures that might be used to urge compliance with these standards; and the role of economic growth in advancing labor rights and standards.

First, it is important that we arrive at some common language about international labor rights or standards. Fields is right: different definitions, involving differing elements, have enabled a degree of confusion to be inserted into the debate. I would assert that much of this confusion has been sown deliberately by those who oppose any labor rights-trade linkage. But be that as it may, it will help the debate if we are all speaking about the same general issues when we examine labor's linkage to trade.

It seems to me that, by beginning with the language of the U.S. Trade Act of 1974 as amended in 1984 to include certain labor standards in the Generalized System of Preferences, Fields has inadvertently introduced a "red herring." That law, the first to set out a definition of labor rights that Beneficiary Developing Countries were obligated to be taking steps to enact and enforce, set out three rights that were considered absolute—freedom of association, the right of collective bargaining, and a prohibition of forced labor. Child labor was referenced only by requiring countries to have established a minimum age for employment, and the fifth area, "acceptable conditions of work with respect to wages, hours of work, and occupational safety and health" was made contingent on level of development. In fact, no complaint has ever been brought on the basis of this fifth area of concern, except as supporting evidence for the effect of failures in the enforcement of one or more of the first three. This means that we do not have to start from a fight against what Fields considers standards versus rights, or an uncertain or shifting lexicon of standards.

Further, no labor organization has proposed that WTO-related labor standards include wages, hours or health and safety. The only addition that has been proposed to the three rights in the GSP law, plus child labor limitations, is non-discrimination in employment. And that constellation of rights tracks exactly the so-called "core labor standards" that are being developed in a solemn declaration at the ILO this year.

Thus, when it comes to content, as against terminology, there is a very wide range of consensus about what labor standards or rights ought to be included. I would simply suggest that, since the ILO has adopted the terminology for these rights as "core labor standards," we utilize that term in this debate.

The only caveat that I have about this limited definition is related to those trade areas where common levels of development make it possible to mesh a broader range of labor standards involving social and job security, benefits and retirement benefits, such as are contained in the European Union's social charter. This broader range of standards becomes important primarily in the context of free labor mobility, as is the case in Europe. In the Mercosur negotiations, a similar package of broader social measures have been adopted as part of the aspiration expressed in that document to move toward labor mobility. But where major movements of labor are not anticipated or desired, such consolidation of standards has not been on the table.

The second area of interest in Fields's paper is the discussion of what kinds of measures might be taken up to defend these core labor standards, or in his terms, these inviolable human rights of workers. Here I find his discussion somewhat lacking. He seems to be saying that by guaranteeing the core labor standards by international agreement, "those productive processes that are deemed deplorable would be effectively banned." By whom? And to what effect? Does he really seek to have an international authority with the power to effectively ban production under terms that contravene these norms? He suggests that "implementation" of these labor rights should be the work of the ILO. Does that suggest that he proposes giving such authority to ban production to the ILO? And, if so, with what enforcement measures to assure compliance? Fields correctly notes the low level of compliance today with these rights by governments all over the world. What would be the implication in international law or trade for the handling of goods made by what he calls "illegitimate processes."

If, as it would appear, he is proposing that banning the production of goods by such "illegitimate processes" automatically converts goods made under these terms into contraband that can be stopped at the border of an importing state, then he has carved out a position that is even more extreme than mine. But, if, on the other hand, he is only considering a symbolic banning of production and the use of international moral suasion to enforce such a ban, then he is left with the current, patently unworkable system.

I would prefer that we look at measures that combine both enticements and punishments to bring states into better compliance with these process norms, or international labor rights. Such a grouping of measures might include an absolute ban in trade of goods made under certain conditions, slavery or bonded labor, for example, whether by children or adults. The other rights, such as freedom of association or collective bargaining, might, if violated in serious ways that remain uncorrected by government action, trigger trade counter measures along the lines of actions that are justified for other unfair trade practices. Whether discrimination falls in this category is a matter of considerably more discussion than I can address here, for it is an area of cultural relativity that makes for more shades of gray than others. But for gross levels of discrimination, as determined by an objective international body like the ILO's committee of experts or a panel similar in process to the Freedom of Association Committee, there might be a legitimizing of trade countermeasures by a country or group of countries which can show injury as a result of these practices.

For matters of health and safety, while I agree on the definition in his paper, in actual practice there are many levels of disputed fact and interpretation that render the absolute less so. For this area, as for discrimination, it might be more productive to consider a range of positive incentives for improvement in performance, which could range from trade benefits to eased levels of credit at the multilateral development banks to development assistance. Trade sanctions would be needed only as a last resort.

The final concern I want to mention is Fields's unwarranted reliance on "economic growth" as the primary vehicle for improvement in observation of labor rights. It is true that, where development does not take place, it is difficult if not impossible to press for improved rights, especially those rights that have an economic cost attached. But economic growth in and of itself guarantees very little. One only has to look at the ongoing plight of America's underclass, migrant workers, petty farmers and ghetto-bound minorities, to recognize that the lifting tide has left too many boats anchored to the bottom on a short rope. Only when economic growth is harnessed to policies that work for distribution of benefits – whether by recognition of collective bargaining rights, minimum wage protections, or employment security measures – does economic growth guarantee the improvement in labor rights protection.

The example drawn of Korea is one on which we have many disagreements. As one who was intimately engaged in the struggle of Korean workers for more than twenty years, I am painfully aware that economic statistics produced year after year by successive Korean governments to demonstrate that wages were tracking productivity gains, were essentially propaganda documents, and that when, in 1987, workers finally achieved the *de facto* right to organize and form unions, they achieved advances in wages that were long overdue, advances that had not been gained by any automatic mechanism of economic growth, but by hard, political struggle and the deaths or imprisonment of thousands of valiant workers. It is important sometimes for economists to look up from their pages of statistics to see the concrete lives and struggles that seem only in retrospect to have been the product of some automatic market mechanism.[1]

That said, I nevertheless found much in Fields's paper to agree with. In particular I am intrigued by his suggestion that the GATT/WTO be modified to include a "social safeguards" clause that would specify that "no nation has to maintain free trade with a country or in a specific product if doing so would require violating a widely held ethical standard or social preference at home." Such a clause, which would of course be subject as all trade provisions are, to possibilities of abuse, would nevertheless respond to a very large percentage of the questions that are currently being raised about free trade by social critics, labor movements and consumers. It is an idea that bears developing.

Note

[1] Editors' note: Gary Fields has pointed out to us that the Korean governments not only published the wage and productivity statistics but also made available to him and others the raw micro data on the basis of which Fields made his calculations and claim that wages tracked productivity gains.

Comment

Dani Rodrik

This is a refreshing and honest paper on a controversial topic. Fields argues that maintaining a sharp distinction between trade policy and labor standards is no longer possible. He also advocates that we distinguish between labor *rights* and labor *standards*. I agree with both points. In these comments, I want to elaborate on some of the themes in the paper.

First, let us be clear about the role of labor standards (or labor rights) in raising workers' earnings. Economists tend to argue that wages are determined primarily by labor productivity, while labor advocates emphasize the role of labor legislation and collective bargaining rights. Table 6.1 displays some regressions which speak to this issue. As column (1) shows, labor productivity is closely linked to wages. In fact, about 90 percent of cross-national variation in wages is explained by productivity. But the other two columns show that labor standards and civil liberties matter too. An index of basic worker rights (based on the number of ratifications for six of the core ILO labor standards) enters with a positive sign in the wage equation and is significant at the 90 percent level (column 2). A broader index of civil and political rights is highly significant (column 3). The estimated coefficient in the last regression suggests that wages in, say, Mexico would increase by 30 percent if that country were to reach the level of democracy that prevails in the United States. That is not small. So while the bulk of cross-national differences in wages is accounted for by productivity, the ability of workers to assert their rights makes a difference too.

Second, we have to be clear about who we are trying to help as we integrate concerns about labor standard in trade policy. Are we trying to help workers abroad, or domestic workers whose earnings might be undercut by weak standards abroad? These two objectives have to be kept separate for two reasons. For one thing, the appropriate instruments to be used in each case likely differ. For another, the distinction forces us to recognize that the objectives may sometimes clash: if we want to help workers at home, this will sometimes have adverse effects on workers abroad (for example, when we restrict market access for foreign products). I happen to believe that both objectives are legitimate ones. In particular, I think it is legitimate under certain conditions—and these include gross violation of core worker rights abroad—to protect domestic workers, by trade restrictions if need be. We do not allow temporary migrant workers to come into the United States and work under sub-standard conditions. But when domestic firms outsource in countries where workers lack basic rights, such as freedom of association, the consequences on workers at home are no different.

Third, what are the best instruments for achieving our goals? It is clear that there is no single approach, and trade policy alone is unlikely to get us too far. When our objective is to assist workers abroad, I think we should treat this as a human rights—rather than trade—issue, and deploy all instrument of foreign policy that are available. This might include trade carrots and sticks, but only as part of a broader portfolio of tools. When we are concerned about workers at home, we should use a mix of tools of as well. Compensation, training, and adjustment assistance may help ease some pressures. Encouraging labeling of products (i.e., "no child labor") can also be effective. But, as Fields recognizes, there is a deeper fairness issue with regard to international competition from low-standards (rights) countries that is not tackled well by compensation and market-based solutions. That is one reason why demands for trade protection resonate so much among the broader public.

TABLE 6.1. Cross-National Determinants of Wages in Manufacturing

Dependent Variable: log labor costs, 1985–89 average			
	(1)	*(2)*	*(3)*
log MVA/worker	0.79*	0.79*	0.81*
	(0.05)	(0.05)	(0.05)
log GDP/cap.	0.27*	0.29*	0.20*
	(0.07)	(0.07)	(0.07)
log price level	0.42**	0.40**	0.50*
	(0.18)	(0.17)	(0.18)
Basic worker rights		0.04***	
(range: 1—6)		(0.02)	
Civil liberties and political			0.60*
rights (range: 0—1)			(0.15)
N	80	80	79
Root MSE	0.30	0.30	0.28
R^2	0.94	0.94	0.95

Note: Regressions include a constant term and dummies for East Asia, Latin America, Sub-Saharan Africa, and OECD members (coefficient estimates not shown). Robust standard errors are reported in parenthesis. Levels of statistical significance are indicated by asterisks: * 99 percent; ** 95 percent; *** 90 percent.

CHAPTER 7

The Simple Economics of Labor Standards and the GATT

Kyle Bagwell and Robert W. Staiger

I. Introduction

How should the issue of domestic labor standards be handled in the GATT/WTO? This question is part of a broader debate over the appropriate scope of international economic institutions such as the GATT (and now its successor, the WTO), where member-countries are considering proposals for a new round of negotiations that would move beyond GATT's existing focus on trade barriers and cover traditionally "domestic" issues such as labor and environmental standards and regulatory reform. Such proposals encroach on traditional limits of national sovereignty, and they raise fundamental challenges to the existing structure of international economic relations among sovereign states. In this chapter we explore some of the linkages between trade policy and labor policy, and we consider several approaches to the treatment of domestic labor standards within a trade agreement.

As currently structured, GATT's approach to labor standards might be most aptly characterized as one of "benign neglect."[1] This characterization reflects two dimensions, the first of which is simply the degree to which GATT members are obligated to uphold a set of minimum standards for labor policies. While there is an explicit provision within GATT articles that allows governments to restrict importation of the products of prison labor, the determination of domestic labor standards is for the most part considered the legitimate domain of each national government, and weak labor standards *do not* constitute a violation of GATT obligations. Rather, as Enders (1996, p. 62) observes, "...the WTO rules place no constraints on a country's right...to regulate [its] labour practices...." This then implies a second dimension to GATT's approach to labor standards, which is essentially that the obligations on trade restrictions (e.g., tariff bindings) that a GATT member *does* accept cannot lawfully and unilaterally be later modified or withdrawn in order to respond to the labor standards of a trading partner, either for the purpose of influencing the labor standards of the trading partner or to offset the cost advantages associated with those standards on a particular product.[2] Hence, for the most part, current GATT rules respect the sovereignty of domestic decisions over labor standards, as they allow each member government to determine its own labor policies without worrying about the ramifications of these choices for either its GATT obligations or those of its trading partners.

It is the wisdom of preserving this national sovereignty over domestic labor policies while at the same time negotiating successive multilateral agreements to liberalize world trade which is now being challenged from various quarters in the United States and elsewhere in the industrialized world. The primary concern voiced by labor interests and social activists is that working conditions and wages in industrialized countries will suffer from trade liberalization as a result of increased import competition from countries where labor standards are weak or not enforced. It is feared that such pressures could fuel a "race to the bottom," in which the labor standards of the industrialized world are compromised in the name of international "competitiveness." These concerns have in turn led to proposals to introduce the issue of labor standards directly onto the negotiating agenda of the WTO, with the purpose of creating a "social clause" for the WTO that would permit restrictions to be placed on imports from countries not complying with a specified list of minimum standards (see, for example, the description of these proposals in Maskus, 1997, pp. 58–62). These proposed changes would allow governments to raise import restrictions in response to the weak labor standards of their trading partners, and if adopted these changes would mark a dramatic departure from the "benign neglect" approach to labor standards that has been followed by GATT over its 50–year history. With the WTO facing proposals for such fundamental changes in its approach to the issue of domestic labor standards, it is a good time to consider the question: how *should* the issue of domestic labor standards be handled in the GATT/WTO?

Much has been written on the interaction between international trade and labor standards (see, for example, Brown, Deardorff and Stern, 1996, Srinivasan, 1996, and the papers dealing with this issue from a legal perspective in the authoritative volumes edited by Bhagwati and Hudec, 1996, as well as the very useful discussion of the issues and literature contained in Brown, Deardorff and Stern, 1997), and no single paper can do justice to the broad set of issues that are involved. However, an important dimension that is absent from this literature is a formal economic analysis of the interaction between negotiations over trade policy and the determination of labor standards.[3] Yet it is within the context of sustained negotiations to liberalize world trade that the need to negotiate international agreements over labor standards has been most forcefully raised, and it is from the backdrop of GATT's successes in securing low levels of negotiated tariffs on a multilateral basis that the case for adding labor standards to the negotiating agenda of the WTO must be evaluated. Hence, an understanding of the interaction between tariff negotiations and the determination of labor policies seems a necessary starting point for assessing the claim that labor standards will suffer as a result of trade liberalization and for considering how the issue of labor standards ought to be approached by the WTO.

In this chapter we evaluate the relative merits of several approaches to the treatment of domestic labor standards within a trade agreement, ranging from one extreme that reflects GATT's current approach of benign neglect all the way to the other extreme of direct negotiations over labor standards to create a social clause for the WTO. Our broader intent in this research is to provide an answer to the question we posed at the outset of this paper. Here we narrow our focus to a more modest goal: we present a simple economic model within which some of the central features of the interaction between trade policy and labor standards may be understood, and we use this analytical structure to draw attention to an observation that has to our knowledge not appeared previously in the literature and that seems to us to be worthy of further discussion. In particular, we show that, while the benign neglect of labor standards within a trade agreement will result in inefficient choices of both trade barriers and labor standards, direct negotiations over labor standards are *not* required to reach efficient outcomes. Rather, as we demonstrate below, more modest changes to existing GATT rules could in principle correct the problems associated with GATT's current approach to labor standards without the need to engage in direct negotiations over these domestic policies.

The basic insight that underlies our findings is quite simple, and can be seen intuitively by considering the following situation. Imagine two college students who live in separate dorm-rooms across a shared courtyard. Both own stereos but each has a distinct taste in music, and each likes to listen to his own music both in his room and when walking in the courtyard. The courtyard is sufficiently large that neither student's stereo can be heard inside the other student's room, but both stereos can potentially be heard in the courtyard. All else equal, each student would prefer that his music dominate that of his neighbor over as much of the courtyard as possible. The louder is one of the stereos turned up relative to the other, the further out into the courtyard it will dominate the other. Hence, each student is aware that by turning up his stereo he can restrict the audible range of his neighbor's music in the courtyard as he simultaneously extends the audible range of his own.

In this setting, consider what problems will arise when the two students set their stereo levels non-cooperatively, and consider as well what kinds of cooperative agreements might be entertained. Without some kind of cooperation, both students will turn up their stereos in a competition to dominate the courtyard, and each student will therefore play his stereo at a level which is louder *inside* his room than he would choose in the absence of the courtyard competition. An obvious solution to this inefficient situation is for the two students to agree to turn down their stereos to mutually acceptable levels, perhaps preserving the relative balance in the courtyard but achieving desired reductions in the sound level inside each room. However, an agreement that simply specified the setting of the volume knob for each stereo would now tempt each student to achieve dominance in the courtyard by less direct means, perhaps for example by reorienting his speakers increasingly in the direction of the courtyard window. Of course, the distortions to in-room listening associated with manipulating speaker locations would create new inefficiencies, and these new inefficiencies could also be handled in the same way as the volume settings, by broadening the agreement to cover both the setting of the volume knob and the placement of the speakers in each room. And in principle this broadening could go on until the negotiations covered every conceivable angle that either student might test in his effort to achieve dominance in the courtyard.

But an alternative approach to negotiations is also possible once the essential features of the problem are understood. Since each student is driven to make inefficient choices regarding his stereo operation by the incentive to affect the *courtyard volume* of his music relative to that of his neighbor, each student could in principle retain the right to unilaterally determine the details of his stereo operation without sacrificing efficiency provided that he faced appropriate restrictions under the agreement that offset this incentive. For instance, an agreement could simply specify courtyard volume levels for each stereo directly, and then let each student decide on how best to satisfy the terms of the agreement (e.g., what combination of volume-knob setting and speaker placement consistent with the agreed-upon courtyard volume would provide him with the best in-room listening).

As it turns out, the analogy between the situation described above and that faced by trade negotiators is surprisingly close in its essentials. In the absence of any form of international (inter-room) agreement, governments (students) will tend to raise tariffs (volume knob settings) to inefficiently high levels in an effort to restrict the market access of foreign products (drown-out competing stereos) and enjoy the lower foreign exporter prices (reduced audible range of competing music) that result. This is the fundamental inefficiency that a trade agreement such as GATT can correct.[4] However, if an agreement is negotiated that covers only direct interventions such as tariffs (volume knob settings), the unilateral urge to limit market access (drown-out competing stereos) will be deflected on to "domestic" policies such as labor standards (in-room speaker location), whose determination will then be distorted as a consequence of negotiated trade liberalization (agreements on the setting of volume knobs). In analogy with the courtyard scenario, a possible solution to this problem in the context of trade negotiations is to introduce labor standards directly onto the negotiating agenda, but it is not necessary to do so: once the source of the unilateral incentive to distort labor standards is understood to be derived from the incentive to limit market access, governments can retain the right to unilaterally determine their own labor standards without sacrificing efficiency provided that they face appropriate restrictions on their choices which offset these incentives. As we establish below, the restrictions that work in principle are closely related to those embodied in current GATT practice, suggesting that more modest changes to existing GATT rules might provide an alternative to the direct negotiation of a social clause.

Throughout the paper we attempt to keep technical material to a minimum, so that the ideas may be highlighted as clearly as possible. We rely primarily on a series of graphs to express our results. A more general mathematical treatment of these and other issues relating to standards and trade policy may be found in Bagwell and Staiger (1998). But it is nevertheless important to bear in mind that our formal analysis abstracts from many of the difficult issues associated with the determination of national labor standards in an international setting. For this reason, we do not interpret our results as implying that bringing labor standards into the WTO is a good idea. To come to such a view, many other complications that we have ignored would have to be considered. Rather, we interpret our results as implying that, *if* the WTO is going to act to address this issue of labor standards, then there are more modest changes to existing GATT rules that ought to be considered as an alternative to a WTO social clause.

The rest of the paper proceeds as follows. The next section presents the benchmark case of the choice of labor standards in a closed economy. In section III we then open this economy to trade and consider how import competition alters the determination of its labor standards. In section IV we introduce tariffs as a second policy variable, so that we may consider how trade policy and labor standards can interact. Here we establish that international negotiations over tariffs alone will lead to a globally inefficient outcome described by partial tariff liberalization and a weakening of labor standards. In section V we take up the issue of how GATT negotiations can be structured to strengthen labor standards and achieve efficient outcomes. Finally, section VI concludes.

II. Labor Standards in a Closed Economy

In this section we present the benchmark case of the choice of labor standards in a closed economy. We choose our set of modeling assumptions to reflect some basic features of the issues described above that we wish to capture. Whenever there is a choice between generality and clarity, we opt for the latter. Hence, rather than making a claim on generality, our model should be seen as simply serving to illustrate some basic points that should be kept in mind in the broader debate over the appropriate handling of labor standards within GATT. As we will be particularly interested in examining how import competition affects the choice of labor standards, we will consider an "industrialized" economy that determines its labor standard in an industry that may face import competition from a "less-industrialized" economy abroad. We first consider the issues involved in determining the labor standard for this industry when it does not face import competition (i.e., in a closed economy), and then in the next section turn to a trading environment.

We focus on a single good x which, with p_x denoting its price, will be consumed by this economy at the rate $C_x(p_x) = 1 - p_x$ and produced at the rate $Q_x(p_x,s) = (1-s) + p_x$. The parameter s lies between zero and one and denotes the economy's *labor standard*, with $s = 0$ corresponding to a "loose" labor standard and $s = 1$ corresponding to a "tight" labor standard. Consider, for example, the possibility that s denotes the stringency of child labor laws. If children of any age could be legally employed in the production of x in this economy, then we would represent this by setting $s = 0$, and the economy's supply of x would be given by $Q_x = 1 + p_x$. At the other extreme, if children were strictly prohibited from working in the x industry, then we would represent this by setting $s = 1$, and the economy's supply of x would then be "shifted in" and given by $Q_x = p_x$. More generally, the labor standard may be set at some intermediate level, in which case the parameter s would be greater than zero but less than one, and the economy's supply of x would lie somewhere in between the two extremes just described.

The top panel of figure 7.1 illustrates the market for x in this closed economy, with x-demand given by the downward-sloping line, and with x-supply given by the upward sloping line intersecting the x-axis at the value $(1-s)$. The "autarky" (closed economy) equilibrium price of good x will equate the country's supply and demand, and is labeled in the top panel of figure 7.1 by p_x^A. Notice that a more stringent labor standard (a higher s) will result in a leftward shift of supply and therefore an increase in p_x^A. This simply reflects the fact that more stringent labor standards will reduce the supply of workers available to the industry, and the market-clearing price will rise as a consequence.

Our partial equilibrium focus allows economic surplus associated with industry x in this closed economy to be measured as the sum of consumer surplus and producer surplus. In the equilibrium depicted in the top panel of figure 7.1, consumer surplus is given by the area under the demand curve and above the market-clearing price p_x^A, while producer surplus is given by the area above the supply curve (and the x-axis) and below p_x^A.

It can be seen by inspection of the top panel of figure 7.1 that the economic surplus in industry x will be smallest when $s = 1$, so that the labor standard is at its most stringent: when $s = 1$ the supply curve intersects the x-axis at the origin, and so the market-clearing price is one-half and the economic surplus is one-quarter, as measured by the sum of the areas of the consumer and producer surplus triangles, each with height one-half and base one-half. On the other hand, economic surplus in industry x achieves its maximum value when $s = 0$, so that the labor standard is at its most lax: when $s = 0$ the supply curve intersects the x-axis at one, and so the market-clearing price is zero

Figure 7.1. Determination of Domestic Labor Standards under Autarky

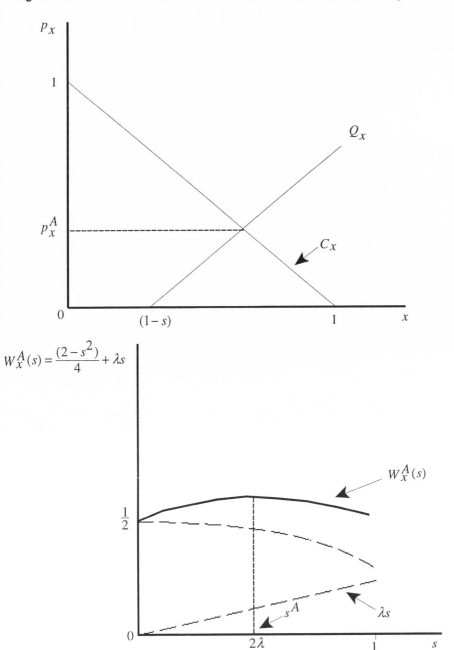

and the economic surplus is one-half, as measured by the area of the consumer surplus triangle, with height one and base one.[5] These observations reflect our implicit assumption that workers excluded from industry x as a result of tightening labor standards (a rise in s) cannot work elsewhere in the economy, and therefore contribute nothing to economic surplus in an alternative use. Hence, from the point of view of economic surplus, labor standards in this simple setting have only economic costs and no economic benefits.

Of course, even if it is costly from an economic standpoint, a society may still decide to exclude certain segments of the population (e.g., children) from the workforce for "non-economic" social reasons, and we assume that the government of this economy does place value on more stringent labor standards for social reasons. In particular, we assume that the government values increases in s at the rate λ.[6] Hence, in determining the stringency of the labor standard to apply to industry x, the government faces a tradeoff between lower economic surplus (as measured in the top panel of figure 7.1) and greater social surplus (as measured by its valuation parameter λ).

In the bottom panel of figure 7.1, we depict this tradeoff by displaying separately the levels of economic and social surplus achieved in this closed economy as a function of the choice of labor standard s. The level of economic surplus is given by the dashed curve in the bottom panel of figure 7.1. This curve plots as a function of s the economic surplus determined in the top panel of figure 7.1, and it is decreasing monotonically as s increases from zero to one. The level of social surplus is given in the bottom panel of figure 7.1 by the straight line out of the origin with slope λ. The sum of economic and social surplus in this closed economy for any choice of s, which we denote by $W_x^A(s)$, is then depicted by the bold curve in the bottom panel of figure 7.1.[7] Henceforth we will refer to $W_x^A(s)$ as the *domestic surplus* associated with a given labor standard s.

We assume that the government chooses its labor standard s in autarky to maximize domestic surplus $W_x^A(s)$, and therefore it chooses the value of s associated with the highest point on the bold curve in the bottom panel of figure 7.1. It is straightforward to show that setting the labor standard at a value of 2λ achieves this maximum, and so the government's chosen labor standard in autarky will be given by $s^A \equiv 2\lambda$. This solution reflects an optimal balance between the attainment of social goals and the economic costs of achieving those goals in a closed economy.

III. How Import-Competition Alters the Determination of Labor Standards

Suppose now that the domestic country has an opportunity to trade with a foreign country, and suppose that the forces of comparative advantage would dictate that the foreign country export good x to the domestic market. In the face of import-competition, how will the domestic government's choice of labor standards be altered? This is the question we now seek to answer.

We consider first how the advent of trade alters the economic surplus associated with industry x when the domestic labor standard is fixed at the level chosen in autarky, s^A. We suppose that foreigners consume good x at the rate of $C_x^*(p_x^*) = 1 - p_x^*$, where p_x^* denotes the price of good x in the foreign country. For simplicity, we abstract from the issue of foreign labor standards, and assume simply that foreign supply of good x is given by $Q_x^*(p_x^*) = 1 + p_x^*$.[8]

The top panel of figure 7.2 depicts the free trade equilibrium between the domestic and foreign country when the domestic labor standard is fixed at s^A. The figure on the left depicts the demands and supplies of the home country as a function of the prevailing home-country price of good x. The figure on the right depicts the demands and supplies in the foreign market as a function of the price of good x prevailing there. Free trade will ensure that a single price of x prevails in the two markets, so that $p_x = p_x^*$, and this common price will be determined in equilibrium so that the difference between demand and supply of good x in the home country (the *domestic import demand*, $M_x(p_x, s^A) \equiv C_x(p_x) - Q_x(p_x, s^A)$) is equal to the difference between supply and demand of good x in the foreign country (the *foreign export supply*, $E_x^*(p_x^*) \equiv Q_x^*(p_x^*) - C_x^*(p_x^*)$). The equilibrium free trade price is labeled p_x^F in the top panel of figure 7.2, and this price will prevail in each market (i.e., $p_x = p_x^F = p_x^*$).

Notice that at the free trade equilibrium price p_x^F depicted in the top panel of figure 7.2, the domestic country enjoys increased economic surplus associated with industry x relative to the economic surplus associated with this industry in autarky (i.e., at p_x^A, where the domestic demand and supply curves intersect). The increase in surplus for the domestic country amounts to the area above p_x^F and below both the domestic demand and supply curves, and in the top panel of figure 7.2 we label this additional surplus $G_x^F(s^A)$. Given the labor standard s^A, $G_x^F(s^A)$ simply measures the additional economic surplus that the domestic country achieves through free trade with its foreign trading partner, or the domestic country's *gains from trade*. Likewise, the gains from trade for the foreign country are given in the top panel of figure 7.2 by the area

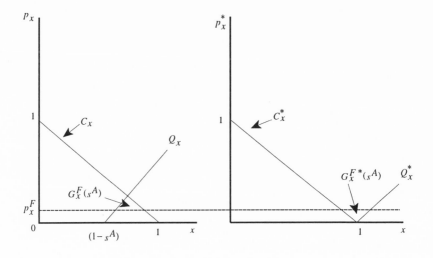

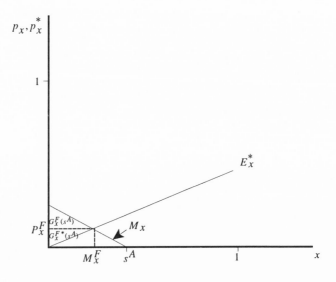

Figure 7.2. Introduction of Trade

below p_x^F and above both the foreign demand and supply curves, and we label this area $G_x^{F*}(s^A)$.

The gains from trade for the domestic country can be measured equivalently as the area above the equilibrium price and below the domestic country's import demand curve $M_x(p_x, s^A)$. Analogously, the gains from trade for the foreign country can be measured equivalently as the area below the equilibrium price and above the foreign country's export supply curve $E_x^*(p_x^*)$. In the bottom panel of figure 7.2, the domestic import demand and foreign export supply curves are depicted, with the equilibrium free trade price and trade volume determined by their intersection (with the latter labeled M_x^F) and the domestic and foreign gains from trade labeled as $G_x^F(s^A)$ and $G_x^{F*}(s^A)$, respectively. The top and bottom panels of figure 7.2 are simply equivalent ways of depicting free trade equilibrium and the gains from trade.

Notice in the bottom panel of figure 7.2 that the domestic import demand curve intersects the x-axis at a value equal to the choice of domestic labor standard, and that the gains from trade are therefore affected by the choice of domestic labor standard. In particular, as can be seen from inspection of the bottom panel of figure 7.2, each country's gains from trade would be larger if the domestic government would tighten its labor standard beyond s^A, as this would shift out the domestic import demand curve and thereby increase the size of each of the gains-from-trade triangles beyond those depicted in the figure.[9] The linkage between domestic labor standards and the gains from trade simply reflects the fact that, as the domestic labor standard is tightened, the two countries become increasingly "different," and they are able to exploit these differences as the basis for trade. This suggests that, when faced with the prospect of international trade, the domestic government may wish to take account of the impact of its labor standard on the gains from trade as it determines its preferred level for this standard.

To highlight the impact that international trade has on the domestic government's choice of labor standard, we therefore decompose the economic and social surplus it achieves with any choice of s under free trade, which we denote by $W_x^F(s)$, into the sum of (i) the domestic surplus its labor standard choice would generate in autarky, $W_x^A(s)$, and (ii) the domestic gains from trade associated with this choice, $G_x^F(s)$. That is, we write the level of free-trade economic and social surplus achieved by the domestic government under any labor standard s as $W_x^F(s) \equiv W_x^A(s) + G_x^F(s)$.

This decomposition is depicted in figure 7.3, the top panel of which depicts the economic and social surplus associated with free trade when the do-

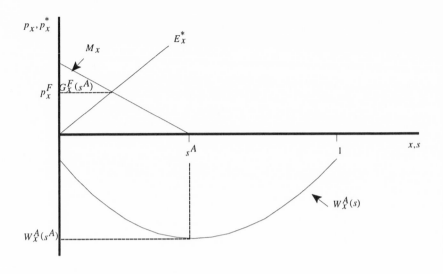

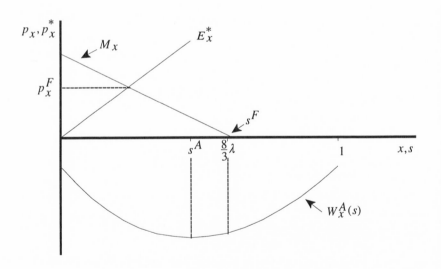

Figure 7.3. Determination of Domestic Labor Standards under Free Trade

mestic surplus, $W_x^A(s)$, is plotted (in an inverted fashion) below the x-axis as a function of s. As was shown in figure 7.1, $W_x^A(s)$ reaches its maximum when $s = s^A$, and this is reflected as well in the top panel of figure 7.3, where it can be seen that a small movement in s away from s^A would leave the value of $W_x^A(s)$ unaltered at its (maximal) value of $W_x^A(s^A)$. Above the x-axis domestic import demand and foreign export supply are plotted. As observed previously, the domestic import demand curve intersects the x-axis at a value equal to the domestic labor standard s, and with the domestic labor standard set at the level determined in autarky this intercept occurs at s^A as depicted. The associated domestic gains from trade are labeled $G_x^F(s^A)$. Therefore, the surplus achieved by the domestic government under the labor standard s^A in the presence of free international trade is given by $W_x^F(s^A) = W_x^A(s^A)$ $+ G_x^F(s^A)$, with the determination of $W_x^A(s^A)$ and $G_x^F(s^A)$ each reflected in the top panel of figure 7.3.

An important implication of international trade for the choice of labor standards can now be seen. As reflected in the top panel of figure 7.3, *when faced with import competition from abroad, the domestic government can always improve upon* s^A *with a small strengthening of its labor standard* (a slightly higher s). This is because a slight strengthening of domestic labor standards from s^A will have no impact on domestic surplus $W_x^A(s)$, but it will increase the domestic gains from trade $G_x^F(s)$. In effect, while s^A reflects the optimal balance between the social benefits of more stringent labor standards and the economic costs of achieving them in a closed economy (i.e., s^A maximizes $W_x^A(s)$), the opportunity to import from abroad reduces the domestic country's economic costs of achieving more stringent labor standards, and makes the choice of tighter labor standards ($s > s^A$) desirable for the domestic government as a result.

The bottom panel of figure 7.3 depicts the end result of this process, where the domestic government has set its labor standard at a level that balances the domestic social benefits of tight labor standards against the domestic economic costs of achieving these goals in an open economy. As depicted, the optimal labor standard level is higher than s^A and given by $s = 8\lambda/3 \equiv s^F$, and at this standard level the additional gains from trade for the domestic country that would be generated by a further tightening of domestic labor standards (the increase in $G_x^F(s)$ associated with a small increase in s above

$_s{}^F$ would just be matched by the reduction in domestic surplus $W_x^A(s)$) that the change in labor standards would generate.

Hence we have:

Observation 1:   Import competition is not an "enemy" of strict labor standards. Countries will adopt more stringent labor standards in the presence of import competition than they would choose to adopt in its absence.

While we have focused on the impact of import competition on labor standards, similar arguments can be used to show that just the opposite forces are at work in export sectors.[10] Hence, more generally trade will induce governments to *reorient* their labor standards toward greater stringency in import-competing industries and greater laxity in export sectors. But the essential point remains, namely, that there is nothing about exposure to international trade per se that leads inexorably to weaker labor standards.

IV. How Trade Liberalization can Weaken Labor Standards

Thus far we have concerned ourselves with the way that trade and labor standards can interact, assuming that trade remains free of impediments when it occurs. We now introduce the possibility that import tariffs may be imposed, and consider how trade *policy* and labor standards can interact. To do this, we proceed in three steps. Our first step is to determine the import tariff and labor standard choices that would be optimal for the domestic government in the absence of any possibility of international policy cooperation with its foreign trading partner. Our second step is to identify inefficiencies associated with these unilateral policy choices, so that the possibility of creating mutual increases in welfare (by eliminating these inefficiencies) can be established and the basis for a cooperative international agreement over trade and labor policies may be understood. Our third and final step in this section is then to consider whether all the potential benefits from international cooperation can be achieved with an agreement over trade policy alone.

As shown in the previous section, the opportunity to import from abroad reduces the domestic country's economic costs of achieving more stringent labor standards, and makes the choice of tighter labor standards desirable for the domestic government as a result. When the domestic government also has an import tariff at its disposal, it has an enhanced ability to "shift the costs" of its more stringent labor standards onto its trading partner through import protection, and this leads it to favor more stringent labor standards than it would choose under free trade. Hence, as we now show, *the ability to impose import protection goes hand-in-hand with tighter labor standards.*

To see this, consider the domestic country's gains from trade in industry x when its labor standard is set at the level which would be chosen under free trade, $_s{}^F$, but when it sets an ad valorem import tariff t on imports of x from the foreign country. Letting $\tau \equiv (1 + t)$, the domestic country's tariff will drive a wedge between the domestic and foreign price of x, and provided the tariff is not set so high as to prohibit imports altogether, the resulting trade volume will ensure that $p_x = \tau p_x^*$. This tariff wedge will alter the gains from trade achieved by each country under the domestic labor standard s^F from the gains each would have received under free trade, and this in turn will upset the tradeoff between domestic surplus and the gains from trade which, under free trade, led the domestic government to choose the labor standard s^F. Consequently, import protection will render s^F sub-optimal, and a link between import protection and labor standards can be established.

Figure 7.4 illustrates. The top panel depicts the domestic surplus ($W_x^A(s^F)$) and the domestic gains from trade ($G_x^T(s^F, \tau)$) associated with the domestic labor standard s^F and a (non-prohibitive) domestic import tariff τ.[11] Domestic surplus is plotted below the x-axis as a function of the domestic labor standard s and, as depicted, the labor standard level s^F is determined so as to balance the reduction in domestic surplus that a further tightening of the standard would generate against the additional domestic gains from free trade that would be created. With the introduction of a domestic import tariff τ, the domestic government increases the price of x prevailing in its own market while it decreases the price of x prevailing in the foreign market relative to the (common) free trade price p_x^F, and in so doing it reduces import volume below the free trade level M_x^F. In the top panel of figure 7.4, the equilibrium domestic and foreign prices associated with the domestic import tariff τ are labeled as p_x^T and p_x^{T*}, respectively, while the equilibrium import volume is labeled M_x^T. The domestic gains from trade $G_x^T(s^F, \tau)$ are now given by the area above p_x^T and below the domestic country's import demand curve *plus* the area above p_x^{T*} and below p_x^T out to M_x^T (which is the tariff revenue collected by the domestic government). The foreign country's gains from trade $G_x^{T*}(s^F, \tau)$ are given by the area below p_x^{T*} and above the foreign export supply curve. The area of the triangle labeled D corresponds to the *dead weight loss* associated with the import tariff τ, as this amount of free trade surplus is lost in the presence of the tariff.

It can now be seen from the top panel of figure 7.4 that the additional domestic gains from trade generated by a slight tightening of the domestic labor

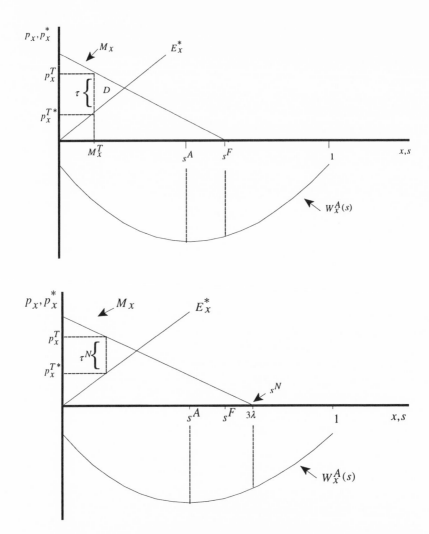

Figure 7.4. Determination of Domestic Labor Standards under Non-cooperative Tariffs

standard beyond s^F will be higher when the domestic government can impose an import tariff than when it is restricted to a policy of free trade.[12] To see this, consider a small increase in s starting from s^F, and suppose that the domestic government were to adjust the level of its import tariff τ to keep the dead weight loss associated with its tariff policy (D in the figure) unchanged. Such a tariff adjustment would certainly be feasible for the domestic government (and if it is not optimal then the domestic government could only increase its gains from trade further by adjusting its tariff to the optimal level). With this tariff adjustment holding D fixed, the increase in the *total* (i.e., domestic plus foreign) gains from trade generated by the rise in s will be the same as the increase in the total gains from *free* trade when s rises. But the domestic country's *share* of this increase will be larger than it would be under free trade, owing to the low foreign price p_x^{T*} received by foreign exporters (and the tariff revenue collected from foreign exporters by the domestic government as a consequence). Therefore, with an import tariff at its disposal, the domestic government can generate larger increases in its gains from trade as it strengthens its labor standard than it would enjoy under free trade. This implies in turn that import protection will render s^F sub-optimal, and that the domestic government will wish to strengthen its labor standard when it can also impose import protection.

The bottom panel of figure 7.4 depicts the domestic government's choice of labor standard and import tariff. For any choice of labor standard, the import tariff will be set to maximize the domestic gains from trade, and it is straightforward to show that setting $\tau = 2 \equiv \tau^N$ achieves this goal. The domestic labor standard is then set where a further tightening would generate losses in domestic surplus ($W_x^A(s)$) which are just matched by the added domestic gains from trade ($G_x^T(s, \tau^N)$). This point is reached by strengthening the domestic labor standard beyond s^F to $s = 3\lambda \equiv s^N$, at which point the domestic government has set its labor standard at a level that balances the domestic social benefits of tight labor standards against the domestic economic costs of achieving these goals in an open (but protected) economy.

Having established that the ability to impose import protection leads the domestic government to choose tighter labor standards, we now proceed to our second step and characterize the labor standard and trade policy choices that would be *efficient* (as measured by governments' own surplus calculations) from a world-wide perspective. We assume that the two countries have a means of redistributing income between them in a lump sum fashion, as this allows us to focus on the policy choices that would maximize their joint surplus. As is well-understood, efficiency cannot be achieved in this environment in the presence of import tariffs, and so efficiency will require that the domestic import tariff be set to zero ($\tau = 1$) so that free trade can prevail. The remaining question concerns the efficient choice of domestic labor standard s. We now show that a further strengthening of domestic labor standards is required for efficiency.

Figure 7.5 demonstrates why this must be so. The top panel of figure 7.5 recreates the determinants of the domestic government's choice of labor standards under free trade, s^F. Recall that this choice balances the reduction in domestic surplus that a further tightening of labor standards would cause against the generation of additional domestic gains from trade $G_X^F(s)$. But to achieve an efficient labor standard, the impact of this standard on *foreign* gains from trade $G_X^{F*}(s)$ must be taken into account as well, and foreign gains from trade also increase with a strengthening of domestic labor standards. Hence, domestic labor standards impart a positive externality on foreign welfare, and efficiency requires that this externality be internalized with more stringent domestic labor standards than would be chosen by the domestic government on its own. The bottom panel of figure 7.5 depicts the determination of the efficient domestic labor standard. When this standard is increased to $s = 4\lambda \equiv s^E$, a further rise in s would lead to a reduction in domestic surplus which is just offset by the increase in domestic and foreign gains from trade. As depicted in the figure, the efficient labor standard (s^E) is more stringent than that which the domestic government would choose in the absence of any international cooperation (s^N), and so *an international agreement that achieves efficiency must call for free trade and tighter labor standards.*

This brings us to the third and final step in considering how trade policy and labor standards can interact. We now wish to determine whether all the potential benefits from international cooperation can be achieved with an agreement on trade policy alone. That is, we suppose initially that tariff and labor policies are set non-cooperatively and that then the domestic and foreign governments are given the opportunity to negotiate a tariff agreement, but that domestic labor policy will continue to be set unilaterally by the domestic government. As before, with international lump sum transfers available, the two governments will negotiate a tariff agreement that maximizes their joint surplus, but they must now take into account the fact that domestic labor policy will be set unilaterally by the domestic government in light of their tariff agreement. The question we now consider is whether the inability to negotiate an agreement on labor standards will alter the content of the tariff agreement or the surplus achieved through negotiation. As we now establish, *international negotiations over tariffs alone will lead to a globally inefficient outcome described by partial tariff liberalization and a weakening of labor standards.*

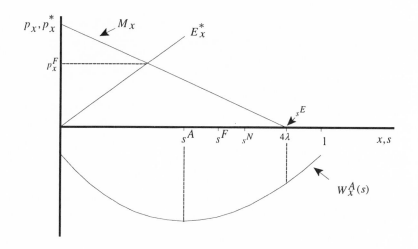

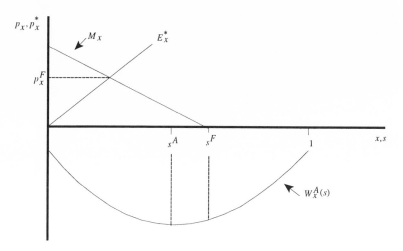

Figure 7.5. Determination of Efficient Tariffs and Labor Standards

Figure 7.6 illustrates the result. The top panel represents the determination of non-cooperative trade and labor policies τ^N and s^N. As established previously, these policies are inefficient, as full efficiency requires that the domestic country's import protection be eliminated and that its labor standard be strengthened to s^E. The domestic government could simply agree to eliminate its tariff, thereby securing one part of the efficient policy combination. However, as domestic labor policy is "off limits" to negotiation by assumption, an agreement which achieved free trade would induce the domestic government to *weaken* its labor standard below s^N to s^F. But efficiency calls for a *strengthening* of domestic labor standards beyond s^N to s^E. Hence, as the domestic government agrees to liberalize its trade policy, it will unilaterally be adjusting its labor standard in the wrong direction from the standpoint of world-wide efficiency and creating further distortions. As a consequence, it will not be efficient to negotiate a tariff agreement that calls for free trade. Instead, (constrained) efficiency will call for a balance between the costs of distortions in trade policy and the costs of distortions in labor standards.

The bottom panel of figure 7.6 shows the determination of the optimal tariff agreement when labor standards are beyond the reach of international negotiations. The agreement calls for tariff liberalization to achieve a tariff below the non-cooperative tariff τ^N, but this liberalization does not go all the way to free trade. Rather, the tariff level τ^G called for in the agreement lies strictly between free trade and the non-cooperative tariff τ^N. At the optimal negotiated tariff τ^G, a slight amount of additional tariff liberalization would create additional domestic and foreign gains from trade (through a further reduction in the dead weight loss D) which would be just offset by the reductions in domestic and foreign gains from trade and the increases in domestic surplus that come with the weaker domestic labor standards that further tariff liberalization would engender. As indicated in the figure, the agreed-upon tariff liberalization to τ^G will induce the domestic government to choose (unilaterally) to weaken its labor standard from s^N to s^G. Hence, the optimal tariff agreement will fail to eliminate tariffs as it leads to weaker labor standards, and consequently the surplus generated by an agreement over tariffs alone cannot achieve the level of surplus attainable with international cooperation over both trade and labor policies.

Thus we have:

Observation 2:   International negotiations over tariffs alone will lead to a globally inefficient outcome described by partial tariff liberalization and a weakening of labor standards in import-competing industries.

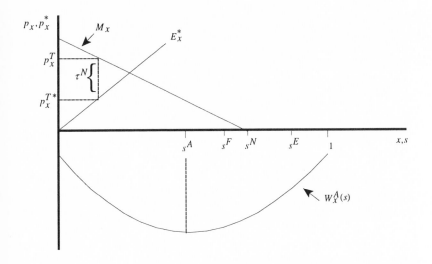

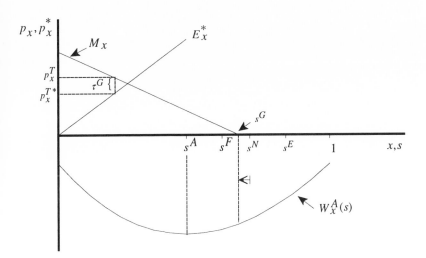

Figure 7.6. International Negotiations over Tariffs Alone

Again we note that this observation reflects our focus on the interaction between labor standards and import competition, and opposite forces will be at work with regard to the choice of labor standards whose central effects are on export sectors. However, this focus does give some credence to the view that successive rounds of GATT-sponsored tariff liberalization may be fueling a "race to the bottom" in which the labor standards of the industrialized world are being sacrificed in the name of international "competitiveness."[13] It is from such a backdrop that proposals to introduce the issue of labor standards onto the WTO agenda are often advanced. In the next section we consider a number of approaches that might be taken to handle the issue of labor standards within the WTO.

V. How GATT Negotiations can be Structured to Strengthen Labor Standards

In the preceding section we showed that tariffs and labor-standards will be set at inefficient levels if they are determined non-cooperatively, and that attempts to address these problems through international negotiations over tariffs alone will lead to globally inefficient outcomes characterized by partial tariff liberalization and a weakening of labor standards. In this section we consider three approaches to negotiations that can achieve efficient outcomes. We begin with the most obvious approach, which is to introduce the issue of labor standards directly on to the agenda of international trade negotiations.

It is clear that direct negotiations over tariffs and labor standards together will allow the domestic and foreign government to negotiate to the efficient outcome of free trade and a domestic labor standard s^E (with a possible need for lump sum international payments across countries). However, it is interesting to note that the addition of labor standards to the negotiating agenda will not only result in an agreement to strengthen labor standards, but will make further tariff liberalization desirable as well. To see this, we refer to figure 7.7, the top panel of which depicts the determination of the optimal tariff agreement when negotiation over labor standards is not allowed. As described previously, in the absence of the ability to negotiate an agreement over labor standards, it will be efficient for the trade agreement to call for partial liberalization of the domestic import tariff to τ^G with the domestic labor standard then set unilaterally by the domestic government at a level s^G that lies below the efficient level s^E. When labor standards are added to the negotiating agenda, it is then possible to implement an agreement on tariffs and labor standards that achieves the efficient outcome of free trade and a domestic labor standard set to s^E, as the bottom panel of figure 7.7 indicates. But this implies that the addition of labor standards to the international negotiating agenda provides new impetus for further tariff liberalization, as the reason for failing to negotiate to free trade in the first place has been removed. Hence, the

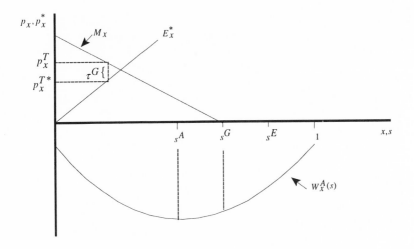

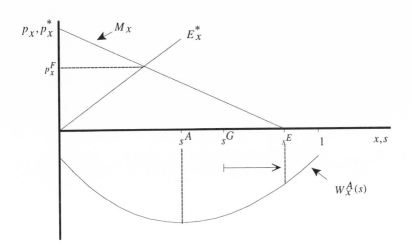

**Figure 7.7. International Negotiations over Tariffs
and Labor Standards**

addition of labor standards to the international negotiating agenda will bring about negotiations which both tighten labor standards and lead to further reductions in tariffs.

While the introduction of direct negotiations over labor standards can address the inefficiencies associated with negotiations over tariffs alone, this approach nevertheless requires that governments completely relinquish their national sovereignty over labor standards, a policy issue that has traditionally been considered a "domestic" concern. In fact, as we have shown above, it is the sovereign control over labor standards and the implied right to set these standards unilaterally that causes the problem. But are there approaches to negotiation that can achieve efficient outcomes and yet allow governments to preserve some degree of sovereignty over the determination of their labor standards? As it turns out, the answer is "yes," and in the remainder of this section we describe two additional approaches to negotiation that will achieve efficient outcomes but that do not require direct negotiations over labor standards.

To understand how it is possible to provide the domestic government with some degree of unilateral control over its labor standards and yet achieve a fully efficient outcome through direct negotiations over tariffs alone, it is helpful to consider more closely the unilateral incentives that the domestic government would have to distort its labor policy choice starting from the fully efficient agreement. The bottom panel of figure 7.7, which characterizes the determination of the fully efficient agreement, can help to reveal these incentives. Recall that this agreement eliminates the domestic import tariff and sets the domestic labor standard at s^E, where the gain in domestic surplus created by a slight reduction in s would just be offset by the associated loss in domestic *and foreign* gains from trade. Of course, from a unilateral perspective, the domestic government will not value the gains from trade that its labor policies create for its trading partner, and it is because of this that the domestic government has a unilateral incentive to weaken its labor policy from s^E. But this suggests that if the domestic government were granted the freedom to make unilateral adjustments to its labor policy, it would face the "right" incentives to make efficient choices *provided that it was obligated to make offsetting adjustments to its tariff which preserved the gains from trade of the foreign country*. The gains from trade for the foreign country are determined in turn by the foreign price of *x*, and so this obligation would amount to a commitment by the domestic government to make offsetting tariff changes which *preserve the foreign export price* as it adjusts its labor standards. This basic logic underlies the final two approaches to negotiations that we now describe.

The first of these alternative negotiation approaches bears a strong resemblance to the findings of Kemp and Wan (1976), who showed that the membership of a customs union could always be increased in such a way as to raise the national income of member-countries without reducing the national income of any non-member country, by adjusting the (common) external tariff of the customs union to preserve export prices. In the present setting, we suppose that the two governments negotiate an agreed level of tariffs, and then that the domestic government is free to unilaterally alter its labor standard provided that it simultaneously makes *Kemp-Wan adjustments* to its import tariff which preserve the foreign export price at the level implied by the negotiated tariff (and the domestic labor standard in place at the time of tariff negotiations).

Figure 7.8 illustrates. We suppose that the two countries have previously engaged in negotiations over tariffs alone (with unrestricted sovereignty granted to the domestic government over its labor standard), so that they begin from the (constrained) efficient tariff and labor policies first characterized in figure 7.6. We then suppose that, in the current round of tariff negotiations, it is agreed that if the domestic government subsequently loosens its labor standard from its existing level it will then be obligated to reduce its tariff to offset the impact of its altered labor standards on the price received by foreign exporters. Conversely, if the domestic government subsequently tightens its labor standard from its existing level, then it is agreed that it will be able to raise its tariff to offset the impact of its altered labor standards on the price received by foreign exporters. As these Kemp-Wan tariff adjustments eliminate the ability of the domestic government to use subsequent alterations of its labor standards to capture a portion of the foreign country's gains from trade under the tariff agreement, they will ensure that the domestic government has the "right" incentives when selecting its labor standard, given any negotiated foreign export price (and foreign gains from trade) that it must preserve. The only task of the current round of tariff negotiations is then to ensure that the domestic government faces the "right" (i.e., efficient) foreign export price when making its unilateral labor standard decisions.

In the top panel of figure 7.8, the efficient foreign export price is labeled p_x^{E*}, and is determined by the free trade equilibrium in which the domestic labor standard is set at its efficient level s^E. Since the domestic labor standard s^G in place at the time of (the current) tariff negotiations is below s^E, efficient tariff negotiations that result in a foreign export price of p_x^{E*} will require the liberalization of the domestic tariff from its initial level of τ^G to a level that is initially below the efficient tariff of zero (i.e., an import subsidy). This is depicted in the top panel of figure 7.8, and notice that a new dead weight loss triangle labeled D' has been created by the tariff agreement given the existing domestic labor standard. Hence, neither the tariff nor the domestic labor standard is efficient at this point.

Following the conclusion of the round of tariff negotiations, the domestic government will then be free to unilaterally adjust its labor standard while making Kemp-Wan adjustments to its import tariff. The bottom panel of figure

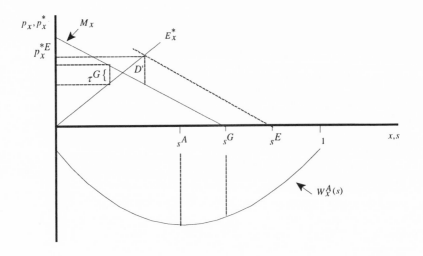

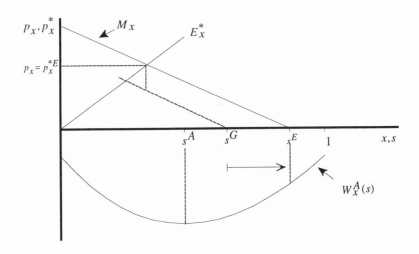

Figure 7.8. International Negotiations over Tariffs alone
with Kemp-Wan Adjustments

7.8 depicts these adjustments. As the obligation to make Kemp-Wan adjustments will prevent the domestic government from capturing a portion of the foreign gains from the tariff agreement by weakening its labor standard, it will have no incentive to do so. On the other hand, as Kemp-Wan adjustments permit the domestic government to raise its tariff as it raises its labor standard, they allow the domestic government to capture *all* the additional gains from trade created by tighter labor standards. But this implies that the domestic government will then choose to raise its labor standard to the efficient level s^E (which, it should be recalled, balanced all the additional gains from trade created by tighter labor standards against the reduction in domestic surplus) and simultaneously raise its import tariff to free trade (from an initial import subsidy). At these (efficient) policy choices, the domestic government can do no better for itself, as it is committed through Kemp-Wan adjustments to the efficient foreign export price and therefore to preserving foreign surplus at its efficient level.[14] Hence, *international negotiations over tariffs alone with Kemp-Wan adjustments will achieve efficient trade and labor policies.*

In figure 7.9 we summarize the relationships derived above and depict the logic of Kemp-Wan adjustments from a slightly different perspective. In this figure we plot the domestic import tariff τ on the horizontal axis and the domestic labor standard s on the vertical axis. The efficient policy combination of free trade and a domestic labor standard set at s^E is labeled as point E in the figure, and this represents the goal of international negotiations. Also depicted running through point E is a "Kemp-Wan" curve (labeled p_x^{E*}) that reflects combinations of τ and s that fix the foreign export price at p_x^{E*}. The curve labeled $s(\tau)$ depicts the domestic country's preferred choice of labor standard s for any level of import protection τ, and it describes a constraint by which international negotiations over tariffs alone must abide as long as the domestic government is granted unrestricted sovereignty over its labor standard. At every point along this curve, the domestic country's indifference curves (labeled W) are vertical. The point on this curve labeled G depicts the (constrained) efficient tariff and labor policies τ^G and s^G, where world surplus is maximized subject to the constraint given by $s(\tau)$: this is reflected in the figure by the tangency at point G between the constraint $s(\tau)$ and the iso-world-surplus curve labeled $W + W^*$. It is from point G that the new "Kemp-Wan" round of tariff negotiations begins. The two-step procedure to move from G to E described above can now be readily seen in figure 7.9. With the labor standard s^G taken as given in the first step, tariff negotiations reduce the import tariff τ along the horizontal line through G until the "Kemp-Wan"

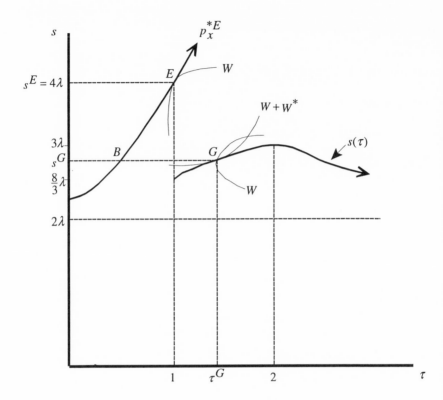

Figure 7.9. The Logic of Kemp-Wan Adjustments

curve p_x^{E*} is hit (at point B in the figure). Then in the second step, the domestic country is granted limited sovereignty to make any Kemp-Wan adjustments to its policy mix that it desires (i.e., it must remain on the curve p_x^{E*}). But as figure 7.9 makes clear, the Kemp-Wan adjustments made by the domestic country will lead the world to the efficient point E, as the policy combination associated with point E provides the domestic country with the highest level of welfare it can achieve along the "Kemp-Wan" curve (as reflected in the tangency between p_x^{E*} and the domestic country's indifference curve at point E). In this way, efficiency can be achieved without international negotiations over domestic labor standards.

While we have shown that direct negotiations over labor standards are not required to achieve efficient outcomes, it is nevertheless important to observe that the loss of domestic sovereignty implicit in the second negotiating approach we have outlined above is substantial, especially when compared to current norms under the GATT/WTO. In particular, the combination of tariff negotiations and Kemp-Wan adjustments as we have described them above require that governments are to be held rigidly to the export prices and trade volumes implied (in light of initial labor standards) by the outcome of their tariff negotiations. By contrast, under current GATT practice the trade volumes implied by a negotiated tariff agreement are not considered rigid commitments. In particular, GATT rules (and more specifically GATT's Article XXVIII) reserve for member-governments the right to unilaterally raise tariffs above previously-agreed-to levels. When a government exercises this right and denies previously negotiated "market access" to its trading partners, its trading partners are then allowed under GATT rules to take *reciprocal* actions which deny it an equivalent degree of access to their markets. As we have emphasized elsewhere (see, for example, Bagwell and Staiger, 1996, 1997, forthcoming), these reciprocal actions will serve to stabilize the export-price effects of a government's initial decision to unilaterally raise its tariffs above previously-agreed-to levels. Hence, under current GATT practice, governments *are* effectively held to the export prices implied by their tariff negotiations. But they are *not* held to the implied trade volumes.

Thus, while the second negotiating approach we have described above would imply that governments must commit to both the export prices and the trade volumes that emerge from a tariff negotiation, GATT's existing emphasis on reciprocity implies that governments are effectively only committing to the export prices that emerge from tariff negotiations. We now ask whether these more limited tariff commitments might be combined with subsequent Kemp-Wan adjustments to again allow governments to reach efficient outcomes through tariff negotiations alone. In particular, in a third and final approach to negotiations we suppose that the two governments negotiate an agreed level of tariffs, and that subsequent to tariff negotiations (i) either government is free to announce that it plans to raise its tariff, at which point its trading partner will then be free to increase its tariff by a reciprocal amount, and (ii) the domestic government is free to alter its labor standard provided that it simultaneously makes Kemp-Wan adjustments to its tariff.

To evaluate this final negotiating approach, we must introduce a second good, y, imported by the foreign country and subject to a foreign import tariff. As this good serves effectively only to provide the foreign government with a means to take "reciprocal" tariff actions in response to the actions of the domestic government, we keep this industry as simple as possible and abstract from issues of labor standards in industry y either at home or abroad. Instead, we assume simply that, with p_y denoting the domestic market price of good y, domestic demand for good y is given by $C_y = 1 - p_y$ while domestic supply is given by $Q_y = 1 + p_y$. Similarly, with p_y^* denoting the foreign market price of good y, we assume that foreign demand and supply of good y are given, respectively, by $C_y^* = 1 - p_y^*$ and $Q_y^* = p_y^*$. Finally, foreign import demand for good y is then defined by $M_y^*(p_y^*) \equiv C_y^*(p_y^*) - Q_y^*(p_y^*)$, while domestic export supply of good y is defined by $E_y(p_y) \equiv Q_y(p_y) - C_y(p_y)$.

Our final task before considering this third approach to negotiations is to define what is meant by *reciprocity* in a tariff agreement. Here we follow our earlier work (see, for example, Bagwell and Staiger, 1997, forthcoming) and assume under the tariff agreement that, if subsequent to implementing the agreement the domestic government wishes to raise its tariff so as to reduce foreign export volume into its markets, then it will be free to do so. However, in this event, the foreign government will be permitted to raise its tariff *reciprocally* so as to reduce by the same amount the domestic export volume into its markets. Of course, the foreign government enjoys a symmetric right to initiate modification of its own tariff and can expect under the tariff agreement a reciprocal response from the domestic government. It can be shown that, in the present context, the implied tariff modifications to any original agreement under reciprocity must satisfy $[p_x^{*o} - p_x^{*m}]M_x^m = [p_y^o - p_y^m]M_y^{*m}$, where the superscript "o" denotes magnitudes implied under the original tariff agreement and the superscript "m" denotes magnitudes associated with the modified tariff agreement. Effectively, this restriction ensures that the export price effects of one government's decision to raise its tariff will be neutralized by the export price effects of the tariff increase permitted under the rule of reciprocity by its trading partner. In our earlier work we assumed that government policies consisted solely of tariffs, and showed that reciprocity as described above could guide governments to efficient tariff agreements. In the present context government policies also include the domestic labor standard, and we now show that, *when combined with subsequent Kemp-Wan adjustments, reciprocity will guide governments through international negotiations over tariffs alone to achieve efficient tariff and labor policies.*

Having described the restrictions on modifications to an original tariff agreement that are allowed under reciprocity, we may now characterize the tariff agreement that will be negotiated under reciprocity with subsequent Kemp-Wan adjustments. Figure 7.10 illustrates. For simplicity, we suppose as before that the two countries have previously engaged in negotiations over tariffs alone (without reciprocity and with unrestricted sovereignty granted to the domestic government over its labor standard). This implies that as the current round of negotiations begins, the two governments will begin from free trade in good y (recall that we have for simplicity assumed away any labor standard issues in industry *y*), and they will begin from the (constrained) efficient tariff and labor policies characterized in figure 7.6 for good *x*. Now suppose that, as depicted in the top panel of figure 7.10, the two governments were to negotiate the same degree of tariff liberalization in industry *x* as they would have negotiated (in the absence of reciprocity) under the Kemp-Wan adjustments of figure 7.8. It can now be seen from the bottom panel of figure 7.10 that the more-limited tariff commitment implied by reciprocity will still allow this outcome to be sustained.

To see this, observe that the third negotiating approach described above will permit the domestic government to make unilateral Kemp-Wan adjustments to its tariff and labor policies in industry *x* without fear of triggering a tariff response from the foreign government, as these adjustments preserve the foreign export price p^*_x and thus do not invite the foreign government to alter its tariff under reciprocity (i.e., so as to induce reciprocal changes in the domestic export price p_y). As we showed previously, these adjustments will achieve the efficient policy mix in the *x* industry, with free trade then prevailing in both industries *x* and *y* and the efficient domestic labor standard s^E in place, as the bottom panel of figure 7.10 indicates. Furthermore, while either country would still be free under reciprocity to raise its tariff, the reciprocal tariff increase that can be imposed by its trading partner under reciprocity as described above is sufficient to eliminate each government's incentive to close its own import markets. Hence, when combined with subsequent Kemp-Wan adjustments, reciprocity will guide governments through international negotiations over tariffs alone to achieve efficient tariff and labor policies.
Gathering the results of this section together, we have:

Observation 3:   Any of the following three approaches to multilateral trade negotiations could allow governments to reach a globally efficient outcome achieved by complete tariff liberalization and a strengthening of labor standards:

(A) Introduce the issue of labor standards directly on to the agenda of multilateral trade negotiations and negotiate commitments over both tariffs and labor standards;

(B) Exclude the issue of labor standards from multilateral negotiations and negotiate commitments over tariffs alone, but subsequent to tariff negotiations allow any country wishing to strengthen its labor standards to increase its tariff levels as well, provided that its tariff adjustments are made to neutralize the export-price effects of its strengthened labor standards; or

(C) Exclude the issue of labor standards from multilateral negotiations and negotiate commitments over tariffs alone, but subsequent to tariff negotiations (i) allow any country to raise its tariffs, provided that its trading partners have the right to reciprocate with tariff increases of their own which serve to stabilize export prices, and (ii) allow any country wishing to strengthen its labor

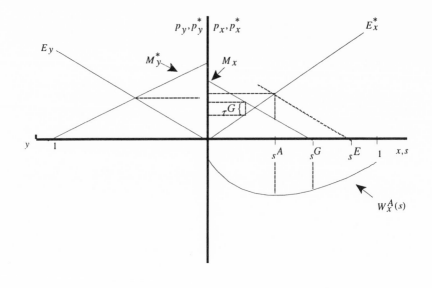

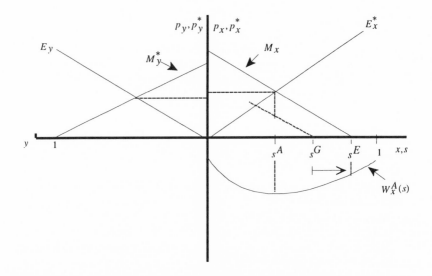

Figure 7.10. International Negotiations over Tariffs alone with Reciprocity and Kemp-Wan Adjustments

standards to increase its tariff levels as well, provided that its tariff adjustments are made to neutralize the export-price effects of its strengthened labor standards.

It is interesting to observe that, from the perspective of the GATT/WTO, approach (C) effectively amounts to permitting countries to credit changes in their labor standards as a "compensatory adjustment" when engaged in Article XXVIII tariff renegotiations. Consequently, our results suggest that relatively straightforward changes to the rules of GATT could allow governments to implement efficient labor standards without the need for direct international negotiations over these policies.

Finally, we note that there is an important distinction between these changes to the rules of GATT and the changes that have been proposed in recent WTO discussions, namely, the formal inclusion of a "social clause" that would permit restrictions to be placed on imports from countries not complying with a specified list of minimum standards. These proposed changes would allow governments to raise import restrictions in response to the weak labor standards of their trading partners, possibly by expanding GATT's Article XX (which currently permits tariffs to be raised against the importation of the products of prison labor) or Article VI (under which countervailing duties can be imposed against imports that are subsidized). In contrast, the changes suggested by our analysis would instead allow governments to raise import restrictions in exchange for tightening their own labor standards. This reorientation linking the permissible level of import protection in GATT to one's *own* labor standards rather than the labor standards of one's trading partners is a fundamental feature of our analysis, and this feature is likely to appear in settings which are much more general than the simple model we have used here to illustrate it.

VI. Conclusion

How should the issue of domestic labor standards be handled in the GATT/WTO? This is a question that is currently before the WTO, where member-countries are considering proposals for a new round of negotiations that would move beyond GATT's existing focus on trade barriers and cover "domestic" issues such as labor and environmental standards and regulatory reform, issues that have traditionally been treated with "benign neglect" within GATT.

In this chapter, we have considered several approaches to the treatment of domestic labor standards within a trade agreement. We have used simple economic arguments to show that, while the benign neglect of labor standards within a trade agreement will result in inefficient choices for both trade barriers and labor standards, direct negotiations over labor standards are *not* required to reach efficient outcomes. Specifically, we have described two alternative tariff negotiating structures that deliver efficient outcomes while preserving varying degrees of national sovereignty over policy choices. A first approach combines tariff negotiations with subsequent *Kemp-Wan adjust-ments*, under which each government is free to alter unilaterally its policy mix so long as trade volumes are not affected. A second approach adds to the first approach GATT's rule of *reciprocity*, under which subsequent to tariff nego-tiations each government is free to alter unilaterally its tariff, but its trading partner is then free to reciprocate with a tariff response which stabilizes export prices. We have shown that both approaches will deliver governments to the efficiency frontier, but that the second approach provides governments with greater sovereignty over their policy choices and bears a strong resemblance to the negotiating procedures spelled out in GATT.

While in principle our results point toward a relatively simple "fix" for the contentious issue of labor standards in the WTO, in practice there are of course a host of important caveats which must be borne in mind. First among these is the "slippery slope" argument that asks of the WTO, "Why stop at labor stan-dards?" To some degree virtually all domestic policy choices of large econo-mies such as the United States will have implications for export prices in the world economy and hence could be the subject of an analysis similar to that which we have undertaken here. Where, then, should the WTO draw the line? Also important is the question of how, given the complexities of the real world, the trade effects of a given change in domestic labor standards could be assessed with any accuracy.[15] These and other arguments might well be of-fered up against the advisability of altering the rules of GATT in the way that our formal results suggest. On the other hand, the direct international negotia-tion of domestic labor standards and the subsequent enforcement of a WTO "social clause" seems itself to be an extraordinarily complex task which is not immune to the "slippery slope" argument, and at the same time this approach crosses a boundary of national sovereignty that has served GATT well for 50 years. Hence, if *anything* is to be done to address the issue of labor standards in the WTO, the new approach that we have highlighted here seems at least worthy of discussion along side the others.

Notes

We thank our discussants, John H. Jackson and T. N. Srinivasan, for very helpful comments. We have also benefited from very useful discussion with conference par-ticipants.

[1] See Dam (1970) and Jackson (1969, 1989) for authoritative accounts of GATT princi-ples and practices. For a very useful discussion of the way labor standards are currently handled in the WTO, see Enders (1996).
[2] This is not to say that GATT members have *no* ability to respond to the labor standard choices of their trading partners. As Enders (1996, pp. 64–65) observes, if the tariff in question is not bound in a GATT schedule, then a country is of course free to raise the tariff for this (or any other) reason, and even where the tariff in question is covered by a GATT binding the country could still raise the tariff through an Article XXVIII modifi-cation, though it would then be obligated to make "compensatory adjustments" under

which it lowered other tariffs or else face a "reciprocal" tariff increase from its trading partner. Moreover, in principle, a claim of "nullification and impairment" associated with a trading partner's labor policies might successfully be brought under GATT's dispute settlement procedures if it could be shown that these labor policies interfered with market access in a way that could not reasonably have been anticipated at the time of the tariff negotiations. In practice, however, the burden of proof and other features of so-called "non-violation" complaints under GATT's dispute settlement procedures make them difficult to carry out, and from 1947 through 1995 only 14 out of the more than 250 GATT dispute proceedings centered on such complaints (see, for example, Petersmann, 1997, pp. 135–176).

[3] For example, Brown, Deardorff and Stern (1996) focus on the welfare and terms-of-trade effects of the imposition of labor standards in the presence of free trade but do not consider the choice of tariff policy, while Srinivasan (1996) considers whether diversity of labor standards alters the case for free trade but is not concerned with whether trade liberalization might alter a country's choice of labor standards.

[4] In Bagwell and Staiger (1996, 1997, forthcoming) we establish that this is the essential inefficiency that underlies the possible gains from a trade agreement in a broad class of settings that include both economic and political motives for member governments.

[5] In fact, the economic surplus associated with industry x in a closed-economy setting takes the very simple algebraic form of $(2 - s^2)/4$.

[6] The parameter λ is taken to be a positive constant. Provided that $\lambda < 1/4$, the chosen labor standard will lie strictly between zero and one.

[7] More specifically, we have $W_x^A(s) = (2 - s^2)/4 + \lambda s$.

[8] It might be objected at this point that we are "throwing the baby out with the bath water." After all, it is the allegation of weak labor standards in less-industrialized countries that gives rise to the fear that free trade with these countries will weaken the labor standards of industrialized countries as well. However, notice that the *channel* through which such pressures must be exerted is trade, regardless of the reasons for that trade. Our approach here is therefore to abstract from the reasons for trade (which could include weak labor standards in the exporting country) and focus on the implications of that trade for labor standards in the import-competing country.

[9] Specifically, for s between zero and one, we have $G_x^F(s) = G_x^{F*}(s) = (s/4)^2$.

[10] A formal confirmation of this can be found in the model detailed in the Appendix to the Comment by our discussant, T. N. Srinivasan.

[11] In the presence of a domestic import tariff τ , the domestic gains from trade function can be written algebraically for any labor standard s as $G_x^T(s,\tau) = [(2\tau - 1)s^2]/[4(1+\tau)^2]$, while the foreign gains from trade function is given by $G_x^{T*}(s,\tau) = s^2/[4(1+\tau)^2]$.

[12] Formally, for $\tau \in (1, \tau^N]$ we have $\partial G_x^T(s,\tau)/\partial s = [s(2\tau - 1)]/[2(1+\tau)^2] > s/8 = \partial G_x^F(s)/\partial s$.

[13] In practice there may also be an important "North-South" asymmetry at work that serves to diminish the extent of interaction between tariff liberalization and the choice of labor standards in export industries, and which thereby serves to further justify our

focus on labor standards in an import-competing industry. In particular, if we think of the group of less-industrialized countries who export labor-intensive goods to their large industrialized trading partners as individually being unable to have significant impacts on export prices in the world economy, then the incentive to distort labor standards in import-competing industries as we have analyzed it above will exist for the industrialized countries, but there will be no analogous incentive to distort labor standards in the export sectors of the less-industrialized countries. Hence, the labor standards issues relevant to the WTO will be those associated with import-competing industries.

[14]Above we have outlined a two-step process that achieves efficient trade and labor policies, under which the domestic government first reduces its tariff in the context of a tariff negotiation with the foreign government and then subsequently raises its tariff and labor standard in a Kemp-Wan fashion. As our discussion indicates, domestic welfare rises throughout the second step of this process while foreign welfare remains unchanged. To ensure that each country gains as well in the first (negotiation) step, it will be necessary for the foreign government to make an international lump-sum transfer to the domestic government in exchange for its tariff cut. The assumption that such transfers are feasible simplifies our analysis, but it is not required for our results (see Bagwell and Staiger, 1998).

[15]The practicality of Kemp-Wan-type tariff adjustments in the context of customs-union formation has been discussed by McMillan (1993) and Srinivasan (1997).

References

Bagwell, Kyle, and Robert W. Staiger. "An Economic Theory of GATT." *American Economic Review*, forthcoming.

Bagwell, Kyle, and Robert W. Staiger. 1996. "Reciprocal Trade Liberalization." NBER Working Paper No. 5488, March.

Bagwell, Kyle, and Robert W. Staiger. 1997. "Reciprocity, Non-discrimination and Preferential Agreements in the Multilateral Trading System." NBER Working Paper No. 5932, February.

Bagwell, Kyle, and Robert W. Staiger. 1998. "Domestic Policies, National Sovereignty and International Economic Institutions." Mimeo, February.

Bhagwati, Jagdish, and Robert E. Hudec (eds.). 1996. *Fair Trade and Harmonization: Prerequisites for Free Trade?*, Volume 2 (Legal Analysis). Cambridge: The MIT Press.

Brown, Drusilla K., Alan V. Deardorff, and Robert M. Stern. 1996. "International Labor Standards and Trade: A Theoretical Analysis." In Bhagwati and Hudec (eds.), *Fair Trade and Harmonization: Prerequisites for Free Trade?*, Volume 1 (Economic Analysis). Cambridge: The MIT Press.

Brown, Drusilla K., Alan V. Deardorff, and Robert M. Stern. 1997. "Trade and Labor Standards." University of Michigan, RSIE Discussion Paper No. 394, March 14.

Dam, Kenneth W. 1970. *The GATT: Law and International Economic Organization.* Chicago: University of Chicago Press.

Enders, Alice. 1996. "The Role of the WTO in Minimum Standards." In van Dijck and Faber (eds.), *Challenges to the New World Trade Organization.* The Hague: Kluwer Law International.

Jackson, John H. 1969. *World Trade and the Law of GATT.* New York: Bobbs-Merrill.

Jackson, John H. 1989. *The World Trading System.* Cambridge: The MIT Press.

Kemp, Murray C., and Henry Wan, Jr. 1976. "An Elementary Proposition Concerning the Formation of Customs Unions." *Journal of International Economics* 6:95–98.

Maskus, Keith. 1997. "Should Core Labor Standards be Imposed through International Trade Policy?" Policy Research Working Paper No. 1817, The World Bank, August.

McMillan, John. 1993. "Does Regional Integration Foster Open Trade? Economic Theory and GATT's Article XXIV." In Anderson and Blackhurst (eds.), *Regional Integration and the Global Trading System.* New York: St. Martin's Press.

Petersmann, Ernst-Ulrich. 1997. The GATT/WTO Dispute Settlement System: International Law, International Organizations and Dispute Settlement. The Hague: Kluwer Law International.

Srinivasan, T. N. 1996. "International Trade and Labour Standards from an International Perspective." In van Dijck and Faber (eds.), *Challenges to the New World Trade Organization.* The Hague: Kluwer Law International.

Srinivasan, T. N. 1997. "The Common External Tariff of a Customs Union: Alternative Approaches." *Japan and the World Economy* 9:447–465.

Comment

John H. Jackson

The notion that I could critique the Bagwell-Staiger paper is rather exaggerated, although Bob Staiger earlier led me through the main points. Leaving the more technical issues for T. N. Srinivasan to comment upon, I would like to raise a couple of issues which I think are important. I found myself rather uncomfortable with the analysis, because I felt that there were some subterranean assumptions being made, and there was lacking a well-defined position. For instance, Bagwell and Staiger focus on efficiency considerations. I must say that the word efficiency always kind of stops me. When one talks about the efficiency of, for instance, a child labor standard, I wonder how uniform the view would be on what that efficiency is across different cultures. Even within a particular nation, I think there would be some differences. You could use an economic efficiency idea that why we want standards on child labor is to protect the future of the workforce, that is, to have the workforce well trained, healthy, etc. I could see a long range concept here which then raises questions: is the government stepping in because of a market failure, because there is a long-range situation with free-riding, etc.? While Bagwell and Staiger wisely refer to *global* efficiency, I think that this concept is going to be even more difficult to apply because of cultural differences, etc.

The notion that you could, when the gains from trade would redound to the other party, adjust with a lump sum, is to my mind dubious. We know how difficult lump-sum payments would be in the real context of trade policy today. Also, one other point I will make is about reciprocity. To some, reciprocity may be an incredibly elusive concept. I recently attended a Council on Foreign Relations dinner at which Alan Greenspan spoke, and it was an extraordinarily good, but off-the-record, session. He gave a very interesting paper that laid out his view of the world financial crisis problems at the moment. At one point, he got into questions of WTO and reciprocity. Basically, he was very negative about the WTO. (This is incidentally, no longer off the record. He has given the speech elsewhere, presumably changed it some and it is now a public document.) He went on to say that one of the problems with the WTO is that it is really based on reciprocity and it is too much the captive of the lawyers who do not understand reciprocity at all. I think I understand reciprocity. In fact, in my book, *The World Trading System*, page 147, I go into this question of reciprocity. I say, for instance, ". . . it may be argued as a matter of economic policy that reciprocity does not make much sense." I then go on to indicate that it is nonetheless a motivator for a lot of trade negotiations. It has been a motivator from the start; it has some very powerful ideas. Also, there is a game theoretic advantage if you hold back a little bit to try and get reciprocity and that induces the other side also to liberalize; then you get a double benefit and not just single liberalization. However, the rules of reciprocity are very fluid. I do not think that you can really base a policy analysis, like Bagwell and Staiger have done, on reciprocity. For instance, there are probably five different ways to evaluate, numerically, reciprocity even in the tariff area. When you move into the rules area, it just becomes completely fluid, virtually impossible, I think, to define reciprocity.

Having said all that, let me turn to *my* comparative advantage. I am a specialist in the field of international economic law. I am not an expert on labor standards or on the linkage of labor standards or human rights or these other things to the GATT/WTO, but I am trying to learn about them. Here are some of my thoughts as they are progressing. First, I am absolutely convinced, as was stated in Fields's paper and in other contexts, that the labor standards questions as well as certain other social policy questions, *must* be linked. They have to become internalized into the GATT/WTO process. It is not possible politically and I do not think conceptually either, simply to put those concepts off and leave them to the rest of the world to take care of. Indeed, the language in the recent "shrimp-turtle" case that was considered in a WTO dispute settlement first level panel concerns me. It sounds a little too much of this old flavor of leaving the rest of these issues to the rest of the world and not to take them on in the GATT/WTO. On the other hand, I think that the U.S. policy involved in that case is very vulnerable. It is a unilateral decision, based on a unilateral U.S. statute, pushed by particular interests that are well-meaning, but which has an impact on other countries that have not been integrated into the U.S. policy-making process. So, I would predict that probably, even if there is an appeal, the bottom line will be still to bring a fair amount of criticism of the U.S. law. I do not think that the WTO can remain isolated from these points. To some extent, maybe the conceptual link can be worked out via the notion of a "market failure." That is, there are certain market failures that stem from a lack of looking at a broader sense of what society is about.

Now, a further question is, if there is going to be a linkage, how are we going to do it? What are the solutions? There are a variety of possibilities. First, we could enunciate a policy and announce it broadly. Now, we can all laugh at that and say, well, it will not get implemented, but the policy has some importance. It has a symbolic importance. Clearly, at a recent conference held at the International Institute of Economics, Renato Ruggiero, Director General of the WTO, in the morning, and USTR Charlene Barshefsky both said labor standards will become part of the WTO. That is official policy by two individuals who have a certain amount of representation behind them. It was just about as clear as you could get it. We did get some policy enunciated at the Singapore Ministerial, incidentally. It was a bit of passing the buck (to the ILO), but I will get to that.

Another possibility is just to leave it to the national sovereigns. Let every country do what it wants. But, we are learning that there are constraints from globalization to that approach. There are a variety of constraints that impact on the acting country itself—the race to the bottom, etc. There are also constraints about how an acting country can impact on other parts of the world and on other countries.

Another possibility is to formulate a rule, a social clause rule, if you want to call it that, to try to bill it as a treaty obligation. But, then again, you have the implementation question. You notice that I have not yet brought this to the WTO; I am just enunciating different possibilities. Yet another possibility is to emphasize adjustment, adjustment assistance or adjustment facilitation, which I think are very important and, indeed, I think will have to be part of the WTO process. A further possibility is other kinds of international coordination or cooperation, such as a rule taking the form of harmonization. That is, an agreement on some kind of a threshold standard which governments are allowed to use in their trade policy as well as in their domestic policy. Or it could be related to some notion of mutual recognition. Still a further possibility is to find other organizations to take on the task like the ILO. One of the troubles here is the ILO does not have much credibility. Some time ago in a talk I raised the question about ILO concerns and the audience laughed. But, I do think the ILO has come farther than that. Finally, there are various possibilities of national unilateral response.

The problem is that it is conceptually hard to plug the labor standards issue into the GATT/WTO. Some of what Bagwell and Staiger are saying in their model has some similarities to countervailing duties which we already have. That is one solution. You call the lack of inadequate standards on some social policy, labor or what have you, as a subsidy and you allow it to be countervailable. That has been talked about. It has been actually mentioned in U.S. statutes, but it poses lots of risks. Another approach is to allow governments to have a trade ban. But that raises the shrimp-turtle problem and the tuna-dolphin problem, and that is very difficult to implement conceptually under the GATT. Another possibility is to have an exception in Article XX. Actually, in some areas, particularly the environment, I think an exception amendment to Article XX could work very well, but I am not sure about labor standards. One of the problems is the so-called "process" versus "product" question. Can we reach processes abroad that are not part of the integral definition of a product without getting on and going down the slippery slope, where everything could be brought in, all sorts of different social problems?

The fundamental question though, and this is going to be my last point, is connected with the political realities and the reality of the existing institutions, namely the WTO and its annex the GATT, where a very large majority of the world is frightened to death of what industrial countries want to do with the social policy arrangements, particularly if they are linked to sanctions of the trade sort, i.e., a raising of a tariff whether it is for reciprocity protection or countervailing duty or what have you. Thus, for example, the WTO environmental committee is getting nowhere because probably three-fourths of the membership of the WTO does not want anything linked. They are just afraid that it is going to be abused by the industrial countries. I must say that they have some grounds for that fear, especially in some of the language that has been used in the political realm as well as by unions. In this connection, the U.S. gasoline reformulation rule, for instance, was interesting because it really involved an overreaching for protectionist purposes. This was evident in testimony in the Congress. The "smoking gun" is on the record, and it is quite intriguing. So, what it comes down to then is how can countries like the United States go into the WTO forum and get a constructive approach to some of the needed linkages? In order to do that, they have to persuade three-fourths of the membership that they will not overreach, that they will not abuse the rules that they formulate, and that there will not be loopholes that are going to injure the trade of those countries. I think this will be tough to accomplish. I do not know what the answer is yet. I have posed this question to various people in the last few months including very top U.S. officials. My sense is that we are all at sea, at the moment, searching for a viable solution.

Comment

T. N. Srinivasan

The paper by Bagwell and Staiger applies the same methodology to analyzing labor standards that the two authors have employed in a series of papers analyzing the roles of GATT's principle of non-discrimination, and the ill-defined notion of reciprocity in multilateral trade negotiations on tariff reductions in reaching an efficient (Pareto Optimal) and stable outcome. In the present paper, they model possible approaches to negotiations over the choice of two policy instruments, namely, tariffs and labor standards. In their model, full-efficiency (defined as maximization of the sum of social welfare of the two countries) requires free trade and a higher level of labor standards than the countries would choose, were they to adopt free trade, but set labor standards unilaterally in a non-cooperative fashion. Clearly with two policy instruments at the disposal of the governments, if they are free to set one of them unilaterally in a non-cooperative fashion, it is intuitive that negotiations to set the other instrument will result in neither instrument being set at levels consistent with full efficiency. To get around this problem, it is again intuitive that a linkage has to be established between the choice of the two instruments.

The authors then consider three alternative ways of linkage that achieve full efficiency. The first of course is to have joint negotiations on tariffs and labor standards so that the interplay between them is fully taken into account. Second is to have negotiations only with respect to tariffs, but if a country chooses to adjust its labor standards unilaterally subsequent to the agreement on tariffs, it can do so only if such an adjustment is accompanied by revisions in tariffs that leave the terms of trade faced by its trading partner unchanged at the level implied by the negotiated tariff (prior to the adjustment in labor standards). The third is to allow partners to change their tariffs and other policies in a reciprocal fashion in response to a country's adjustments in its labor standards after tariff negotiations, these reciprocal actions serving to maintain the terms of trade as in the second alternative.

The authors work with a very simple *partial equilibrium* model and their analysis is lucid and admirably transparent. I am not, however, entirely persuaded that the particular way they have introduced labor standards in the model, namely, that the imposition of higher labor standards reduces the intercept of the home supply curve, captures all the essential features of labor standards. As a matter of fact, one could equally well describe what they call labor standards, as standards for obscenity or pornography! Thus, if I may caricature, in their model, producers are 'lewds' who reduce supply if faced with more stringent standards. The government consists of 'prudes' whose welfare increases with the stringency of the standards. Consumers are 'neutral' (I resisted the temptation to use the word 'neutered'!) individuals who care only about the price they pay for the product and not, one way or the other, about the obscenity standards set by the government!

A more appropriate way of introducing labor standards would recognize that while more stringent standards raise production costs, they also raise consumer welfare. I describe, in the Appendix, a *general equilibrium* model in which labor standards are a public good that enters (positively) in the welfare of consumers and in the production function of producers (negatively, by raising costs). The government mandates labor standards acting as a Stackleberg leader and maximizes consumer welfare. In such a model, it is not necessarily the case that the mandated labor standards become progressively more stringent as one moves from autarky to free trade, then to non-cooperative Nash equilibrium in tariffs, and finally to full efficiency as in the authors' model. I am not sure whether monotonicity is essential for the authors' analysis. If it is, my example is a cause for concern.

Returning to the paper, the authors seem to imply that joint negotiations on tariffs and labor standards to achieve full efficiency is the analogue of introducing a social clause in the WTO. I am not persuaded. There is no need for negotiations on *both* to take place in the WTO. One can easily imagine tariffs and trade policy instruments being negotiated in the WTO, and labor standards being negotiated in the International Labor Organization, but with the two negotiations being coordinated to ensure mutual consistency towards achieving global efficiency.

The GATT (and now the WTO) articles do not define *reciprocity*, thus leaving the concept vague and open to many interpretations. The authors define reciprocity as requiring that if one country's action reduces the volume of its imports from its trading partners, the latter can reciprocate in a way that reduces their imports from that country by the same volume. Since this is only one of the many possible ways in defining reciprocity, it is not clear whether the authors' results would hold under alternative definitions of reciprocity.

Reference is made to the fact that GATT articles allow a country to prohibit imports of products made by prisoners. I cannot resist in this connection to refer to the hypocrisy of the United States in accusing China of exporting products made by prison labor. UNICOR, a corporation wholly owned by the U.S. Federal Government, run by the Bureau of Prisons in the United States,[1] operates 100 factories, sells over 150 products including "prescription glasses, safety eyewear, linens, monogrammed towels, executive office furniture, bedroom sets, gloves, brooms and brushes of all kinds, even targets for target practice. They also make cables and electronic component parts for Army tanks, jet fighters and the Patriot missile." Its gross sales in 1995 were around $500 million, of which wages paid to prisoners were about $35 million! According to Mr. Schwlab, Assistant Director of Corporate Management of

UNICOR, prisoners are "not covered by the Fair Labor Standards Act, minimum wage laws. They don't get retirement benefits, unemployment compensation, etc. They're workers, but they're not employees." Besides publicly owned UNICOR, private industry has been attracted and allowed to operate within prisons, and as the owner of one such private company agreed, it was a fantastic deal all the way around and he liked "the financial advantages of a prison business, namely, getting to hire the cream of the crop from a pool of cheap prison labor, not to mention the use of ... brand new air-conditioned factory space, rent free." The cost advantage of UNICOR and any private business operating with prison labor should be obvious. Yet, as the narrator of the story put it, without realizing the absurdity of the economic reasoning involved,

> Back in 1934, when Congress created UNICOR, it restricted its sales to one and only one customer, the federal government. The reason: to prevent UNICOR's cheap prison labor from undercutting private industry in the commercial marketplace. But Congress also armed UNICOR with one big advantage: It gets first crack at the government's business, even at the expense of private companies competing for the same work.

Clearly, any sale to government by UNICOR displaces what another producer, *domestic* or *foreign*, would have made! It is irrelevant that UNICOR is not allowed to export or sell to the domestic private sector. Yet those in the United States and the OECD, who accuse less developed countries with lower labor standards than their own as engaging in social dumping, fail to see that the operation of UNICOR has the same effect!

Let me conclude by highlighting a point made by the authors in the concluding paragraph of their paper. It is this. Almost all purely domestic policies could affect export prices. As such, if a country's exercise of one such policy, namely, that relating to the choice of labor standards, is made actionable by its trading partners through trade sanctions, countervailing duties or whatever, the demand to make the exercise of other domestic policies actionable through trade policy instruments would become irresistible. Once the first step on a slippery slope is taken by linking labor standards and trade sanctions, it will not stop at that step. The next steps could well be the linking of other domestic policies such as building codes, zoning laws, etc. and trade sanctions. This would be extremely unfortunate. Far more efficient policies other than trade sanctions are available to address the genuine concerns in rich countries about conditions of work (particularly child labor) in poor countries (Srinivasan, 1998). The inclusion of a social clause in the WTO, mandating the use of trade sanctions to enforce particular labor standards, is totally unwarranted.

Appendix

Consider the labor standards as a mandate by the government. Producers and consumers treat it as a public good. Higher labor standards, denoted by *s*, enter consumer's utility function positively but affects the input $l(s)$ of labor per unit of output of one of the two goods (good 1) in a Ricardian model of production. Government is a benevolent Stackleberg leader which mandates the level of *s* so as to maximize consumer welfare, taking into account the reaction of producers and consumers to the mandated level *s*.

First consider autarky. Let x_i denote the production (which equals consumption c_i) of good *i*, *i* = 1, 2. The labor input per unit of output of good 1 is $l(s)$ with $l'(s) > 0$, $l''(s) > 0$. Let the labor per unit of output of good 2 be constant at unity. Let the aggregate labor endowment, supplied inelastically by the consumer, be *L*. Let the consumer's utility function *U* be Cobb-Douglas:

$$U = \alpha \, Log \, c_1 + \beta \, Log \, c_2 + (1 - \alpha - \beta) \, Log \, s$$
with $\alpha > 0$, $\beta > 0$, $\alpha + \beta < 1$.   (1)

Let *s* be restricted to the unit interval. In autarky $c_i = x_i$ and, hence, using the factor endowment constraint

$$l(s)c_1 + c_2 = L \tag{2}$$

we get

$$U = \alpha \, Log \, c_1 + \beta \, Log \, (L - l(s)c_1) + (1 - \alpha - \beta) \, Log \, s \tag{3}$$

Suppose

$$l(s) = (1 - s)^{-\gamma}, \gamma > 0 \tag{4}$$

Then the first-order condition for a maximum of U is:

$$\frac{\alpha}{c_1} - \frac{\beta l(s)}{L - l(s)c_1} = 0 \tag{5}$$

or

$$c_1 = \left(\frac{\alpha}{\alpha + \beta}\right)\frac{L}{l(s)} = \left(\frac{\alpha}{\alpha + \beta}\right)L(1 - s)^{\gamma}. \tag{6}$$

Substituting in (3), the maximized value of *U* as a function of s is

$$\tilde{U}(s) = \alpha \, Log\left(\frac{\alpha}{\alpha + \beta}\right) + \beta \, Log\left(\frac{\beta}{\alpha + \beta}\right) + (\alpha + \beta) Log \, L$$
$$+ \alpha\gamma \, Log \, (1-s) + (1-\alpha-\beta) \, Log \, s. \tag{7}$$

The government maximizes $\tilde{U}(s)$ by setting *s* at

$$s^A = \frac{(1 - \alpha - \beta)}{\alpha\gamma + (1 - \alpha - \beta)}. \tag{8}$$

Second, let us turn to free trade. It is convenient to derive the offers, and choice of labor standards, for any given relative price *p* of good 1 in terms of good 2. Since $l(s)$ rises from one to infinity as *s* rises from 0 to 1, it is seen from figure 7.11 that the production possibility frontier (PPF) pivots around A from AB with a slope (i.e. tangent of angle ABO) of unity at $s = 0$ to AO with

Figure 7.11. Offers and Choice of Labor Standards under Free Trade

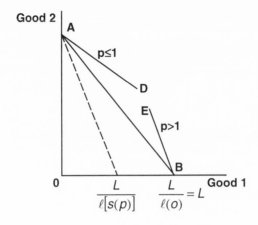

a slope of zero at $s = 1$. This means that for any $p \leq 1$ (i.e. a terms of trade line such as AD) the economy will specialize in producing good 2 whatever is the value of s in [0,1] and welfare from the consumption of the two goods will remain unchanged as s varies. Since consumers prefer higher s, it follows that the aggregate (i.e. the welfare from goods consumption and the enjoyment of s) welfare maximizing value of s under free trade at p, denoted by $s^F(p)$, is unity for $p \leq 1$.

Suppose $p > 1$ so that the terms of trade line is parallel to BE. If s is set at zero so that the PPF is AB, the economy will specialize in the production of good 1 since $p > l(0) = 1$. As s is increased from zero to $s(p)$ where $l[s(p)] = p$, the economy continues to specialize in good 1 since $p \geq l(s)$. Welfare from the consumption of the two goods *falls* because of the increase in the labor needed to produce good 1. However the increase in s increases consumer welfare as they enjoy higher labor standards.

With production specialized in good 1, the output of good 1 is $L/l(s)$. Income is $pL/l(s)$ so that the consumption of good 1 is $\left(\dfrac{\alpha}{\alpha + \beta} \right) \dfrac{L}{l(s)}$ and that of

good 2 is $\left(\dfrac{\beta}{\alpha + \beta} \right) \dfrac{pL}{l(s)}$. Thus, aggregate welfare $U(p,s) = \alpha \, Log \left(\dfrac{\alpha}{\alpha + \beta} \right)$

$+ \beta \, Log \left(\dfrac{\beta}{\alpha + \beta} \right) + (\alpha + \beta) \, Log \, L + \beta \, Log \ p - (\alpha + \beta) \, Log \, l(s) +$

$(1 - \alpha - \beta) \ Log \ s = C + \beta \, Log \ p - (\alpha + \beta) \, Log \ l(s) + (1 - \alpha - \beta) \, Log \ s$ (9)

where

$$C = \alpha \, Log \left(\frac{\alpha}{\alpha + \beta} \right) + \beta \, Log \left(\frac{\beta}{\alpha + \beta} \right) + (\alpha + \beta) \, Log \, L \tag{10}$$

Now

$$\frac{\partial U}{\partial s} = -\frac{(\alpha + \beta)}{l(s)} l'(s) + \frac{(1 - \alpha - \beta)}{s}$$

$$= -\frac{(\alpha + \beta)\gamma}{(1 - s)} + \frac{(1 - \alpha - \beta)}{s}$$

$$= \frac{[(1 - \alpha - \beta) + \gamma(\alpha + \beta)](\tilde{s} - s)}{s(1 - s)} \tag{11}$$

where

$$\tilde{s} = \frac{(1 - \alpha - \beta)}{(1 - \alpha - \beta) + \gamma(\alpha + \beta)} \tag{12}$$

It follows therefore that if $s(p) \le \tilde{s}$, $U(p,s)$ increases in s for s in $[0, s(p)]$. If $\tilde{s} < s(p)$, $U(p,s)$ increases as s increases from zero, reaches a maximum at $s = \tilde{s}$, and then decreases as s increases from $\tilde{s}$ to $s(p)$.

As s is further increased above $s(p)$, $p < l(s)$ and the economy specializes in the production of good 2. Once again welfare from the consumption of the two goods is unchanged while the increase in s increases welfare. This means that aggregate consumer welfare increases as s increases in $[s(p), 1]$.

Thus if $s(p) \le \tilde{s}$, then aggregate welfare $U(p,s)$ increases as s increases from zero and the aggregate welfare maximizing value b is $s^F(p) = 1$. If $s(p) > \tilde{s}$, since $U(p,s)$ increases with s in $[0, \tilde{s}]$, then decreases as s increases in $[\tilde{s}, s(p)]$ and then again increases as s further increases from $s(p)$ to 1, it follows that the aggregate welfare maximizing value $s^F(p)$ is given by

$$s^F(p) = \tilde{s} \quad if \ U(p, \tilde{s}) \le U(p, 1) \tag{13}$$

$$= 1 \quad if \ U(p, \tilde{s}) > U(p, 1) \tag{14}$$

Now with $s(p) > \tilde{s}, l(s(p)) \equiv p > l(\tilde{s})$. Hence at $\tilde{s}$, the economy is specialized in good 1 and hence

$$U(p, \tilde{s}) = C + \beta \, Log \, p - (\alpha + \beta) \, Log \, l(\tilde{s}) + (1 - \alpha - \beta) \, Log \, \tilde{s} \tag{15}$$

At $s = 1$, $l(s) = \infty$, the economy is specialized in the production of good 2 with its output being L. Income is L, consumption of good 1 is $\left(\frac{\alpha}{\alpha + \beta} \right) \frac{L}{p}$ and that of good 2 is $\left(\frac{\beta}{\alpha + \beta} \right)^L$. Thus welfare $U(p,1) = C - \alpha \, Log \, p$.

Thus,

$$U(p,1) - U(p,\tilde{s}) = (\alpha + \beta)[\, Log \; l(\tilde{s}) - Log \; p] - (1 - \alpha - \beta) \, Log \; \tilde{s} \qquad (16)$$

The first term of (16) is negative while the second is positive. If $\gamma(\alpha + \beta)$ is very small, then $\tilde{s}$ will be close to unity, $l(\tilde{s})$ will be very large implying $U(p,1) - U(p,\tilde{s})$ will be positive so that $s^F(p) = \tilde{s} \approx 1$. One cannot rule out $U(p,1) - U(p,\tilde{s})$ being negative so that $s^F(p) = 1$.

Putting all the results together, $s^F(p) = 1 > s^A$ if either $p \leq 1$, or $p > 1$ and $U(p,\tilde{s}) > U(p,1)$. $s^F(p) = \tilde{s} < s^A$ if $p > 1$ and $U(p,\tilde{s}) \leq U(p,1)$. The equilibrium p is determined by the intersection of home and foreign country offer curves. Since we have not specified anything about the foreign offer curve, it is clear that equilibrium p could be such that, depending on the foreign offer curve, $s^F(p) = 1 > s^A$ and $s^F(p) = \tilde{s} < s^A$ are *both* possible outcomes.

Third, let us consider non-cooperative (Nash) tariff-setting. It is convenient to postulate a foreign offer curve (that presumably depends on foreign tariffs), $M = F(E)$ where M is *home net imports* of good 2 and E is *home net exports* of good 1. Thus, $F'(E)$ is the home's marginal terms of trade. Since home's maximum output of good 1 is L (when s is set at zero so that $l(s) = 1$) and of good 2 is also L, by definition exports of either good cannot exceed L. Thus the relevant range for E is $E \leq L$ and for M is $M \geq -L$. Let us assume that in this range, $F'(E) \geq 0$, $F''(E) < 0$. For simplicity let us assume $F(E) = E^\theta$ for $E > 0$, $0 < \theta < 1$ and $F(E) = -(\,|\,E\,|\,)^\theta$ for $E < 0$.

Suppose at a social optimum the economy is specialized in the production of good 1 so that $c_1 = \dfrac{L}{l(s)} - E$ and $C_2 = F(E)$. Then welfare

$$W(E,s) = \alpha \, Log \; C_1 + \beta \, Log \; C_2 + (1 - \alpha - \beta) \; Log \; s$$

(17)

The first-order conditions for a maximum of (17) (since $c_2 > 0$ implies $E > 0$) are:

$$-\frac{\alpha}{c_1} + \frac{\beta}{c_2} F' = 0 \qquad (18)$$

$$\frac{\alpha}{c_1} \frac{-Ll'(s)}{(l(s))^2} + \frac{(1 - \alpha - s)}{s} = 0 \qquad (19)$$

Substituting for $l(s)$ and $F(E)$ in (18) and (19) and solving one gets

$$s \equiv s^{01} = \frac{1 - \alpha - \beta}{(\alpha + \beta\theta)\gamma + (1 - \alpha - \beta)} \qquad (20)$$

$$F \equiv E^{01} \equiv (\frac{\beta\theta}{\alpha + \beta\theta}) \frac{L}{l(s^0)} \qquad (21)$$

$$c_1 \equiv c_1^{01} = (\frac{\alpha}{\alpha + \beta\theta}) \frac{L}{l(s^0)} \qquad (22)$$

$$c_2 \equiv c_2^{01} = (E^{01}) \qquad (23)$$

Suppose at a social optimum the economy is specialized in the production of good 2 so that $c_1 = -E$, $c_2 = L \, | - | E |^{\theta}$. Since c_1 and c_2 do not depend on s, welfare is an increasing function of s so that the optimal $s^{02} = 1$. The optimal choice of E is determined by the first-order condition

$$-\frac{\alpha}{c_1} + \frac{\beta}{c_2} \, \theta |E|^{\theta-1} = 0 \qquad \text{or}$$

$$\frac{\alpha}{E} + \frac{\beta\theta |E|^{\theta-1}}{L - |E|^{\theta}} = 0 \qquad \text{or}$$

$$\alpha \, [L - | E |^{\theta}] - \beta\theta \, | E |^{\theta} = 0 \qquad \text{or}$$

$$|E|^{\theta} = \frac{\alpha L}{\alpha + \beta\theta} \tag{24}$$

$$E \equiv E^{02} = -(\frac{\alpha L}{\alpha + \beta\theta})^{1/\theta} \tag{25}$$

$$c_2 \equiv c_1^{02} = |E^{02}| \tag{26}$$

$$c_2 = L - |E^{02}|^{\theta} \tag{27}$$

Whether it is socially optimal to specialize in good 1 or good 2 depends on whether $W(E^{01}, s^{01}) \overset{>}{\underset{<}{-}} W(E^{02}, s^{02})$. Since $s^{01} < s^A < s^{02} = 1$, it is clear that one cannot rule out the possibilities that the optimal labor standards associated with a noncooperative Nash equilibrium exceeds or falls short of its autarky (or for that matter free trade) value.

It is also clear from the above even without explicitly writing down foreign welfare function and maximizing the sum of home and foreign welfare that the value of labor standards associated with such a maximum could exceed or fall short of its free trade value.

Note

[1] The description of the activities of UNICOR and the quotations in this paragraph are taken from the transcript of the program "60 Minutes" broadcast by CBS on October 20, 1996. [Transcript prepared by Burrelle's Information Services, Box 7, Livingstone, N.J.]

Reference

Srinivasan, T. N. 1998. "Trade and Human Rights." In Alan V. Deardorff and Robert M. Stern (eds.), *Constituent Interests and U.S. Trade Policies.* Ann Arbor: University of Michigan Press.

CHAPTER 8

A Transactions Cost Politics Analysis of International Child Labor Standards

Drusilla K. Brown

I. Introduction

Child labor is perhaps the most painful face of poverty. The specter of small children working long hours in dangerous and brutal working conditions is difficult for most members of the industrialized world to fully comprehend. Even worse is the thought of a small child delivered into bonded labor in order to discharge a parent's debt. UNICEF (1991) estimates that there are 80 million children aged 10–14 worldwide whose work is "so long or onerous that it interfered with their normal development." Labor force participation rates for smaller children aged 6 to 11 have been recorded as high as 25 percent in some communities. (For examples, see Grootaert and Kanbur, 1995.)

A natural response for an economist is to begin to search for some evidence of a correctable market failure that could justify a market intervention, thereby at least reducing the level of child labor. Noneconomists are likely to simply want to do away with the practice through legal prohibitions enforced with some sort of economic sanctions. The search for suitable corrective tools, however, has yielded frustratingly little in terms of policy recommendations that might be expected to reduce child labor in the near term in a manner that can reasonably be expected to serve the working child's interests. The fact of the matter is that in many low-income countries, the economic value of a child is still active at the margin.

For example, Hoffman (1988) surveys cross-country motivations for having children. The results, reported in table 8.1, clearly demonstrate the economic value of child-bearing in developing countries. Of respondents in Indonesia (Japanese), 94.1 percent identified economic/utility as a reason for having children and no other reason was offered more often than 29 percent of the time. Similarly high rates were reported for Indonesia-Sudanese (79.6%), the Philippines (71.3%) and Thailand (74.6%). Even for Turkey, an economic motivation was cited by 54 percent of respondents and was the most common reason offered. By comparison, only 6 percent of respondents in the United

TABLE 8.1. Advantages of Having Children Reported by Mothers (percent)

REASON	COUNTRY								
	U.S.	Turkey	Indonesia (Japanese)	Indonesia (Sudanese)	Philippines	Thailand	Korea	Taiwan	Singapore
Economic-Utility	6	54	94.1	79.6	71.3	74.6	35.7	44.4	46.8
Primary Ties and Affection	66.1	34.3	14	34.7	46.1	12.9	36.8	44.8	58.6
Stimulation/Fun	60	21.7	12.8	38.2	58.2	9.2	46.8	68.6	70.9
Self-Fulfillment	35.3	10.4	28.6	41.5	8.9	4.7	23.7	38.1	21.2
Adult Status	21.9	13.8	2.1	4.7	5.9	2.0	5.8	8.3	9.1
Achievement	11.1	4.6	7.8	7.7	3.4	1.8	30.1	2.8	3
Morality	6.8	6.7	0.5	0.4	1.9	1.9	2.3	0.4	0.2
n	1259	1539	984	965	1567	2288	1433	2103	904

Source: Adapted from Hoffman (1988).

States identified economic motivation as important. Rather, American parents seem largely motivated by the search for primary ties and affection.

Beyond the economic motivations for bearing children, there are several other reasons why it is difficult to identify the problems concerning child labor that are amenable to corrective measures. Some are enumerated below.

1. Banning child labor will very likely make the family poorer, thus lowering the welfare of the child. Appropriate labor market outcomes are dependent on income level. For many families, the work of children is essential to the survival of the family.

2. Subsidizing a mother's wages can have perverse results if the objective is to increase the formal education of her children. In the case of girls, work in the home frequently makes it possible for the mother to engage in market work. The opportunity cost to the family of formal education, then, is the wage earned by the mother, rather than the child's wage. A rise in the mother's wage can, at some income levels, increase female child labor in the home by drawing the mother into the work place. A similar relationship has been established between adult male wages and the home work of their male children.

3. Child labor in some cases is used to reduce risk associated with a poor harvest or other instability in family income. Legal restrictions against child labor or mandatory schooling are not likely to be effective in manipulating the behavior of a family close to subsistence.

4. Child labor that arises simply because the well-being of children has low value in the family is particularly hard to address with any policy tool. Prohibiting or circumscribing child labor may actually lower the value of the child to the family.

5. Identifying inappropriate child labor is difficult. Some labor, particularly apprenticeships, may be more education than work. Children may acquire marketable skills, even though reading, writing and arithmetic are not among them. In communities where the quality of formal education is extremely poor, work may provide higher-valued skills than formal schooling.

6. The outright banning of child labor is unlikely to eliminate the practice. However, it will remove it from the scrutiny of any regulatory agency.

Historically, the most effective strategies for reducing child labor have been the byproduct of economic growth. Once adult wages reach a threshold level, child labor begins to decline. Furthermore, technological change and mechanization reduce the demand for the skills possessed by children by virtue of their small size and nimble fingers.

Some standard market failure stories that one might appeal to in order to justify market intervention seem to miss the mark in terms of the welfare of children. For example, one might point to a failure in the market for education due to the externality generated by an educated populace. However, the welfare loss that is the target of the policy prescription in this case is born by someone other than the child. Correcting the market failure may improve the welfare of the general population, but only inadvertently addresses a source of child poverty. Presumably, the focus of attention should be on market failures that directly affect the welfare of the working child. Arguments based on child labor that result from incomplete markets for managing risk by marginally viable households have more appeal. In this case, improving access to insurance directly raises expected family income and lowers the probability of falling below subsistence.

II. Trade Sanctions and Child Labor

Among the most popular proposals in industrialized countries for dealing with child labor is to tax or prohibit imports of goods produced by children. Perhaps the most airtight (if not compelling) case for trade sanctions has been made by Basu and Van (1998). In their model, children are offered for market work only if the adult wage leaves the family below subsistence. Once subsistence is reached, children are withdrawn from the labor force and sent to school. As a consequence, there is a discontinuity in the labor supply curve at the subsistence wage. Labor demand is generated by competitive firms who hire only labor and the production function exhibits diminishing marginal productivity of labor.

The labor market for this economy is depicted in figure 8.1. As can be seen, there are two labor market equilibria. At point A, firms pay a high wage, W_h, and families send children to school. However, the equilibrium at point B is characterized by a low wage, W_l, which is below the subsistence wage, W_s. At the low-wage equilibrium, families are forced to offer their children for work. The policy recommendation that emerges from the Basu-Van analysis is that if child labor is legally prohibited then the low-wage equilibrium will be eliminated. Presumably, the market will then find its way to the high wage-no child labor equilibrium.

The special market characteristics that are necessary to support a prohibition against child labor in the Basu-Van model are difficult to guarantee. In fact, the point has been made many times in many contexts that a prohibition against child labor can leave children in far worse occupations at lower wages than the ones prohibited.

Furthermore, attempts by high-income countries to enforce a ban on child labor with import tariffs could have the effect of lowering the wages of children who continue to work. One example of this type of analysis is developed by Maskus and Holman (1996). They consider a two-good model in which child labor is specific to the labor-intensive export sector of a developing country. The importing country may attempt to punish the exporter for producing goods with child labor by imposing an import tariff.

If the price received by the exporter falls, so will the demand for children. Some children will, indeed, leave the work force for home work, alternative employment or school. This could raise social welfare if there is a negative externality generated by child labor and the alternative employment is better for the child than working in the export sector. However, the wage for those

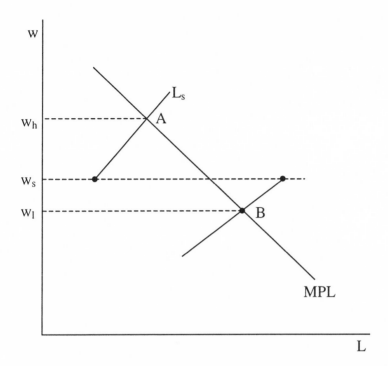

Figure 8.1

children who remain employed in the export sector will decline, thus making them worse off.

Not only will children who remain in the work force be made worse off but there is no guarantee that the children who leave the work force will find themselves in more desirable occupations. It is possible that a prohibition against work introduces a constraint in the parent's resource allocation problem which causes them to find that the next best alternative for the family is to place the child in a less onerous form of home work or, even better, to place the child in school. However, it is equally likely that the alternatives for the child will be worse rather than better.

III. Product Labeling

Freeman (1994) has suggested an alternative approach. He sorts all labor standard issues into those that are *process*-related and those that are *outcome*-related. *Process*-related issues such as freedom from forced labor, freedom of association, and the right to organize, are supported as fundamental human rights to which we can all agree and can be achieved independent of income level. These rights are most appropriately administered with legal prohibitions.

Outcome-related labor market characteristics such as minimum wages, maximum hours of work, hazardous working conditions, and minimum age of work are all functions of the income level of each country. Blanket requirements across all countries are not feasible or even desirable. Whatever labor standards that are established must be sensitive to specific market conditions.

In Freeman's view, the failure that necessitates intervention in the labor market stems from the negative external effect that a consumer experiences knowing that he is consuming a good produced under working conditions that the consumer finds distasteful. Freeman's proposed solution is to place a *label* on the product to characterize the conditions under which the good was produced. If the negative externality is significant, then presumably the consumer would be willing to pay a higher price for goods produced under *desirable* working conditions rather than *undesirable* working conditions.

There are already in existence several labeling efforts particularly targeting child labor. The Child Labor Coalition was formed in 1989 and consists of religious, human rights, and union groups. Their objective is to inform consumers in high-income countries about child labor employed and conditions of work in the production of goods such as rugs in South Asia. The coalition has sponsored the *Rugmark* campaign that provides a label certifying that the product was not produced using child labor. The United States has sought to use the ILO to extend the *Rugmark* label to clothing and other products. In addition, several firms have voluntarily established a code of conduct regulating labor practices. Some examples are Levi Strauss, Liz Claiborne, Nike, Reebok, Sears, Timberland, and Walmart.

However, if the net impact of labeling is to switch demand away from goods produced by children, the consequence for child workers could actually be quite negative. Those who leave the tradable goods sector may find poorer employment prospects elsewhere. Those who remain employed in the tradable goods sector may remain there only at reduced wages.

In order to guarantee that the label benefits the intended target (the worker), the worker and the label must remain connected to each other through the product. For example, the objective may be to change a production process that is hazardous to workers. A firm that changes the hazardous practice at some cost labels the product to this effect. The consumer pays a higher price for the good, which finances the change in the hazardous practice. The employee, now working in safer conditions, is the beneficiary (as is the socially-conscious consumer).

However, in the case of child labor, the intended beneficiary (the child) and the label are no longer connected. A label that identifies a product as having been produced with adult labor may raise the price of that good. As a consequence, the adult wage may rise. The impact on the working child, who is now in a new occupation, is undetermined. If labeling is to be beneficial for children, its success must rely on secondary effects that emerge in the general equilibrium.

ADULT

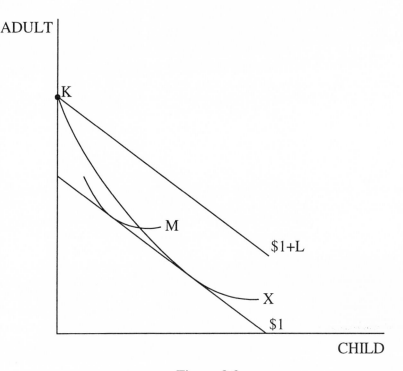

CHILD

Figure 8.2

In fact, the outcome from labeling where child labor is concerned can be quite perverse. Consider, for example, a two-good two-factor model of a price-taking developing country. Both the import-competing and export sectors employ adult and child labor, which are imperfect substitutes. The export sector, X, is taken to be child labor-intensive as compared to the import-competing sector, M. Factor market equilibrium for adult (A) and child (C) labor is depicted in figure 8.2. The unit value isoquants for each sector are shown to be tangent to a $1 isocost line. The slope of the isocost line is, of course, the relative wage rates of child and adult labor.

Now introduce product labeling. A premium, L, is paid by Western consumers for a dollar's worth of the X-good that is labeled as has having been produced using adult labor only. In order to qualify for the label, producers in the X-sector must produce using an adult-only technology. That is, X producers must use the technique of production denoted by point K in figure 8.2.
In order to be viable, the adult-only technology must cost no more than $1+L. If the $1+L isocost line falls short of the adult-only technology, point K, then no firms will label. Child labor practices will continue as is. However, if the $1+L isocost line intersects the A-axis exactly at point K, as shown in figure 8.2, then firms are indifferent between using adult-only technology, applying the label and receiving the label premium or continuing with their current

practice of hiring both adults and children. Some X-sector firms may decide to adopt the adult-only technology. In this case, the impact of production and factor employment can be seen by examining the Edgeworth Box in figure 8.3. The pre-labeling equilibrium is given by point H where the factor proportions rays, R_x and R_y, intersect. After labeling, $O_y L_A$ amount of adult labor is deployed to the adult-only firms in the X sector. The adult labor remaining and all child labor supplied are then distributed between the X and M sectors with equilibrium at point J. As the Rybczynski Theorem would lead us to expect, production of the import-competing good contracts and production of the export good expands.

We are now in a position to draw two conclusions. First, since both factor employment and wages are unchanged, labor income must be unchanged. Furthermore, since the labeling premium was just barely enough to cover the increased cost of the adult-only technology, profits are unchanged. However, it is clear that Western consumers are paying more for the labeled goods than before. As a consequence, it must be the case that the labeling premium, L, has been completely dissipated due to the use of the inefficient adult-only technology. The only social benefit obtained is the good feeling that Western consumers experience knowing that they are consuming a good that was not produced by child labor. However, the amount of child labor and each child's family income are unchanged. Children are no better off than they were before labeling.

Second, the one impact that labeling does have is to expand the export sector and contract the import-competing sector at fixed world prices. So we can conclude that the developing country will trade more. If we now relax the assumption that the developing country is a price-taker, we can conclude that a terms-of-trade deterioration is possible. Further, since child labor is the relatively abundant factor, the Stolper-Samuelson Theorem tells us to expect a decline in the wage-rate for child labor.

Returning to figure 8.2, if the $1+L$ isocost line intersects the Adult-axis above point K then all exporting firms will want to adopt the adult-only technology. The resultant increase in the demand for adult workers will raise the adult wage relative to the wage of child workers, ultimately stemming the flow of X-sector firms adopting the adult-only technology. The new labor market equilibrium is depicted in figure 8.4. The wage of child labor has fallen relative to the adult wage, as indicated by the flattened isocost line. The X-sector firms using an adult-child technology have now adopted a more child-labor intensive process given by point N in response to the lower relative cost of child labor.

Firms in the import-competing M-sector will also attempt to reduce cost by substituting children for adult labor. However, since the M-sector is adult labor-intensive as compared to the X-sector, the rise in the adult wage must raise costs for M-sector firms as compared to the X-sector firms that use the adult-child technology. Therefore, if X-sector firms are breaking even, the M-sector firms must have negative profits. This can be seen in figure 8.3, in

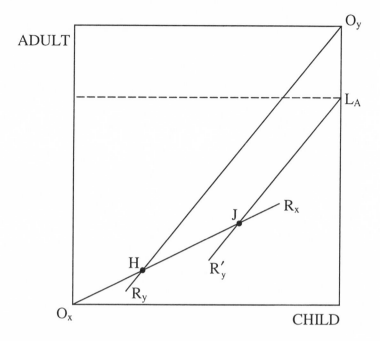

Figure 8.3

which the M-sector unit value isoquant now lies uniformly above the $1 iso-cost line. As a consequence, no import-competing firms will survive once labeling is introduced.

The fact that the M-sector is eliminated is not a surprising result. The introduction of a labeled good has essentially converted the two-good two-factor price-taking economy into one of three goods and two factors. Consequently, it is virtually certain that one of the three sectors will not be able to break even in the post-labeling equilibrium.

Since the M-sector has been eliminated, the relative wages of adult and child workers is determined so as to make X-sector firms indifferent between using an adult-only technology and an adult-child technology. Therefore, the adult wage will rise until the additional cost of producing X using the adult-only technology is just barely covered by the labeling premium, L. X firms using the adult-only technology are once again breaking even on the $1+L iso-cost line at point K.

The impact on children in all three cases appears to be either zero or negative. Of course, the adults in the labor force are likely to be the parents of the children in the labor force. One might hope that raising the adult wage in the third case might reduce the need for the child's contribution to family in-

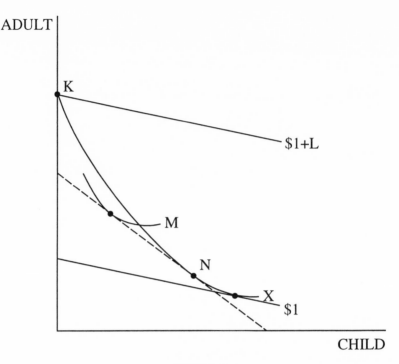

Figure 8.4

come. Furthermore, the fall in the child's wage lowers the opportunity cost to the family of formal schooling. However, it must be kept in mind that, at least for this example, the total payment to a typical family (adult plus child workers) is virtually unchanged. As in the previous case, much if not all of the labeling premium has been dissipated through the use of the inefficient adult-only technology. Product labeling will raise the welfare of children only if the labeling premium is far more than the amount necessary to compensate firms for the higher cost of the adult-only technology. In order to succeed, the labeling premium has to be large enough to raise the adult wage to the threshold level at which child labor begins to decline. In other words, when labeling succeeds, it succeeds because it provides an income transfer to families, not because it provides a disincentive to the firm to hire children.

There is a more fundamental weakness with the labeling approach. The issue that presumably should concern Western consumers is not whether they are offended by consuming goods produced by a child. Surely, the real issue is the working child's welfare. As a consequence, the consumer must distinguish between child labor that actually serves the child's interest and child labor that is somehow exploitative, reflective of the child's low standing in the family, etc. Labeling does little to address the sources of market failure that result in inefficient child labor and miserable outcomes for children. For example, a breakdown in the market for insurance for subsistence families may result in too much child labor. However, labeling, will either reduce the child's wages or, at best, leave them unchanged. For a subsistence family, the child is likely to be on the downward-sloping part of the labor supply curve. That is, a cut in the wage will induce the child to work more in a now more desperate struggle to keep the family above subsistence. The result, obviously, is to worsen the child's expected outcome.

It would take an extraordinary amount of sophistication on the part of the consumer and quite a detailed label if the consumer is to distinguish between child labor that is inappropriate by some standard and child labor that is actually in the interest of the child. Confronted with a label that says that this product was produced by a child, it is quite likely that the working child's welfare will rise if the good is purchased, thereby raising the child's wages, rather than if it is shunned by the consumer. What one would actually need to see is a label that says something like, "this good was produced by a *child* in a community in which the elasticity of supply of child labor is negative," in which case you should buy the product, or "this good was produced by *adult* labor in a community where the elasticity of child labor with respect to parental wages is negative," in which case you should buy the good.[1]

Buying the goods produced by a child, thereby raising the child's wages, generally should expand the child's opportunity set.[2] So the presumption is that one should buy child-produced goods, not avoid them. There are two reasons why this may not be the case. One possibility is that the child's earnings are being expropriated by other family members. The second is that either the child or the parent making decisions for the child under-appreciate the value of education or the negative consequences of hazardous and/or grueling working conditions. In other words, the market-failure that is occurring must be within the child's household.

In addition, labeling does not address market failure associated with child labor if the disutility of children working is a public good, as Freeman points out. Labeling can, however, play a role in transferring resources from a Western consumer to poor children. For example, a product label can state that some fraction of the purchase price has been donated to an educational institution or a community agency.

IV. The Transactions Cost Politics (TCP) of International Labor Standards

There are several aspects of the treatment of labor standards in the international arena that reflect the transactions costs of political bargaining.[3] Consider, for example, the allocation of monitoring tasks across international agencies. As an historical matter, the characterization and monitoring of labor standards has been allocated to the much-maligned International Labour Organization (ILO). Currently, the ILO is the single international agency that addresses labor standards. However, the ILO has been given little real enforcement power. As a consequence, their activities have been constrained to promulgating conventions that establish minimal labor standards, monitoring, disseminating information and providing technical assistance. Product labeling is the most aggressive that the ILO has become in attempting to penalize countries or producers with poor labor practices.

The ILO Secretariat did attempt to connect labor standards and international trade with the objective of improving enforcement. The ILO and the World Trade Organization (WTO) were to work together in monitoring the protection of core labor standards. However, the working party suspended future discussion of the use of trade sanctions in 1995.

Multitask Agencies

One aspect of the incentive system faced by multitask agencies has been brought to bear in understanding the exclusive assignment of labor issues to the ILO. It is argued that the appropriate international *trade* standards to which we should and can agree can be established with much greater clarity than is the case for *labor* standards. Further, it is far easier to observe compliance with international trade law than with international labor law. As a result, a WTO that is assigned both monitoring tasks will assign greater effort to monitoring of trade violations than to monitoring labor violations. Therefore, labor issues should be assigned to a separate agency so as to increase the monitoring effort labor standards receive.

However, the interpretation that monitoring assignments across international agencies arise from the difficulty of observing labor standards enforcement relative to trade standards enforcement is not consistent with the historical evolution of the issue. The United States has, for some time, attempted to draw labor standards under the umbrella first of the General Agreement on Tariffs and Trade (GATT) and then the WTO. The apparent purpose is to attempt to use the enforcement mechanisms of the GATT, and now the WTO, to improve compliance with what the United States considers to be fair labor standards.

Most recently the United States placed the issue of labor standards on the agenda for the WTO Ministerial Meeting held in Singapore in December 1996. The Clinton Administration claimed that its objective was to signal U.S. workers that competition from low-wage countries would not be intensified due to the denial of basic human rights. Administration officials went to some lengths to dispel the view that the United States sought to erect trade barriers or to discriminate against low-wage competitors. Most importantly, Administration officials claimed that they were not seeking to use trade sanctions to uphold labor standards. However, the U.S. delegates did want the WTO ministers to link the maintenance of an open world trade system to the promotion of core labor standards such as freedom of association, prohibition of forced labor and elimination of exploitative child labor. Furthermore, they did seek to establish a working party to identify links between labor standards and WTO rules.

However, it was not to be. The U.S. position received little support from many European trade ministers and was vigorously countered by the trade ministers of South East Asia and India, who opposed any discussion of trade and labor standards in the WTO. The Singapore Ministerial Declaration that was adopted on December 13, 1996 stated:

"We renew our commitment to the observance of internationally recognized core labour standards. The International Labour Organization (ILO) is the competent body to set and deal with these standards, and we affirm our support for its work in promoting them. We believe that economic growth and development fostered by increased trade and further trade liberalization contribute to the promotion of these standards. We reject the use of labour standards for protectionist purposes, and agree that the comparative advantage of countries, particularly low-wage developing countries, must in no way be put into question. In this regard, we note that the WTO and ILO Secretariates will continue their existing collaboration."

Labor standards were only mentioned in the Singapore Ministerial Declaration to the effect that: (1) the ILO was the appropriate body for addressing labor standards internationally; (2) economic growth and trade are the appropriate tools for promoting standards; (3) the use of labor standards for protectionist purposes is rejected; and (4) the comparative advantage of low-wage countries should not be questioned. In effect, the Ministerial unequivocally placed labor standards under the jurisdiction of the ILO.

Clearly, the pressure to divide trade and labor monitoring tasks between the WTO and ILO is driven by those principals, such as India, who seek minimal enforcement of labor standards, not by those principals who seek to intensify enforcement, such as the United States. Therefore, it is unlikely that the allocation of the labor monitoring task to the ILO is intended to improve enforcement as the multitask agency argument discussed above would suggest.

Multiprincipal Agencies

An alternative explanation for the division of labor and trade standards monitoring, which is more consistent with recent history, is that labor issues would receive far too much attention in the WTO, rather than too little. Excessive monitoring of labor issues could stem from the fact that the WTO must respond to multiple principals with conflicting objectives.

The fundamental objective of international trade negotiations is to alleviate the prisoner's dilemma. Each country's interests lie in optimal protection of its own sectors but little or no intervention by its trade partners. However, the collective interest is served when all countries follow an "open" trading regime. Defining a set of rules of fairness regulating international trade is easy when compared to developing an international protocol on issues like labor standards. Most importantly, the trade rules can serve the interests of all participants without regard to specific country characteristics such as stage of economic development. Optimal labor market characteristics, however, depend heavily on each country's level of income. Labor market standards that do not threaten the interest of the poorest countries have been frustratingly elusive. Even if developing countries were to agree that a set of standards is desirable, achieving them may be difficult or impossible.

An enforcement mechanism that the participants in an international trade and labor organization might adopt would specify a relationship between a vector of trade and labor standards, S, and actual performance, A, to a vector of punishments, P, for deviations from those standards. If the punishment parameter, t, is uniform across all standards, then we have

$P=t(A-S)$.

In a negotiated agreement there will be a trade-off between the power of the incentive, t, and the stringency of the standard, S. Since there is a large group of countries who have poor labor-market conditions and will have difficulty meeting even minimal labor market standards, one outcome could be to set a weak punishment parameter. This is sub-optimal, however, since it produces a set of low-power incentives for an open trading regime on which all participants were able to agree. A more attractive alternative would be to adopt very weak standards for labor market performance while setting a stiffer punishment parameter.

An optimal approach, however, is to represent the punishment parameter as a matrix, which has been partitioned between trade and labor standards. For example, where the L (T) subscript denotes labor (trade) standards (S), performance (A), punishment parameter (t) and punishment (P).

$$\begin{bmatrix} P_L \\ P_T \end{bmatrix} = \begin{bmatrix} t_L & 0 \\ 0 & t_T \end{bmatrix} \begin{bmatrix} A_L - S_L \\ A_T - S_T \end{bmatrix}$$

Under this configuration it would be possible to set the trade penalties suitably high to reflect the consensus on the desirability of an open trading regime. The power of incentives for achieving labor standards would be considerably lower, reflecting the diversity of optimal labor standards that are appropriate across countries.

The partitioned configuration was pursued by the United States during the Singapore Ministerial. The Clinton Administration proposed setting the punishment parameter for labor standards at zero in the hope that it could obtain a set of rigorous labor standards. However, the WTO charter is an incomplete contract. It would ultimately fall to a working party to interpret the operational consequences of the WTO's charter. The United States was clearly signaling an intent to use the interpretation process to reduce labor standards to their trade equivalent. Ultimately, the United States could not credibly pre-commit not to pursue the link between labor standards and WTO trade rules, thereby using the power of the trade punishment parameter against labor standards violations.

The outcome of the WTO Ministerial was to accept the notion of partitioning of penalties and to accept a rigorous definition of labor standards. However, in order to prevent any possibility that trade penalties would apply to labor standards violations, labor standards were partitioned right out of the WTO. The ILO, a distinctly different entity, would address the issue of international labor standards. Much is made of the weakness of the ILO and the absence of enforcement powers. However, a more charitable view of the agency is that labor standards have been allocated to the ILO precisely because it has no power to punish. The low power of the incentives used by the ILO is entirely appropriate given the general inability to identify a set of uniform labor standards that can be applied in all settings.

Designing the charter of a multitask/multiprincipal agency is difficult when the intensity of enforcement should vary markedly over the various tasks. This is particularly the case if one of the principals would like to apply the high enforcement power of one set of tasks inappropriately. It may be necessary to sort tasks across agencies so that the maximum enforcement power of the agency is consistent with the task that it undertakes that should have the lowest intensity of enforcement. The end result is that some agencies may have a very small range of tasks and virtually no power of enforcement, as is the case with the ILO.

This is not unlike the fundamental transactions cost that bedevils multiprincipal and multitask agencies. When several principals are attempting to affect decision-making in an agency, they will provide positive incentives for desirable actions and negative incentives for undesirable actions. To the extent that the principals disagree or tasks vary in observability, bargaining can produce a set of low-powered incentives. Holmstrom and Milgrom (1991) and Dixit (1996) have shown that the power of incentives can be improved if some of the actions of the agent and principals can be controlled in an *all-or-nothing* manner.

A similar principle applies here. The United States would like to apply the high-powered punishments for trade barriers to labor-standards violations. Given this fact, the impact must be to either lower the punishments for trade barriers or lower the labor-standards, neither of which is optimal. The optimal solution is to prohibit the United States from switching punishments that are intended for trade violations over to the labor-standards violations. Partitioning tasks across international agencies is a particularly effective strategy for enforcing the prohibition.

Sorting tasks by international agency can also be understood as a strategy for coping with the comparatively rigid rules that are optimal for regulating international trade while leaving the flexibility for managing international labor standards. Clear and transparent trade standards reduce the ambiguities that must be left to interpretation by a dispute resolution panel. Clarity and simplicity have the potential, therefore, to improve compliance. Meaningful labor standards, by contrast, must be flexible and responsive to individual country conditions. Sorting trade and labor enforcement by international agency can help diminish the tension between rigid rules that improve commitment to principles of trade liberalization and the flexibility that outcome-related labor standards require.

Agency Shopping

If the United States is to successfully press its case for labor standards internationally, it is going to need to meet four preconditions. First, it needs leverage. The United States threatened to walk out of the WTO Ministerial if it did not get its way with labor standards. However, such a threat lacked credibility. Given the current set of issues still unresolved in the WTO, the United States is asking for more than it has to offer. As a consequence, walking out would gain the United States nothing but could potentially cost a great deal. Second, the United States needs a mechanism that will allow standards to vary with the individual country characteristics. Third, the policy device must reasonably be expected to actually improve the welfare of the intended beneficiaries of the policy. Fourth, the consequences of intervention will probably require popular support within the targeted country.

The Clinton Administration thinks that it has found such an agent in the International Monetary Fund (IMF). As is well known, the standard IMF package offers loans to bridge a balance of payments crisis, but in return demands that the country government conform to certain fiscal, monetary and exchange rate policy prescriptions. However, during the financial crisis in Asia in November and December 1997, the IMF substantially broadened the concept of *IMF Conditionality*. The South Koreans call the new regime *IMF Plus.*

IMF Plus includes the standard conditions concerning monetary, fiscal and exchange rate policy prescriptions. However, the South Koreans were subject to additional conditions concerning trade policy and other market reforms and even went so far as to stipulate accounting practices that must be adopted by Korean firms. The intent of IMF Plus is to eliminate the practices of "crony capitalism" that are believed to be a central contributor to the financial crisis. The IMF targeted eight reform areas that include foreign ownership of equity capital, foreign participation in banking and insurance, and barriers to industrial imports. Note that all of the conditions have previously been sought by the United States with limited success in rounds of trade liberalization.

Indonesia was subject to similar conditions. The long list of reforms imposed on Indonesia included such items as setting the price of gasoline and the manner in which plywood was sold. Corrupt business practices used to enrich President Suharto's family and friends were also to be curtailed.

However, the Administration has already signaled its intent to press further. Under the right circumstances, future IMF conditions will address the *quality* as well as the *quantity* of fiscal spending. For example, the Administration officials have already suggested that it might be appropriate to attempt to force governments in a financial crisis to divert expenditure on military armaments and palaces to expenditure on education. Such a change in IMF policies obviously raises serious questions about national sovereignty. However, sovereignty aside, there are several reasons why the Clinton Administration is far more likely to enjoy success working through the IMF than through the WTO.

First, balance of payments crises provide the United States the leverage that it lacks in the WTO. Experience with the Latin American debt crisis in the 1980s strongly suggests that the economic and social turmoil that results from a severe and unrelieved financial crisis can be catastrophic and long-lived. By comparison, the IMF, in conjunction with the industrialized countries, moved swiftly to relieve the financial pressure in Asia. Although the financial crisis in Asia has taken its toll, a decade-long economic collapse seems unlikely.

The Clinton Administration identified the Asian crisis as a clear threat to the economic welfare of the United States, but also saw a military threat, as well. As a consequence, the South Korean government attempted to bargain over the conditions of IMF Plus precisely because they realized that the Clinton Administration officials perceived U.S. interests to be so closely tied to the financial stability of East Asia. However, the United States was unmoved. It was the view of U.S. Treasury officials that without fundamental market reform, the preconditions for financial stability would not be met. Another crisis would occur. This belief gave the Administration officials the credibility they needed to press for the reforms they believed were appropriate.

Similar reasoning could apply to fiscal and financial reform that the United States would like to press on many developing countries in Asia and Africa. For example, to the extent that there is a break-down in the market for education that can be alleviated through government action and poor educational opportunities play a significant role in slow economic development, the IMF will have the leverage that it needs to press for a reallocation in government spending against a country in a financial crisis.

The role that the IMF would play in the domestic politics of its target countries is also somewhat different than for conventional IMF conditionality. When the IMF's policy prescription is one of fiscal and monetary contraction, the immediate impact is negative. It is commonly argued that the IMF, by imposing conditions for loans, can help a government credibly commit to a plan of fiscal and monetary contraction that would otherwise be politically nonviable.

However, if the Clinton Administration turns its focus to the content of fiscal policy rather than its level, the impact of the new IMF conditions will be redistributive rather than contractionary. IMF conditions that require a reduction in spending on a repressive police force, for example, and increased spending on education, electrification, etc. could have a "populist" quality. The role, then, of the IMF would be to strengthen the hand of the political entities who seek a more equitable distribution of wealth and a more efficient fiscal structure.

Finally, using the IMF as a vehicle provides the flexible rules that outcome-related labor standards require. As discussed above, the characteristics of an efficient labor market outcome depend heavily on the level of income and economic development as well as the precise nature of whatever market-failure that may be contributing to unnecessarily poor outcomes for children.

Tailoring labor standards to individual country conditions is virtually impossible in an organization like the WTO where great emphasis is placed on uniform rules applying to all countries. However, the IMF commonly undertakes individual country studies that are intended to ferret out the origins of a financial crisis. The Clinton Administration will be sorely tempted to take the opportunity to identify circumstances that are contributing to slow or negative growth and impose conditions on those practices, as well.

Breakdowns that occur within family decision making that have negative consequences for children will remain unattended by an IMF channel. But market failures can be addressed, particularly those that slow economic growth, which is ultimately the greatest source of child poverty.

V. Conclusions

The foregoing discussion gives little hope that arms-length intervention on behalf of working children is likely to be beneficial. Neither trade sanctions nor incentives offered by consumers to improve the lot of children necessarily improve their welfare as a group. This paper reviews some of the issues that pertain to the treatment of child labor in the international arena. A review of the standard prescriptions for reducing child labor provide little hope that the welfare of children can be improved in the absence of world-wide economic growth, development and increased adult wages.

Familiar prescriptions such as import tariffs levied against goods produced with child labor are likely to leave children with lower wages and/or in more damaging occupations. Similarly, product labeling, intended to identify goods produced without child labor, can have adverse consequences for working children. It is shown that some, if not all, of the premium paid for labeled goods is dissipated due to the use of an efficient technology by firms that hire adults only. Child labor practices are altered only if the premium paid is sufficient to raise adult wages above the threshold at which child labor begins to decline. As a consequence, if the labeling premium is effective in improving the welfare of children, the reason is that the label premium raises family income, not because it provides a disincentive to firms to hire children.

The allocation of the task of monitoring child labor to the ILO rather than the WTO is also analyzed using the transactions cost politics approach. One interpretation of the separation of the multiple tasks of monitoring trade and labor standards between the two agencies stems from the fact that fair trade standards can be established without regard to level of income of participating countries. This is not the case for many labor market outcomes that depend critically on the level of economic development. As a consequence, compliance with fair trade standards is more easily observable than compliance with labor standards. In an agency with the responsibility of monitoring both trade and labor standards, compliance with trade standards would receive closer scrutiny, while labor would be inadequately monitored. However, as an historical matter, the separation of monitoring tasks between the two agencies has been sought by those principals who want little or no monitoring of labor standards, not by those principals who seek greater monitoring.

An alternative explanation is that, the separation of monitoring tasks across agencies stems from the fact that international agencies are controlled by multiple principals. The discrepancy between the ability of the principals to agree on trade rules relative to labor standards argues in favor of high trade standards with strict punishments for protection and labor standards with weak punishments.

Partitioning the labor and trade monitoring tasks between two agencies allowed each standard and the associated punishment for deviations to be set at the highest level to which the principals were able to agree. The comparatively strict rules of the WTO reflect the high degree of consensus for an open trading regime. By comparison, the low level of agreement on labor standards is reflected both in the weak language of the ILO and the absence of any meaningful enforcement mechanism.

We also found that sorting trade and labor enforcement by international agency can help diminish the tension between rigid rules that improve commitment to principles of trade liberalization and the flexibility that outcome-related labor standards require. Sorting also improves the credibility of a commitment to the principle that efficient labor market conditions vary with stage of development and that cross-country variations should not be punished with trade sanctions. As a consequence, the U.S. position on child labor may be best served by embracing the ILO, accepting its limited capacity of enforcement and attempting to work with country-specific incentive schemes rather than punishment.

Finally, we turned to the issue of agency shopping. The United States, having failed to achieve its objectives with regard to labor standards in the WTO, has most recently turned to the IMF as a vehicle.

Notes

[1] This is not as far-fetched as it sounds. There are some such elasticities estimated. For example, Levy (1985) estimated that for Egypt, a 10 percent increase in women's wages would lead to a 15 percent decline in the labor of children aged 12–14 and a 27 percent decline in the labor of children aged 6–11.

[2] There is an added complication in that it is difficult to establish the connection between goods prices and the underlying factor returns. For example, in a two good-two factor world, if the export good is also child-labor intensive, then a fall in its price will

lower the wage paid to children. However, in a world of many goods and factors, there is no reliable link from the price of any particular good to a factor price.
[3] For an introduction to Transactions Cost Politics see Dixit (1996).

References

Aggarwal, Mita. 1995. "International Trade, Labor Standards, and Labor Market Conditions: An Evaluation of the Linkages," USITC, Office of Economics Working Paper No. 95–06–C (June).

Basu, Kaushik, and Pham Hoang Van. 1998. "The Economics of Child Labor." *American Economic Review* 88:412–27.

Brown, Drusilla K., Alan V. Deardorff, and Robert M. Stern. 1998. "Issues of Environmental and Labor Standards in the Global Trading System." In Stanley W. Black (ed.), *Globalization, Technological Change and Labor Markets*. Amsterdam: Kluwer Academic Press.

Dixit, Avinash K. 1996. The Making of Economic Policy: A Transaction-Cost Politics Perspective. Cambridge: The MIT Press.

Feldstein, Martin. 1998. "Refocusing the IMF." *Foreign Affairs*, March/April, vol. 7, no. 2.

Freeman, Richard B. 1994. "A Hard-Headed Look at Labor Standards." In Gregory K. Schoepfle and Kenneth A. Swinnerton (eds.), *International Labor Standards and Global Economic Integration: Proceedings of a Symposium*. Washington, D.C.: U.S. Department of Labor, Bureau of International Labor Affairs.

Grootaert, Christiaan, and Ravi Kanbur. 1995. "Child Labour: An Economic Perspective." *International Labour Review*, Vol. 134, No. 2.

Hoffman, L. W. 1988. "Cross-Cultural Differences in Child-Rearing Goals." In R. A. LeVine, P. M. Miller, and M. M. West (eds.), *Parental Behavior in Diverse Societies: New Directions for Child Development*. San Francisco: Jossey-Bass.

Holmstrom, Bengt, and Paul Milgrom. 1991. "Multitask Principal-Agent Analysis: Incentive Contracts, Asset Ownership, and Job Design," *Journal of Law, Economics, and Organization* 7, Special Issue, 24–51.

Krueger, Alan. 1997. "International Labor Standards and Trade," *Annual World Bank Conference on Development Economics 1996*. Washington, D.C.: The World Bank.

Levy, Victor. 1985. "Cropping Pattern Mechanization, Child Labour, and Fertility Behaviour in a Farming Economy: Rural Egypt," *Economic Development and Cultural Change* (Chicago), Vol. 33, No. 4. July.

Maskus, Keith E., and Jill A. Holman. 1996. "The Economics of Child Labor Standards." In process.

Organization for Economic Cooperation and Development (OECD). 1996. Trade, Employment and Labour Standards: A Study of Core Workers' Rights and International Trade. Paris: OECD

Rodrik, Dani. 1996. "Labor Standards in International Trade: Do They Matter and What Do We Do About Them?" In Robert Lawrence, Dani Rodrik, and John Whalley, *Emerging Agenda for Global Trade: High Stakes for Developing Countries*. Washington, D.C: Overseas Development Council.

UNICEF. 1991. *The State of the World's Children 1991*. Oxford University Press.

Comment

Mark Silbergeld

I have the following points of agreement with Brown's paper:

- Child labor is perhaps the most painful aspect of poverty.
- Effective intervention is appropriate and necessary.
- There are significant and very difficult-to-address cultural aspects to the problem.
- Work skills may be more crucial than formal learning for many people in an economy, to the point where it begins to emerge from poverty.
- There are valid distinctions among various situations in which children work, e.g., among children helping parents and the community harvest food, children working at home and children working in factory conditions.
- Some efforts to address child labor by avoiding the goods may make the situations of some individual child laborers worse.
- The WTO may not be an effective forum for addressing the issue (but when steps are taken through other *fora*, the WTO should agree not to treat them as discriminatory trade practices).

My points of disagreement and considerations that Brown has omitted are:

- The social dimensions of the problem make a market analysis useful but hardly dispositive of the policy issues.
- Government measures alone are inappropriate to attack the problem.
- Improvements in general working conditions for all workers in poor countries are a part of the solution to the plight of working children.
- Labor condition information and individual citizen decisions in the market place based on that information are actually part of the political solution even if they do not alone suffice as economic disincentives to child labor.
- Programs based on positive incentives for improved labor conditions are more likely to contribute to a solution than those that are solely negative (such as trade bans).
- Citizens have a right to information about labor conditions and to act on it—the most basic notion of market economics, consumer sovereignty, suggests that each consumer should be able to evaluate both the probable outcomes of purchasing or avoiding goods produced under adverse condi-

tions that cannot be ameliorated immediately and the appropriateness of participating in economic transactions involving goods produced under such situations.

- The most important aspect of such programs and of citizen actions to prefer products made under more favorable working conditions may be political—to send a message to governments that child labor and other unacceptable working conditions are important to address effectively through public as well as private decisions.

- Even proposed public actions that clearly violate trade agreements help to signal that legally-grounded positive, public programs, whether bilateral, multilateral or through established international institutions, may be politically necessary in order to preserve public acceptance of orderly trade agreements.

- Bilateral and multilateral efforts would be facilitated if the Congress would renew the President's Fast Trade trade negotiations authority with the power to negotiate labor (as well as environmental) conditions in trade agreements.

- Brown suggests that consumers should not switch demand away from child-produced goods because that may worsen the conditions for those children. Does this imply that consumers should prefer child-produced goods to assure their present ("preferred") condition and to create "preferable" conditions for these children now working or living under worse conditions?

- This could be a problem in which the conditions for some may have to become temporarily worse for some in order to improve for many—the potentially positive political effects of consumers' preference shifts are too great for the campaign against child labor to ignore.

Comment

Avinash K. Dixit*

While the main focus of Brown's paper is on issues of political economy of international agreements on trade and labor standards, and the design of organizations to implement such agreements, it begins with some economic analysis, and I will begin likewise. Brown restates an argument of Basu and Van (1998) for trade sanctions. She criticizes the conclusions of the model using other more general ones. But I think that the model can be countered in its own terms, and that it supports exactly the opposite conclusion.

Basu and Van construct a two-dimensional model where adult and child labor are maintained as two distinct quantities. I use the simpler version of Brown, where labor is aggregated into efficiency units. My figure 8.5 reproduces the discontinuous labor supply curve of Brown's figure 8.1. The portion SC is for below-subsistence wage rates, when families offer the children's labor on the market, and the portion SA for higher wages when only adults work. Brown superimposes on this a downward-sloping labor demand curve. Then there can be two equilibria, and, if industrial countries refuse to buy goods produced using child labor, they can help select the upper (better) equilibrium.

But in the context where enough goods are traded in world markets, the wage is determined by the world prices of the goods. The labor demand curve is horizontal at this wage. The height of this horizontal curve (the real wage) shifts as the world prices change, according to the well-known Stolper-Samuelson effect.

Here the export good of the less-developed country is likely to be relatively more labor-intensive. If industrial countries admit this good into their countries without restraint, its relative price will be high and therefore the real wage will be high. If industrial countries impose import tariffs or equivalent restrictions, the price of this good will be low and therefore the wage will be low. Thus we have the very real possibility that under protectionism in industrial countries the labor demand curve in the less-developed country will be in the position DP, supporting the low-wage equilibrium where child-labor prevails, whereas free trade would shift the curve upward to DT, supporting the high-wage, adult-labor-only, equilibrium. Thus industrial countries' protection is likely to aggravate the problem of child labor in the LDCs.

Brown later shows how the product labeling policies that are often advocated to counter child labor in less developed countries can lower the eco-

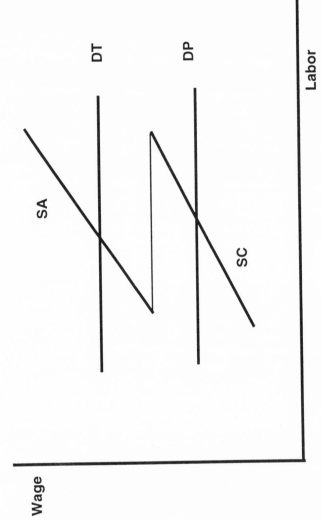

Figure 8.5

Segments of labor supply curve: SC—with child labor,
 SA—only adult labor
Labor demand curves under alternative trade policies of
 industrial countries: DT—free trade, DP—import tariffs

nomic well-being of the very children it is intended to help. I argue that trade restrictions can be similarly counterproductive.

For me the most interesting part of the paper is the analysis of political bargaining among countries over trade and labor issues and implementation of the resulting agreements by international organizations. Brown points out that the countries can be regarded as multiple principals who attempt to influence the actions of the organization, which is then regarded as their common agent. The general theory of such situations tells us that if trade and labor standards are implemented by the same agency, then the interaction between the tasks will lower the power of incentives for both tasks, and therefore lower the efficacy of implementation of both. This suggests using separate agencies for the two. Separate agencies also make it easier to endow each with a specific mission or culture, thereby better aligning the objective function of each agency with that of the principal most directly concerned with its output, thus reducing the extent of the moral hazard problem.

This is a nice use of transaction cost ideas to the issue of the design of international organizations. But it is only a beginning; there are many other aspects of the situation that need to be taken into account. Perhaps the most important is a very unusual aspect of these agencies—their task is to monitor and penalize actions of the principals themselves. Each principal is happy to have the other principals disciplined in this way, but each dislikes and resists being subjected to the same discipline. This calls into question the credibility of the incentive contracts between the principals and the agent. All the other principals must cooperate in disciplining any one of them. That usually relies on the nature of the repeated relationship among the principals. In other words, the right model should be that of a repeated game of common agency, and an equilibrium with tacit cooperation based on credible penalties for defectors. To construct such a model is far beyond the scope of a discussant, but I would guess that the repeated game feature will contribute to the resolution of some of the difficulties of low-powered incentives that exist in static common agencies.

In the concluding part of the paper, Brown examines the "realpolitik" of how the United States can pursue its case for labor standards using different international organizations including the International Monetary Fund and the Generalized System of Preferences in GATT. This reminds me of the discussions that were common in the early and mid-1980s as to which route through the U.S. trade laws was optimal to pursue for protectionist interests—the relative merits of the escape clause, anti-dumping laws, or Section 301. I think the analogy is more than a mere coincidence. The high-minded concern for the welfare of children in less-developed countries is all too often a mask for the selfish objectives of organized interests in the United States, just as the arguments of national security and strategic trade policy in the 1980s were often concocted by these interests.

Basically, child labor is a sad concomitant feature of poverty. It prevailed in Victorian England and nineteenth century U.S. just as it does in many less-developed countries today. The United States began to get rid of its child labor in the early decades of the twentieth century, largely through enactment of compulsory schooling laws. It was only in 1938 that the Fair Employment Act directly banned child labor. If we take 1910 as the earliest date of the shift in the U.S. practice, gross national income per capita at that date translates to about $7,000 at 1995 prices. This needs chaining of different data on income and price indexes, so it may be subject to some errors, but these are unlikely to change the figure drastically either way.

How does this compare with incomes in typical LDCs whose child labor practices are currently criticized in the U.S. and invoke calls for protectionist responses? The World Development Report for 1997 gives the following 1995 incomes per capita (measured in PPP-corrected dollars) for a sample of these countries:

Bangladesh	640
India	1400
China	2920
Philippines	2850
Indonesia	3800
Brazil	5400
Mexico	6400

It was not until the U.S. income per capita had rises to a level higher than any of these that we started to get rid of our own child labor practices. It seems we have no moral standing to criticize the others.

I believe that if we were really concerned with children in less-developed countries, we should be advocating not protection but precisely the opposite policies. The surest way to eliminate child labor is to raise adult incomes in these countries. That is most likely to be achieved through the expansion of trade with them, and particularly direct investment which raises labor demand there, not restrictions on these activities.

Note

* I thank Gary Fields and Harvey Rosen for valuable discussions.

Reference

Basu, Kaushik and Pham Hoang Van. 1998. "The Economics of Child Labor." *American Economic Review* 88:412–427.

CHAPTER 9

The Role of Interest Groups in the Design and Implementation of U.S. Trade Policies

Claude E. Barfield, Phyllis Shearer Jones, Robert Naiman,
Mike Jendrzejczyk, and Nancy Dunne

Claude E. Barfield

My remarks will address the privatization of U.S. trade policy and the consequences involved. The point of my remarks is not particularly novel: it is that ideological and policy goals are powerfully and differentially reshaped by the characteristics of individual national political systems and traditions. In the case at hand, the history of U.S. trade policy over the past several decades provides a rich and fascinating chronicle of this intermix of policy objectives played out and reshaped by strategically placed political actors and interest groups.

Even before the movement toward greater private sector and non-government organization (NGO) involvement in U.S. trade policy, the U.S. system was more open and interest-group friendly than most other national political systems. One need only analyze the role and power of the central trade bureaucracy in the European Union to see the differences. Though the EU system recently may have moved slightly in the direction of a more open U.S. style of decisionmaking, the EU trade bureaucracy still operates with much greater power and insulation from private sector pressure than does its U.S. counterpart. From trade negotiations to the execution of administrative policies such as antidumping or countervailing duty orders, Brussels operates with less transparency and less overt pressures from outside interested parties.

In the United States, on the other hand, interest groups have always played a large role in policy formulation and execution; and in the trade area this role has dramatically increased in scope and depth over the past several decades. There are several reasons for this evolution.

First, the United States has never developed a large trade bureaucracy, and indeed has never established a Department of Trade as have most of its trading partners. The Office of the U.S. Trade Representative, nominally a part of the Executive Office of the President, has a staff of only about 100 professionals.

Though it is backed up by a much larger bureaucracy in the Commerce Department, the arrangement does not make for continuous realtime analysis and execution of trade policy—whether in the process of trade negotiations or in the formulation of responses to alleged unfair trade practices by U.S. trading partners. Thus, the U.S. government is heavily dependent upon interested parties to provide it with the analytical and political case for further trade liberalization in a particular sector or for retaliations against the infraction of existing trade rule in a particular sector.

Second, beginning in the 1970s, Congress in successive trade acts(1974, 1984 and 1988) has mandated ever closer relations between U.S. trade officials and the private sector and concomitantly ever greater weight for private sector interests in the formulation and execution of U.S. trade policy.[1] The result is a raft of private sector advisory committees that keep a running tab on the actions and proposals of U.S. trade officials. In actual negotiations— whether plurilateral as in NAFTA or multilateral as in the Uruguay Round— Congress has dictated that private sector representatives be continuously consulted. Though they are not actually in the room sitting at the side of U.S. negotiators, they are just outside the door and must be continually updated on offers and counteroffers. Two direct results are evident from this forced marriage: bigtime new employment opportunities for corporate trade experts and the sight of hordes of lobbyists descending on Geneva whenever there are serious multilateral or, more recently, sectoral negotiations going on.

What are some of the more serious consequences after two decades of increased private sector involvement in U.S. trade policy. First, there are definite positive developments that have grown out of this evolving relationship between government and business. For instance, when powerful elements of the private sector get behind an issue, they can generate a much larger groundswell of support and clout than the U.S. trade bureaucracy could possibly have mobilized alone. As illustration, one need only look back to the astonishingly rapid rise to top priority of two issues during the runup to the start of the Uruguay Round: one was trade in services and the other was intellectual property. The movement to place these issues at or near the top of U.S.—and then GATT—priorities was wholly conceived and brought about by private sectors companies acting in concert: in services, with a group of financial, construction, telecommunications and entertainment companies which formed the Coalition of Service Industries; and on intellectual property, with the pharmaceutical industry, supplemented by computer software and entertainment companies. Neither area had been on the U.S. trade policymakers radar scope in 1982—and in the case of intellectual property, the rise to prominence came only in the year before the start of the round in 1987.

Clearly, in the above cases, the strong public/ private coalition was a force for more open markets and trade liberalization. But privatization also has downsides and certain negative consequences. First, given the paucity of independent knowledge by government officials, often it is the most powerful company or sector or the "squeakiest wheel" that sets the trade agenda and gets the greatest attention. There has been little or no attempt over the past several decades to evaluate and judge just which interventions by the USTR or the Commerce Department would have the greatest payoff for the U.S. economy. One view of the result of this random intervention came last year from the U.S./Japan Chamber of Commerce which, in a report on U.S. trade agreements and actions against Japan over the past two decades, concluded that in most cases little benefit had accrued to the complaining sector or to the U.S. economy.

In addition, there have been a number of occasions when the USTR and the Commerce Department, largely staffed by lawyers and not by economists or technologically trained officials, have simply misread technological trajectories or market trends and actually entered into actions that hurt U.S. consumers and the economy. The most notorious example of this phenomenon was the Semiconductor Agreement with Japan in 1987, which established a cartel and placed a floor price on DRAM semiconductor chips—thereby producing the transfer of $4/5 billion in rents from U.S. consumers and companies to Japanese companies, according to studies by Kenneth Flamm of the Brookings Institution. USTR and Commerce both bought the wholly erroneous idea that DRAMs were the key to future technological dominance in the computer field and then compounded this error with an intervention which did little to help the semiconductor companies(already exiting the field in the direction of upscale designer chips and microprocessors) but also undercut the competitiveness of U.S. computer companies who were forced to pay exorbitant prices for chips to go into their computers. A similar story—that is, U.S. government officials not understanding the technological components of a trade conflict—could be told with regard to the action forcing Japan to open up a regional market for Motorola's wireless phone technology—which, it turned out, forced upon Japan a soon-to-be-obsolete analog technology instead of the oncoming digital technology in these phones.

A third downside of overwhelming private sector influence is a strong tendency—abetted again by the lawyer's mentality which pervades U.S. trade policymaking—to pay much greater attention to short-term payoffs and tactics at the expense of longer-range U.S. interests. This is manifest in the increasing demand by U.S. trade negotiators for ever tighter reciprocity in trade agreements even when—as with the recent telecommunications agreement—it is often difficult to discern just what constitutes reciprocity. The demand that ever "i" be dotted and every "t" crossed was a major factor in the unfortunate decisions of the United States to torpedo the initial financial services and telecommunications agreements in the WTO negotiations. Similarly, the shortsighted decision to attempt to negotiate an investment agreement in the OECD rather than the WTO not only has not worked but also seems to have backfired. The rationale was that one could get a much better agreement by just negotiating in the OECD with advanced economies—in reality, it has proved impossible to get agreement among advanced countries; and in addition, one result of the OECD negotiations has been to heighten the suspicion of developing countries as well as their determination not to accede to an agreement handed to them from "on high" by the OECD countries. Unfortunately, they have also stiffened their opposition even to negotiations on investment in the WTO.

Clearly, from an economist's perspective the U.S. has adopted a second- or third-best system. But given the proposals for a different system—most center on beefing up USTR or creating a Department of Trade and Industry—this may not be a bad compromise. Yes, under the present system, we have random interventions; and yes, these interventions have political origins that have little connection to economic realities. More *sophisticated* intervention, however, by a Department of Trade and Industry bureaucracy would only compound the negative consequences of the present system and foster the illusion of more *scientific* trade retaliation or subsidy to counter alleged foreign public largesse. It was this specter that Charles Schultz probably had in mind when, in response to Laura Tyson's recommendation for "cautious activism" in which the Commerce Department would attempt just such interventions for "strategic industries," he replied that the last thing he wanted was to have a situation where Commerce Department officials woke up each morning worrying about whether this or that plant(or industry) should be let die or subsidized to keep alive.

Note

[1] To some extent, this has also been true with the role of NGOs, but to date these groups have not achieved nearly the power and influence of corporations.

Phyllis Shearer Jones

I am President and CEO of Elan International, a company specializing in business development, international trade promotion and government/public relations. I was asked to speak on this panel because I bring a perspective from both the private and public sectors on the issue of the role of interest groups in the design and implementation of U.S. trade policies. Prior to Elan International, I spent four years with IBM as a Program Director, International Trade, and two and a half years as a political appointee in the job of Assistant United States Trade Representative for Intergovernmental Affairs and Public Liaison. While at IBM I was responsible for representing IBM's interests in such issues as NAFTA, GATT, and Antidumping. During my tenure at the Office of the United States Trade Representative (USTR), my role switched to that of meeting with and receiving various calls and letters from a number of interest groups on trade policy issues. Based on these experiences, I will share with you what I learned about how interest groups affect trade policies and what makes certain interest groups more effective than others.

Before NAFTA, most Americans did not pay much attention to trade policy development. Policies were created in Washington, D.C. by a certain group of individuals, and the general public did not get involved. NAFTA changed all of that. Labor and Ross Perot brought NAFTA to the attention of the general public. They wanted to defeat NAFTA, and so they spent large sums of money on media campaigns and lobbying efforts. USA NAFTA , a group of organizations that supported NAFTA, also spent many dollars and time on lobbying efforts. Companies were asking their employees and suppliers to get involved and to write letters in support of NAFTA. At IBM, we sent out information over our internal e-mail network asking employees at certain plant locations to voice their opinions on the subject. We did not want the employees to feel that management was "forcing" them to get involved and support NAFTA. So we provided them with information on its benefits to IBM and asked them to make their voices known to Congress if they were inclined even if they did not support NAFTA. One of our employees staffed our e-mail hotline to answer questions. In the end, we succeeded in getting NAFTA passed but it was a wake-up call to those who support open trade because so many different groups got involved in the anti-NAFTA lobbying effort. Groups who tend to be against free trade quite often stay active in the trade debate even when there is no trade legislation under serious contention. This makes the job harder for free traders who tend to be active when legislation is under consideration. Advocates of open trade should continue to educate the public on its benefits even when there is no legislation pending because during each new lobbying campaign free traders almost have to start from scratch with their education efforts.

At USTR, I would hear from various interests groups on subjects such as opening Japan's auto and auto parts markets, intellectual property, China, information technology, telecommunications, financial services, agriculture, labor, environment, the World Trade Organization and on and on. It was interesting to observe the various strategies of the different interest groups. It was also interesting to see which ones were effective. Throughout this panel discussion, it is evident that interest groups have a key role in trade policies. But what makes one more effective than another?

Here are some of my observations on why some interest groups are more effective than others on a particular issue:

1. They have a clear message which has emotional and intellectual appeal.
   "NAFTA will create jobs."
   "NAFTA will cause jobs to shift to Mexico."
   "Leghold traps are cruel to animals."
These examples are not all from winning campaigns, but, if the group did not win, they certainly made it more difficult for the other side. We all remember Ross Perot's "great sucking sound" describing jobs going to Mexico because of NAFTA. The environmentalists created an ugly picture when they showed pictures of animals caught in leghold traps or when they demonstrated the traps breaking pencils in half.

2. Successful interest groups enlist champions to actively support their issues such as Congressional members, the Administration, media, or the President himself.

3. They try to get as large of a constituency as possible so that members of Congress who rely on votes know that there is plenty of support for an issue. This is why USA NAFTA and GATT NOW were formed to show Congress that there was support for these agreements. Anti-NAFTA and anti-GATT forces were making an impact on members of Congress, so these groups were organized to demonstrate that these agreements had support.

4. Groups who are successful take the time to define the impact of allowing a particular piece of trade policy to pass or not to pass in a clear, "digestible" message.

" We will have to move our plant to Mexico and lose 500 jobs in your Congressional district if NAFTA does not get passed."

" High tariffs are costing my industry millions of dollars so we need to get GATT implemented as soon as possible."

"We will lose the U.S. chip industry if these antidumping provisions get implemented."

When I was at IBM, I learned the value of the one-page, white paper to leave behind. You should be able to explain your point on one page when you speak to a member of Congress or one of his/her staff to get their attention. Quite often while at IBM, I had to explain complex antidumping issues and leave behind a one page summary. That was challenging. For those of you that know about how complex these laws are, you can appreciate my challenge. Also, I noticed that lobbyists who visited USTR were able to get more interest in their issue when they took the time to write up their points in a short, clear paper.

5. There are others things I could mention about characteristics of effective interest groups but in the interest of time I will mention one last thing. Effective interest groups stay in the game for a long time and they do not give up.

There are plenty of examples I could have discussed and other points that I could have mentioned, but these can be left in the discussion to follow. What I have sought to do in this brief presentation is to give you my perspective on the role that interest groups play in U.S. trade policies.

Robert Naiman

I would like to entitle my remarks as "The Role of [Public] Interest Groups in [Opposing] U.S. Trade Policy." I could speak on the time allotted to me about how Public Citizen's Global Trade Watch tries to influence Congress in such and so a way. That would first of all be mindnumbingly boring. Secondly, to speak about Public Citizen as an "interest group" would implicitly endorse the idea that whereas multinational corporations represent the general interest, groups like Public Citizen which advocate for the interests of working families, consumers, and the environment represent a special interest. Finally, the notion that there is any theory which could say something interesting and useful about the role of an "interest group" without reference to whether that group advocates for or against corporate rule is one which I wholeheartedly reject.

Rather, the more interesting and useful question that I prefer to address is: what is the role of *public* interest groups in U.S trade policy? And I prefer to answer it mainly by example. For the short answer is: Public Citizen takes advantage of every opportunity we can find or create to tell the truth about the failed economic model, the failed trade model, the deformed model of democracy which is being pushed by the Clinton Administration, the multinational corporations, the leadership of both political parties, the editorial boards, the professors of economics.

So the most appropriate thing is for me to do is to take the time I have to tell you about that failed model. Failed from the point of view of the general public. From the point of view of transnational capital, it is a bonanza.

Let us start with the MAI, the Multilateral Agreement on Investment. This proposed agreement, which has been under negotiation in the OECD for more than two years, would dramatically increase the power of multinational corporations relative to national governments. Specifically, it would bar governments from passing any law or regulation which, in either intent or effect, disadvantages foreign corporations relative to domestic companies. It would furthermore bar performance requirements such as those provided by the Community Reinvestment Act. Moreover, it would give corporations a powerful new tool to intimidate governments—it would allow corporations to sue governments for alleged breaches of the treaty.

The MAI is thus a treaty of significant consequence. It is a major threat to any meaningful democracy, because it tries to exclude major decisions about the direction and nature of investment from popular control. It is instructive that for most of the time that the MAI was being negotiated, there was essentially no press coverage of the MAI in any of the mass media, including the daily newspapers. This shows two things. First, that the Clinton Administration and its corporate allies know very well what they are trying to do, and how deep the public opposition is to their project of dismantling democracy. Thus, they have attempted to conduct the MAI negotiations in secret. One should qualify what one means by the word secret here. The advocates of corporate rule tried to keep the negotiations really secret as long as they could. But when that eventually failed, they tried to keep the negotiations secret in practice. Secret in practice means keeping it out of major news media. If a handful of activists found out about the treaty, but failed to alert the general public, it would be almost as good. The negotiations could proceed, because the secrecy that matters is secrecy from the general public. And for two years this strategy essentially worked, which tells you something about our news media. In a society without formal press censorship, such a strategy could only work with the de facto collaboration of the major news media.

One example is kind of instructive. After joining in the news blackout of the MAI for two years—I can tell you from personal experience that Public Citizen spent a lot of energy trying to get them to run something—anything— about the MAI—the *Washington Post* finally broke its silence on April 1, 1998. In an editorial piece by Fred Hiatt, the *Post* ridiculed critics of the MAI who maintained that the MAI was being negotiated in secret. Remember, this is from the paper that refused to report anything about the MAI for two years. This is the standard practice of denial on these issues. First, pretend they do not exist at all. When that is no longer tenable, ridicule the critics as paranoid delusionals, cowering in terror of space aliens and black helicopters.

Consider now what the evidence was that the Post provided to its readers that the critics of the MAI were not playing with a full deck. The evidence of the Post was that the OECD had earlier posted the text of the treaty on the world wide web. Obviously, then, it is ridiculous to call the MAI a "secret" treaty, if the text is posted on the world wide web by those who are negotiating it. Of course, this begs the question of why the *Washington Post* refused to do any reporting on the MAI for two years.

But what the *Post* did not tell its readers is that, long before the OECD posted the text of the MAI on its web site, Public Citizen published a leaked draft copy of the MAI text on its web site. This missing piece of information puts the decision of the OECD to post the text in a rather different light. By the time the OECD published the text, it was well known to activists and researchers around the world that one could get the MAI text at the Public Citizen web site, along with useful commentary and other links. Thus, the decision by the OECD to post the text on its own site represents no evidence of openness on the part of the OECD, in direct contradiction to the implication of the Post.

As both its supporters and critics correctly anticipated, the exposure of the MAI to public scrutiny has dealt it a severe blow. For now, the MAI remains stymied as a vehicle for the transnational corporate agenda. But that does not mean that the agenda is necessarily stymied. The transnational corporate agenda is simple—remove as many restrictions as possible on the activities and profits of transnational corporations—and when its partisans are stymied in one arena, they move the same agenda to another arena.

This has already happened with the MAI once, and now is happening again. The MAI actually began life not in the OECD, but in the WTO, where it was known as the Multilateral Investment Agreement (MIA). The MIA was blocked in the WTO by developing countries, who saw that its restrictions on national economic policy would be a disaster for small countries struggling not only to attract investment, but also to manage it, especially in a global economy of increasingly destabilizing speculative capital flows. Thus the agenda was moved to the OECD in the form of the MAI, with the idea that it would be easier to reach agreement in an arena where developing countries were not represented. Once the OECD reached agreement, it was thought, the text could be offered to developing countries on a take-it-or-leave-it basis. At that point some developing countries would surely sign, in order to get a "Good House-keeping Seal of Approval" to attract foreign investment, and competitive pressures would force other countries to follow suit.

Fortunately, as we have seen, this scenario has been blocked, at least for now, by the exposure of the MAI to public scrutiny in the developed countries. Now enter the International Monetary Fund, a publicly financed institution perhaps unrivalled in world affairs for its combination of power and lack of accountability to democratic governance. The IMF has certainly not been exempt from public criticism. For years, governments and nongovernmental organizations throughout the developing world have complained bitterly about the brutal austerity policies that the IMF has imposed. For example, a former IMF economist estimates that six million children have died each year since 1982 as a result of IMF/World Bank "structural adjustment" policies. In the wake of the IMF's bungled handling of the Asian financial crisis, vigorous and public critics of the IMF have included even Russian "shock therapy" architect Jeffrey Sachs and World Bank chief economist—and former Chairman of President Clinton's Council of Economic Advisers—Joseph Stiglitz. Characteristically, however, the IMF marches on, ignoring its critics, refusing to change its policies, fully backed by the Clinton Administration. Indeed, the Clinton Administration has shown its enthusiastic approval for IMF policies—mainly made by the U.S. Treasury in any event—by asking Congress to give $18.5 billion in new money to dramatically expand the IMF. In response to this request for a 45% increase in the U.S. contribution, many of the usual liberal critics of the failed economic model have been silent. Indeed, it is mainly Republican opposition in the House, motivated partly by anti-abortion and other factors, that has so far stood in the way of another ringing victory for the IMF's independence from democratic accountability.

What institution could be more well-suited as a place to move the MAI agenda? That's just what the partisans of corporate rule thought, and that is why they are trying to sneak the MAI into the IMF, in the form of amendments to the IMF charter. Indeed, even as we speak (April 1998), the IMF is meeting here in Washington, largely shielded from public scrutiny, preparing to amend its charter so that the IMF would be formally empowered to police "capital account liberalization" for all member countries. In other words, they are seeking to force member countries to remove restrictions on capital flows across borders, a central feature of the MAI.

But of course, these are not the only horses that the partisans of corporate rule are backing. There is, for example, the Crane sub-Saharan Africa Trade Bill, which conditions GSP (Generalized System of Preferences) benefits for sub-Saharan African countries on, among other things, whether they conform to IMF structural adjustment programs and provide MAI-style "national treatment" for foreign investment.

Let me close by addressing the issue of who is being forthright with the public about the effects of corporate globalization. Given their belief in the overwhelming gains from trade, supporters of the dominant model have been a little bit at a loss to explain the public opposition which defeated the President's request for fast-track authority. Since the advocates of the dominant free trade model are unwilling or unable to reconsider their own views, they are left to complain that the public is uneducated and simply does not understand the great benefits of trade. For example, "the costs are localized and the benefits are dispersed." A variation on this complaint is that the ignorant masses have been led astray by the demagogues at Public Citizen and the like who have spread disinformation and tricked the public with horror stories of lost jobs and environmental degradation.

Of course, given the overwhelming imbalance of media resources in favor of the corporations and their allies, such an act of deception, in the absence of evidence, would be quite a feat. But in fact what is happening is that the disinformation of the Clinton Administration and its corporate supporters is starting to unravel in the face of reality. In the case of the MAI, for example, the Clinton Administration dismisses the concerns of critics, saying that state and local laws will be protected by "reservations." But the Administration knows that by design, any provision of law which does not have a full carve-out under the MAI will eventually be subject to the "standstill and rollback" provisions of the MAI, which means that eventually parties to the agreement will be required to remove laws which do not conform to the MAI, even if the parties took reservations for such laws.

Moreover, the underlying analysis that sustains the belief in the so-called "efficiency gains from trade" is fundamentally flawed. Increasingly free-trade boosters such as the Institute for International Economics admit that the "losers" under the free trade regime—which happens to include the majority of wage and salary earners in the United States—are not being compensated. Yet even in the paper models of the free trade economists, the net gains to society from increased trade are very slight. The significant "gains from trade" in the real world are mainly an upward redistribution, transferring income and wealth from those at the bottom towards those at the top. Thus any attempt to save the "free trade model" by actually trying to compensate the losers is likely doomed to fail, because, if the "winners" were really forced to compensate the "losers," there would be hardly anything left over for the winners, and they would likely conclude that the game was not worth the candle. Indeed, the failure of the Gephardt/AFL-CIO model of fast track—which would have tried to incorporate largely unenforceable labor and environmental standards into fast track authority—to gain any meaningful corporate support reflects this reality. The "winners" don't have any interest, apparently, in rescuing the model if they are forced to compensate the losers.

Mike Jendrzejczyk

As the only representative of human rights NGOs on this panel, I want to make it clear that I generally have no problem with increasing trade and commercial contacts—with a few notable exceptions—and see U.S. trade policy as a potentially effective tool to help promote human rights, good governance and the rule of law. Secondly, I strongly believe that it is in the interest of the United States to implement, consistently and effectively, existing trade laws that take account of human rights—in some cases with very specific statutory requirements. Here I am referring mainly to Generalized System of Preferences (GSP) benefits and Overseas Private Investment Corporation (OPIC) political risk insurance and loan guarantees, both of which are conditioned on respect for internationally recognized worker rights. I am also referring to MFN (Most Favored Nation) trading status and the Jackson-Vanik provisions on free emigration. The Clinton administration, like others before it, has tended to fudge or totally ignore these statutory requirements when it is politically expedient.

As an NGO, the role of Human Rights Watch/Asia is to try to press for the effective implementation of the laws, to provide good solid documentation to policy makers (in USTR, on the Hill, the media, and in other agencies), as well as to use debate on trade policy to raise broader human rights/governance issues.

Most recently, OPIC gave Vietnam a clean bill of health in the form of a worker rights determination, despite the fact that OPIC's own investigations in Vietnam led to the conclusion: "Vietnam has a long way to go before its laws and practices conform fully to international norms in such areas of freedom of association and collective bargaining...."

On the other hand, we had one rather positive experience—though the outcome was ultimately disappointing—with GSP in the case of Indonesia. In 1992, we filed a petition challenging Indonesia's access to GSP benefits in light of pervasive worker rights violations. In response to our 20 page petition, documenting worker rights abuses, the lawyers for the Indonesian government filed with USTR over 1,000 pages of documents and exhibits. But in 1993, USTR threatened to suspend GSP unless there were serious labor reforms and then set a deadline several months down the road. This began a process of intense negotiations between Washington and Jakarta, and a series of reciprocal delegations and discussions, while domestic pressure within Indonesia also mounted for major labor reform (wildcat strikes, demonstrations and protests, etc.) Together, the domestic and international pressure had an enormous impact on the Indonesian government. We also found ourselves in dialogue with U.S. companies, worried about the effect of a decision to withdraw GSP, and thus willing to use their influence with Jakarta to help produce a constructive solution.

But, in February 1994, USTR suddenly withdrew the threat of suspension on the basis of some limited commitments and gestures of labor reform by the

Indonesian government. Then the pressure was off, prematurely, without USTR waiting to see if the government would fulfill its promises. This was clearly a political decision: President Clinton was preparing to go to Jakarta in November for a bilateral summit meeting with President Suharto and to attend the APEC meeting in Bogor (Asia Pacific Economic Cooperation forum). The White House was anxious to remove the GSP dispute as a point of tension in the relationship.

I would like to briefly discuss a few other examples of how human rights and trade policy intersect and how NGOs try to influence policy.

Regional Trade Blocs (APEC)

My own experience has been mainly in the context of APEC, the trade forum established in 1993 to press for trade liberalization in the Asia-Pacific region. I have attended every APEC summit, beginning in Seattle in 1993 and most recently in Vancouver, B.C. last November. The Canadian government put a real emphasis on the role of "civil society," even funding some NGOs from the region to come to Vancouver. Beyond the bilateral meetings between U.S. and Asian leaders, which provide a useful channel for dialogue on human rights, there are the various APEC working groups. The group on Human Resources Development, or HRD, is the one structure within APEC that could address crucial issues such as the exploitation of migrant workers—now being severely impacted by the Asian economic crisis, in South Korea and in Southeast Asia —as well as issues such as the treatment of women workers, health and safety concerns, and other labor-related issues which are already on the HRD agenda, at least in principle.

Two years ago, APEC was hosted by the Philippines and President Ramos attempted to get migrants on the agenda, but this was vetoed by other governments. The United States did little to support this initiative, in part because of concern about the implications of its own poor track record of treatment of migrant laborers.

In September 1997, a meeting of ministers in Seoul agreed to ask the HRD working group to organize a tripartite project on labor issues with participation from labor, management, and government. This was discussed at an HRD meeting in Bali in January 1998; for the first time, labor unions were theoretically invited to participate, and this was somewhat of a breakthrough (though the governments chose who would come and labor participation was severely limited, especially from countries where independent unions are nonexistent or tightly restricted). The NGOs and unions with a direct stake in the outcome had little or no direct input. It is increasingly clear that it will take years for the HRD working group to be in a position to tackle substantive, structural problems—such as migrants. And it is a very closed, non-transparent process. But, despite all the built in problems and political constraints, APEC is just too important to ignore.

We met with the U.S. ambassador to APEC several times to discuss these issues, as well as with U.S. Labor Department officials and others. Access is not the problem. It is more a question of political will, combined with the fact that APEC essentially is a consensus-driven process. Here in the United States, there is no obvious constituency for addressing complex, sensitive issues such as human rights and worker rights in the region and their relevance to trade liberalization —though the AFL-CIO has participated in some of the HRD meetings as part of the official U.S. delegation—to balance off the enormous business interests driving the APEC agenda. Hundreds of NGOs from throughout the region have staged parallel conferences and seminars during many of the APEC summits, but they have had little impact on policy making.

We have also tried unsuccessfully to introduce the idea of a dialogue on corruption between the APEC Business Advisory Council and NGOs and others throughout the Asia-Pacific region concerned about governance and the corrosive effect of corruption. Here is an issue—dramatically highlighted by the recent Asian currency crisis—where there is an overlapping agenda and where the United States could be a catalyst or convener.

World Trade Organization (WTO)

I do not believe that the WTO is likely to adopt a social clause that explicitly recognizes the linkages between trade, human rights, worker rights and good governance any time soon. There is a campaign underway supported by various international trade unions to urge the WTO to set up a working party on the relationship between labor standards and trade at the May 18–19, 1998 ministerial meeting in Geneva. The United States should support this effort, as well as to encourage an invitation to the secretary general of the ILO to attend the meeting; he was initially invited to the first WTO ministerial in Singapore, but then disinvited due to opposition from certain governments.

But there are other policy issues related to WTO that are also important. With China's accession to the WTO a topic of ongoing negotiations, I think the Congress should insist on having a vote on whether and when the president should agree to China's WTO entry. Clearly China's membership, on the right terms, would be desirable and useful in the long run, further integrating China into the international system of norms. But there are trade-offs and complex political judgments to be made regarding the timing of China's entry, as well as the level of political will in Beijing to deliver on commitments of major structural reforms. Any decision about WTO entry also must take account of the social implications of these reforms, including greater social unrest and the possibility of increased repression.

In addition, a Congressional debate would provide a useful vehicle to raise questions about China's reliability as a global trading partner, given the lack of an effective, impartial judiciary to enforce agreements on market access or intellectual property rights, as well as human rights and rule of law concerns more generally. Such a debate would exert pressure on the White House to give human rights and worker rights questions a higher priority in U.S.-Sino relations. I would admit that my organization is fairly opportunistic in looking for, and creating, such openings for debate in order to influence policy, recognizing that the MFN annual renewal process for China is of diminishing effectiveness.

I also believe that many members of Congress are interested in having a voice in such a momentous decision—and not only those with an overtly protectionist agenda or who favor isolating China. Needless to say, the Executive Branch has a very different perspective on this question. The challenge for us is to find creative ways to play on the tension between Congress and the Executive Branch over decision making authority on such a key trade issue.

Nancy Dunne

Let me begin by telling you about some unusual experiences that I have had recently, like the animal warden who came to *The Financial Times* to show me an animal trap. He stuck his hand in it and it closed, and didn't hurt him at all. Then, before coming to the conference, I had a voice-mail message from someone from an "anti-minnow" expansion group that was forming, and they wanted to send me their press kit.

I love interest groups; in my case, it is such an easy way to do my job. They arrange all of the arguments nicely and neatly for you, and you know whom to call because they give you their cards. Business lobbyists have raised this ad-hoc group coalition to an art form. I want to explain what it is like to be a journalist seeing all of this, because my situation is different from most other people who deal with business and economic issues. First of all, I usually don't get a press kit. I usually get invited to a press conference. And at the press conference I get my press kit, and the press kit is full of all these great bios of everybody you ever wanted to know, and pictures, and reports, and surveys, and it all looks so expensive that you don't want to throw it away. You know the amount that journalists get paid...I think that's the trick. You don't even have to listen to the speeches because they have the text of all of the speeches in there, and you don't even have to go to the press conference because, if you don't go, they will send everything to you. The point to all of this is that if you see that there is a big press briefing on the hill or in the press club, then you know that there's some money behind an issue. And you can't necessarily find out whose money, but you know it is there and therefore you know maybe you should pay attention to it.

Coalitions, once they get formed, usually hire a lobbyist. They have to make their case before Congress, and their target is usually a committee chairman. And if not a committee chairman, than a sub-committee chairman. And, if they get a sub-committee chairman, they can maybe get the ranking member and that is absolutely the best, since it is desirable to have bipartisan coalitions. Bipartisan support looks great to us journalists because it means maybe something might happen and we had better pay attention. After an issue has been written about for the first time, efforts are made to keep it going. What coalitions are really good at is getting letters from Congress to an administration official or the President. And if they can get a lot of people from Congress to sign their letters, that's good too. And then they send these letters to journalists, and we get to write about them. The coalitions are also great at proposing exclusive interviews with really important people that you just can't possibly turn down. And they are always ready to be helpful. They'll turn up in your office, with more data that you absolutely must have; they'll fax you anything by deadline. This is all very good for me. I couldn't do my job without it. Sometimes these people from these interest groups are the only ones that will talk to me! I can't call members of Congress. They're busy doing important things. So, I'm very grateful to the interest groups.

Fortunately now, there are so many interest groups on both side of an issue that you can write an article that is balanced. Now it may not be true, but it's balanced. You know that everybody's got their spin and you try to balance it all out. Interest groups do a lot that journalists do not get to see. It has been mentioned how the advisory groups can practically sit in on trade negotiations. They are also the ones that will tell you about them, fortunately. These trade advisors can be extremely powerful. They put out a report and they manage to get everybody behind it. It is extremely impressive, and the press takes notice.

From the other point of view, a lobbyist friend recently described to me how he achieved his biggest coup, which was to get financial services included in the Uruguay Round. It all began when his company, a big financial services company, couldn't get credit cards into Japan, Korea, or Brazil, and they were having big problems with processing costs and check clearing. Competition with foreign banks made it unprofitable, and they decided that they really needed to have some rules for financial services like manufacturers have for their products. The farmers were having problems getting their products into Europe. There was a lot of buzzing about a new round and the financial services people were there ready and waiting to try and push for it. They tried first in 1982, then in 1984, and finally in 1986 the negotiation was launched. It was supposed to be finished in 1990. And it was at that point that the Multilateral Trade Negotiation coalition was formed to try to get the round through.

The backers for the coalition included the Business Round Table, the Chamber of Commerce, the Emergency Committee on American Trade (which has had an emergency for 20 years and never goes out of business) and others. It was headed by Bill Brock who was a Republican former U.S. Trade Representative and Bob Strauss who was a Democratic former U.S. Trade Representative. The efforts really grew. They sent people out around the country talking to editorial boards everywhere saying what the Uruguay round would mean for everybody. They had reports on every state, and were able to say what the negotiations would mean to any state, including benefits to agriculture, services, banks, insurance companies, etc. They stayed very much involved with the negotiations, over a period of years. They often called journalists who responded with stories about what was happening in the negotiations. And by the time the round was finally completed, there was a positive attitude in the country, even despite some vocal opposition. That is, the public felt pretty much favorably inclined, the newspapers supported it, and the Congress was convinced despite the opposition.

Without interest groups, there would not be any trade policies. There have always been interest groups involved with trade. Initially it was farmers, then companies, and even labor unions. Initially they wanted restrictive trade policy against bringing products in because they did not want competition. After a while when companies became more committed to exports and when U.S. products got better, they wanted negotiations to open new markets. All this is really nothing new, what is new really is the involvement of so many other types of groups, non-economic groups. This started about 25 years ago, with the 1974 trade legislation, which was the first time the MFN, most favored nation status, was linked to immigration policies, with the goal of getting the Jews out of the Soviet Union. I have been told that this was the first time there were non-economic issues linked to a trade negotiation. This legislation also provided the authority to negotiate the Tokyo Round, and it was the first trade legislation that said that labor rights should be considered fair labor standards as explicit negotiating goals. This is an aim that the United States has yet to achieve. The issue of labor rights has not been resolved because trade unions, which were once very liberal on trade, have become pretty much the strongest opponents to trade liberalization.

Trade policy was once a backroom issue inside the beltway. To this day my mother still asks me what a GATT is. Now the opponents of trade liberalization have pushed the policy discussions out in the open. They put the MAI on the Internet. Even the White House has the WTO and the NAFTA on the Internet. Trade has become an issue for talk shows and phone-in shows where people call in and scream about how their jobs have been lost because of NAFTA or GATT. I think that it is all good, that finally the impact of trade has been brought home to the public. We live in a democracy, and it is important that an economic issue that was once the sole province of insiders has now gone out to the court of public opinion.

About the Authors

Kyle Bagwell

Kyle Bagwell is Professor of Economics at Columbia University. His fields of research are Industrial Organization and International Trade. Within the field of Industrial Organization, he has worked on a variety of topics, including entry deterrence, predation, collusion and pricing to signal product qualify. In joint research with Robert Staiger, he has also contributed to the field of International Trade. Bagwell and Staiger propose a modeling framework with which to interpret and evaluate GATT's central features (reciprocity, MFN, enforcement). He received his Ph.D. from Stanford in 1986 and was previously a Professor of Economics at Northwestern University. He has served on the editorial board of a number of journals.

Claude E. Barfield

Claude E. Barfield is a Resident Scholar and Director of Trade and Science and Technology Policy Studies at the American Enterprise Institute in Washington, D.C. His areas of research and expertise include international trade, science and technology policy, and U.S. competitiveness. He has recently directed the publication of three major multiauthored studies by the institute: *Science for the 21*[st] *Century: The Bush Report Revisited* (1997); *The Future of Biomedical Research* (1997); and *The United States and East Asia: Trade and Investment for the Next Decade* (1997). In 1996 he directed *International Trade in Financial Services: Harmonization vs. Competition Among National Regulatory Systems* (1996) and served as coeditor (with Bruce Smith of the Brookings Institution) of *Technology, R&D, and the Economy (1996).*

Steven M. Beckman

Steven M. Beckman is the Assistant Director of the Governmental and International Affairs Department of the UAW Washington Office. Since June 1985, he has been responsible for developing UAW positions and policies on all aspects of international trade and investment issues. He represents the UAW in meetings with officials in Executive branch agencies, Members and staff in Congress, and with various business, academic, government and general audiences on international trade and related issues. He received his B.A. from Harvard University and an M.A. in Economics from the University of Massachusetts.

Jagdish Bhagwati

Jagdish Bhagwati is the Arthur Lehman Professor of Economics and Professor of Political Science at Columbia University, New York. He was Ford International Professor of Economics at MIT until 1980 and was also Economic Policy Advisor to the Director-General, GATT. He is a Fellow of the American Academy of Arts & Sciences and the Econometric Society. Five volumes of his collected essays have been published by MIT Press. His recent book, *Protectionism* (MIT, 1988) was an international best seller and has been translated into several languages. His latest book, *India in Transition*, based on the Radhakrishnan Lectures at Oxford, was published in June 1993 by Clarendon Press. He was also adviser to the Indian Finance Minister on India's economic reforms. He is the recipient of several honorary doctorates, prizes and other awards.

George J. Borjas

George J. Borjas is the Pforzheimer Professor of Public Policy at the John F. Kennedy School of Government, Harvard University. He is also a Research Associate at the National Bureau of Economic Research. Professor Borjas received his Ph.D. in economics from Columbia University in 1975. Prior to moving to Harvard in 1995, he was a Professor of Economics at the University of California at San Diego. Professor Borjas has written extensively on labor market issues. His research on the economic impact of immigration is widely perceived as playing a major role in the debate over immigration policy in the United States and abroad. Professor Borjas was born in Havana, Cuba, and migrated to the United States in October 1962.

Drusilla K. Brown

Drusilla K. Brown is an Associate Professor of Economics at Tufts University. She received her Ph.D. from the University of Michigan in 1984. Her research focuses primarily on the use of Applied General Equilibrium Models to evaluate preferential trade agreements. In addition, Professor Brown has worked on the theoretical issues concerning international labor standards.

Alan V. Deardorff

Alan V. Deardorff is John W. Sweetland Professor of International Economics and Professor of Economics and Public Policy at the University of Michigan. He received his Ph.D. in economics from Cornell University in 1971 and has been on the faculty at the University of Michigan since 1970 where he served as Chair from 1991 to 1995. He is co-author, with Robert M. Stern, of *The*

Michigan Model of World Production and Trade and *Computational Analysis of Global Trading Arrangements* and has published numerous articles on aspects of international trade theory and policy. His work on international trade theory has dealt primarily with theories of the patterns and effects of trade. With Professor Stern and with Drusilla K. Brown he has developed a series of computable general equilibrium models of world production, trade, and employment that have been used to analyze the effects of both multilateral and regional initiatives for trade liberalization. Professor Deardorff's current research interests include: the interactions among domestic economic policies in an international environment, the role of international trade and trade policy in determining inequality within and among nations, and the determinants of bilateral trade patterns.

Avinash K. Dixit

Avinash Dixit is the Sherrerd University Professor of Economics at Princeton University. He received his B.A. from Cambridge University and his Ph.D. from M.I.T. He has previously held faculty positions at the Universities of California (Berkeley), Oxford and Warwick, and has been a Visiting Professor at M.I.T. and a Visiting Scholar at the I.M.F. His research interests include international trade, political economy, industrial organization, public finance, and investment under uncertainty. His books include *Thinking Strategically* (1995, with Barry Nalebuff), and *The Making of Economic Policy: A Transactions Cost Politics Perspective* (1996).

Nancy Dunne

Nancy Dunne is a Washington trade correspondent. She has been a member of the Financial Times staff in Washington for almost 24 years. Ms. Dunne covered a broad array of subjects, including agriculture, economics, politics, and the criminal justice system before moving into trade issues when the Uruguay Round was first being pushed. She speaks frequently and has traveled extensively around the United States to explore the impact of trade policies. Before joining the *Financial Times*, Ms. Dunne wrote radio commercials and a consumer column for the *Milwaukee Sentinel*. She is a graduate of the University of Missouri School of Journalism.

Gary S. Fields

Gary Fields is Professor of Industrial and Labor Relations and Economics at Cornell University, where he is also Chairman of the Department of International and Comparative Labor. He teaches courses on labor economics and economic development and does research on labor markets and income distribution, mostly in the developing world. His books include *Retirement, Pensions, and Social Security* and *Poverty, Inequality, and Development*. He holds B.A., M.A. and Ph.D. degrees in economics from the University of Michigan. Fields spent the 1997/98 academic year as a visiting scholar at the Russell Sage Foundation in New York City.

Pharis Harvey

Pharis Harvey is the Executive Director of the International Labor Rights Fund in Washington, D.C. An ordained minister of the United Methodist Church, he serves this position under appointment of the World Division of the General Board of Global Ministries. He has a divinity degree from Yale University and a bachelors' degree from Oklahoma City University. He also is the author of *Trading Away the Future: Child Labor in India's Export Industries*. In October 1996, he received the Letelier-Moffit Human Rights Award for "Lifetime Achievement."

John H. Jackson

John H. Jackson teaches international law, and international economic law. From 1966 to 1998 he was professor of law at the University of Michigan, and currently is University Professor of Law at the Georgetown University Law Center in Washington, D.C. His many books include *World Trade and the Law of GATT* (1969), *The World Trading System: Law & Policy of International Economic Relations*, (1989, 2nd ed., 1997); and a casebook on *Legal Problems of International Economic Relations* along with William Davey and Alan Sykes (3d ed., 1995). He is also the author of numerous articles.

Mike Jendrzejczyk

Since April 1990, Mr. Jendrzejczyk has been the Washington Director of Human Rights/Asia (formerly Asia Watch), a private, independent human rights monitoring organization, and a division of the New York-based Human Rights Watch. From 1988–1990, he worked on the staff of the International Secretariat of Amnesty International in London (UK), and from 1984–1987, he was the Campaign Director for Amnesty International/USA in New York. Mr. Jendrzejczyk has represented Human Rights Watch/Asia before Congressional committees and on missions abroad. He also represented HRW/Asia in NGO activities during several Asia-Pacific Economic (APEC) conferences. He has published articles on human rights concerns in the *International Herald Tribune, Los Angeles Times, The Washington Post, Christian Science Monitor, The Asian Wall Street Journal, The Asahi Shimbun, Japan Times, The Boston Globe*, and elsewhere.

Phyllis Shearer Jones

Phyllis Shearer Jones is President and CEO of Elan International, a management consulting firm that assists clients in growing their organizations domestically and/or internationally. From 1995–1997, she was the Assistant United States Trade Representative for Intergovernmental Affairs and Public Liaison at the Office of the United States Trade Representative (USTR). Prior to her tenure at USTR, she spent nineteen years with the IBM Corporation in various management and staff positions in sales, marketing, strategy and planning, and international trade. Ms. Jones holds degrees from the University of Pennsylvania (B.A. in Mathematics and a B.S. in Economics from the Wharton School) and an MBA from Harvard University.

John J. Kirton

John Kirton is Associate Professor of Political Science, Research Associate of the Centre for International Studies, and Director of the G7 Research Group, at the University of Toronto. He has served as team leader of the Commission for Environmental Cooperation's project on NAFTA's environmental effects, as Chair of the North American Environmental Standards Working Group, on the Canadian Government's International Trade Advisory Committee, and on Canada's National Round Table on the Environment and the Economy's Foreign Policy Committee. His 14 books include *Trade and the Environment: Legal, Economic and Policy Perspectives*, (1998); *The Halifax Summit, Sustainable Development, and International Institutional Reform*, (1995); and *Trade, Environment and Competitiveness*, (1992, 1993).

Edward E. Leamer

Edward Leamer is the Chauncey J. Medberry Professor of Management and Professor of Economics at UCLA. He received a B.A. degree in mathematics from Princeton University and a Ph.D. degree in economics and an M.A. degree in mathematics from the University of Michigan. After serving as Assistant and Associate Professor at Harvard University, he joined the University of California at Los Angeles in 1975 as Professor of Economics and served as Chair from 1983 to 1987. In 1990 he moved to the Anderson Graduate School of Management and was appointed to the Chauncey J. Medberry Chair. Professor Leamer is a Fellow of the American Academy of Arts and Sciences, and a Fellow of the Econometric Society. He is a Research Associate of the National Bureau of Economic Research and an occasional visiting scholar at the International Monetary Fund and the Board of Governors of the Federal Reserve System. He currently serves on Governor Pete Wilson's Council of Economic Advisors.

Lawrence Mishel

Lawrence Mishel is the Research Director of the Economic Policy Institute and specializes in the field of productivity, competitiveness, income distribution, labor markets, education and industrial relations. He is the co-author of *The State of Working America*, a comprehensive review of incomes, wages, employment and other dimensions of living standards which is published biennially. He holds a Ph.D. in economics from the University of Wisconsin, an M.S. in economics from American University, a B.S. from Pennsylvania State University and has published in a variety of academic and nonacademic journals.

Robert Naiman

Robert Naiman is Senior Researcher at Public Citizen's Global Trade Watch, longtime critic of U.S. foreign policy and U.S. trade policy, author of several reports on the negative impact of NAFTA and "free trade" on workers, the environment, and democracy.

Joaquin F. Otero

Jack Otero is President of OTERO Global Resources, Inc., a consulting firm which specializes in foreign affairs, governmental and community relations, international labor-management strategies and dispute resolution. From August 1996 through January 1998, he served as President of FPS International, a Washington, D.C. public relations and communications firm. Prior to joining FPS International, Mr. Otero served as Deputy Undersecretary and Assistant Secretary-Designate for International Affairs, U.S. Department of Labor, during the first Administration of President Clinton. Mr. Otero also represented the U.S. Government at the UN-affiliated International Labor Organization (ILO) in Geneva. Mr. Otero began his career as a railway employee in 1955 in St. Louis, Mo. He soon joined the Transportation—Communications Union (TCU) and later served as International Vice-President of TCU from 1971 to 1993. He was the first Hispanic-American labor leader ever to be elected to the AFL-CIO Executive Council. Mr. Otero, a Cuban-American, is a well-known national Hispanic leader. In 1993, he received the "Hispanic Hero of the Year" award from the U.S. Hispanic Leadership Conference

J. David Richardson

J. David Richardson was educated at McGill University (B.A.) and the University of Michigan (Ph.D.). In Fall, 1991, he became Professor of Economics (and International Relations, from Fall, 1997) at Syracuse University. Prior to that, he had been Professor of Economics at the University of Wisconsin, Madison. He has also taught at Wheaton College (Illinois), the University of Michigan, and the Foreign Service Institute of the U.S. Department of State. He is a Research Associate of the National Bureau of Economic Research, Cambridge, Massachusetts and spends two days each week as a Visiting Fellow at the Institute for International Economics, Washington, D. C. He has been a Visiting Scholar at the Board of Governors of the Federal Reserve System and a consultant to the Organization for Economic Cooperation and Development, to the Economic Council of Canada, to the Ford Foundation, and to Educational Testing Service. He writes extensively on international trade policy and its effects.

Dani Rodrik

Dani Rodrik is the Rafiq Hariri professor of international political economy at the John F. Kennedy School of Government, Harvard University. He is also a research associate of the National Bureau of Economic Research, research fellow of the Centre for Economic Policy Research (London), advisory committee member of the Institute for International Economics, senior advisor of the Overseas Development Council, and advisory committee member of the Economic Research Forum for the Arab Countries, Iran and Turkey. He was previously professor of economics and international affairs at Columbia University, New York. He has been the recipient of an NBER Olin Fellowship, a Hoover Institution National Fellowship, and a World Bank McNamara Fellowship. He has given the Alfred Marshall Lecture of the European Economic Association in August 1996 and the Raul Prebisch Lecture of UNCTAD in October 1997. He holds a Ph.D. in economics and an MPA from Princeton University, and an A.B. (summa cum laude) from Harvard College. Rodrik's research interests cover international economics, economic development, and political economy. He has published widely on issues related to trade policy and economic reform in developing economies. Professor Rodrik was born in Istanbul, Turkey in 1957, and is a national of Turkey.

Gregory K. Schoepfle

Gregory Schoepfle has been with the U.S. Department of Labor since 1975. He began as a Senior Economist (1975–80) and moved to Supervisory Economist (1980–83) in the Office of Productivity and Technology, Bureau of Labor Statistics. After that he became Senior International Economist (1983–83) in the Office of International Economic Affairs, Bureau of International Labor Affairs. Since 1984, Mr. Schoepfle has served as Director of Foreign Economic Research. Prior to joining the U.S. Department of Labor, he was an Assistant Professor in the Economics Department at the State University of New

York at Stony Brook. He has also served as a Professorial Lecturer in Economics at The American University. Mr. Schoepfle's research publications have covered various aspects of U.S. trade policies, including the domestic employment effects of preferential and free trade agreements, labor market adjustment issues, and the linkage between internationally recognized labor standards and trade. Schoepfle holds a Ph.D. and an M.S. in Economics from Purdue University and an A.B. in Mathematics from Oberlin College.

Mark Silbergeld

Mark Silbergeld is co-director of the Washington, D.C. office of Consumers Union, publisher of *Consumer Reports* magazine. He has had extensive experience in a wide range of policy areas including international trade, federal trade regulation, and federal food safety and product safety regulation. In 1996, Mr. Silbergeld was conferred one of the consumer community's highest honors when he received the Esther Peterson Consumer Service Award from the Consumer Federation of America. In 1993, he was honored with the Commissioner's Special Citation from the U.S. Food and Drug Administration for his work on the domestic processes of international harmonization of food standards. He serves as an officer or director of several nonprofit organizations. He is president of the Alliance of Nonprofit Mailers, vice president and chair of the important Policy Resolutions Committee of the Consumer Federation of America, secretary of the Alliance for Justice, a board member of the Center for the Study of Services and Consumers Unions and a member of the government relations committee of Independent Sector. He is a former member and chair of the Maryland Consumer Council. Mr. Silbergeld joined Consumers Union in 1972 as an attorney in the Washington, D.C. office. Prior to that, he worked as an attorney for Ralph Nader's Public Interest Research Group. Mr. Silbergeld is a graduate of Indiana University and of the Law School of Washington University in St. Louis.

T. N. Srinivasan

T. N. Srinivasan is the Samuel C. Park, Jr. Professor of Economics and Chairman of the Department of Economics at Yale University. He was a Professor, and later Research Professor, at the Indian Statistical Institute, Delhi (1964–1977). He has also taught at numerous universities, including the University of Minnesota, MIT, Johns Hopkins University, and Stanford University. In addition, Professor Srinivasan has worked extensively with the World Bank, serving for three years as a Special Adviser to the Development Research Center (1977–1980), as a member of the Editorial Board of the *World Bank Review* (1986–1991), and returning for numerous short-term consultancies with the *World Development Report* (1991) and the Economic Development Institute (1995). Professor Srinivasan has published extensively on International Trade,

Development, Agricultural Economics and Microeconomic Theory. His most recent book is *Developing Countries and the Multilateral Trading System: From the GATT (1947) to the Uruguay Round and the Future Beyond.* He has co-edited several journals. Professor Srinivasan is a Fellow of the Econometric Society and the American Academy of Arts and Sciences and holds a Ph.D. in Economics from Yale University.

Robert W. Staiger

Robert Staiger is Professor of Economics at The University of Wisconsin-Madison and a Research Associate of the National Bureau of Economic Research. He received his Ph.D. from The University of Michigan in 1985 and was an Assistant Professor and then an Associate Professor of Economics at Stanford University until coming to Madison in 1993. He also spent a year in Washington as a Senior Staff Economist for the Council of Economic Advisers. His research interests are primarily in the area of international trade policy, and more specifically on the economic analysis of international trade agreements.

Robert M. Stern

Robert M. Stern is Professor of Economics and Public Policy in the School of Public Policy and Department of Economics at the University of Michigan. He has been an active contributor to international economic research for more than three decades and a consultant to several U.S. Government agencies and international organizations. He has collaborated with Alan Deardorff since the early 1970s and more recently with Drusilla Brown (Tufts University) in the development of the Michigan Model of World Production and Trade and its application to a variety of trade policies. His current research includes computational analysis of the expansion of NAFTA and assessment of India's post-1991 economic reforms, as well as issues of trade and labor standards.

David van Hoogstraten

David van Hoogstraten is currently attorney-advisor, Oceans, Environment and Science at the U.S. Department of State. Prior to that he was Coordinator of Trade and Environment at U.S. EPA and Assistant General Counsel for International Activities. He teaches trade and environmental law at George Washington University Law School. He holds BA and MA degrees from the University of Pennsylvania and a JD from the University of Wisconsin.

STUDIES IN INTERNATIONAL TRADE POLICY

Studies in International Trade Policy includes works dealing with the theory, empirical analysis, political, economic, legal relations, and evaluations of international trade policies and institutions.

General Editor: Robert M. Stern